W9-AYM-042

COOKING WITH SMOKE, THE REAL WAY TO BARBECUE

SMOKE & SPICE

CHERYL AND BILL JAMISON

REVISED EDITION

HARVARD
COMMON
PRESS

Brimming with creative inspiration, how-to projects, and useful information to enrich your everyday life, Quarto Knows is a favorite destination for those pursuing their interests and passions. Visit our site and dig deeper with our books into your area of interest: Quarto Creates, Quarto Cooks, Quarto Homes, Quarto Lives, Quarto Drives, Quarto Explores, Quarto Gifts, or Quarto Kids.

Copyright © 2014 by Cheryl Alters Jamison and Bill Jamison
Photographs copyright © 2014 by Gabriella Marks

First published in 2014 by Harvard Common Press,
an imprint of The Quarto Group, 100 Cummings Center,
Suite 265-D, Beverly, MA 01915, USA.
T (978) 282-9590 F (978) 283-2742 www.QuartoKnows.com

All rights reserved. No part of this book may be reproduced in any form without written permission of the copyright owners. All images in this book have been reproduced with the knowledge and prior consent of the artists concerned, and no responsibility is accepted by producer, publisher, or printer for any infringement of copyright or otherwise, arising from the contents of this publication. Every effort has been made to ensure that credits accurately comply with information supplied. We apologize for any inaccuracies that may have occurred and will resolve inaccurate or missing information in a subsequent reprinting of the book.

Harvard Common Press titles are also available at discount for retail, wholesale, promotional, and bulk purchase. For details, contact the Special Sales Manager by email at specialsales@quarto.com or by mail at The Quarto Group, Attn: Special Sales Manager, 401 Second Avenue North, Suite 310, Minneapolis, MN 55401 USA.

Printed in China

Library of Congress Cataloging-in-Publication Data
Jamison, Cheryl Alters.
   Smoke & spice : cooking with smoke, the real way to barbecue / Cheryl and Bill Jamison.
— Third edition.
     pages cm
  Includes index.
 ISBN 978-1-55832-836-5 (alk. paper)
1. Barbecuing. 2. Smoked foods. 3. Spices. I. Jamison, Bill. II. Title. III. Title: Smoke and spice.
  TX840.B3.J36 2014
  641.6'16--dc23

                               2013036553

PHOTOGRAPHY BY Gabriella Marks; FOOD AND PROP STYLING BY Stacy Pearl; SMOKE WRANGLING BY Mike Whistler
COVER DESIGN BY Night & Day Design
TEXT DESIGN & ILLUSTRATION BY Richard Oriolo

To that merry band of barbecue fanatics who've done so much over the past few decades to bring an old American craft back to its homegrown roots—especially to Wayne and PJ Whitworth and the late Jim Quessenberry.

CONTENTS

PART THREE:
GREAT ACCOMPLISHMENTS FROM INDOORS

PREFACE TO THE NEW REVISED EDITION

FROM THE TIME WE FIRST started writing cookbooks, almost twenty-five years ago, we've focused our work on underappreciated foods and the cultures that surround them. Our dozen-plus cookbooks so far have dealt with topics like Texas and New Mexico home cooking, border traditions that Americans share with northern Mexico, and breakfast outside the box—subjects that don't make much buzz when chefs and other culinary pros gather.

Imagine our shock, then, when the cookbook that seemed to us the most clearly out of the mainstream happened upon a trend. When we decided to write *Smoke & Spice*, even our long-term publisher initially balked at the idea. Who could possibly be interested in an old-fashioned style of cooking that takes more time than a turtle running a marathon and envelops you for the duration in a clinging cloud of smoke? We had trouble finding anyone except our meat-market bookkeeper who thought that real barbecue was cookbook material. We didn't care, though, because we love barbecue and knew that it would be great fun to cook, eat, and write about.

Smoke & Spice just happened to appear during a period when Americans wanted to spend more time outside, when we finally got fed up with burned birds for outdoor dinners, when we began to give credibility to genuine American cooking. These and lots of other reasons that we don't understand caused a revival of interest in real, smoke-cooked barbecue. The book came out in 1994 and lots of people bought it, probably at the insistence of wives who worried that Dad was going to burn down the neighborhood.

Two decades later, barbecue continues to soar in popularity. The kinds of barbecue joints that once thrived only in the "barbecue belt" of the South now pop up in all corners of the country, in almost every town with more than a single stoplight. The joints keep getting fancier, too, serving their meat and sides on real ceramic plates, which sometimes even sit on an actual tablecloth. Tending the pit outside may be a professional chef trained in the culinary arts, and one of the diners inside might be an accredited restaurant critic wowed by the wonders of smoked meat. Americans everywhere now seem to have accepted barbecue as our true red-white-and-blue national folk food.

This enormous shift in mood and attitude made it imperative for us to take a fresh look at our book, even though it had already been extensively revised once in 2003. We didn't want to tamper with the original recipes, but we wanted the pages to reflect the important changes that have occurred in the last decade in barbecue culture and cooking. So we've added new dishes, about fifty in all, recharged the practical information and tips, and updated our stories about the landscape of the barbecue craft.

We had almost as much fun revisiting *Smoke & Spice* as we did writing the original version twenty years ago. We hope you share some of that joy with us as you cook and eat from this new edition. If so, you may just be in hog heaven for years to come.

A PASSION, A PASTIME, AND A PARTY

IT'S TIME TO GRADUATE from grilling. American cooks have been enrolled in "Introductory Barbecue" for a half century now, since the days when we all liked Ike. We've enjoyed cooking outdoors, but we're weary of wieners and charred chicken, yearning more and more for the full flavor of old-time, real barbecue, the kind popularly known as "Bar-B-Q," food that dances on your senses and gets your lips to rejoicing.

This is a complete guide to the genuine article, where we move beyond searing and sizzling into really smoking. Some of the hundreds of books on barbecue grilling acknowledge and applaud this advanced art, but they usually suggest that a home cook can't hope to match the results of a professional pitmaster in the Carolinas, Kansas City, Memphis, or Texas. At best, they may say, you can add a few wood chips to a conventional grill or slather a smoky sauce over food. Bunk.

In the last few decades there's been a revolution in home smoking equipment and supplies, the subject of the first two chapters. The new developments allow anyone to make great barbecue—real, honest-to-goodness 'Q'—in their backyard, on their balcony, or even inside, often in ways that avoid the potential health hazards of grilling. All you need to succeed are the right resources and a little learning about the barbecue craft and its delightful, part-and-parcel culture. The cooking isn't more complex than grilling—just the taste—and it's actually much more fun.

LET'S JOIN THE PARTY

TODAY WE USE THE TERM "barbecue" in a multitude of ways, but in the American past, it mainly meant a big, festive community gathering. An English visitor in the eighteenth century described the custom to friends back home, saying that Americans were "extremely fond of an entertainment they call a Barbacue," which was "a large party" that "generally ended in intoxication." George Washington probably even slept at one. In his diary, the first president noted that he once went to Alexandria, Virginia, for a "barbicue" that lasted three days.

When workers laid the cornerstone for the nation's capitol in 1793, the leaders of the new republic celebrated with a huge barbecue. Right before the outbreak of the Civil War, Scarlett O'Hara met Rhett Butler at a barbecue in *Gone with the Wind*. Throughout American history, when churches wanted to lure the less devoted, when politicians needed to attract a crowd for a campaign speech, when folks had any cause for festivity, they held a barbecue and invited everyone.

The cooks didn't grill hamburgers at these affairs. They dug a long, deep pit in the ground, filled this trench with logs, burned the wood down to low-temperature coals, and then slow-roasted whole animals and fish suspended above the smoky fire. That was barbecue then, and it's still the essence of the art. To get real with barbecue, you have to return to the roots, and that means *celebrating* a meal with friends and family by *smoking food slow and low over smoldering wood.*

That's been a grand tradition in the United States from the beginning, but many Americans lost touch with the legacy about the time they discovered frozen vegetables and TV dinners. We were moving to cities and suburbs in droves then and couldn't tear up our streets and backyards to build underground pits. Only the predominantly rural regions of the South, Southwest, and Midwest maintained the memory of real barbecue. The rest of us learned to make do with high-heat charcoal grilling and began calling it barbecue simply because it was done outdoors.

Grilling is a fine method of cooking, but it doesn't produce food with the hearty, woodsy resonance of slow-smoked fare. Those who have tasted true barbecue know the difference, and they are almost certain to be passionate about the distinction. For them, smoked ribs are as superior to a grilled pork chop as a lottery win is to taxes. In the same vein, anyone who has spent an afternoon barbecuing with children or friends understands why Americans made that their traditional party of preference. It's a national pastime older than baseball and just as spirited. When you add the fun to the flavor of the food, you don't need a diploma to tell you that you've reached a new level of barbecue bliss.

PART ONE

HONEST-TO-GOODNESS BARBECUE

THE SECRETS OF SUCCESS

REAL BARBECUE IS BRAGGING FOOD. Maybe it's the great smoky flavor or maybe it's the adulation of the eaters, but somehow all pitmasters develop into natural boasters, cocky enough to milk a bull. They learn to tell tall tales, wear odd clothes, act in wacky ways, and otherwise promote their aura as magicians of meat.

When asked about their secrets, experienced pitmasters prance around the answer like Elvis in concert, hinting of mysterious ingredients in their special dry rub, marinade, or sauce. It's all part of the fun of barbecue, but beginners shouldn't be deceived about the main secret of success. While everything you do makes some difference in your results, the only critical consideration is your smoking equipment and how you use it.

A lot of devices will work, including your old kettle grill, homemade contraptions, inexpensive water smokers, and sure-fire metal pits. We cover the various options in this chapter, focusing on the strengths and limitations of each. Specific information about using the equipment—and other barbecuing advice—is scattered throughout the recipe chapters in a range of "BBQ tips." As long as you know your equipment and understand some barbecue basics, you're just a little practice short of your own bragging rights.

BARBECUE BASICS

THE TWO ESSENTIALS of real barbecue are a low cooking temperature and a cloud of wood smoke. You need sufficient heat to cook the food—the main difference from smoke curing—but you want to keep the temperature just above the level that meat will register inside when done. Since pork needs to be cooked to an internal temperature of at least 160°F, you barbecue it at 180°F to 220°F, a good range for other food as well.

In smoke curing, by contrast, a combination of salt and smoke is used to preserve food rather than cook it and temperatures are generally held below 100°F. That's what makes a barbecued pork shoulder an entirely different animal than a cured country ham. Both processes are likely to reduce the moisture content of meat—concentrating flavor—but barbecuing does little or nothing for preservation. If you find yourself with leftovers, they must be refrigerated like anything else you cook.

Grilling goes in the opposite direction with heat. Much of the time you want the highest temperature possible in grilling because the goal is to sear meat on the outside to crisp and brown the surface. The method works best with tender cuts, like a good steak or chop, which are relatively free of connective tissue. Traditional barbecue meat, on the other hand, is as tough as John Wayne's boots. Spareribs, beef brisket, and the like require slow cooking at a low temperature to break down their stubborn tissues, the reason they were ideal for barbecue from the beginning. When you barbecue steaks, fish, or vegetables, as we do in many of our recipes, you do it to add smoky flavor, not because the slow cooking is needed for tenderness.

The rich smokiness you want in all barbecue should come from smoldering wood, not from fat or oil dripping on coals or hot metal. The difference is enormous, both in taste and in health risks. The smoke produced by burning fat contains benzopyrene, a carcinogen that sticks to food. The effect is almost unavoidable in grilling, but it isn't a problem in barbecuing if you have a water reservoir or pan beneath the meat, an option with much of the equipment.

The use of water or other liquids is a bit controversial in barbecue circles. People in the past didn't add water to their pits in any fashion, and many pitmasters disdain the practice today, contending that barbecuing must be a dry cooking process. In truth, though, most methods of barbecuing have always involved the circulation of moisture-laden air over food, making the process much "wetter" than cooking in a conventional oven. We believe water has a proper place in barbecuing, depending on how it's used and what you're cooking. Traditional barbecue meats benefit from losing moisture as they cook, shrinking their size, but many nontraditional foods benefit from bumping up the humidity inside the smoker. As long as you avoid cooking the food with steam instead of smoke, the extra moisture helps to prevent lean meat and fish from getting too dry.

COOKING TIMES AND TEMPERATURES

THOUGH CRITICAL IN BARBECUING, a low cooking temperature isn't always easy to measure or maintain. Even major equipment manufacturers sometimes fail to put useful thermometers on their smokers, telling complainers like us that barbecuing is an "inexact art." There's a lot of truth in that statement, but the art isn't as inexact as their thinking. As with any other cooking process, if you can gauge the cooking temperature and control fluctuations, you can make a reasonably reliable estimate of the time required for barbecuing anything.

That's exactly what we do in our recipes. We provide an approximate cooking time based on optimum barbecuing temperatures around 200°F. We've tested the times on a wide range of equipment, but you may need to make adjustments for your particular smoker and climate. If your thermometer reads a little high, the weather is windy or cool, you lift the lid often to check the food, or your smoker doesn't retain heat well—all common situations—you may find that you need to cook longer than we suggest. The opposite conditions could push you in the opposite direction. Rely on your personal experience and add or subtract time as needed to our recipes.

Approximations of cooking times—ours or your own—aren't fully useful unless you have a thermometer and a way to control the heat level of your smoker. The best smokers come with industrial-quality thermometers, but the gauges on less expensive models are seldom so reliable. Any type of instrument that reads something like "warm," "ideal," and "hot" isn't worth much more than the beer concession at a Baptist picnic. Replace it with a true thermometer fitted in the same opening or get a small oven thermometer that sits on the grate next to the food, basically the same options that are available to people without any form of temperature gauge on their smoker.

The most practical solution, if your equipment has a vent or other opening on the lid, is to use a portable candy thermometer that has a head facing outward. Insert the probe into the opening, placing the tip as close as possible to the cooking area without touching the food, and position the head so that it's not blocking all air circulation and is clearly visible. You can check the temperature without lifting the lid, a major advantage over an oven thermometer inside the smoker. If you have to remove the cover to see your thermometer, you release substantial heat and slow the cooking process beyond the time projected in a recipe.

A thermometer is most useful when you have the means to fine-tune the cooking temperature—with air vents or the amount of fuel you're burning—but it's a valuable tool even when you lack much control. In that situation, common with water smokers, you can at least add or subtract cooking time based on whether the internal temperature is higher or lower than the range suggested in a recipe.

A thermometer is particularly important when you're first getting the feel of new equipment or making the transition from grilling to smoking on old equipment. With a season or two of experience, you may be able to gauge the cooking temperature in other ways. You'll learn how much flame you want in your log pit, or how much heat your electric water smoker is generating under normal conditions in your climate with your extension cord. If you're burning charcoal, and tracking the cooking temperature over time, you'll develop a good sense of how many briquettes or hardwood lumps are needed to produce and maintain a 200°F fire in your size and type of smoker.

However you manage it, you need to make sure you're cooking slow and low. The principle is vital in barbecue, and however inexact the art may be, measurements of your success are as useful as in any other form of cooking. If you can confirm that you're smoking steady between 180°F and 220°F, you can count on the approximate cooking times in our recipes. More important, you can count on great 'Q' from a wide range of equipment.

LOG-BURNING PITS

THE BEST WAY TO BARBECUE is with a log fire, which is how it all began. In the early years the only equipment Americans needed was an ax and a shovel. They cleared trees along a stretch of open land, cut the branches into logs, and loaded the wood into a long pit several feet deep. They burned the logs down to smoldering coals and cooked their food over the smoky fire for a full night or longer, adding wood as necessary to maintain a steady, low temperature.

Originally the pits were open on top and the meat was hung above the fire or placed on a ground-level grate. Many people still barbecue in a similar style, but around the beginning of the twentieth century, the country's first commercial Bar-B-Q joints introduced important changes in the technology.

Much of the credit goes to immigrant German butchers, who knew little at first about American barbecue but a great deal about old-country methods of smoking sausage and pork. In meat markets from the Carolinas to Texas, they introduced Southerners to the European art of charcuterie and learned in turn from their customers about American smoked meats. The two traditions merged easily in places such as the Kreuz Market in Lockhart, Texas, where the butchers built a large brick pit in the back of the shop to smoke all kinds of fare. For barbecuing, the pit offered many advantages over an open underground trench. The brick walls elevated the working level enough to keep the cooks out of the chiropractor's office, and the newfangled metal lid trapped heat and smoke inside to make the cooking process more efficient and even. The homespun inventors also placed the fire farther from the food, often moving the burning logs from directly underneath the meat to the far end of the long pit opposite an outside vent.

Hundreds of other barbecuers created their own similar closed pits, simple but ingenious contraptions that carried an old legacy into a new age. No one has really improved on the design in the century since, and in recent decades it has become the model for a big breakthrough in home barbecue equipment.

Starting around 1980, several small but dynamic companies began manufacturing log-burning metal pits. Many of them had an offset firebox at one end and a chimney at the other, just like that ancient brick pit at Kreuz Market, but some were more vertical in shape with the wood directly under the food. All of these smokers keep the fire well away from the meat, get good smoke circulation, and maintain a constant low temperature for extended periods, regulating the heat with damper controls. You check the temperature every 20 to 30 minutes and add wood as needed, maybe once an hour.

The advantage of burning logs is the density of wood smoke they produce. Like the lava rocks in a gas or electrical grill, most charcoal doesn't generate smoke unless fat or food falls on it. So a major part of the heat source in any kind of charcoal, gas, or electrical device cooks food without smoking it, regardless of how many wood chips or chunks you use. You can barbecue many things well with this kind of equipment, as our recipes show, but you can never quite match the smokiness of the meat at a great Bar-B-Q joint.

PRIME LOG PITS

TOP-OF-THE-LINE LOG PITS do produce that full flavor from traditional barbecue meats, and they do it to perfection. If you are set on making the best pork shoulder or beef brisket in town, this is the way to go. The premier pits, made by custom fabricators, weigh several hundred pounds and cost in the same range as a high-quality gas grill. The weight and the expense come from the use of thick, heavy-gauge metal that's capable of standing up to serious log fires for a lifetime of use.

When we went shopping for a log pit years ago, our choice was a moderate-size model from Pitt's & Spitt's. The Houston company has changed hands since then, but in the past at least, the craftsmanship on all their products was outstanding in looks, durability, and capability. The pits feature an offset firebox with ¼-inch plate walls, stainless steel parts, an accurate industrial thermometer, a water reservoir with a drain, and superior smoke drafting. Visit the virtual showroom at pittsandspitts.com. Other leading manufacturers of similar pits include Big Hat Bar-B-Q (bighatbbq.com), BBQ Pits by Klose (bbqpits.com), and Lang BBQ Smokers (langbbqsmokers.com).

When you compare the range of choices among companies and among models, be sure to look at all the features, not just the cost. Consider the heft of the firebox and the lightness of the lid. Decide the value of a water reservoir, which helps to keep meat juicy and eliminates the possible carcinogenic effects of fat dripping on hot metal. Examine the quality of the metal fabrication, even the sturdiness of the wheels. All the details matter because a prime log pit should provide a lifetime of barbecue bliss.

POPULAR VALUE PITS

ONE OF THE FEW LIABILITIES of the top log pits is their size. The heavy-duty construction is an asset in barbecuing, but it makes the pits fairly expensive and bulky. If your bank account or outdoor space is limited, you might want to look at other ways to cook with wood.

The best alternatives are the moderately priced, lighter-weight pits that are becoming widely available in warehouse clubs and large hardware shops. They look similar to their big brothers and function much the same, but the thinner metal of the firebox is more suitable for wood chunks than for large logs. What you sacrifice in capability and features, you make up in savings. Regular retail prices start around $300, and you can find bargains for less.

For all kinds of pit smokers, the fullest list of fabricators that we've found is at smokingmeatforums.com/a/smoker-manufacturer-list.

OUTDOOR OVENS

ANOTHER GOOD OPTION for barbecuing is a smoker oven. They generally produce less smoky flavor than a log or chunk pit, but they are easy and economical to use. Cook-shack (cookshack.com) makes one of our favorites. Primarily a manufacturer of commercial barbecue equipment, the company also offers a model suitable for home use that operates just like the bigger restaurant ones. Powered by electricity, it burns wood chunks in a tightly sealed oven that you turn on and don't touch again until you're done.

Bradley Smoker (bradleysmoker.com), a Canadian firm, sells an oven that looks similar but operates a little differently. An electrically powered smoke generator burns special "Bradley Bisquettes," compressed hardwood chips about the size of a hockey puck. An automatic mechanism feeds the fire as needed with new bisquettes, which are produced from a variety of woods such as alder, apple, and hickory.

Oregon's Traeger Wood Pellet Grills (traegergrills.com) look much different from the Bradley Smokers but operate in a similar way. You set the grill at an appropriate smoking temperature and load a supply of wood pellets. A patented auger mechanism feeds the wood into a small, efficient firebox under the cooking grate.

All these smokers are distinctive additions to the patio, marking you as a special kind of outdoor cook, but none of them compare in individuality to the Big Green Egg (biggreenegg.com). A charcoal smoker and grill, it's modeled on the Japanese kamado, a clay oven that looks like an oversized egg. The thick ceramic walls efficiently retain heat and moisture, keeping food naturally juicy without the use of a water pan. With the possible exception of a French rotisserie, nothing cooks chicken more perfectly.

The grill-style oven that we use the most, and like the best, is the Hasty-Bake (hastybake.com). Fired by charcoal, it's equally adept as a grill and a smoker, which isn't always the case with products that claim both capabilities. The flexibility comes from an adjustable firebox and a side door for loading fuel. You can regulate the temperature by raising or lowering the firebox, and you can add charcoal and wood without opening the lid and releasing heat. Several companies make grills with the same features, but the Hasty-Bake is the original, first built in 1948.

CHARCOAL AND GAS GRILLS

IN ADDITION TO the Hasty-Bake, you can also barbecue in many conventional grills that lack an adjustable firebox. The challenge is greater because it's more difficult to maintain constant low temperatures for long enough to get the right result. Some grills manage that task better than others. Check out the capabilities of your grill by starting with foods that require relatively short smoking times, such as boneless chicken breasts, fish, and vegetables.

A grill cover is necessary for smoking, along with an ample supply of wood chips and chunks presoaked in water. The rest is straightforward, if not simple. On the most common grills, you cook with indirect heat by placing the food over a pan of water on the opposite side of the grill from the fire and wood. Consult the owner's manual for specific indirect cooking instructions for your grill.

The key to success is a low cooking temperature. That's easier to attain initially with charcoal grills but easier to maintain during a slow cooking process with gas grills. If your charcoal grill has vents, as many popular models do, close them most of the way to hold down the intensity of the fire, and try not to lift the lid except to add more wood or charcoal. Many gas grills are limited in their range of cooking temperatures, and simply won't go low enough for real barbecuing, but when they do, they hold a steady heat level with less fuss.

VERTICAL WATER SMOKERS

WATER SMOKERS (also called vertical smokers) seem ubiquitous these days, appearing in almost every store that sells outdoor products. They deserve their popularity in many respects, providing a solid combination of value and versatility, of ease and efficiency. Starting in price below $50, they are relatively simple to use, require minimal attention during operation, and yield fine results with many foods, particularly items that benefit from a moist cooking process. The most serious shortcoming pertains to traditional barbecue meats such as beef brisket and pork shoulder, which remain excessively fatty because of the added moisture.

All water smokers look much the same and operate on similar principles. Shaped like something a dinosaur dropped on the patio, they have a domed lid (often fitted with an imprecise thermometer), one or two grates for food, a pan for holding water or other liquids, and a charcoal, electric, or gas heat source on the bottom. The water helps keep the temperature low and prevents the undesirable smoke produced by fat from falling into the fire. It also adds considerable moistness to food, much more than you get from a water reservoir in a log pit. When you want a crisp, crunchy finish in a dish, you may need to cook without the water pan, or perhaps remove the pan during the last stages of cooking.

Among the various models, the electric versions are the most reliable and convenient, at least if you have a handy power outlet. They cost more initially than their charcoal counterparts, but the fuel is much cheaper over time. Their primary advantage is a steady, dependable cooking temperature. The temperature will vary a little between different smokers and climates, and will drop some in cold weather or when you're using an extension cord, but it does remain fairly constant during the cooking process on any particular day. Gas water smokers share that strength, but they get pricey and aren't as widely available.

Charcoal models fluctuate in cooking temperature, following a standard bell curve. They fire up gradually, reach a peak temperature that can approach 300°F when the coals are at their hottest, and then drop steadily as the charcoal dies down. You can mitigate the effect by lighting only a small circle of coals in the center, and allowing them to ignite the others over time, but you will still get temperature variations. You have to rely on the average heat level, which can be difficult to determine accurately, in order to estimate the cooking time required for a dish. Compounding this potential problem, weather variables such as cold and wind affect the temperature more in charcoal smokers than in electric ones, and they take longer to regain heat any time you lift the lid. With a little experience, the cooking process becomes easy, but many people find it frustrating at first.

HOMEMADE SMOKERS

BARBECUING WAS AMERICA'S ORIGINAL and most popular form of outdoor cooking until grilling surged into the forefront after the Second World War. Equipment was a major reason for the shift. By the 1950s factories were turning out basic, cheap grills faster than Formica, but those who wanted a barbecue smoker for home use had to make it for themselves. That's still a good option for some people, even with the solid commercial products available today. A lot of barbecue cook-off champions work on homemade equipment, sometimes expensively fabricated pits in special shapes ranging from armadillos to whiskey bottles.

Most do-it-yourselfers start with 55-gallon metal drums—well-scrubbed ones that never contained anything toxic. They are moderately easy to convert into a smoker and, most important, they project an authentic homespun feel, letting everyone know you're no drugstore dude.

A single drum cut in half horizontally, the most common design, is better for grilling than for smoking, but it can manage either. You split the barrel lengthwise, adding hinges on the back and a handle in front for a lid. Any kind of heavy metal grid can serve as a grate for holding the food. The most difficult part is attaching legs, usually accomplished by welding or bolting angle irons to the drum.

To avoid that job, you can use the barrel vertically, which elevates the working area to a comfortable height and also improves the smoke circulation needed for real barbecue. Among several options for rigging it, you can cut one end from the drum, place the opening over a brick fire pit, and hang meat from hooks secured to the vented top.

A double-barrel configuration is even better for barbecuing, though the construction is more complex. The bottom drum serves as an offset firebox, allowing you to keep the flame at an optimum distance from the food. Some experts recommend using parts from wood stoves for such elements as the firebox door, cast-iron supports, flues, and chimneys with dampers. Wood stove dealers and large hardware stores should have sources.

An experienced welder can build any of these barrel smokers, but a few tips may help you to get it right. Remove any existing paint as well as you can and refinish all surfaces with a high-temperature paint. Install a good thermometer near the cooking area, so you can check the temperature easily. Make sure you have a well-controlled flow of air from the firebox, across the food, and out through a chimney or vent at the opposite end of the smoker. A baffle may help insure proper smoke circulation. If you want to burn logs instead of charcoal, as you should, line the bottom of the barrel with sand and firebrick to keep the wood from burning through and to reinforce the heat-retention properties of the thin metal.

A brick pit is another option for anyone with a lifetime address and basic masonry skills. A simple brick rectangle with a metal grate and lid will work, though it's better to add an attached outside firebox at one end of the pit and a chimney at the other, both fitted with mechanisms for regulating air circulation. Even someone who isn't handy at all can make a temporary version of a similar pit. Just stack concrete blocks about four feet high in a cleared, level area—perhaps a driveway—borrow a grate from your grill or oven, and use heavy-duty aluminum foil as a lid.

What you can barbecue well depends on what you build. A double-barrel pit or a sophisticated brick pit has the same kind of broad range as a store-bought log-burner, though they are trickier to master. Other homemade options are more limited in capabilities, but any that can handle a true wood fire have more potential than a manufactured charcoal smoker.

Whether you build or buy, your equipment is your key to barbecue success. You may be inclined after a while to give more credit to your skills and secrets, but you won't be bragging about much if you ever forget that the fire comes before the food.

FUELS AND TOOLS

IF SOMEONE EVER DISCOVERS a way to fix real barbecue by pushing a button, life will be as dull as a dance at a bankers' convention. Cooks add the soul to barbecue, and they do it through their fuels and tools.

WOOD

CIGARS PRODUCE SMOKE and so does burning fat, but you don't want to cook with either one. The smoke flavor in real barbecue should come mainly from wood. If you aren't using it in one form or another, you aren't barbecuing.

Only hardwoods work. Soft, resinous woods, such as pine, cedar, and spruce, contain too much sap, which makes their smoke harsh and foul-tasting. Avoid plywood, construction scraps, or anything you cannot identify as an appropriate, untreated hardwood.

The most common barbecue woods are listed in the flavoring chart on page 14. Many pitmasters swear by a certain wood, particularly hickory or oak, but the differences are less substantial than the similarities. Usually people prefer what grows in their neck of the woods, and that always seems to suit the food they fix.

If you have a log-burning pit, the optimum kind, your choice of woods will be limited to your region anyway unless you're willing to pay some heavy freight charges. To find out what's available, check the yellow pages for firewood dealers.

Most backyard barbecuers get their smoke flavor from wood chips or chunks, both sold in small bags in stores that carry outdoor cooking supplies. Chips should be soaked in water or another liquid—perhaps beer, wine, or juice—for a minimum of 30 minutes, preferably longer, so they will smoke instead of flame. When they are well saturated, you

WOOD FLAVORING CHART

ALDER The traditional wood for smoking salmon in the Pacific Northwest, alder also works well with other fish. It has a light, delicate flavor.

APPLE AND CHERRY Both woods produce a slightly sweet, fruity smoke that's mild enough for chicken or turkey, but capable of flavoring a ham.

HICKORY Hickory is the king of the woods in the Southern barbecue belt, as basic to the region's cooking as cornbread. The strong, hearty taste is perfect for pork shoulder and ribs, but it also enhances any red meat or poultry.

MAPLE Mildly smoky and sweet, maple mates well with poultry, ham, and vegetables.

MESQUITE The mystique wood of recent decades, mesquite is also America's most misunderstood wood. It's great for grilling because it burns very hot, but below average for barbecuing for the same reason. Also, the smoke taste turns from tangy to bitter over an extended cooking time. Few serious pitmasters use mesquite, despite a lot of stories about its prevalence in the Southwest.

OAK If hickory is the king of barbecue woods, oak is the queen. Assertive but always pleasant, it's the most versatile of hardwoods, blending well with a wide range of flavors. What it does to beef brisket is probably against the law in some states.

PECAN The choice of many professional chefs, pecan burns cool and offers a subtle richness of character. Some people call it a mellow version of hickory.

place them on top of a charcoal fire right before the food goes on the grate. One handful produces a mild smoke flavor in anything that cooks for less than an hour. For a deeper smoke taste, add more chips, and replenish them periodically over an extended cooking time, whenever the vented smoke starts dying out, perhaps as often as every 30 minutes.

Wood chunks work better than chips for most barbecuing and are a little more versatile. You can cook with them straight from the bag, burning them down to embers. Or presoak them and put them on a charcoal fire for a few hours. The dry chunks produce a lot of smoky flavor, but they tend to burn unevenly, making it difficult to maintain a steady temperature unless you have an offset firebox and a good thermometer. Several soaked chunks used in combination with charcoal result in the same flavor as a handful of chips, but they last longer, an asset in slow and low cooking.

BBQr's Delight (bbqrsdelight.com) offers an alternative to chips and chunks that we use often. The Arkansas company makes compressed pellets of wood that are denser than any tree and produce considerable smoke for their compact size. They don't require soaking, and they work well in any grill or smoker. The pellets come in a range of wood flavors, including such unusual choices as black walnut and sassafras.

CHARCOAL

MANY PEOPLE WHO COOK with charcoal pick up any old bag that's handy or cheap. This can be a mistake. Charcoal varies as much as the moods of a stuck-up Hollywood starlet and has almost the same chance of being a real stinker.

The problem is in the contents. Standard charcoal briquettes are made by turning sawdust to carbon in a combustion process that excludes oxygen. This burns away the wood flavor, but even worse things may happen after that point. To bind the carbonized wood into briquettes and promote ignition, many manufacturers add other substances, sometimes including petroleum products, coal, and sodium nitrate. When lit, these briquettes pollute the air, and they may do a little jig on your taste buds as well.

The advantage of the standard briquettes is that they provide even, constant heat for a considerable period of time. With practice you can control their rate of burning to maintain the low, steady temperatures needed for real barbecue, and you can avoid the need to add more coals to the fire on a frequent basis. By themselves the briquettes won't provide any wood smoke flavor, but you can get that with the addition of wood chips or chunks.

Recently, some manufacturers have started putting in the wood for you, making briquettes studded with noncarbonized pieces of hardwood. It's a convenient way to get the kind of smoke you want, but you may still have the undesirable additives, and you lose control over the amount of wood you're burning in the charcoal fire.

We prefer to add chips or chunks ourselves, and we prefer to use briquettes bound together with vegetable starches only. Likely to be labeled "all-natural" briquettes, they offer the strengths of their conventional cousins without the drawbacks, and they burn for as long as, or longer than, any kind of charcoal on the market. Many standard supermarkets and large stores carry them today, but they are most readily available at grocery chains that specialize in "natural" products.

Lump hardwood charcoal, sometimes called chunk charwood, is another good option when used in combination with wood chips or chunks. It is carbonized, like all charcoal, but it's left in irregular shapes instead of being compressed into briquettes, eliminating the need for fillers and binders. It burns cleanly, ignites easily, and produces a steady fire. The main problem with lump hardwood charcoal is that it burns hotter than briquettes, so you have to be careful about controlling the temperature. The solution is to reduce the amount used in cooking and to keep the lumps spread slightly apart from each other.

That's merely an extension of what you do with any charcoal fire in barbecuing. Except in a water smoker, you use fewer coals than you would for grilling the same food and you keep them loosely spaced rather than stacked together. The number of coals needed varies with the kind of equipment, but a good starting point for experimentation is 20 to 50 briquettes or 10 to 25 handfuls of hardwood lumps, depending on the size of the firebox and its distance from the food. If you need to add more charcoal after an hour or two, preheat it in a charcoal chimney or other metal container and use tongs to place the pieces in the fire.

FIRE STARTERS

STARTING A LOG FIRE in a barbecue pit is similar to doing the same thing in a fireplace or wood stove. You stack a few logs carefully to allow room for air to circulate around them, and ignite the wood with kindling. Just don't use resinous kindling, such as fatwood, in a pit. We put a few chunks of hardwood under the logs and get them burning with one of the many non-petroleum fire starters on the market today.

To begin a charcoal fire, we recommend using the metal chimneys designed for the purpose and sold in almost any store that carries outdoor cooking supplies. You just light crumpled newspaper in the bottom of the sheet metal cylinder, and that ignites the charcoal you pile in the top portion. If you need to heat additional coals later, the chimneys are ready-made for the purpose. Best of all, they're inexpensive and hassle-free. Electric fire starters are equally easy to use, but the odd blend of technologies seems to us a little like drinking bourbon with root beer.

Charcoal is ready for grilling purposes as soon as it's covered completely with a thin layer of gray ash. For barbecuing, you can let it burn down a few minutes longer, until it's thickly coated with ash and no red glow is visible. You should be able to hold your hand about 5 inches above the coals for a minimum of 5 seconds.

BARBECUE TOOLS

HEAT-RESISTANT GLOVES The best way to remove food from a smoker, or to shift it around, is with your hands, securely wrapped in heat-resistant gloves. Never puncture your vittles with a fork. Tongs work with small items, but if you point a pair of the overgrown tweezers at a 10-pound brisket, the poor pincers are going to wilt in your paws. Kitchen or welder's mitts offer good protection for your hands, but we prefer neoprene gloves designed for firemen. They can handle anything and they clean quickly. Besides, the big, black, shiny mitts have a certain pitmaster sex appeal.

MOPPING BRUSHES Mopping or basting is a big part of barbecuing, as we explain in the next chapter. Cotton string dish mops work best, but pastry brushes or even nylon paint-brushes do an adequate job. Clean them thoroughly at the end of the day, even dunking cotton mop heads in boiling water.

KITCHEN SYRINGE Some foods, especially poultry, benefit from the injection of spices and liquid into the meat to add flavor and moistness. This is done with an inexpensive kitchen syringe, an oversized needle resembling something a veterinarian might use to inoculate a cow. To use, push the plunger down to expel any air and then dip the needle into your injection liquid. Draw the plunger back slowly until the syringe fills fully and then inject the liquid deep into the food in several spots. Be sure to clean the syringe after each use with hot, soapy water.

INSTANT-READ MEAT THERMOMETER In addition to a cooking thermometer, most bar-becuers will want a thermometer that can give an instant reading of the internal tempera-ture of meat. You don't need to check traditional barbecue meats for doneness because they are cooked for so long, but you'll want that capability with many other foods. Some of the handiest models are designed to clip in your pocket. Chefs and serious barbecue aficionados today often opt for the expensive but oh-so-accurate whiz-bang digital Thermapen, avail-able online from many sources.

FIREPLACE POKER OR SHOVEL For a pit in particular, and some other smokers as well, you need a metal poker or handheld shovel to move around coals, logs, and ashes. You can find them at any store that carries fireplace or wood stove supplies.

WIRE BRUSH It's important to keep your cooking grate clean so food doesn't stick or taste like what you cooked the last time. Instead of soap or other scouring agents, use a heavy-duty wire brush, available at hardware stores. Some are designed specifically for cleaning grills, but general-purpose versions also work. Scrub the grate when it's hot, preferably right after cooking or, if you forget, the next time you fire up the smoker.

STURDY WORKTABLE An outdoor cook shouldn't be running to the kitchen to work. You want your supplies, sauces, and refreshments handy, and you need an area for prepping, cutting, and serving the day's feast. A card table will work, but the more you barbecue, the more you'll want something larger and heavier.

TIDBIT UTENSILS If you're planning to cook bite-size morsels or fish in your smoker, it's worth investing in a portable grate with a small mesh that prevents food from falling through. A set of metal skewers is also useful.

DRIP PAN To barbecue on a covered charcoal grill, you need a drip pan to place beneath the food alongside the coals. If you use a regular kitchen pan, instead of a disposable aluminum one, wrap it in foil or spray it with a nonstick cooking spray to make cleaning easier. Fill the pan halfway with water or another liquid.

SMOKE-PROOF DISHES Use pans and dishes that won't discolor easily from smoke, such as cast-iron pots or something that can be cleaned with relative ease, such as a Pyrex dish. Disposable foil pans are a good option, too. Heavy-duty foil can be fashioned into trays for lightweight food or used for wrapping various items. Other baking dishes and heatproof utensils can be used with barbecuing, but they may require a lot of scrubbing to remove the dark smoke color, particularly if you're smoking in a wood-burning pit.

COOKING ACCESSORIES An apron may feel funny at first, but you learn quickly why people wear them. The same is true of potholders, paper towels, a cutting board, plastic trash bags, aluminum foil, and other normal kitchen fixtures.

GIMME CAP Professional chefs wear toques. Barbecue cooks wear caps, usually the "gimme" kind people give away or sell cheaply to promote a business, team, or event. They just look right, and they're certainly handy when you've forgotten the pot holders, paper towels, or fly swatter.

INDOOR STOVETOP SMOKING

THE NEWEST RAGE IN SMOKE COOKING is doing it indoors. The result is not quite true barbecue, but it's close enough to fool a foreigner and tasty enough to inspire yelps of joy in a Carolina pork lover. If you live in a Manhattan townhouse, or a high-rise apartment anywhere, indoor smoking may be your only option anyway, and during winter it may make more sense in any situation than outdoor barbecuing.

The "barbecue pit" of choice is a crafty, inexpensive device called a stovetop smoker. We use one made by a Colorado Springs company, Camerons (cameronssmoker.com), but the Max Burton brand sold in some stores and websites is similar in most respects, including price. You place wood dust or chips—packaged with the smokers—in the bottom of a rectangular pan. A drip tray and food grate go directly above. You cook over the front and back burner of a stove, using low to moderate heat to gently ignite the wood and generate a puff of smoke, which is trapped inside the pan by a tight-fitting lid and absorbed by the food during the cooking process.

Stovetop smokers excel with chicken breasts, fish fillets, and other ingredients of a comparable size that respond well to a light smoke flavor. Manufacturers suggest you can also cook larger cuts of meat by removing the lid and wrapping a foil tent around the food, but we find the process cumbersome and unproductive. On most home stoves, the lowest possible cooking temperature falls between 275°F and 300°F, a higher range than you usually get in outdoor smokers. While you need to reduce cooking times in recipes slightly to accommodate the heat difference, the results remain similar for dishes that suit the mode.

All the unsmoked dishes in the book—from rubs to sauces to sides—obviously work well for an inside kitchen. Thirty-some barbecue recipes that also translate well, and shine in a stovetop smoker, are listed below, along with page numbers. Each will put a spark in a snowy day.

SMOKING SLOW AND LOW

SPICING UP YOUR LIFE

THE FIRST STEP IN BARBECUING, MOST OF THE TIME, IS THE APPLICATION OF A DRY RUB, PASTE, OR MARINADE TO THE FOOD YOU'RE FIXING. THEN, AFTER YOU START COOKING, YOU OFTEN "MOP" THE FOOD WITH A LIQUID CONTAINING SOME OF THE SAME INGREDIENTS. THESE ARE VITAL PROCESSES IN BARBECUING, BEST APPROACHED WITH PLAYFUL EXUBERANCE, EVEN IF YOU'RE A LITTLE SQUEAMISH ABOUT WORKING WITH RAW MEAT.

Flavor is the main function of the various potions, and their role is frequently more important to the taste of barbecue than anything you add at the end. Sometimes a dry rub, paste, marinade, or mop becomes the basis of a finishing or table sauce—the subject of a separate chapter—but even then, they have worked much of their wizardry before the cooking is completed. In barbecuing, you don't get a real treat without some serious foreplay.

DRY RUBS

DRY RUBS ARE COMBINATIONS of dried spices massaged into food before cooking. Originally developed long ago for preservation, rubs in barbecuing help seal in flavor, add another dimension to the taste, and form a savory crust. While the technique is old, it wasn't widely used in American cooking outside of barbecue circles until recently, when New Orleans chef Paul Prudhomme created blackened redfish and other dishes using his line of seasoning blends.

The appropriate ingredients in dry rubs vary with the kind of food you're cooking, but some items are more common than others. Salt and sugar probably appear more often than anything else, in both commercial and homemade rubs, though they are also the most controversial ingredients. Some pitmasters say that salt draws the moisture out of meat, and everyone agrees that white or brown sugar burns on the surface of food. We follow the course of moderation, using salt and sugar when they round out the taste of a rub, but keeping the quantity in careful balance with other ingredients. From a flavor standpoint, if nothing else, they are normally better in a supporting rather than starring role.

Garlic powder, onion powder, and lemon-pepper seasonings are a close second in popularity, particularly in homemade rubs. They all work better in a dry spice mix than they do in most kitchen preparations, but by themselves their potential for adding punch is pretty limited. We usually supplement them, or even supplant them, with black pepper and dried chiles, plus some combination of secondary seasonings, such as dry mustard, cumin, sage, thyme, allspice, cinnamon, nutmeg, and ginger.

When applying a rub, add it thoroughly and evenly. Generally you don't skimp on the amount, though some dishes benefit from a lighter touch. If you're cooking chicken or other poultry, spread the seasoning both over and under the skin, being careful to avoid tearing the skin. If you're rubbing vegetables, cover them first with a thin layer of oil.

Always wash your hands well with soap and hot water before moving on to other tasks.

After coating the food, let it absorb the spices in the refrigerator, wrapped in plastic. We favor zipper-top plastic bags or industrial-size food-safe plastic bags, depending on the size of the item. Oven-roasting bags, the type used for Thanksgiving turkeys, work too. As we indicate in our recipes in later chapters, fish fillets and shrimp need to sit for 30 to 45 minutes before cooking, big cuts of meat like an overnight sleep, and other kinds of food require some amount of time in between.

The following collection of master rubs illustrates typical spice blends for different dishes. We repeat all the instructions when we use one of these in a particular recipe—so you don't have to turn back here—but it may help in understanding rubs to see a sample set of them in one place. Also, if you want to make up a batch of your own custom rubs at the beginning of the barbecue season, as we do each year, you'll find this a useful starting point. Figure that 2 cups of rub will yield enough to flavor a couple of briskets, a half dozen slabs of ribs, or 8 to 10 chickens.

GETTING OUT THE VOTE

A group of African American leaders in Virginia during the Reconstruction era published a broadside invitation to a barbecue, proclaiming "We, a portion of the . . . colored voters of Richmond City and Henrico County, intend giving a barbecue to our colored political friends, on Friday afternoon, at 3 O'clock, July 2, on Vauxhall Island, Mayo's Bridge. Every colored voter in favor of the equal political and civil rights of the colored and white man is earnestly invited to attend and participate."

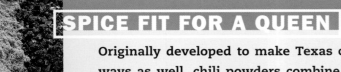

SPICE FIT FOR A QUEEN

Originally developed to make Texas chili con carne, but now used in many other ways as well, chili powders combine dried red chiles (usually anchos) with other spices, such as cumin and garlic. One of the oldest and best brands is Gebhardt's, created by German immigrant William Gebhardt in 1896. A New Braunfels resident, he loved the spicy stews made at that time by the fabled San Antonio "Chili Queens" and developed his powder to emulate their seasonings.

Wild Willy's Number One-derful Rub

This is our main all-purpose rub, good on ribs, brisket, chicken, and more.

MAKES ABOUT 2 CUPS

3/4 cup paprika or Spanish smoked paprika

1/4 cup freshly ground black pepper

1/4 cup kosher salt or coarse sea salt

1/4 cup sugar

2 tablespoons chili powder

2 tablespoons garlic powder

2 tablespoons onion powder

2 teaspoons cayenne

Mix the spices thoroughly in a bowl. Store covered in a cool, dark pantry.

BBQ *tip* In the two decades since we published the first edition of *Smoke & Spice*, the number of commercially available dry rubs has grown from a handful to enough to sand a new Sahara. It makes sense to keep a few store-bought favorites on hand to shake effortlessly over food you are smoking for simple weekday meals. Be aware, however, that you may pay a lot for the convenience. Some companies load up rubs with inexpensive spices that have the flavor of sawdust, and others rely heavily on salt or sugar as the primary ingredients (the ones listed first on the label). As always, buyers must beware.

Southern Succor Rub

We use this on many cuts of pork, from shoulder to tenderloin. MAKES ABOUT 2 CUPS

1/2 cup freshly ground black pepper

1/2 cup paprika

1/2 cup turbinado sugar

1/4 cup kosher salt or coarse sea salt

4 teaspoons dry mustard

2 teaspoons cayenne

Mix the spices thoroughly in a bowl. Store covered in a cool, dark pantry.

BBQ tip The late Jim Quessenberry, one of the planet's all-time premier pitmasters, gave us the idea of using turbinado sugar in rubs. A coarsely granulated raw sugar, turbinado has a light molasses flavor and doesn't break down under barbecuing temperatures to the same extent as other sugars. You can find turbinado sugar at natural food stores and many supermarkets.

Sweet Meat Rib Rub

When you're rubbing down pork or beef ribs, this brown sugar–rich blend will make a fine crust for your meat. MAKES ABOUT 1 1/4 CUPS

3/4 cup packed dark brown sugar

2 tablespoons dry mustard

2 tablespoons onion powder

2 tablespoons kosher salt or coarse sea salt

1 tablespoon freshly ground black pepper

1 tablespoon cayenne

Mix the spices thoroughly in a bowl. Store covered in a cool, dark pantry.

IT TOUCHES US ALL

"Barbecue is a metaphor for American culture in a broad sense, and . . . is a more appropriate metaphor than any other American food. Barbecue alone encompasses the highbrows and the lowbrows, the sacred and the profane, the urban and the rural, the learned and the unlettered, the blacks, the browns, the yellows, the reds, and the whites." Lolis Eric Elie, *Smokestack Lightning* (1996, Farrar, Straus and Giroux)

Poultry Perfect Rub

Chicken and other poultry can take a variety of rubs well, depending on the flavor you want, but this is often our top choice. MAKES ABOUT 2 CUPS

3/4 cup paprika

1/4 cup freshly ground black pepper

1/4 cup celery salt

1/4 cup sugar

2 tablespoons onion powder

2 tablespoons dry mustard

2 teaspoons cayenne

Zest of 3 to 4 lemons, dried and minced (see BBQ tip)

Mix the spices thoroughly in a bowl. Store covered in a cool, dark pantry.

BBQ *tip* Lemon zest can be air-dried overnight. If you're in a hurry to get your poultry in the pit, dry the zest in a 225°F oven or smoker for 8 to 10 minutes.

Seafaring Seafood Rub

Try this complexly flavored blend on swordfish, striped bass, and shrimp.

MAKES ABOUT 3/4 CUP

1/4 cup kosher salt or coarse sea salt

2 tablespoons celery seed

4 teaspoons garlic powder

4 teaspoons ground ginger

4 teaspoons freshly ground black pepper

2 teaspoons paprika

2 teaspoons packed brown sugar

1 teaspoon ground mace or nutmeg

1 teaspoon cayenne

1/2 teaspoon ground allspice

Mix the spices thoroughly in a bowl. Store covered in a cool, dark pantry.

CAROLINA PIONEER

Skilten Dennis may have been the earliest commercial barbecue cooker in North Carolina. He smoked a few hogs in an underground pit to feed a Baptist church convocation in 1830, offering take-out pork from the back of a wagon. His great-great-grandson, Pete Jones, re-stoked the legacy in 1947 by opening the Skylight Inn barbecue restaurant in Ayden, North Carolina, now under the skilled stewardship of Pete's grandson Sam.

Cajun Ragin' Rub

This blend dances on your taste buds. Pair it with pork ribs or shoulder or boudin sausage, or use it with shrimp or a meaty fish, such as snapper or redfish.

MAKES ABOUT 1¹/₄ CUPS

¹/₄ cup celery salt

¹/₄ cup freshly ground black pepper

¹/₄ cup ground white pepper

¹/₄ cup packed brown sugar

2 tablespoons garlic powder

1 to 1¹/₂ tablespoons cayenne

1 tablespoon dried thyme

2 teaspoons dried sage

Mix the spices thoroughly in a bowl. Store covered in a cool, dark pantry.

BBQ tip Many good cooks frown on the use of garlic powder, onion powder, and similar commercial products that appear in rub recipes because most supermarket versions simply don't offer much flavor or substance. For superior results, mail-order these seasonings and other spices from specialty companies such as Penzeys Spices (penzeys.com), Pendery's World of Chiles & Spices (penderys.com), and Vanns Spices (vannsspices.com).

Smoky Salt

Use this robust salt in place of plain salt in or on nearly anything, from rubs to sauces, pea soup to peanuts. MAKES 1 CUP OR MORE

1 cup or more kosher salt or coarse sea salt

When you are planning to smoke any other dish, pour the salt into a shallow pan or tray in a thin layer. Place the pan in the smoker so that juices from the other dish or dishes cannot drip into the pan. Smoke for 20 to 30 minutes. To test whether the flavor is bold enough for you, sprinkle a bit on a cracker and taste. Continue to smoke longer if you wish. When cool, store covered in a cool, dark pantry.

Forget France. Paris, Texas, abutting the Piney Woods in the eastern side of the state, is loaded with down-home barbecue eateries. There are almost a dozen places to pick up your favorite meat, approximately one for every 2,000 residents. The single McDonald's in town is far, far behind in the count.

Sweet Sensation

These spices match the sweetness and succulence of tender cuts of pork, such as tenderloin or rib roast. MAKES ABOUT 1 CUP

1/4 cup ground allspice

1/4 cup packed brown sugar

1/4 cup onion powder

2 tablespoons kosher salt or coarse sea salt

2 teaspoons ground nutmeg

2 teaspoons ground cinnamon

2 teaspoons dried thyme

Mix the spices thoroughly in a bowl. Store covered in a cool, dark pantry.

VARIATION: MAPLE SWEET SENSATION Replace the brown sugar and half of the allspice with maple sugar, available widely throughout maple-tree territory. Smoke the rubbed meat over maple wood, too, if you have the opportunity.

BBQ *tip* To avoid contaminating a large batch of rub, pour or spoon out the amount you expect to use in a small bowl, so that the remaining portion doesn't get touched by your hands while you are rubbing down raw meat. When you have leftover rub, seal it in plastic zipper-top plastic bags or in jars. Keep the spice blend in a cool pantry or refrigerator until your next round of barbecuing, or try it with other preparations, such as grilling, broiling, or sautéing.

Basic Black Rub

Hardly a recipe, but as essential to an outdoor cook as a little black dress is to a woman. Try it on swordfish, albacore tuna, sea scallops, or a burger.

MAKES ABOUT 1/2 CUP

6 tablespoons coarsely ground black pepper

3 tablespoons kosher salt or coarse sea salt

Mix the spices thoroughly in a bowl. Store covered in a cool, dark pantry.

Trail Dust

When you want the distinctive flavor of Worcestershire without the liquid, perhaps to put a real crust on burgers or a steak, here's a simple combo. MAKES ABOUT 1 CUP

1/2 cup Worcestershire powder

1/4 cup freshly ground black pepper

1 tablespoon kosher salt or coarse sea salt

Mix the spices thoroughly in a bowl. Store covered in a cool, dark pantry.

Java-Chile Rub

We developed this rub for pork chops, but it also works well on many cuts of beef and on quail or other game birds. Ground coffee fades in flavor quickly, so make it in small batches. MAKES ABOUT 1 CUP

1/2 cup ground coffee

3 tablespoons ground pasilla or ancho chile

3 tablespoons kosher salt or coarse sea salt

2 tablespoons packed brown sugar

1 tablespoon coarsely ground black pepper

Mix the spices thoroughly in a bowl. Store covered in a cool, dark pantry.

VARIATION: ESPRESSO RUB Substitute stronger ground espresso for half of the ground coffee. Reduce the brown sugar to 2 teaspoons so the coffee flavor comes through like that morning jolt of double espresso.

SURF'S UP

Hundreds of websites deal with barbecue in one way or another, often promoting cook-offs, sauces and rubs, catering businesses, smoking equipment, and the like. Some of the sites, such as amazingribs.com and thesmokering.com, provide links to numerous other sites. From them you can surf yourself silly through wave after wave of barbecue boasting.

Southwest Heat

Hard to beat when you want some heat. Good on beef, from steak to burgers, on pork chops, even on trout. Some people like to add a few tablespoons of onion powder or onion salt to this kind of blend. MAKES ABOUT 1¹/₂ CUPS

¹/₂ cup ground New Mexican red chile

¹/₂ cup ground ancho chile

3 tablespoons kosher salt or coarse sea salt

3 tablespoons ground cumin

1 tablespoon dried oregano, preferably Mexican

Mix the spices thoroughly in a bowl. Store covered in a cool, dark pantry.

VARIATION: SOUTH-OF-THE-BORDER SMOKY HEAT For a smoky Mexican version of the rub, substitute ground chipotle chile for half of the ancho chile.

BBQ tip Chiles in a rub should leave an afterglow in the throat, not a raging conflagration. Dried ground chiles, such as ancho or New Mexican red, offer earthy savor and sweetness with a moderate level of firepower. Powders made from jalapeños and chipotles (smoked ripe jalapeños) turn up the thermostat a little higher, and cayenne or habanero chiles can shoot the mercury right out the top.

Jamaican Jerk Rub

This rendition of the popular Jamaican spice mix is a slam-dunk with pork but also tasty on chicken and even salmon. MAKES ABOUT 1¹/₂ CUPS

6 tablespoons onion powder

6 tablespoons onion flakes

2 tablespoons ground allspice

2 tablespoons freshly ground black pepper

2 tablespoons cayenne

2 tablespoons sugar

1¹/₂ tablespoons dried thyme

1¹/₂ tablespoons ground cinnamon

1¹/₂ teaspoons ground nutmeg

¹/₄ teaspoon ground habanero chile (optional)

Mix the spices thoroughly in a bowl, being careful to keep the incendiary habanero powder off your bare hands and away from sensitive body parts. Store covered in a cool, dark pantry.

Simple Chinese Five-Spice Medley

Used on our West Coast Baby Backs, this fragrant blend adds a lovely anise-like Asian note to any pork or chicken dish. MAKES ABOUT 1 CUP

1/2 cup five-spice powder

1/2 cup packed brown sugar

Mix the spices thoroughly in a bowl. Store covered in a cool, dark pantry.

BBQ tip You can usually find five-spice powder in the Chinese section of your supermarket or certainly in Asian markets. To make a fresher version, grind up equal amounts of cinnamon sticks, star anise, cloves, fennel seeds, and Szechwan peppercorns. The mixture will keep for several months in an airtight jar in a cool pantry.

PASTES

A PASTE IS A WET VERSION of a dry rub, a combination of seasonings bound together in a thick emulsion by liquid or fat. Occasionally called "slathers" or "wet rubs," they add both flavor and moisture to food. Typical core ingredients range from stock to lemon juice, from oil to fresh herbs. Pureed garlic, onions, anchovies, horseradish, mustard, or even peanut butter might bind the mixture.

Dry rubs are great on traditional barbecue meats, such as beef brisket and pork butt, which don't need extra moisture, but pastes work better on game and other lean meats. They usually impart a milder taste than rubs, making them suitable for delicate fish or seafood preparations. Pastes are also a good way to add herb flavors, allowing you to coat a chicken with basil or a lamb chop with mint.

A paste needs to be thick enough to adhere to the food but thin enough to smear easily. As with dry rubs, you massage it into every surface and then put the food in the refrigerator in a plastic bag to soak for an appropriate period. Pastes with fresh herbs lose their potency after a few days, but others keep for several weeks when refrigerated.

The paste preparations that follow show some of the possibilities. If none of these sounds exactly right for your favorite food, they may at least inspire your own creations.

Some paste recipes promise more than others. We came across one, based on mustard, that claimed equal effectiveness as a flavoring agent and as a medicinal plaster for combating bronchial infections.

Primo Paste

This is a basic, general-purpose paste, good for a range of lean foods, particularly turkey. MAKES ABOUT 1 CUP

1 whole head of garlic, cloves peeled

6 tablespoons coarsely ground black pepper

6 tablespoons kosher salt or coarse sea salt

1/4 teaspoon cayenne or ground chipotle chile

6 tablespoons garlic-flavored oil (see BBQ tip on page 211)

In a mortar and pestle or with a food processor, mash the garlic with the salt, black pepper, and cayenne or chipotle. Add the oil to form a thick paste. Refrigerate the paste, covered, for up to 2 weeks.

BBQ *tip* Oil-based pastes work especially well on fish and lean meats, such as venison, cabrito, and chicken. Experiment with oils of varied flavors, infused with garlic, basil, or other herbs. Unrefined or lightly refined oils, such as corn or peanut, add their own pleasing taste.

Sweet and Hot Mustard Paste

Mustard makes a fine base for a paste, since it naturally clings to any food you wish to pair it with. Wonderful on salmon steaks, chicken thighs, and pork.

MAKES ABOUT 3/4 CUP

1/4 cup sweet hot mustard

1/4 cup minced onion

Juice of 1 large lemon

2 teaspoons minced fresh dill or sage or 1 teaspoon crumbled dried dill or sage

1 teaspoon kosher salt or coarse sea salt

Mix the ingredients in a bowl. Use immediately or cover and refrigerate overnight.

Roasted Garlic Mash

This paste adds depth to dishes that smoke quickly, such as boneless chicken breasts or other poultry parts, flaky white fish fillets, small whole fish, or beef tenderloin. If you like, add a teaspoon of ground cumin, oregano, or black pepper to the mixture. MAKES ABOUT 1/2 CUP

2 whole heads of garlic

2 tablespoons kosher salt or coarse sea salt

2 teaspoons extra-virgin olive oil or vegetable oil

Break the garlic heads apart into individual cloves, but don't peel them. Place them in a cast-iron or other heavy skillet and dry-roast over medium heat until soft and brown, 6 to 8 minutes, shaking or stirring as needed to color evenly. Peel the garlic (a quick task once roasted) and transfer to a small bowl. Using the back of a large fork, mash the garlic lightly. Add the salt and oil and continue mashing until you have a rough puree. Cover and refrigerate until ready to use. The mixture will keep for at least a week, though it loses some complexity over time.

Name-Your-Herb Paste

Mix and match your favorite herb flavors and fragrances in this paste. We like mint with trout and lamb, basil on chicken and tuna, parsley for beef, cilantro with shrimp and salmon, and sage on cabrito, duck, and pork. Mint plus cilantro is good for sea bass or fresh sardines. Lamb and chicken take to a combination of mint, basil, parsley, and cilantro—if you believe, as we generally do, that more is more.
MAKES ABOUT 1 1/2 CUPS

1 1/2 cups fresh herb leaves (mint, basil, flat-leaf parsley, cilantro, or sage)

10 to 14 garlic cloves

1 teaspoon table salt

3/4 cup oil, preferably olive or another type of flavorful oil that complements your recipe

In a food processor, combine the herbs, garlic, and salt. Process until the herbs are finely chopped. Add the oil in a slow stream, mixing thoroughly. The paste should be refrigerated in a covered container and used within a day or two.

Yucatecan Seasoning Paste

Called a *recado,* this mild mixture works magic on pork, whole chickens, and also fish such as snapper or grouper. The red stain comes from annatto seed, an ingredient in the achiote paste, which is available at Hispanic or Latino markets and in the Mexican foods section of many supermarkets. **MAKES ABOUT 1 CUP**

3.5-ounce package achiote paste
1/2 medium onion, chunked
1/2 cup freshly squeezed orange juice
1 tablespoon freshly squeezed lemon juice
1 teaspoon kosher salt or coarse sea salt

Place the ingredients in a blender or food processor and process until a smooth, thick puree is formed. Cover and refrigerate until needed. The mixture keeps at least a week.

Pan-Asian Pandemonium

A little soy, a little fish sauce, and a little ginger equal a lot of pizzazz. Use a light coating of this on fish steaks, shrimp, chicken, beef short ribs, or small cuts of pork.

MAKES ABOUT 3/4 CUP

1/2 cup roughly chopped scallions
2 walnut-size chunks fresh ginger, peeled
3 tablespoons freshly squeezed lime juice
2 tablespoons reduced-sodium soy sauce
1 tablespoon Asian fish sauce
1/2 to 1 tablespoon Asian chile garlic paste

Place the ingredients in a blender or food processor and process until a smooth, thick puree is formed. Cover and refrigerate until needed. The mixture keeps at least a week.

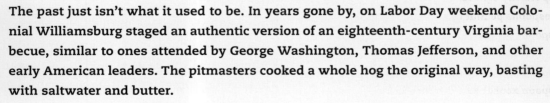

PRESIDENTIAL PIG

The past just isn't what it used to be. In years gone by, on Labor Day weekend Colonial Williamsburg staged an authentic version of an eighteenth-century Virginia barbecue, similar to ones attended by George Washington, Thomas Jefferson, and other early American leaders. The pitmasters cooked a whole hog the original way, basting with saltwater and butter.

"No taste for a barbecue!' exclaimed Major Heyward. "You surprise me, Mr. Fenni-more; no taste for a barbecue! Well, that shews [sic] you were not raised in Virginia. Time you should see a little of the world, sir; there's nothing in life equal to a barbe-cue, properly managed—a good old Virginia barbecue. Sir, I would not have you miss it for the best horse on my plantation." James Hall, *Kentucky: A Tale* (1834, London)

Kentucky Pride

This smoky, sweet paste can enhance better cuts of pork and beef.

MAKES ABOUT 1¹/₄ CUPS

1 medium onion, preferably a sweet variety, chunked
¹/₄ cup bourbon
2 tablespoons packed brown sugar
2 tablespoons freshly ground black pepper
1 tablespoon vegetable oil
1 teaspoon table salt

Combine the paste ingredients in a food processor or blender and process until the onion is finely chopped and a thick puree forms. Refrigerate the paste, covered, for up to 2 weeks.

VARIATION: TEXAS PRIDE Substitute beer or tequila for the bourbon and match the paste with chicken or game birds.

Thunder Paste

A more exotic blend that's superb on chicken and shrimp. MAKES ABOUT 1 CUP

1 small onion, chunked
¹/₃ cup freshly squeezed orange juice
2 tablespoons peanut oil
2 teaspoons ground anise
1 teaspoon turmeric
1 teaspoon curry powder
1 teaspoon kosher salt or coarse sea salt

¹/₂ teaspoon ground allspice
¹/₂ teaspoon ground cinnamon

Combine the paste ingredients in a food processor or blender and process until the onion is finely chopped and a thick puree forms. Refrigerate the paste, covered, for up to 2 weeks.

MARINADES

NORMALLY A COMBINATION of acid, oil, and spices, marinades are liquid flavoring agents used to bathe food before cooking. Like pastes, they aren't as common in barbecuing as dry rubs, but they are gaining favor. Some marinades tame an undesirable taste, as a buttermilk soak does for wild game, but most often they are intended to complement and enrich the food's natural flavor.

The acid might be vinegar, lemon or other fruit juice, milk, yogurt, or wine. The fat in a marinade is normally a vegetable oil, since butter and bacon drippings coagulate when chilled. The proportions depend a lot on the type of food you're cooking, with the amount of oil increasing substantially with fish and lean cuts of meat. Spices and herbs are used in assertive quantities because their pungency is diminished by the soaking process.

Some people think marinades tenderize meat, but that's not quite accurate. Actually the liquid softens tissue, a subtle but important distinction. Food marinated for too long becomes mushy and flabby. Extra time doesn't help the flavoring process either, because marinades don't penetrate much beyond the surface of the food and don't need to go any deeper.

Prepare marinades right before they are needed and don't reuse them with other raw foods. If you plan to use a marinade for mopping or basting, or as part of a sauce, first boil the mixture vigorously to kill any harmful bacteria.

Marinate food in a glass, stainless steel, or plastic container; aluminum can react with the acid. Choose a shallow dish just larger than the food, a zipper-top freezer bag, or, for big cuts of meat, an industrial-size food-safe plastic bag or an oven-roasting bag. Bag-wrapped food is easier to stash in the fridge and requires only about half the amount of liquid to cover the food.

Turn food you are marinating once or twice during the process to make sure you're saturating all surfaces. Figure that 2 cups of marinade will flavor about 2 pounds of meat.

James Beard helped inspire the suburban resurgence of outdoor cooking after the Second World War. His *Cook It Outdoors* (1941, M. Barrows and Company) and the 1960 *Treasury of Outdoor Cooking* (Golden Press) are gems of their era. *The Complete Book of Outdoor Cookery* (1955, Doubleday & Company), which Beard co-authored with Helen Evans Brown, remains a grilling classic.

James Beard's Basic Barbecue Marinade

The master of American cooking, James Beard, used a marinade similar to this on many outdoor dishes. Its slight Asian accent mates well with salmon, pork, chicken, and duck. MAKES ABOUT 2 CUPS

1/2 cup reduced-sodium soy sauce

1/2 cup dry sherry

1/2 cup strong brewed tea

2 tablespoons honey

2 tablespoons peanut oil

1 teaspoon freshly ground black pepper

1/2 teaspoon ground anise

1/2 teaspoon ground cloves

1 garlic clove, minced

Whisk the ingredients together in a large bowl. The marinade can be covered and refrigerated for several days.

James Bond's Basic Barbecue Marinade

If you like vodka martinis as much as James Bond does, you'll relish this marinade on seafood and chicken. MAKES ABOUT 2 1/2 CUPS

1 1/2 cups vodka

1/2 cup dry vermouth

3 tablespoons vegetable oil

3 tablespoons minced onion

Juice of 1 large lemon

Combine the ingredients. Mr. Bond would implore you to shake it rather than stir it. The marinade is best the day it's made.

Red Wine Marinade

A stout, classic combo for beef and venison. MAKES ABOUT 2¾ CUPS

2 cups dry red wine

½ cup red wine vinegar

¼ cup oil, preferably olive or another type of flavorful oil that complements your recipe

10 to 12 fresh sage leaves or 2 teaspoons dried sage

2 garlic cloves, halved

Combine the ingredients in a food processor or blender. The marinade is best the day it's made.

BBQ tip Don't waste money on expensive wines for marinades, but do use something that's good enough to drink—you will be eating it in your food, after all.

Stout Beer Marinade

No barbecue is complete without beer, so you might as well give your food a swig, too. Stout adds a pleasantly yeasty, malty character to ribs and other pork, but if you want a less assertive taste, you can substitute a pale ale or other lighter beer. Just avoid "lite" beer, which is simply too lightweight. MAKES ABOUT 2½ CUPS

12 ounces stout or other dark beer such as a porter

1 medium onion, sliced thin

3 tablespoons vegetable oil

3 tablespoons white or cider vinegar

2 tablespoons molasses

2 tablespoons mustard, preferably brown, Dijon, or honey-Dijon

2 teaspoons bruised caraway seeds (optional)

1 teaspoon kosher salt or coarse sea salt

Whisk the ingredients together in a medium-size bowl. This is best used the day you assemble it.

VARIATION: GINGER BEER MARINADE Combine the beer, onion, oil, and molasses with a thumb-size chunk of fresh peeled ginger, sliced into thin rounds, then bruised with the side of a knife. It's also a winner with pork.

Jalapeño-Lime Marinade

This feisty mixture adds a kick to shrimp and chicken. MAKES ABOUT 1½ CUPS

⅓ cup pickled jalapeño slices

¼ cup pickling liquid from a jar or can of pickled jalapeños

Juice of 2 limes

¼ cup corn oil

3 tablespoons minced fresh cilantro

4 scallions, sliced

3 garlic cloves, halved

1 teaspoon kosher salt or coarse sea salt

Puree the marinade ingredients in a food processor or blender. The marinade is best the day it's made.

VARIATION: LIME-JALAPEÑO MARINADE Turn around the flavors and the name for a marinade that's better on pork butt or shoulder. Simply replace the lime juice with a 6-ounce can of thawed frozen limeade concentrate.

Red-Eye Marinade

An eye-opener any time of day—try it with pork or beef. MAKES ABOUT 3 CUPS

2 cups strong brewed coffee

1 medium onion, chunked

½ cup cider vinegar

¼ cup molasses

1 teaspoon table salt

Blend the ingredients in a blender. The marinade is best the day it's made.

BBQ tip Since marinades flavor only the surface of food, the larger the surface area relative to weight, the more of the marinade taste you will get. A flank steak, for example, drinks up the juice like a jilted cowboy out on the town.

MACHO MARINADE

Former Houston Oilers star Earl Campbell concocted a marinade for beef brisket that was as powerful as his running game. He based the unusual mixture on brown sugar—as much as two pounds' worth—black pepper, garlic, meat tenderizer, and Lawry's sauce. You wouldn't want to trot out onto the field right after that kind of meal.

Cheryl's Cider Soak

Here's a fruity favorite of ours for pork, duck, and game birds. We skip the oil when we use the soak for ribs or other fatty cuts of pork. MAKES ABOUT 2 3/4 CUPS

1 1/2 cups apple cider or juice

3/4 cup cider vinegar

1/2 medium onion, minced

3 tablespoons vegetable oil (optional)

1 1/2 tablespoons Worcestershire sauce

1 teaspoon ground cinnamon

1 teaspoon dried thyme

Combine the ingredients in a food processor or blender. The marinade can be covered and refrigerated for several days.

VARIATION: CHERYL'S CIDER SPRITZ When you want to use a spray bottle to help flavor and moisten a dish like ribs, leave the onion, oil, and thyme out of the "soak" and simply stir the remaining ingredients together. Pour into the spray bottle and you are good to go.

BBQ *tip* Cheryl's Cider Soak is a good example of a marinade that can do double-duty as a mop. For basting food, simply heat the ingredients in a saucepan and apply the warm liquid to the vittles while they're cooking. If you marinated meat in the mixture first, bring the marinade to a vigorous boil before using it as a mop.

Korean Kick

The traditional flavoring for Korean dishes like kalbi, or beef short ribs, but darned fine on other beef or pork, and amazingly tasty on chicken, too. MAKES ABOUT 2 CUPS

1 1/2 cups *ganjang* (Korean soy sauce) or Japanese soy sauce such as Kikkoman

1/4 cup plus 2 tablespoons granulated sugar or packed light brown sugar

1/4 cup toasted sesame oil

6 to 8 garlic cloves, halved

3 to 4 scallions, limp green tops discarded, chopped roughly

2 tablespoons *gochujang* (Korean red pepper paste) or sriracha (optional)

Combine the ingredients in a food processor or blender. The marinade is best the day it's made.

Mojo Marinade

Among all the great flavors in *nuevo* latino—and *viejo* latino—cooking, mojo may translate best to barbecue. The tangy citrus and herb concoction is excellent for small cuts of pork, chicken breasts, and the occasional smoked onion. Always set some aside for a table sauce, its original purpose. MAKES ABOUT 2 1/2 CUPS

3/4 cup freshly squeezed orange juice, plus 2 tablespoons grated orange zest

3/4 cup freshly squeezed lime juice

3/4 cup extra-virgin olive oil

6 to 8 garlic cloves, minced

1/3 cup chopped fresh cilantro

2 teaspoons ground cumin

2 teaspoons dried oregano

1 teaspoon kosher salt or coarse sea salt, or more to taste

Whisk the ingredients together in a bowl. Use within a few hours for best flavor.

VARIATION: SPIKED MOJO MARINADE Juice up the marinade with 1/4 cup light or dark rum. It adds a little extra caramelization on the surface of the food, not to mention a little extra marination for the cook.

MOPS

MOPS, OR BASTES, PLAY an important role in traditional barbecuing. These liquids that you apply to meat during the cooking process are an old and honored way of keeping food moist and adding an extra layer of flavor. Their usefulness today, however, varies considerably, depending on the kind of cooking equipment you have. We include mops in most of our barbecue recipes, but we make them optional because the design of some smokers precludes or discourages basting. See page 45 for guidance on whether "To Mop or Not."

A mop can be something as simple as beer or meat stock, or a combination of ingredients as complex as an IRS form. Butter or oil is a primary element when cooking fish, chicken, and other food that dries out easily. It's also common to use vinegar or lemon juice, some Worcestershire, and a healthy dose of the same seasonings you used in your rub, paste, or marinade. In some cases, the marinade itself simply becomes the mop after a vigorous boiling.

You usually baste the food with a cotton-string tool that resembles a miniature floor mop, often available at restaurant supply stores or businesses specializing in outdoor cooking supplies. Keep the liquid warm during the cooking process to kill any bacteria the tool might pick up from the surface of the food and to avoid lowering the temperature of the food. When you're working with a pit, the baste can simmer in a heavy pan on top of the firebox; otherwise you may need to keep it hot on the stove inside. Replenish the liquid as needed. The long cooking concentrates the flavor and creates an increasingly robust brew that is sometimes boiled and served as a table sauce with the meat.

Foods with little or no fat may require regular mopping, as our recipes indicate, but don't overdo it. Every time you lift the lid of your smoker, you lower the temperature inside and increase the cooking time. That's desirable only if the fire gets too hot, when it helps to release heat and cool the meat with a little moisture.

We suggest many different bastes in our recipes later in the book, but the ones that follow are representative of the range. They demonstrate the core principles and ingredients, and may give you ideas for developing special mops of your own.

Southern Sop

This is one version, among hundreds, of the traditional pork baste used throughout the South. MAKES ABOUT 3 1/2 CUPS

2 cups cider vinegar

1 cup water

3 tablespoons freshly ground black pepper

2 tablespoons kosher salt or coarse sea salt

1 tablespoon Worcestershire sauce

1 tablespoon paprika

1 tablespoon cayenne

Combine the ingredients in a saucepan. Heat the mop and use it warm.

THE OL' BASTER

C. Clark "Smoky" Hale won renown in barbecue circles as an "Ol' baster" extraordinaire. In his folksy *Great American Barbeque Instruction Book* (1985, Abacus Publishing), Smoky argues that the basting sauce or mop is the secret of great barbecue, capable of making "a pine knot tender and delicious."

The equipment you use for barbecuing determines whether and how often you baste food while it cooks. We list mops as "optional" in most of our barbecue recipes, but you should use them if they are appropriate to your style of smoker. In a few cases, we suggest basting food before or after cooking, rather than during the process, and in those unusual situations, the mop works well with any kind of equipment.

WOOD-BURNING PITS Mops were made for pits. If you burn logs or wood chunks in a manufactured or homemade pit of traditional design, basting your food will improve its quality. Mop as often as the recipes indicate.

OUTDOOR OVENS Never apply a mop during cooking in an oven that operates on electrical power. It's not only dangerous but, in some cases at least, also unnecessary. In ovens that seal as tightly as the Cookshack, for example, food retains its internal moisture and doesn't require any basting. Follow the manufacturer's directions with other brands of smoker ovens.

CHARCOAL AND GAS GRILLS You should baste food in a grill, but not as often as you do in a wood-burning pit because grills generally lose more of their heat when you lift the lid. In a conventional charcoal grill, we mop only when we have the top off to add charcoal or pieces of wood. In an oven-style grill, such as the Hasty-Bake, we mop with about half the frequency we would in a wood-burning pit.

VERTICAL WATER SMOKERS Basting isn't really necessary in a water smoker because the cooking process itself adds moisture to food. We like to mop occasionally for the flavor value, but we limit the frequency for the same reason we do in a charcoal grill—heat loss. We baste every 1 to 2 hours, or when we have the lid off for another purpose.

Basic Beer Mop

Anything from Texas brisket to Boston butt will happily lap up this brew. If you think more spice is nice, add a few slices of pickled or fresh jalapeño or serrano chile.

MAKES ABOUT 3 CUPS

12 ounces beer

1/2 cup water

1/2 cup cider vinegar

1/4 cup vegetable oil

1/2 medium onion, chopped or sliced in thin rings

2 garlic cloves, minced

1 tablespoon Worcestershire sauce

1 tablespoon Wild Willy's Number One-derful Rub (page 26) or other dry rub or seasoning that complements the flavor of your dish

Combine the ingredients in a saucepan. Heat the mop and use it warm.

Lemon Splash

A delicious baste for chicken, fish, and seafood. Use the stock and rub that match your main ingredient. MAKES ABOUT 3 CUPS

1 1/2 cups chicken or fish stock

1/2 cup freshly squeezed lemon juice

1/2 medium onion, chopped

1/2 cup unsalted butter

1 tablespoon Worcestershire sauce

1 tablespoon yellow mustard

2 teaspoons Poultry Perfect Rub (page 28) or Seafaring Seafood Rub (page 28)

Combine the ingredients in a saucepan. Heat the mop and use it warm.

VARIATION: TARRAGON VINEGAR SPLASH This makes a good change of pace on the same foods as the lemon version. Substitute tarragon vinegar for the lemon juice and Dijon mustard for the yellow mustard.

CHEFS AT THE PIT

At Atlanta's recently opened Heirloom Market BBQ, two professional chefs smoke the meat and make the sides. Chef Cody Taylor, who calls himself a Texas hillbilly even though he has cooked at a Ritz-Carlton, grew up on barbecue. His partner, Chef Jiyeon Lee, grew up on kimchi in South Korea and brings a lively Asian accent to the food. They decided to open the restaurant as the answer to a shared question: "What can we enjoy doing the next ten years?"

Lightning Mop

We developed this for our Hot Times Jalapeño Turkey Breast, page 212, but it's also good with other poultry and shrimp dishes. MAKES ABOUT 4 CUPS

3 cups chicken or turkey stock
1/2 cup vegetable oil
1/4 cup minced pickled jalapeños
1/4 cup jalapeño jelly

Combine the ingredients in a saucepan. Heat the mop and use it warm.

VARIATION: ASIAN LIGHTNING MOP Drop the jalapeños and the jalapeño jelly. Instead add 1/4 cup reduced-sodium soy sauce, 1 tablespoon packed brown sugar, 1 tablespoon or more Asian chile garlic paste or sauce, and 3 tablespoons water. Still good on poultry and shrimp, and also on flank steak.

Pop Mop

Unless you brag too much, no one is likely to guess the source of the curiously sweet flavor in your food. The mop is especially good on onions. It makes a good injection liquid for pork, too. MAKES ABOUT 3 CUPS

3 cups Dr Pepper, Cherry Dr Pepper, Coca-Cola, or RC Cola
2 tablespoons vegetable oil

Combine the ingredients in a saucepan. Heat the mop and use it warm.

Garlic-Herb Butter

Everything's better with butter. We developed this for turkey breasts, but it's also good with other poultry, shrimp and trout dishes, steaks, and more. Add a couple of teaspoons of salt if you aren't already using it in another seasoning on your food.

MAKES ABOUT 1 CUP

1 cup unsalted butter
2 to 12 garlic cloves, minced
1/4 cup packed minced mint, tarragon, or flat-leaf parsley leaves or 2 tablespoons packed minced rosemary or sage leaves

Combine the ingredients in a saucepan. Heat the butter and use it warm.

PORK YOU CAN PULL APART

WHEN YOU'RE TALKING BARBECUE IN THE SOUTH, YOU'RE TALKING PORK. TO EXPRESS A PREFERENCE FOR BARBECUED BEEF OR SMOKED FISH IS AKIN TO ANNOUNCING THAT YOU'RE THE GRANDCHILD OF GENERAL WILLIAM TECUMSEH SHERMAN. YOU CAN EVEN STIR UP A HELL OF AN ARGUMENT OVER THE PART OF THE PIG YOU LIKE. IN SOME AREAS OF THE CAROLINAS YOU GO WHOLE HOG OR NOTHING, BARBECUING THE ENTIRE ANIMAL AND EATING IT ALL in a variety of forms. Just a county away, folks won't touch anything except the shoulder; down the road, the ribs are the only cut that matters.

If you get beyond the feud about parts, you're still confronted with passionate differences about saucing and serving the pork. Some pitmasters base their sauce on ketchup, others won't let a tomato through the door. Some think spice is nice, others are set on sweet, and still others won't abide anything on their meat. The pork may be pulled, chopped, or minced. If you order a dinner plate, the accompaniments could be anything from hush puppies to burgoo. If you opt for a sandwich, you can usually count on a white bun or bread, but you never know whether the coleslaw will be inside or on the side.

In truth, barbecued pork is good any of these ways and many others. Our favorite version is always what's in front of us at the moment, and right now that's a whole heap of deliciously different recipes.

DOWNTOWN MR. BROWN

Leonard Heuberger conceived the most famous barbecue sign in the country, a fixture for many years at Leonard's in Memphis. A neon pig in top hat and tails, swinging a cane, announces, "Mr. Brown Goes to Town."

The Renowned Mr. Brown

In old Southern slang, "Mr. Brown" is the dark, smoky outside part of barbecued pork, usually the shoulder. This is the traditional cooking style, perfected by generations of pitmasters to give Mr. Brown his deserved renown. SERVES 8 TO 10

SOUTHERN SUCCOR RUB

1/4 cup freshly ground black pepper

1/4 cup paprika

1/4 cup turbinado sugar

2 tablespoons kosher salt or coarse sea salt

2 teaspoons dry mustard

1 teaspoon cayenne

6-pound to 8-pound pork butt (Boston butt)

SOUTHERN SOP (OPTIONAL)

2 cups cider vinegar

1 cup water

3 tablespoons freshly ground black pepper

2 tablespoons kosher salt or coarse sea salt

1 tablespoon Worcestershire sauce

1 tablespoon paprika

1 tablespoon cayenne

Vaunted Vinegar Sauce (page 370), Golden Mustard Barbecue Sauce (page 371), or Carolina Red (page 371) (optional)

1. The night before you plan to barbecue, combine the rub ingredients in a small bowl. Massage the pork well with about half of the rub. Transfer the pork to a plastic bag and refrigerate it overnight.

2. Before you begin to barbecue, remove the pork from the refrigerator. Pat down the butt with another coating of rub. Let the pork sit at room temperature for about 45 minutes.

3. Prepare the smoker for barbecuing, bringing the temperature to 200°F to 220°F.

4. If you plan to baste the pork (see page 45, "To Mop or Not"), stir any remaining rub together with the mop ingredients in a saucepan and warm the mixture over low heat.

5. Transfer the pork to the smoker and cook it for about 1½ hours per pound, or until it's falling-apart tender. Mop the pork about once an hour in a wood-burning pit, or as appropriate for your style of smoker.

6. Remove the pork from the smoker and let it sit until cool enough to handle, about 15 minutes. Pull off chunks of the meat and either shred or chop them as you wish. Make sure each serving has some of the darker, chewier Mr. Brown along with the lighter interior meat. If you wish, serve the pork with your choice of sauce—our favorite for Mr. Brown is Vaunted Vinegar Sauce.

BBQ *tip* Butchers normally cut pork shoulder into two big pieces, the Boston butt and the picnic, both likely to weigh 6 to 8 pounds. If you want to cook the whole shoulder, an overnight job, you may have to order in advance. Most backyard cooks and restaurants are satisfied with just the butt, the portion with the least bone.

Red-Eye Butt

Anything as tasty as a barbecued shoulder warrants a little experimentation. Here we add some extra tang, using an old American pork enhancer—coffee—and we speed up the cooking time by starting with just half of a Boston butt, a common supermarket cut. SERVES 4 TO 6

RED-EYE MARINADE AND MOP

2 cups strong brewed coffee

1 medium onion, chunked

1/2 cup cider vinegar

1/4 cup molasses

1 teaspoon table salt

1/2 pork butt (Boston butt), 3 1/2 to 4 pounds

Bar-B-Q Ranch Sauce (page 375) or Espresso Barbecue Sauce (page 375) (optional)

1. The night before you plan to barbecue, combine the marinade ingredients in a blender. Pour the marinade over the pork in a plastic bag. Refrigerate the meat overnight.

2. Before you begin to barbecue, drain the pork, reserving all of the marinade and adding 1 cup water to it if you plan to baste the meat. If your smoker isn't appropriate for basting, save only 1 cup of the marinade. Let the pork sit at room temperature for 30 to 40 minutes.

3. Prepare the smoker for barbecuing, bringing the temperature to 200°F to 220°F.

4. Bring the reserved marinade to a boil over high heat. Reduce the heat to a simmer and cook for several minutes. Keep the liquid warm over low heat.

5. Transfer the pork to the smoker and cook it for 4 hours. Baste the meat with the warmed marinade at 45-minute intervals in a wood-burning pit, or as appropriate for your style of smoker (see page 45, "To Mop or Not"). After 4 hours, wrap the pork in heavy-duty foil, pouring about 1/2 to 1 cup of the warmed marinade and the onion solids over the meat. Discard any remaining marinade. Seal the edges of the foil well. Return the pork to the smoker and cook it to the fall-apart stage, about 2 more hours.

6. Allow the pork to sit at room temperature for 10 to 15 minutes before pulling the pork apart in shreds. Offer your choice of sauce on the side if you wish.

VARIATION: JAVA-CHILE BUTT For a quicker approach to the coffee accent, skip the marinade; instead, rub the meat with Java-Chile Rub (page 31), saving at least 1 tablespoon of the mixture. Let the butt sit at room temperature while you fire up your smoker. If you want to use a mop, combine 1 cup white or cider vinegar mixed, 1 cup water, and the reserved tablespoon of dry rub.

BBQ tip Pork works better than any other meat for barbecuing on a charcoal grill. The Red-Eye Butt is particularly well suited, and so is The Renowned Mr. Brown (page 51), using half of a butt instead of the full cut.

Perfect Picnic

The bony portion of a pork shoulder, the picnic, is as delectable as the butt end, but slightly different in flavor, closer in taste to ham. SERVES 8 TO 10

PERFECT PICNIC RUB

5 tablespoons freshly ground black pepper

1/4 cup turbinado sugar

3 tablespoons paprika

2 tablespoons kosher salt or coarse sea salt

1 tablespoon dry mustard

2 teaspoons onion powder

1 teaspoon cayenne

6-pound to 8-pound pork picnic

PICNIC MOP (OPTIONAL)

3 cups cider vinegar

1 cup water

1 medium onion, minced

1/4 cup freshly ground black pepper

2 tablespoons kosher salt or coarse sea salt

1 tablespoon dry mustard

4 garlic cloves, minced

1 teaspoon cayenne

Golden Mustard Barbecue Sauce (page 371), Vaunted Vinegar Sauce (page 370), or Creole Classic Barbecue Sauce (page 382) (optional)

1. The night before you plan to barbecue, combine the rub ingredients in a small bowl. Massage the pork well with about half of the rub. Transfer the pork to a plastic bag and refrigerate it overnight.

2. Before you begin to barbecue, take the pork from the refrigerator. Pat down the pork with another coating of rub. Let the pork sit at room temperature for about 45 minutes.

3. Prepare the smoker for barbecuing, bringing the temperature to 200°F to 220°F.

4. If you plan to baste the pork (see page 45, "To Mop or Not"), stir any remaining rub together with the mop ingredients in a saucepan and warm the mixture over low heat.

5. Transfer the pork to the smoker and cook it until the internal temperature reaches 170°F to 180°F, about 1½ hours per pound. Mop the meat every 50 to 60 minutes in a wood-burning pit, or as appropriate for your style of smoker.

6. Remove the pork from the smoker and let it sit until cool enough to handle, about 15 minutes. Pull off chunks of the meat, then either shred or chop them as you like. If you wish, serve the pork with your choice of sauce.

SERVING SUGGESTION A smoked picnic makes for a memorable small-scale "pig-picking." Add Creamy Coleslaw (page 390), Candied Sweet Potatoes (page 399), Carolina Jerusalem Artichoke Pickles (page 434), and maybe a pot of Brunswick Stew (page 392). For a prodigious finish, offer Prodigal Pecan Pie (page 442) for dessert.

BBQ tip The time needed to bring a smoker to the proper temperature for barbecuing varies from less than 5 minutes to as much as 1 hour, depending on the style of smoker, your fire-building techniques, the moisture content of the wood or charcoal, and the weather. Our recipe instructions assume an average warm-up time of 30 to 45 minutes. If your smoker requires more or less time, you may need to adjust the sequence of recipe steps accordingly.

Citrus-Marinated Pork Butt

We based this idea on *lechón asado*, a celebratory spit- or pit-roasted favorite in Puerto Rico, Mexico, and other Latin American countries. To turn this into a tasty sandwich, pile the pork and fixings onto a crusty roll or section of French bread, or onto warm corn tortillas. SERVES 6 TO 8

1/2 pork butt (Boston butt), 3 to 3 1/2 pounds

YUCATECAN SEASONING PASTE
3.5-ounce package achiote paste

1/2 medium onion, chunked

1/2 cup freshly squeezed or reconstituted frozen orange juice

1 tablespoon freshly squeezed lemon juice

1 teaspoon kosher salt or coarse sea salt

CITRUS MOP (OPTIONAL)
1 cup water

1/2 cup white vinegar

One-half 6-ounce can frozen orange juice concentrate, thawed

1/4 cup freshly squeezed lime juice

1 tablespoon vegetable oil

CITRUS SAUCE
1/2 cup sugar

1/2 cup white wine vinegar

1/2 cup freshly squeezed lime juice

One-half 6-ounce can frozen orange juice concentrate, thawed

2 tablespoons light rum

1 garlic clove, minced

1/2 teaspoon kosher salt or coarse sea salt

2 tablespoons unsalted butter

2 to 3 large ripe avocados, peeled, pitted, and diced shortly before serving

2 medium to large oranges, peeled and cut into segments

Thin-sliced scallion rings

Minced fresh cilantro

Lime wedges, for garnish

1. At least 4 hours and up to the night before you plan to barbecue, cut the butt in half lengthwise, forming two long strips. Place the pork in a plastic bag or shallow, nonreactive dish.

2. Place the seasoning paste ingredients in a blender or food processor and process until a smooth, thick puree is formed. If you are planning to baste the meat (see page 45, "To Mop or Not"), set aside 1 tablespoon of the seasoning paste. Rub the rest of the mixture thickly over the pork and refrigerate.

3. Prepare the smoker for barbecuing, bringing the temperature to 200°F to 220°F.

4. Let the pork sit at room temperature for 30 minutes.

5. If you are going to baste the meat, combine the mop ingredients with the reserved 1 tablespoon of paste and warm over low heat.

6. Transfer the pork to the smoker and cook until the internal temperature reaches 165°F to 170°F, about 3 hours. Baste the meat with the warm mop at 45-minute intervals in a wood-burning pit, or as appropriate for your style of smoker. After the pork reaches the desired internal temperature, wrap the two pieces together tightly in heavy-duty foil. Return the pork to the smoker and cook it until very tender and falling apart, about 1 more hour.

7. While the pork smokes, make the sauce. Warm the sugar over low heat in a heavy saucepan. When the sugar is melted and golden brown, pour in the vinegar, watching out for the steam that immediately forms. Raise the heat to medium and add the lime juice, orange juice concentrate, rum, garlic, and salt, and simmer for 5 minutes. Stir in the butter and warm the sauce over low heat.

8. Remove the pork from the smoker and let it sit until cool enough to handle, about 15 minutes. Neatly shred the pork and arrange it on a platter. Spoon several tablespoons of sauce over the pork, then pour the rest of the sauce into a small bowl to pass separately. Scatter avocado chunks, orange segments, scallions, and cilantro over the pork, garnish with the lime wedges, and serve.

VARIATION: MOLASSES-BRINED PORK BUTT
Replace the Yucatecan Seasoning Paste with a marinade of 1 cup white vinegar, 1 cup water, $1/2$ cup molasses, and $1/4$ cup kosher salt or coarse sea salt. (There's no need to set any of it aside as in step 2, however.) The flavors of the citrus mop and sauce blend well with the deep molasses nuances of the marinade.

BBQ tip You have more control over your cooking temperature in a log-burning pit than in other kinds of smokers, but the mechanisms of control are not always well explained in the owner's manual. First in importance is the size and intensity of the fire. In an efficient, well-constructed pit you seldom need more than three logs burning at once, or more than a small flame going. The air intake control is a close second in significance. You open it to increase the draft—which stirs the flame and raises the heat—or close it to dampen the blaze and reduce the temperature. The outtake adjustment on the smoke stack is most useful in reining back a fire that's gotten too hot. Unless that happens, leave it fully open to keep the smoke circulating freely. If it's shut down for an extended period, food will get sooty.

Boston Bay Jerked Pork

Jamaica's Boston Bay is the spiritual home of jerk pork, where the meat is cooked over smoldering allspice wood at several small enterprising shacks. The first time we visited the country, over 30 years ago, an escort from the tourism office tried everything to keep us away from the jerk shacks, mistakenly thinking we would prefer fancy Continental-style restaurants. Finally he realized we were serious about sampling the then little-known specialty, a savory, smoky delight. For home barbecuing, we like to match the jerk rub with the robust flavor of the pork picnic, but the lively seasoning also works well with the butt portion of a shoulder and with ribs. **SERVES 8 TO 10**

JAMAICAN JERK RUB

6 tablespoons onion powder

6 tablespoons dried onion flakes

2 tablespoons ground allspice

2 tablespoons freshly ground black pepper

2 tablespoons cayenne

2 tablespoons sugar

1½ tablespoons dried thyme

1½ tablespoons ground cinnamon

1½ teaspoons ground nutmeg

¼ teaspoon ground habanero chile (optional)

6-pound to 8-pound pork picnic

JERK MOP (OPTIONAL)

3 cups cider vinegar

1 cup water

1 medium onion, sliced thin

4 garlic cloves, sliced thin

Mango-Habanero Hellfire (page 387), Jamaican Barbecue Sauce (page 383), or South Florida Citrus Sauce (page 386) (optional)

1. The night before you plan to barbecue, combine the rub ingredients in a small bowl. Massage the pork well with about half of the rub. Transfer the pork to a plastic bag and refrigerate it overnight.

2. Before you begin to barbecue, take the pork from the refrigerator. Pat down the pork with another coating of rub. Let the pork sit at room temperature for about 45 minutes.

3. Prepare the smoker for barbecuing, bringing the temperature to 200°F to 220°F.

4. If you plan to baste the pork (see page 45, "To Mop or Not"), stir any remaining rub together with the mop ingredients in a saucepan and warm the mixture over low heat.

5. Transfer the pork to the smoker and cook it until falling-apart tender, about 1½ hours per pound. Mop the meat every 50 to 60 minutes in a wood-burning pit, or as appropriate for your style of smoker.

6. Remove the pork from the smoker and let it sit for about 15 minutes, until cool enough to handle. Pull off chunks of the meat, then either shred or chop them as you like. If you wish, serve the pork with your choice of sauce.

Memphis Mustard Pork Sandwich

This is a tasty variation on the standard pork sandwich, based on a version we had in Memphis at Payne's, a former gas station converted mainly in its menu of fuels. The slaw and sauce can be made a day ahead of serving, if desired. SERVES 6 TO 8

MEMPHIS MUSTARD SLAW

2 cups chopped cabbage

1/2 cup minced onion

2 1/2 tablespoons yellow mustard

1 1/2 tablespoons white vinegar

3/4 teaspoon sugar

1/4 teaspoon table salt

MEMPHIS MAGIC BARBECUE SAUCE

3 tablespoons unsalted butter

1/4 cup minced onion

1 cup white vinegar

1 cup tomato sauce

1/4 cup Worcestershire sauce

2 teaspoons sugar

1 teaspoon table salt

1/2 teaspoon freshly ground black pepper

1/8 teaspoon cayenne or crushed red chile flakes

Dash of Tabasco or other hot pepper sauce

About 3 cups pulled or chopped smoked pork shoulder, such as meat from The Renowned Mr. Brown (page 51), Red-Eye Butt (page 52), Perfect Picnic (page 53), or Going Whole Hog (page 58), warmed

6 to 8 Yeast Buns (page 413) or spongy white bread buns

1. To make the slaw, mix all the ingredients in a bowl. Refrigerate, covered, for at least 30 minutes.

2. To make the sauce, melt the butter in a heavy saucepan over medium heat. Add the onion and sauté until softened. Mix in the remaining ingredients and simmer until the sauce has thickened and reduced, about 25 minutes. Refrigerate the sauce, too, if you are not planning to use it within the next hour. It can be served cold or reheated.

3. To serve, place the pork on a serving platter along with the buns. Let each person make his or her own sandwich, piling portions of the slaw, pork, and sauce on the bun, then squishing the bun together so that the meat juices and sauce mingle. Chow down.

VARIATION: CRACKLIN' CORNBREAD SANDWICH

In some scattered spots, particularly in Kentucky, people like their barbecue sandwiches on cornbread. If you want to try the idea, pile the pork on Cracklin' Cornbread (page 408).

BBQ tip Resist any upscale urge you may have to improve on the soft, spongy white buns traditionally used for barbecue sandwiches, unless you want to try cornbread. A "whole-grain sesame seed sourdough baguette" won't soak up enough juice to do the sandwich justice. Besides, it wouldn't be sloppy enough either. If you're itching to do something more, we give you a recipe later in the book for white bread Yeast Buns (page 413), so you can bake your own.

Going Whole Hog

If you have a large barbecue pit, a few assistants, and an urge for the ultimate challenge, you should tackle a whole hog. The quintessential barbecue meat of the South for a couple of centuries, it remains the first choice of many prominent pitmasters. Among all the experts, no one did a better job than the late Jim Quessenberry, founder and leader of the Arkansas Trav'lers barbecue team. We had the honor of cooking with the Trav'lers one year at the Memphis in May World Championship Barbecue Cooking Contest, where Jim taught us his techniques.

As he said, "The most important factor in whole hog is in fact the hog, himself." Bribe your butcher for the best animal in the area, preferably a heritage breed such as Berkshire. Jim got his hogs from a Mennonite farmer in Tennessee who custom-raised them on corn for a firm white meat that's as mild as turkey. The butcher should gut the hog, skin it, and trim the outside fat to a ¼-inch thickness. Use only a seriously sizeable wood-burning pit for whole hog barbecue and be committed to having someone tend the fire for some 20 hours of cooking time.

SERVES HALF OF ARKANSAS

1 full-grown hog, 120 to 150 pounds, skinned and trimmed

10 to 15 cups Southern Succor Rub (page 27)

2 apples, plus a couple of plump pimiento-stuffed green olives or dried apricots (optional)

QUESSENBERRY'S QUINTESSENTIAL HOG MOP

12 cups (3 quarts) cider vinegar

6 cups water

¾ cup kosher salt or coarse sea salt

Golden Mustard Barbecue Sauce (page 371), Carolina Red (page 371), or Vaunted Vinegar Sauce (page 370) (optional)

1. Fire up the pit, preferably with a combination of hickory and oak, and bring it to a temperature of 250°F.

2. Rub the hog thoroughly with the rub and lift it onto the pit, belly side down. If the pit has an off-set firebox, position the head facing away from the fire. The front legs should be stretched out so that they run alongside the head and the back legs pointed the other way. Cover the hams, tail, snout, and ears loosely with aluminum foil. If you're worried about your friends freaking out over a porker in a pit, you can make your meal look a little more festive by putting an apple in its mouth before you begin. (You'll replace it with the second apple at the end of cooking.)

3. Combine the mop ingredients in a large saucepan and warm over low heat.

4. Every hour or so, sprinkle on more rub or mop the meat with the vinegar mixture, alternating between the two applications. If you run low on mop, extend the batch with more water and vinegar, or simply mix up some more. Remove the foil in the last couple of hours of smoking so that the hams and other parts can brown nicely.

5. Maintain a steady cooking temperature of 200°F to 250°F until the internal temperature of the meat is at least 165°F to 170°F, and up to 180°F, especially in the shoulder area—this will take 18 to 20 hours. Check the internal temperature in several areas, to make sure none of the meat is underdone. It's pretty hard to seriously overcook the hog unless your fire is too hot.

6. While the fire dies, allow the hog to sit in the pit for about 2 hours before carving. Replace the browned and shriveled apple in the hog's mouth with the fresh apple, and arrange olives or dried apricots over the eyes if you like.

7. Serve the pork straight from the pit, simply picking at the tender meat with forks and fingers, covered if necessary with insulated washable mitts. (Use plastic bags over a pair of cloth oven mitts in a pinch.) Have a large cutting board and a cleaver and some large disposable foil pans or baking sheets nearby on a table with a washable surface. This will all be something of a mess, but if you've gotten this far, it shouldn't deter you. In the foil pans, mix the pulled pork and your choice of sauce. Serve with more sauce on the side.

BARBECUE BOOKS GALORE

If you want to pig out on barbecue books, follow our footsteps to the country's best dealer in outdoor cookbooks, Pig Out Publications in Kansas City. Owner Karen Adler, who is also a cookbook author and publisher herself, stocks virtually everything on the market, from bestsellers to obscure gems. Buy from her online shop, pigout publications.com, or even better, call 913-789-9594 for an appointment to browse the offerings in person at the BBQ Book Nook.

Miss White's Delights

Most of the time Southerners serve pork shoulder in a sandwich, a simple concept that's been perfected to a folk art. This traditional sandwich, Carolinas-style, blends a bit of The Renowned Mr. Brown (page 51) with a pile of stringy "pulled" pieces of "Miss White," the luscious inside meat. The slaw and sauce can be made a day ahead of serving, if desired. SERVES 6 TO 8

CAROLINA SANDWICH SLAW

2 cups chopped cabbage

2 tablespoons minced onion

2 tablespoons white vinegar

1 1/2 tablespoons mayonnaise

2 teaspoons sugar

1/4 teaspoon kosher salt or coarse sea salt

Generous grinding of black pepper

VAUNTED VINEGAR SAUCE

1 cup white vinegar

1 tablespoon sugar

1 teaspoon kosher salt or coarse sea salt

1/2 teaspoon freshly ground black pepper

1/2 teaspoon cayenne or crushed red chile flakes

About 3 cups pulled or chopped smoked pork shoulder, such as meat from The Renowned Mr. Brown (page 51), Red-Eye Butt (page 52), Perfect Picnic (page 53), or Going Whole Hog (page 58), warmed

6 to 8 Yeast Buns (page 413) or spongy white bread buns

1. To prepare the slaw, mix all the ingredients in a bowl. Refrigerate, covered, for at least 30 minutes.

2. To prepare the sauce, combine all of the ingredients in a bowl and stir until the sugar dissolves. Refrigerate the sauce, too, if you are not planning to use it within the next hour. It can be served cold or reheated.

3. Place the pork on a serving platter along with the buns. Let each person make his or her own sandwich, piling portions of the coleslaw, pork, and sauce on the bun, then squishing the bun together so that the meat juices and sauce mingle. Devour immediately.

SERVING SUGGESTION Offer Peppery 'Pups (page 406), our Carolinas-style hushpuppies, on the side and maybe Moon Pies (see page 459) for dessert.

BBQ tip Don't try to slice a barbecued butt with a knife to make sandwiches or anything else. If it's cooked right, the meat will be easy to pick or pull apart when it's still warm, and that's the time-honored way to serve it. Allow the pork to cool a little, but not for too long, and use gloves or a fork. The only role for a knife is to chop or mince the pieces of meat after they are pulled off, and that's an optional step.

The TBS SuperStation ranked the website of the Ugly Brothers (uglybrothers.net) the top "Guy Food" site on the Internet. Les, Big, and Bud Ugly, a barbecue cook-off team, say they pursue "inner peace through the artistic and scientific practice of slow-smoked pig meat." As you might guess, they're from California.

Spicy Seoul-ful Pulled Pork Sandwich

Tiny Heirloom Market BBQ in Atlanta has a grand international take on the classic pulled pork sandwich. Our Korean-seasoned recipe is inspired by what the Market serves to folks who patiently stand in a line at the door. In this case, you make a portion of our Korean Kick marinade and use it as a sauce. SERVES 6 TO 8

CUCUMBER-RADISH SLAW

1 large English cucumber, peeled, halved lengthwise, seeded, and sliced in thin half-moons

1 bunch mild radishes, tops and tails trimmed, halved and sliced thin

1 tablespoon minced onion

3/4 cup rice vinegar

1/2 cup granulated sugar

1/2 teaspoon table salt

KOREAN KICK (SAUCE)

3/4 cup *ganjang* (Korean soy sauce), or Japanese soy sauce such as Kikkoman

2 tablespoons toasted sesame oil

3 tablespoons granulated sugar or packed light brown sugar

3 garlic cloves

1 or 2 scallions, limp green tops discarded, chopped roughly

1 tablespoon *gochujang* (Korean red pepper paste) or sriracha

About 3 cups pulled or chopped smoked pork shoulder, such as meat from The Renowned Mr. Brown (page 51), Red-Eye Butt (page 52), Perfect Picnic (page 53), or Going Whole Hog (page 58), warmed

6 to 8 Yeast Buns (page 413) or spongy white bread buns

1. To make the slaw, mix all the ingredients in a bowl. Refrigerate, covered, for at least 30 minutes.

2. To make the sauce, combine all of the ingredients in a blender and puree until smooth. Pour the sauce into a serving bowl and refrigerate if you wish. It can be served cold or warm.

3. To serve, place the pork on a serving platter along with the buns. Let each person make his or her own sandwich. Pile portions of the pork, slaw (use a slotted spoon), and sauce on a bun, and serve right away.

OPEN-FACED CRISPY, CRUNCHY, SWEET, AND TANGY PULLED PORK SANDWICH Studded with bacon, cheese, and pickles, this has become one of our very favorite go-to lunches when we have leftover pulled pork. Heat up a griddle and, for each diner's sandwich, toast both sides of a slice of a favorite soft white sandwich bread or "Texas toast," the double-thick white bread. (Outside of Texas and the South, that's more likely found in the frozen food aisle.) While toasting the bread on the griddle, also use it to heat a generous 1/2 cup pulled pork per person, crisping it in places. Arrange a couple of slices of pepper Jack or other good melting cheese over each warm slice of toast. Top with a pair of slices of crisp smoky bacon and the warm pork, and cover with Bodacious Bread-and-Butter Pickles (page 433) or other bread-and-butter pickle slices. Dill pickle slices make a nice variation, if you like. Drizzle with a tomato-based barbecue sauce, such as our Bour-B-Q Sauce (page 381), Espresso Barbecue Sauce (page 377), or Struttin' Sauce (page 369). Eat with a fork and knife.

PULLED PORK SLIDERS WITH PICKLED RED ONIONS Make a batch of pickled onions by combining 1 thinly sliced red onion with 1 cup red wine vinegar, 3 ounces thawed frozen orange juice concentrate, and a good pinch of salt. Refrigerate for at least several hours, though they will keep for weeks chilled. Use small slider buns or split basic white bread rolls and toast if you wish. Pile high with warm pork and pickled onions, and add a swoosh of mustard or mustard-based barbecue sauce such as Golden Mustard Barbecue Sauce (page 371). Secure with bamboo skewers if you wish.

PULLED PORK CROQUETTES Mix 1 pound well-seasoned pulled pork with 1 large egg, 1/4 cup sour cream, 1/4 cup panko bread crumbs, a teaspoon or two mustard of your choice or a mustard-based barbecue sauce, and an optional splash of hot red pepper sauce. Pat the mixture into 12 ovals about 1/2 inch thick. Roll each croquette in additional panko bread crumbs. Cover the surface of a large heavy skillet with 1/4 inch vegetable oil. Fry the croquettes over medium heat until medium-brown and crispy, about 5 minutes per side. Serve hot, topped with spoonfuls of ranch dressing, mustardy barbecue sauce, or mayonnaise.

PULLED PORK PATTIES OVER GARLIC CHEESE GRITS Make 6 pulled pork patties using the recipe for croquettes on page 63, forming six ½-inch-thick rounds from the mixture rather than a dozen ovals. Keep them warm while preparing the grits or, even better, make them simultaneously. Make the grits by first bringing 4 cups water, 2 minced garlic cloves, and ¾ teaspoon table salt to a boil in a large heavy saucepan over high heat. Whisk in 1 cup stone-ground grits, a handful at a time. Reduce the heat to a bare simmer and cook the grits until thick and soft, about 30 minutes. Give the grits a stir occasionally as they cook, more often toward the end, to avoid scorching. Scrape them up from the bottom each time. Properly cooked grits should never be gritty in texture. Stir in 2 tablespoons unsalted butter and 4 ounces (1 cup) grated mild cheddar and remove from the heat. If you're really in a rush, "quick" (5- to 10-minute) grits work tolerably in this recipe, with the cooking time reduced accordingly. Spoon the warm grits into bowls or onto plates. Top each portion with a pork patty. Add a fried or poached egg and a shower of mild cheddar and serve.

PULLED PORK SOPES Sopes are delightful fried Mexican corn masa "boats" covered in a mix of toppings. To make the sopes, mix 2 cups masa harina, ¼ cup all-purpose flour, ½ teaspoon table salt, and ½ teaspoon baking powder in a medium-size bowl, then stir in 2 tablespoons vegetable oil and 1¼ cups water. Form the dough into 18 to 20 golf ball–size balls. Press the balls into flat disks about 2½ inches in diameter. Turn the outside edge of each disk up slightly to cradle the fillings. Fry in batches (flared side down) in 350°F vegetable oil, until crisp and golden, 2½ to 3 minutes. Top each sope shell with a couple of tablespoons warm pulled pork, cooked black or pinto beans, crumbled queso fresco or cotija cheese, and some avocado slices or guacamole. Serve right away with salsa.

PULLED PORK AND PORK BELLY BREAKFAST SANDWICHES ON ENGLISH MUFFINS You can use leftover Wood-Smoked Pork Belly (page 103) or simply bake a side of pork belly the day before you want to make the sandwiches. Place the uncooked belly, skin side down, in a roasting pan. Season assertively with Sweet Meat Rib Rub (page 27) or salt, pepper, and a couple of tablespoons brown sugar. Add 1 cup water to the roasting pan, pouring it around but not over the meat. Bake in a 300°F oven until soft and tender with a crispy top, 4 to 4½ hours. Slice as much meat as needed to cover an English muffin half, saving the rest for other meals. Toast the English muffin halves and smear each with mayonnaise. Cover with a layer of pork belly and another layer of warm pulled pork. Add an egg cooked any way to each sandwich, and maybe a slice of cheese. If you don't want to mess with the pork belly, just fry up some breakfast sausage patties for the sandwiches instead. And, oh heck, if you want, put the ingredients between a couple of buttermilk pancakes instead of English muffin halves.

PORK-STUFFED SWEET POTATOES Pierce plump sweet potatoes in several places with the tines of a fork. Place on a baking sheet covered with a silicone baking mat or parchment paper. Bake the sweet potatoes in a 400°F oven until tender, about 45 minutes. Make an end-to-end slit in each sweet potato, then push in from the ends just a bit to push up a bit of the soft center. Add a pat of butter to each and a sprinkling of salt and pepper. Spoon $1/3$ to $2/3$ cup warm pork over each. Mix in or drizzle over the top Honey-Mustard Barbecue Sauce (page 371) or another favorite sauce with some sweetness. Snipped chives or sliced green scallion rings are a nice finishing touch.

PULLED PORK AND GREEN CHILE STEW Sauté 1 large chopped onion and a couple of minced garlic cloves in a couple of tablespoons vegetable oil. When they are softened, pour in a 14.5-ounce can chopped tomatoes and juice, 4 cups reduced-sodium chicken stock, and a 10- to 12-ounce baking potato (peeled or unpeeled) chopped in bite-size chunks. Simmer until the potato begins to soften, about 15 minutes. Add 2 to 4 cups chopped mild to medium New Mexico–style green chile (fresh, thawed frozen, or jarred are preferable but canned can be used), and at least 2 cups pulled pork. Continue cooking about 15 minutes more. Serve hot.

PULLED PORK AND BEANS Switch up the emphasis by mixing a 15-ounce can of your favorite brand of baked beans with 2 cups pulled pork and $1/4$ to $1/2$ cup of a favorite barbecue sauce, such as Jalapeach Barbecue Sauce (page 384) or Smoked Onion Sauce (page 383). Bake in a 350°F oven until bubbly and hot throughout, about 30 minutes.

Lone Star Spareribs

In Kansas City, Memphis, and other rib capitals, most barbecuers cook in a "wet" style, applying a sauce near the end of the cooking and again before serving. In Texas, where people love to be contrary, the ribs are often left "dry," as they are here. SERVES 6

BARBECUED RIB RUB

1/3 cup freshly ground black pepper

1/4 cup paprika

2 tablespoons sugar

1 tablespoon kosher salt or coarse sea salt

1 tablespoon chili powder

1 1/2 teaspoons garlic powder

1 1/2 teaspoons onion powder

3 full slabs pork spareribs, "St. Louis cut" (trimmed of the chine bone and brisket flap), preferably 3 pounds each or less

BASIC BEER MOP (OPTIONAL)

12 ounces beer

1/2 cup water

1/2 cup cider vinegar

1/4 cup vegetable oil

1/2 medium onion, chopped or sliced in thin rings

2 garlic cloves, minced

1 tablespoon Worcestershire sauce

1. The night before you plan to barbecue, combine the rub ingredients in a small bowl. Apply about half of the rub evenly to the ribs. Place the slabs in a plastic bag and refrigerate them overnight.

2. Before you begin to barbecue, take the ribs from the refrigerator. Pat them down with the remaining rub, reserving 1 tablespoon of it if you plan to use the mop. Let the ribs sit at room temperature for 30 to 40 minutes. Prepare the smoker for barbecuing, bringing the temperature to 200°F to 220°F.

3. If you are going to baste the ribs (see page 45, "To Mop or Not"), mix the mop ingredients with the reserved 1 tablespoon rub in a large saucepan. Warm the mop liquid over low heat.

4. Transfer the meat to the smoker. Cook the ribs for 5 to 6 hours, turning and basting them with the mop about once an hour in a wood-burning pit, or as appropriate in your style of smoker.

5. When ready, the meat should be well-done and falling off the bones. Allow the slabs to sit for 10 minutes before slicing them into individual ribs.

BBQ tip We suggest different cooking times for our various rib recipes, but you may want to adjust the times for your taste. Spareribs are usually done in 3 1/2 to 4 hours, when you can crack them apart with a gloved hand. At that point the meat is firm, chewy, and juicy. If you prefer the ribs crunchier, leaner, and falling apart, as we do with "dry" styles, cook them longer, about 5 hours for a 3-pound slab or up to 6 hours for a larger slab. If you like super-tender ribs, cook them for 5 hours in the "naked-foiled-naked" style that barbecue teams call 3-2-1: Cook for 3 hours in the smoker as described in our recipes, then wrap in foil and return to the smoker for the next 2 hours for the meat to steam and simmer, then unwrap and continue cooking naked for about 1 hour more so the ribs' surface will get crispier and chewy in spots.

Southern Rib Sandwich

The idea will sound weird to the uninitiated, but a rib sandwich is viewed as a little hunk of heaven to aficionados. Expand "the recipe" by as many intrepid eaters as you've rounded up, using the end ribs from the smaller, tapered end of a rack of ribs smoked your favorite way. SERVES 1

1 or more slices spongy white bread

3 to 4 smoked spare ribs, cut into individual bones

Golden Mustard Barbecue Sauce (page 371), Memphis Magic (page 374), Bour-B-Q Sauce (page 381), or other favorite barbecue sauce

Place the bread on a plate. Top it with the individual ribs, piled in a crisscross kind of stack. Drizzle—or ladle—your choice of barbecue sauce over the ribs, and serve immediately. Alternatively, pile the bread over the ribs. Eat in any way you can manage, preferably with a pile of wet napkins.

CRACKLIN' RIBS

Most Memphis barbecue restaurants serve their ribs wet, but the Rendezvous downtown has probably sold more dry ribs than any place in the country. Layered with spices, the ribs come out of the kitchen as crunchy as corn chips, a perfect accompaniment to the barrels of beer served nightly in the raucous rathskeller.

Kansas City Sloppy Ribs

Kansas City folks love to make a mess with ribs, layering them with so much sweet, hot sauce that you're licking your fingers as often as you're licking your chops. Oh, mercy! SERVES 6

KC RIB RUB

1 cup packed brown sugar

1/2 cup paprika

2 1/2 tablespoons freshly ground black pepper

2 1/2 tablespoons kosher salt or coarse sea salt

1 1/2 tablespoons chili powder

1 1/2 tablespoons garlic powder

1 1/2 tablespoons onion powder

1 to 2 teaspoons cayenne

3 full slabs pork spareribs, "St. Louis cut" (trimmed of the chine bone and brisket flap), preferably 3 pounds each or less

Cheryl's Cider Spritz (page 42) (optional)

Struttin' Sauce (page 369), Boydesque Brew (page 368), Smoked Onion Sauce (page 383), or other sweet, tomato-based barbecue sauce

1. The night before you plan to barbecue, combine the rub ingredients in a bowl. Apply about one-third of the rub evenly to the ribs. Place the slabs in a plastic bag and refrigerate them overnight.

2. Before you begin to barbecue, take the ribs from the refrigerator. Sprinkle the ribs lightly but thoroughly with more rub, reserving the rest of the mixture. Let the ribs sit at room temperature for 30 to 40 minutes.

3. Prepare the smoker for barbecuing, bringing the temperature to 200°F to 220°F.

4. Transfer the meat to the smoker. Cook the ribs for about 4 hours, turning and sprinkling them with more dry rub about halfway through the time. If you wish, spray the ribs with Cheryl's Cider Spritz every 45 minutes or so. In the last 45 minutes of cooking, slather the ribs once or twice with your favorite sweet tomato-based barbecue sauce.

5. When ready, the meat will bend easily between the ribs, and the sauce will be gooey and sticky. Allow the slabs to sit for 10 minutes before slicing them into individual ribs. Serve with more sauce on top or on the side and plenty of napkins.

GUESS I'LL TAKE THE PORK

The Skylight Inn in Ayden, North Carolina, always wins acclaim from serious eaters as one of the best barbecue joints in the South. Proprietor-and-pitmaster Sam Jones smokes whole hogs overnight, chops up a mixture of the pork with a good share of the dark exterior portions, and serves it in a sandwich or on a real plain plate. That's it folks, but it's so good you won't be left wanting.

Way back in 1860, an author identified only as "an ex-member of Congress" published a book called *My Ride to the Barbecue*. He described the feast in this fashion: "There appeared to be about half a hundred whole carcasses of full-grown and well-fattened sheep and hogs, each having two long iron rods run through its length. . . . These were all laid across a trench (the projecting ends of the rods resting upon each side thereof), which was about a hundred feet in length by four deep, and in the bottom of which was a bed of glowing coals, that was replenished from time to time from large log fires kept constantly burning close by for that purpose. At suitable intervals along the sides of the trench were iron vessels, some filled with salt, and water; others with melted butter, lard, etc., into which the attendants dipped linen cloths affixed to the ends of long, flexible wands, and delicately applied them with a certain air of dainty precision to different portions of the roasting meat."

BBQ tip Rib cuts can get confusing. Pork spareribs come from the belly of the hog, next to the bacon, and are great for barbecuing because of their combination of meat, fat, and pork flavor. Butchers used to discard the tough cut until they discovered it could be tenderized through slow smoking. Loin ribs, baby back ribs, and country ribs are all "better," more expensive cuts. They taste good barbecued, too, but they don't depend as much on the process for their flavor.

BBQ tip Barbecue sauces and other glazes added to meat in the last hour of cooking are often important to the flavor of a dish, particularly ribs, but you need to adjust their use to your style of smoker. Like mops, they work best in a wood-burning pit, where they should be applied the maximum number of times suggested in a recipe. With a charcoal grill, water smoker, or other kind of equipment that loses a lot of heat when the lid is raised, we normally use glazes only once during the cooking. With some electric-powered smokers, such as a Cookshack, you should wait to apply the sauce when you remove the food from the oven.

Bourbon-Glazed Ribs

This Kentucky-inspired recipe is our personal favorite for "wet" spareribs. They're finished at the end with a mellow glaze that also serves as a table sauce. SERVES 6

BARBECUED RIB RUB

1/3 cup freshly ground black pepper

1/4 cup paprika

2 tablespoons sugar

1 tablespoon kosher salt or coarse sea salt

1 tablespoon chili powder

1 1/2 teaspoons garlic powder

1 1/2 teaspoons onion powder

3 full slabs pork spareribs, "St. Louis cut" (trimmed of the chine bone and brisket flap), preferably 3 pounds each or less

BOURBON MOP (OPTIONAL)

3/4 cup bourbon

3/4 cup cider vinegar

1/2 cup water

BOUR-B-Q SAUCE

1/4 cup unsalted butter

1/4 cup vegetable oil

2 medium onions, minced

3/4 cup bourbon

2/3 cup ketchup

1/2 cup cider vinegar

1/2 cup freshly squeezed orange juice

1/2 cup pure maple syrup

1/3 cup molasses

2 tablespoons Worcestershire sauce

1/2 teaspoon freshly ground black pepper

1/2 teaspoon table salt

1. The night before you plan to barbecue, combine the rub ingredients in a bowl. Apply about half of the rub evenly to the ribs. Place the slabs in a plastic bag and refrigerate them overnight.

2. Before you begin, take the ribs from the refrigerator. Pat them down with the remaining rub. Let sit at room temperature for 30 to 40 minutes.

3. Prepare the smoker for barbecuing, bringing the temperature to 200°F to 220°F.

4. If you plan to baste the meat (see page 45, "To Mop or Not"), mix the mop ingredients and warm the mixture over low heat.

5. Transfer the meat to the smoker. Cook the ribs for about 4 hours, turning and mopping them every 1 1/2 hours in a wood-burning pit, or as appropriate in your style of smoker.

6. Prepare the sauce so that it is ready to apply approximately 45 minutes before the meat is done. In a large saucepan, melt the butter with the oil over medium heat. Add the onions and sauté until they begin to turn golden. Add the remaining ingredients, reduce the heat to low, and cook until thickened, approximately 40 minutes, stirring frequently.

7. Brush the ribs with sauce once or twice in the last 45 minutes of cooking. Return the remaining sauce to the stove and simmer until reduced by one-third, 15 to 20 minutes.

8. When the slabs are ready, the meat will bend easily between the ribs, and the sauce will be gooey and sticky. Allow the slabs to sit for 10 minutes before slicing them into individual ribs. Serve with the reduced sauce on the side.

SERVING SUGGESTION We like these ribs best with a simple salad like Killed Salad (page 418), which means there will still be room for Run for the Roses Pie (page 443) afterward.

BBQ *tip* The preferred size of spareribs for barbecuing is "3 and down," meaning 3 pounds or smaller, a variable that depends on the weight of the pig when butchered. Don't fret if all you can find are larger slabs, but do smoke them a little longer.

Apple City Baby Back Ribs

This recipe is inspired by the award-winning ribs made by the Apple City BBQuers from Murphysboro, Illinois, one of the most successful barbecue contest teams in the country. SERVES 3 TO 4

CHERYL'S CIDER SOAK

1 1/2 cups apple cider or juice

3/4 cup cider vinegar

1/2 medium onion, minced

1 1/2 tablespoons Worcestershire sauce

1 tablespoon vegetable oil

1 teaspoon ground cinnamon

1 teaspoon dried thyme

2 slabs baby back ribs, preferably 1 1/4 to 1 1/2 pounds each

RIB RUB

1/4 cup packed brown sugar

4 teaspoons onion powder

1 teaspoon ground cinnamon

1 teaspoon dry mustard

1 teaspoon kosher salt or coarse sea salt

1/2 teaspoon dried thyme

APPLE RIB MOP (OPTIONAL)

1 1/2 cups apple cider or juice

1/2 cup cider vinegar

4 teaspoons Worcestershire sauce

Apple City Apple Sauce (page 384), Espresso Barbecue Sauce (page 377), or Boydesque Brew (page 368)

1. The night before you plan to barbecue, combine the soak ingredients in a large glass measuring cup. Place the slabs of ribs in a plastic bag or shallow dish and pour the marinade over the ribs. Refrigerate them overnight.

2. Prepare the smoker for barbecuing, bringing the temperature to 200°F to 220°F.

3. Remove the ribs from the refrigerator and drain them, discarding the marinade. In a bowl, mix the dry rub ingredients and pat the ribs with about half of the mixture. Let the ribs sit at room temperature for 25 to 30 minutes.

Barbecue cook-offs go hog wild with names. Some of our favorites from over the years include "Swine Days" in Natchez, Mississippi, "When Pigs Fly" in McPherson, Kansas, "Squealing on the Square" in Laurens, South Carolina, and "Hogtoberfest" in Roanoke Rapids, North Carolina. We're not so sure about the naming folks in Ashburn, Georgia, who host their cook-off at the Fire Ant Festival.

4. If you plan to baste the meat (see page 45, "To Mop or Not"), mix the cider, vinegar, and Worcestershire sauce in a saucepan. Warm the mop liquid over low heat.

5. Transfer the meat to the smoker. Cook the ribs for approximately 3 hours, turning and basting them with the mop every hour in a wood-burning pit, or as appropriate in your style of smoker. About 45 minutes before the ribs are done, brush them with your choice of sauce, and repeat the step shortly before you remove the meat from the smoker.

6. When the slabs are ready, the meat will bend easily between the ribs, and the sauce will be gooey and sticky and caramelized in spots. Allow the slabs to sit for 5 to 10 minutes before slicing them into individual ribs. Serve with more sauce on the side.

BBQ tip The Apple City BBQuers took their name from the apples that grow in their neighborhood and they took their wood from the same trees. The sweet wood works well with many pork dishes, though we usually like to mix it with hickory.

Thai-phoon Baby Backs

The layered Thai flavors in these ribs will wash over you like a South Seas storm. As is common on the home turf of the seasonings, we serve the pork as finger food with a dipping sauce that's both sweet and fiery. SERVES 3 TO 4

THAI-PHOON MARINADE

1½ cups crushed pineapple from a 20-ounce can, remainder reserved for dipping sauce

2 tablespoons Asian fish sauce

¼ cup freshly squeezed lime juice

3 garlic cloves, halved

1½ stalks lemongrass, chopped

2 slabs baby back ribs, preferably 1¼ to 1½ pounds each

THAI-PHOON DIPPING SAUCE

2 tablespoons peanut oil

½ stalk lemongrass, chopped

2 garlic cloves, sliced thin

¾ cup white or cider vinegar

¼ cup sugar

2 tablespoons Asian fish sauce

1 to 2 teaspoons crushed red chile flakes

1 to 2 tablespoons minced fresh cilantro (optional)

1. At least 2 hours before you plan to barbecue, and preferably the evening before, puree the marinade ingredients in a food processor. Place the ribs in a plastic bag or nonreactive dish, pour the marinade over them, and refrigerate for at least 2 hours, or up to overnight. Turn the meat occasionally.

2. Prepare the smoker for barbecuing, bringing the temperature to 200°F to 220°F.

3. Remove the ribs from the refrigerator, drain them, and if you wish to mop the meat (see page 45, "To Mop or Not"), reserve the marinade in a saucepan. Let the ribs sit at room temperature for 25 to 30 minutes. If reserving the marinade, bring it to a boil over high heat with ½ cup water and boil for several minutes. Keep the mop warm over low heat.

4. Transfer the meat to the smoker. Cook the ribs for approximately 3 hours, turning and mopping twice in a wood-burning pit, or as appropriate in your smoker.

5. When done, the ribs will have a thin lacquered coating on the surface and will pull apart easily. Allow the slabs to sit for 5 to 10 minutes before slicing them into individual ribs.

6. While the ribs cook, prepare the dipping sauce. Warm the oil in a small saucepan over medium heat. Add the lemongrass and garlic and sauté briefly, until the garlic is lightly colored. Add the reserved crushed pineapple, vinegar, sugar, fish sauce, and chile flakes, raise the heat to high, and cook until reduced by one-third and rather syrupy, about 2 minutes. Stir in the cilantro, if desired, and remove from the heat. Serve the ribs warm, with the dipping sauce. If the sauce gets too thick for easy dunking, simply add a bit more water.

West Coast Baby Backs

At the time we wrote the original edition of this book, much of the country's Asian-inspired cooking was still centered on the West Coast, hence the name for these soy- and star anise–scented little babies. Today, they are as at-home in St. Louis as in San Francisco or Seattle. SERVES 3 TO 4

SIMPLE CHINESE FIVE-SPICE MEDLEY
1/3 cup five-spice powder
1/3 cup packed brown sugar

2 slabs baby back ribs, preferably 1¼ to 1½ pounds each
1/4 cup reduced-sodium soy sauce
West Coast Wonder barbecue sauce (page 379) or Plum Good Slopping Sauce (page 387) (optional)

1. At least 2 hours before you plan to barbecue, and preferably the evening before, mix the rub ingredients in a small bowl. Rub the ribs with the soy sauce, followed by a liberal coating of the spice mixture. Reserve the remaining rub. Place the ribs in a plastic bag and refrigerate them overnight, or for at least 2 hours.

2. Prepare the smoker for barbecuing, bringing the temperature to 200°F to 220°F.

3. Remove the ribs from the refrigerator. Pat them down with the remaining rub. Let the ribs sit at room temperature for 25 to 30 minutes.

4. Transfer the meat to the smoker. Cook the ribs for approximately 3 hours, turning and sprinkling them with the remaining dry rub about halfway through the cooking time.

5. When done, the ribs will have a thin coating of crispy spices on the surface and will pull apart easily. Allow the slabs to sit for 5 to 10 minutes before slicing them into individual ribs. Serve warm, with barbecue sauce if you wish.

SERVING SUGGESTION Add some sliced water chestnuts and minced red bell pepper to cooked white rice, and serve it along with steamed broccoli spears drizzled with a little soy sauce. Finish with creamy 'Nana Pudding (page 463) or Key Lime Pie (page 447).

BBQ tip Perfectionists and cook-off contestants strip the membrane from the bone side of ribs before cooking, but this step isn't really necessary, particularly if you smoke the meat longer than it needs for doneness. If you wish to do this, work a butter knife under the membrane until you've loosened a section large enough to grasp. Then use a paper towel to help grip it to pull it all away.

"There may be religious, political, athletic, or sexual images that stir deeper emotions—*may* be—but nothing in the realm of Southern food is regarded with more passionate enthusiasm by the faithful than a perfectly cooked and seasoned pork shoulder or slab of ribs." John Egerton, *Southern Food* (1987, Knopf)

Double-Crusted Baby Backs with Fennel and Coriander

When we first penned *Smoke & Spice*, many of us in the food world were complaining that pork had become too lean and had lost much of its flavor. Since that time, farmers started working once again with older breeds, like the Berkshire, known for its succulent marbling. We particularly love ribs from a heritage breed with a dry rub, because the crusty surface contrasts so dramatically with the juicy meat.

SERVES 3 TO 4

FENNEL AND CORIANDER RUB

2 tablespoons crushed fennel seeds

2 tablespoons crushed coriander seeds

2 teaspoons kosher salt or coarse sea salt

2 teaspoons packed brown sugar

2 slabs baby back ribs, preferably 1¼ to 1½ pounds each

1. At least 2 hours before you plan to barbecue, and preferably the evening before, mix the rub ingredients in a small bowl. Rub the ribs with half of the rub. Place the ribs in a plastic bag and refrigerate them overnight, or for at least 2 hours.

2. Prepare the smoker for barbecuing, bringing the temperature to 200°F to 220°F.

3. Remove the ribs from the refrigerator. Pat them down with the remaining rub. Let the ribs sit at room temperature for 25 to 30 minutes.

4. Transfer the meat to the smoker. Cook the ribs for approximately 3 hours, turning and sprinkling them with the remaining dry rub about halfway through the cooking time.

5. When done, the ribs will have a thin coating of crispy spices on the surface and will pull apart easily. Allow the slabs to sit for 5 to 10 minutes before slicing them into individual ribs. Serve warm.

Cajun Country Ribs

Country-style ribs come from the blade ends of pork loin. Meaty and full of flavor, they pair well with hearty Louisiana spices. SERVES 4

CAJUN RAGIN' RUB

2 tablespoons celery salt

2 tablespoons freshly ground black pepper

2 tablespoons ground white pepper

2 tablespoons packed brown sugar

1 tablespoon garlic powder

1 1/2 teaspoons cayenne

1 1/2 teaspoons dried thyme

1 teaspoon dried sage

Four to six 10-ounce to 14-ounce country-style rib sections

QUICK SOUTHERN SOP (OPTIONAL)

1 1/2 cups cider vinegar

3/4 cup water

1 tablespoon Worcestershire sauce

Creole Classic Barbecue Sauce (page 382), Memphis Magic (page 374), or other spicy tomato-based barbecue sauce

1. The night before you plan to barbecue, combine the rub ingredients in a small bowl. Apply about half of the rub evenly to the ribs. Place the ribs in a plastic bag and refrigerate them overnight.

2. Prepare the smoker for barbecuing, bringing the temperature to 200°F to 220°F.

3. Remove the ribs from the refrigerator. Pat them down with a liberal sprinkling of the remaining rub, reserving 1 tablespoon if you plan to use the mop. Let the ribs stand at room temperature for 25 to 30 minutes.

4. If you are going to baste the meat (see page 45, "To Mop or Not"), mix the vinegar, water, Worcestershire sauce, and reserved 1 tablespoon rub in a saucepan. Warm the mop liquid over low heat.

5. Transfer the meat to the smoker. Cook the ribs for 2 1/2 to 3 hours, basting them with the mop at 45-minute intervals in a wood-burning pit, or as appropriate in your style of smoker.

6. When ready, the meat will be well-done and quite tender, with a coating of crispy spices on the surface. Serve hot.

SERVING SUGGESTION Mix cultures tastefully, serving the ribs with Kraut Salad (page 428), Sweet Potato Biscuits (page 411), and Santa Fe Capirotada (page 464) for the finale.

Maple-Bourbon Ham

In Virginia, Kentucky, and other nearby states, traditional country hams are cured in a bed of dry salt for some 5 weeks, smoked in an old-fashioned smokehouse for up to 2 months, and hung to age for almost a year. Barbecuing a ham is much simpler, and many people find the result even tastier. SERVES 10 TO 12

12- to 14-pound bone-in cooked ready-to-eat ham

MAPLE-BOURBON PASTE

2 tablespoons pure maple syrup

2 tablespoons freshly ground black pepper

2 tablespoons Dijon or honey-Dijon mustard

1 tablespoon bourbon or other sour-mash whiskey

1 tablespoon vegetable oil

1 tablespoon paprika

1 tablespoon onion powder

2 teaspoons kosher salt or coarse sea salt

MAPLE-BOURBON MOP (OPTIONAL)

1/4 cup pure maple syrup

1/4 cup bourbon or other sour-mash whiskey

1/4 cup cider vinegar

3 tablespoons vegetable oil

2 teaspoons Dijon or honey-Dijon mustard

MAPLE-BOURBON GLAZE

3/4 cup pure maple syrup

1/4 cup plus 2 tablespoons bourbon or other sour-mash whiskey

3 tablespoons Dijon or honey-Dijon mustard

2 tablespoons unsalted butter

2 tablespoons minced onion

1 tablespoon cider vinegar

2 teaspoons yellow mustard seeds, cracked

1 teaspoon freshly ground black pepper

1. The night before you plan to smoke the ham, score the fatty side of the ham in wide criss-cross cuts through the fat layer, about 1/4 to 1/2 inch deep. Combine the paste ingredients in a small bowl. Apply the gooey, sticky paste evenly to the ham, pretending you're a kid playing in something that will appall your mother. We find it easiest to manage the task if we arrange a large plastic bag on the counter, set the ham in the bag, rub the meat with the paste, and then pull the bag up snug and close it. Refrigerate the ham overnight.

2. Before you begin to barbecue, take the ham from the refrigerator and let it sit at room temperature for 45 to 60 minutes.

3. Prepare the smoker for barbecuing, bringing the temperature to 200°F to 220°F.

4. If you plan to baste the meat (see page 45, "To Mop or Not"), mix the mop ingredients in a saucepan. Warm the mop liquid over low heat.

5. Transfer the ham to the smoker. Cook for 5 1/2 to 6 hours, basting the meat with the mop about once an hour in a wood-burning pit, or as appropriate in your style of smoker.

6. Meanwhile, combine the glaze ingredients in a small bowl. Brush the ham with the glaze twice during the last hour of cooking. The ham is ready when thoroughly heated through.

7. Let the ham sit for 15 minutes before carving.

If you like smokehouse-style country hams, you'll love the Loveless Motel and Café, just outside Nashville, Tennessee. The small roadhouse eatery specializes in hams and jams, and the kitchen does a magnificent job with both. You can even order by phone (615-646-9700) or online (lovelesscafe.com).

Ginger-Glazed Ham

This is a substantially different but equally luscious approach to barbecued ham.

SERVES 10 TO 12

SOUTHERN SUCCOR RUB

2 tablespoons freshly ground black pepper

2 tablespoons paprika

2 tablespoons turbinado sugar

1 tablespoon kosher salt or coarse sea salt

1 teaspoon dry mustard

1/2 teaspoon cayenne

12-pound to 14-pound bone-in cooked ready-to-eat ham

PINEAPPLE MOP (OPTIONAL)

1 1/2 cups chicken stock

1 1/2 cups pineapple juice

3 tablespoons vegetable oil

2 teaspoons dry mustard

1 teaspoon ground cloves

GINGER GLAZE

2/3 cup ginger preserves or jelly

2 to 3 tablespoons pineapple juice

1/4 teaspoon dry mustard

Pinch of ground cloves

1. The night before you plan to barbecue, combine the rub ingredients in a small bowl. Apply the rub evenly to the ham. Place the ham in a plastic bag and refrigerate it overnight.

2. Before you begin to barbecue, take the ham from the refrigerator and let it sit at room temperature for 45 to 60 minutes.

3. Prepare the smoker for barbecuing, bringing the temperature to 200°F to 220°F.

4. If you plan to baste the meat (see page 45, "To Mop or Not"), mix the mop ingredients in a saucepan. Warm the mop liquid over low heat.

5. Transfer the ham to the smoker. Cook for 5 1/2 to 6 hours, basting the meat with the mop about once an hour in a wood-burning pit, or as appropriate in your style of smoker.

6. Meanwhile, combine the glaze ingredients in a small bowl. Brush the ham with the glaze twice during the last hour of cooking. The ham is ready when thoroughly heated through and infused with smoke flavor.

7. Let the ham sit for 15 minutes before carving. Save some of the leftovers for Monday Night Ham Loaf (page 106).

SERVING SUGGESTION Ham has always made a Sunday dinner special. Prepare a crock of Supper Spread (page 107) and serve it with crackers as a taste teaser. Accompany the ham with Country Collard Greens (page 400), Mayme's Macaroni and Cheese (page 405), Corn and Watermelon Pickle-lilli (page 438), and Buttermilk Biscuits (page 410) with peach butter or jam. Sweet Potato Pudding (page 462) slides down easily for dessert.

BBQ tip Ham leftovers are a little gift for the cook. Cut them into tiny cubes and mix them into biscuit dough before baking. If your biscuits are already baked, slice the ham thin and arrange between two warm halves, with a dollop of mustard or chutney. Add little shreds to a pot of greens or make the best ham and cheddar sandwich that ever met your mouth.

GIVE A CURTSY, BOYS

The Blue Ridge BBQ & Music Festival in June in Tryon, North Carolina, gives awards to cooks, of course, but has also honored pigs that are almost too pretty to barbecue. Bring your pit to enter the cook-off, the official state championship event, and in appropriate years dress up a shapely pig to get it crowned Queen of the North Carolina Hogs. If you don't make the cut either way, there's still plenty of great music to enjoy. Jim Tabb, the dean of North Carolina barbecue, founded the festival to honor the state's proud pork heritage.

Weeknight Pork Tenderloin

One of the dishes that participants in our cooking classes love the most is smoked pork tenderloin. Because of its long, thin shape, it's among the quickest and easiest meats to transform with smoke. Enjoy it as an entrée or add it to salads, pastas, or other dishes. SERVES 4

1¼-pound to 1½-pound pork tenderloin

1 to 2 tablespoons vegetable oil

2 to 3 tablespoons Wild Willy's Number One-derful Rub (page 26), Southwest Heat (page 32), or your favorite store-bought dry rub

South Florida Citrus Sauce (page 386), Smoked Onion Sauce (page 383), or other favorite barbecue sauce (optional)

1. Prepare your smoker for barbecuing, bringing the temperature to 200°F to 220°F.

2. Cut the tenderloin down one of its long sides, cutting to within about ½ inch of the other side. Fold the tenderloin open like a book, and press down along the seam so that it will stay open. Lightly pound the tenderloin as needed to even its thickness to about ½ inch. Rub with 1 to 2 teaspoons of the oil, and then with the dry rub. Let it sit at room temperature for 30 minutes.

3. Warm a heavy skillet over high heat, and add the remaining oil. Sear the tenderloin well, about 1 minute per side. Transfer the tenderloin to the smoker. Cook until the internal temperature reaches 160°F, about 1½ hours. Brush the tenderloins lightly, if you wish, once during the last 30 minutes of cooking with your choice of barbecue sauce. Let the meat sit for 10 minutes before carving. Serve with additional sauce on the side.

VARIATION: YUCATECAN PORK TENDERLOIN Use Yucatecan Seasoning Paste (page 36) in place of the dry rub for seasoning. Serve with Sauce Olé (page 379), Mango-Habanero Hellfire (page 387), or Fiesta Salsa (page 349), and black beans and white rice.

BBQ tip We think North of the Border, a small company down the road from our home, makes some of the best commercial dry rubs and other barbecue condiments available today. Proprietors Gayther and Susie Gonzales consistently get the balance of seasonings just right. For this simple pork tenderloin, we often use their green chile rub, known as P.C. Willy's, or their smoky Montezuma Chipotle Seasoning. For a spicy finishing sauce for either preparation, consider the company's Chipotle Catch Up or Chipotle Barbeque Sauce. Buy North of the Border products online at northoftheborder.net.

Sweet and Fruity Pork Tenderloin

This tenderloin is dressed up for a fancy occasion in honey and spice and everything nice. SERVES 4

SWEET SENSATION RUB

1 tablespoon ground allspice

1 tablespoon packed brown sugar

1 tablespoon onion powder

1½ teaspoons kosher salt or coarse sea salt

½ teaspoon ground nutmeg

½ teaspoon ground cinnamon

½ teaspoon dried thyme

Two 12-ounce to 14-ounce tenderloins

Vegetable oil

TENDERLOIN MOP (OPTIONAL)

1½ cups chicken stock

2 tablespoons vegetable oil

1 tablespoon cider vinegar

1 tablespoon honey

Jalapeach Barbecue Sauce (page 384) or Jamaican Barbecue Sauce (page 383)

1. The night before you plan to barbecue, combine the rub ingredients in a small bowl. Massage the tenderloins with a thin film of the oil followed by a couple of tablespoons of the rub. Wrap them in plastic and refrigerate overnight.

2. Prepare your smoker for barbecuing, bringing the temperature to 200°F to 220°F.

3. Remove the tenderloins from the refrigerator and let them sit at room temperature for 30 minutes.

4. If you plan to baste the meat (see page 45, "To Mop or Not"), stir together the remaining rub with the other mop ingredients in a small saucepan and warm the mixture over low heat.

5. Warm a heavy skillet over high heat. Quickly sear the tenderloins on all sides. Transfer the tenderloins to the smoker. Cook for 2 to 2¼ hours, turning the meat and basting it with the mop about once every 30 minutes in a wood-burning pit, or as appropriate in your style of smoker. Brush the tenderloins lightly with Jalapeach Barbecue Sauce or Jamaican Barbecue Sauce during the last 30 minutes of cooking.

6. The tenderloins are ready when the internal temperature reaches 160°F. Let the meat sit for 10 minutes before carving. Serve with additional sauce on the side.

SERVING SUGGESTION Provide a decorative bowl of Curry Pecans (page 344) and a pitcher of Cham-gria (page 483) for openers. With the pork, serve roasted potatoes and carrots and Blue Corn Muffins (page 412). Finish off with a Key Lime Pie (page 447).

Purely Pork Chops

Like the Weeknight Pork Tenderloin (page 82), these chops are a simple smoke job but lusciously succulent. SERVES 6

SOUTHERN SUCCOR RUB

1 tablespoon freshly ground black pepper

1 tablespoon paprika

1 tablespoon turbinado sugar

1½ teaspoons kosher salt or coarse sea salt

½ teaspoon dry mustard

¼ teaspoon cayenne

6 bone-in center-cut pork chops, ½ to ¾ inch thick

CHOP MOP (OPTIONAL)

½ cup cider or white vinegar

Old-Fashioned High-Cholesterol Great-Tasting Southern Sauce (page 372), Apple City Apple Sauce (page 384), Smoked Onion Sauce (page 383), or other barbecue sauce (optional)

1. At least 2 hours, and preferably 4 hours, before you plan to barbecue, combine the rub ingredients in a small bowl. Massage the chops with several tablespoons of the rub. Place the chops in a plastic bag and refrigerate for 1½ to 3½ hours.

2. Prepare the smoker for barbecuing, bringing the temperature to 200°F to 220°F.

3. Remove the chops from the refrigerator and let them sit at room temperature for 30 minutes.

4. If you plan to baste the chops (see page 45, "To Mop or Not"), warm the vinegar in a small saucepan over low heat.

5. Warm a heavy skillet over high heat. Quickly sear the chops on both sides and transfer them to the smoker. Cook the meat for 55 to 65 minutes, turning and basting it with the mop once or twice in a wood-burning pit, or as appropriate in your style of smoker.

6. The chops are ready when the internal temperature reaches 160°F. Serve hot, with your choice of barbecue sauce on the side if you wish.

VARIATION: POP CHOPS Marinate and/or mop the chops with Pop Mop (page 47), using Dr Pepper, Coca-Cola, or RC Cola.

DUELING DICTIONARIES

The North Carolina Pork Producers Association improved on Mr. Webster in its definition of barbecue: "1. The premiere ethnic food of North Carolina. 2. Pig pickin'. 3. Catalyst for great debate. 4. A method of cooking. 5. Pig as a culinary art. 6. A cultural rite. 7. All of the above."

Stuffed Chops

These tender chops are stuffed with a moist cornbread dressing. SERVES 6

KENTUCKY PRIDE PASTE

1/2 medium onion, preferably a sweet variety, chunked

2 tablespoons bourbon

1 tablespoon packed brown sugar

1 tablespoon freshly ground black pepper

1 1/2 teaspoons vegetable oil

1/2 teaspoon table salt

6 bone-in double-thick center-cut pork chops, about 1 1/2 inches thick, cut with a pocket for stuffing

STUFFING

1/4 cup unsalted butter

1/2 medium green bell pepper, seeded and chopped fine

1/2 small onion, chopped fine

1 celery rib, chopped fine

1 cup dry cornbread crumbs

1 dozen pitted prunes, chopped

2 tablespoons chopped fresh parsley

1 tablespoon minced fresh sage or 1 1/2 teaspoons dried sage

1/4 teaspoon dry mustard

Table salt to taste

1 to 3 tablespoons chicken stock or water

DRUNK CHOP MOP (OPTIONAL)

1 cup cider or white vinegar

2 tablespoons bourbon

2 tablespoons water

1. At least 2 hours, and preferably 4 hours, before you plan to barbecue, combine the paste ingredients in a food processor or blender. Massage the chops inside and out with the paste.

Place the chops in a plastic bag and refrigerate for 1 1/2 to 3 1/2 hours.

2. Prepare the smoker for barbecuing, bringing the temperature to 200°F to 220°F.

3. Remove the chops from the refrigerator and let them sit at room temperature for 20 to 30 minutes.

4. To make the stuffing, melt the butter in a small skillet. Add the bell pepper, onion, and celery, sautéing until soft. Spoon the mixture into a bowl and stir in the remaining ingredients, adding only enough water or stock to bind the stuffing loosely. Stuff the chops with equal portions of the mixture.

5. If you plan to baste the chops (see page 45, "To Mop or Not"), warm the vinegar, bourbon, and water in a small saucepan over low heat. Keep the mop warm over low heat.

6. Warm a heavy skillet over high heat. Quickly sear the chops on both sides and transfer them to the smoker. Cook for 1 3/4 to 2 hours, turning and basting the meat with the mop about every 30 minutes in a wood-burning pit, or as appropriate in your style of smoker.

7. The chops are ready when the internal temperature reaches 160°F. Serve hot.

VARIATION: GERMAN STUFFED CHOPS Replace the paste with one made of 3 tablespoons brown mustard, 2 teaspoons vegetable oil, and 1 teaspoon kosher salt or coarse sea salt. In the stuffing, eliminate the cornbread crumbs, prunes, and parsley. Instead, mix in 1¼ cups fresh rye bread crumbs, 1 cup sauerkraut, and 1 teaspoon brown mustard with the other stuffing ingredients. Prepare as described.

SERVING SUGGESTION For a casual supper, pair the chops with Sweet Sally's Sweet Potato Salad (page 426). Poach apple slices in apple juice and cinnamon and top with crystallized ginger for dessert.

Pork Loin Mexicana

In this succulent loin, tropical fruits combine with spice for a south-of-the-border flavor reminiscent of Veracruz. The preparation is a bit involved, but you'll know it was worth it with every bite. SERVES 4

SWEET SENSATION RUB

1 tablespoon ground allspice

1 tablespoon packed brown sugar

1 tablespoon onion powder

1 1/2 teaspoons kosher salt or coarse sea salt

1/2 teaspoon ground nutmeg

1/2 teaspoon ground cinnamon

1/2 teaspoon dried thyme

3 1/2-pound to 4-pound boneless center-cut pork loin, with a pocket sliced lengthwise through the center

FRUIT SALSA

1 cup freshly squeezed orange juice

2 ripe Roma or other plum tomatoes

1 small ripe banana, chopped

1/2 medium onion, minced

1 fresh jalapeño, minced

2 teaspoons extra-virgin olive oil

1 teaspoon ground red chile, preferably ancho or New Mexican, or chili powder

2 garlic cloves, minced

Dash of cider vinegar

FILLING

6 to 8 ounces uncooked Cha-Cha Chorizo (page 100) or other chorizo or spicy sausage

1 large egg

1/2 medium onion, minced

3 scallions, sliced

MEXICANA MOP

Juice of 2 oranges

1/2 cup water

1/2 cup cider vinegar

1 tablespoon extra-virgin olive oil

2 garlic cloves, minced

1. The night before you plan to barbecue, combine the rub ingredients in a small bowl. Massage the pork with the rub inside and out. Wrap the meat in a small plastic bag and refrigerate overnight.

2. Before you begin to barbecue, prepare the salsa by combining all the ingredients in a small bowl. Cover and refrigerate it until needed.

3. Prepare the smoker for barbecuing, bringing the temperature to 200°F to 220°F.

4. Remove the pork from the refrigerator and let it sit at room temperature for 30 minutes.

5. In a small bowl, combine the filling ingredients. Stuff the loin with the chorizo mixture and tie it with kitchen twine in several places.

6. Mix the mop ingredients in a small saucepan and keep the liquid warm over low heat.

7. Warm a heavy skillet over high heat. Add the loin and sear it quickly on all sides. Transfer the pork to the smoker. Cook for 2½ to 2¾ hours, basting the loin at 30- to 40-minute intervals in a wood-burning pit, or as appropriate for your style of smoker.

8. After the initial cooking period, remove the pork from the smoker and wrap it in heavy-duty foil, pouring about 2 tablespoons of the mop and ¼ cup of the salsa over the meat. Discard any remaining mop. Seal the edges of the foil well. Return the pork to the smoker and cook to an internal temperature of 160°F, 1 to 1¼ hours.

9. Allow the pork to sit at room temperature for about 10 minutes before slicing. Serve slices topped with spoonfuls of the salsa. Offer the remaining salsa on the side.

VARIATION: CUBANO-MEXICANO SANDWICH Use the pork (or just some leftovers) to make a barbecue-style Cuban sandwich. Use Cuban bread or a crusty roll and smear with mustard. Then pile on pork slices, thinly sliced ham and Swiss cheese, a spoonful of black beans, and a few avocado or dill pickle slices. Toast in a sandwich press, in a skillet, or on a griddle.

BBQ tip If you run short of mop in any recipe, extend it with additional splashes of the main liquid or even a little water. While we call for specific proportions, always feel free to take liberties—that's part of the fun of barbecuing.

OUT-OF-LUCK LUAU

Stan Gambrell, who coordinated the first Big Pig Jig in Vienna, Georgia, in 1982, got a kick out of the cooking style of one of the competing barbecue teams that year. He wrote that they "insisted on burying their pig in the ground Hawaiian style, and kept insisting that the hole be dug wider. And wider. And WIDER. We dug the way they said they wanted it, but when judging time came and they tried to dig up their pig, they never could find it."

East L.A. Pork Tacos

Shoulder chops start out a little tougher and fattier than their center-cut cousins, but many pork fans prefer their richer flavor and cheaper cost. Cooked in this style, they'll be plenty tender and taste great, too. Many well-stocked supermarkets carry achiote, as do Mexican, Latin American, and East Indian markets. SERVES 4 TO 6

BORRACHO MARINADE AND OPTIONAL MOP

2 cups freshly squeezed orange juice

2/3 cup tequila

Juice of 2 limes

Juice of 1 lemon

1/2 medium onion, minced

1 tablespoon extra-virgin olive oil

3 garlic cloves, minced

2 teaspoons dried oregano, preferably Mexican

1 teaspoon achiote paste

1 teaspoon cumin

Several dashes of Melinda's Original Habanero XXXtra Hot Pepper Sauce or other fiery habanero hot sauce

Six 12-ounce to 14-ounce shoulder pork chops

Warm corn tortillas

Chopped onion and fresh cilantro, and lime and orange wedges, for garnish

Sauce Olé (page 379) or additional habanero hot sauce

1. The night before you plan to barbecue, combine the marinade ingredients in a blender or food processor. Pour the marinade over the pork in a plastic bag. Refrigerate the chops overnight.

2. Prepare the smoker for barbecuing, bringing the temperature to 200°F to 220°F.

3. Drain the pork, reserving all of the marinade if you plan to baste the meat during cooking. Let the chops sit at room temperature for 30 minutes.

4. To make the optional mop (see page 45, "To Mop or Not"), bring the marinade to a boil over high heat and boil for several minutes. Keep warm over low heat.

5. Transfer the chops to the smoker. Cook for 2 1/2 to 2 3/4 hours, basting at 45-minute intervals in a wood-burning pit, or as appropriate for your style of smoker.

6. When done, the pork will pull easily away from the fat and bone. Allow the chops to sit at room temperature for 10 to 15 minutes and pull the pork into shreds. Arrange the pork on a platter with the warm tortillas and garnishes. Serve with Sauce Olé or additional habanero hot sauce.

BBQ tip Most authorities today agree that pork is done enough to eat when the internal temperature reaches 150°F or even a little less. Most barbecuers cook the meat to a temperature of at least 170°F, when it begins to fall apart, and some go as high as 190°F.

Creole Crown Roast

A crown pork roast, elegantly presented and carved at the table, symbolizes a special occasion. Call your butcher ahead for the roast, formed by tying the rib section of the loin into a circle. SERVES 8 TO 10

CREOLE RUB

2 tablespoons celery salt

1 tablespoon packed brown sugar

1 tablespoon paprika

1 tablespoon freshly ground black pepper

1 tablespoon ground white pepper

1 1/2 teaspoons garlic powder

1 1/2 teaspoons dried thyme

1/2 teaspoon cayenne

5-pound crown pork roast (10 to 12 chops)

1 to 2 tablespoons Worcestershire sauce

CREOLE MOP (OPTIONAL)

2 cups chicken or beef stock

2 cups water

1/4 cup Worcestershire sauce

1/4 cup unsalted butter

1. The night before you plan to barbecue, combine the rub ingredients in a small bowl. Massage the roast well with the Worcestershire sauce and then with about half of the rub. Transfer the roast to a plastic bag and refrigerate it overnight.

2. Before you begin to barbecue, remove the roast from the refrigerator. Pat down the roast lightly with another coating of rub, reserving the remainder. Let the roast sit at room temperature for 40 to 45 minutes.

3. Prepare the smoker for barbecuing, bringing the temperature to 200°F to 220°F.

4. If you plan to baste the roast (see page 45, "To Mop or Not"), stir any remaining rub together with the other mop ingredients in a saucepan and warm the mixture over low heat.

5. Transfer the roast to the smoker and cook until the internal temperature reaches 160°F, 4 3/4 to 5 hours. Mop the pork every 40 to 45 minutes in a wood-burning pit, or as appropriate for your style of smoker.

6. Remove the pork from the smoker and let it sit at room temperature for 10 to 15 minutes. Carve the roast, slicing downward between each bone to cut into individual chops.

SERVING SUGGESTION Serve the crown roast as the centerpiece for a Mardi Gras meal. Sip Firewater (page 475) first, then sit down to an initial course of Shrimp Rémoulade (page 262). Present the roast with twice-baked potatoes, Maque Choux Peppers (page 292), and sautéed chayote squash. Offer pralines and coffee laced with bourbon for dessert.

BBQ tip When mops include butter or oil, much of the fat drips away from the food it's protecting, leaving behind moist meat and a hint of flavor.

Ca-Rib-bean Roast

Caribbean flavors, including a little rum, provide a lively accent for a pork roast.

SERVES 4 TO 5

CA-RIB-BEAN RUB

1 tablespoon packed brown sugar

2 teaspoons ground allspice

2 teaspoons onion powder

1 teaspoon kosher salt or coarse sea salt

1/2 teaspoon dried thyme

1/2 teaspoon ground nutmeg

2 1/2-pound to 2 3/4-pound pork rib roast

1 tablespoon dark rum

CA-RIB-BEAN MOP (OPTIONAL)

1 cup chicken or beef stock

1 cup water

1/2 cup cider vinegar

1/4 cup dark rum

2 tablespoons vegetable oil

MANGO SAUCE

1 mango, peeled, pitted, and chopped

1/2 medium onion, chopped

2 tablespoons mango chutney

1/2 cup chicken stock

2 to 3 tablespoons dark rum

2 tablespoons cream of coconut

Splash or two of Pickapeppa sauce (optional)

Kosher salt or coarse sea salt to taste

1 1/2 teaspoons unsalted butter

1. The night before you plan to barbecue, combine the rub ingredients in a small bowl. Massage the pork well with the rum and then with about half of the rub. Transfer the pork to a plastic bag and refrigerate it overnight.

2. Prepare the smoker for barbecuing, bringing the temperature to 200°F to 220°F.

3. Remove the pork from the refrigerator. Pat down lightly with another coating of rub. Let sit at room temperature for 30 to 40 minutes.

4. If you plan to baste the pork (see page 45, "To Mop or Not"), reserve 1 teaspoon of the remaining rub and stir the rest with the other mop ingredients in a saucepan. Warm the mixture over low heat.

5. Transfer the pork to the smoker, fattier side up, and cook until the internal temperature reaches 160°F, 4 3/4 to 5 hours. Mop the meat every 40 to 45 minutes in a wood-burning pit, or as appropriate for your style of smoker.

6. While the roast cooks, prepare the sauce. In a food processor, puree the mango, onion, and chutney, adding a bit of stock if necessary. Pour into a saucepan and add the remaining stock, rum, cream of coconut, and reserved 1 teaspoon rub. Warm over medium heat and simmer for about 20 minutes. Add Pickapeppa and salt to balance the savory and sweet flavors. The sauce can be kept warm or refrigerated and then reheated. Whisk the butter into the warm sauce just before serving.

7. Remove the pork from the smoker and let it sit at room temperature for 10 to 15 minutes. Carve the roast and serve with the sauce.

Hill Country Links

If you own or can borrow a meat grinder, you can stuff your own sausage links for barbecuing. MAKES ABOUT 2 DOZEN SAUSAGES, SERVING 12 OR MORE

4 pounds pork butt, with fat

2 pounds beef chuck or round steak, with fat

1 large onion, minced

6 garlic cloves, minced

2 tablespoons minced fresh sage or 1 tablespoon dried sage

1 tablespoon kosher salt or coarse sea salt

1 tablespoon coarsely ground black pepper

1 to 2 tablespoons chile caribe or other crushed dried red chile of moderate heat

1/2 to 1 teaspoon cayenne

4 yards hog sausage casings (see BBQ tips)

Vegetable oil

1. At least the evening before you plan to barbecue the sausages, grind the pork and beef together, using the coarse-grind blade of a meat grinder. Add the rest of the ingredients, except the casings and oil. If you wish, grind the mixture again. Refrigerate, covered, overnight.

2. Prepare the casings, soaking them in several changes of water over several hours.

3. With the stuffing attachment of a meat grinder, stuff the cold sausage mixture into the casings, making 1-inch-thick links about 5 inches long. With your fingers, twist the casing and tie off the individual sausages with kitchen twine. Cut between the links. If you end up with any air bubbles, prick the casing in those spots with a needle. The sausage is ready to barbecue, but it can be refrigerated for several days or frozen for at least a month.

4. Prepare the smoker for barbecuing, bringing the temperature to 200°F to 220°F. Rub the sausages lightly with the oil.

5. Transfer the links to the smoker and cook until the skin of the sausage looks ready to pop, 2 to 2¼ hours. Always err on the side of caution with the timing and cut one of the sausages open to check for doneness before eating any of them. Serve hot.

VARIATION: HILL COUNTRY JALAPEÑO-CHEESE LINKS Eliminate the sage and chile caribe. Add 1 cup shredded medium cheddar and several finely chopped fresh jalapeños (to taste) to the ground pork and beef mixture.

BBQ tip Sausage casings are the intestines of various farm animals. You want casings from a pig in this instance. Inexpensive and hard to damage, the casings generally come packed in brine. These days most casings come "preflushed," eliminating the need to clean the casing interiors with running water. You'll want to soak them, though, to eliminate the brine. When stuffing the sausages, it's easiest to work with the casings in sections no longer than a yard long, and to have the meat well chilled.

LINKS TO THE PAST

The same German butchers who helped create modern Texas barbecue also made great link sausage, which they smoked with the brisket in the pit at the back of the meat market in venerable central Texas joints such as the City Market in Luling and Smitty's in Lockhart. The links are still as popular as beef in that area of the state.

BBQ *tip* If you plan to make a lot of sausage, some sausage companies and meat markets sell casings in bulk. You can usually get casings for 100 pounds of sausage and change back from a twenty-dollar bill. The brined casings keep, refrigerated, for up to a year.

SHOULD BE PROUD

Roger and Dawn Hubmer, with their children Paul and Laura, raise hogs and then barbecue some of them for the family's catering business. Their Prairie Pride Farm near St. Clair, Minnesota, prides itself on tasty, naturally raised pork that is perfect for the pit. It's great to see the current revival of farms like this, practicing sustainable agriculture and placing priority on flavor. For more information, visit the Hubmers online at prairiepridepork.com.

Store-Bought Hot Brats

If you don't want to grind and stuff your own sausage, you can start with a store-bought variety and still add an abundance of smoky, barbecue taste. Around the barbecue cook-off circuit, nationally distributed Johnsonville bratwurst from Sheboygan, Wisconsin, is a popular choice. Personally, we prefer brats with more spice—nutmeg, coriander, ginger, or caraway—though they are a little harder to find. SERVES 6

1 dozen 4-ounce to 6-ounce uncooked bratwursts

Vegetable oil

1 to 2 teaspoons Wild Willy's Number One-derful Dry Rub (page 26) or other savory seasoning blend (optional)

Alabama Great White (page 385) or Golden Mustard Barbecue Sauce (page 371) or other mustardy barbecue sauce (optional)

1. Prepare the smoker for barbecuing, bringing the temperature to 200°F to 220°F.

2. Rub the brats lightly with oil and sprinkle them with rub if you wish. Let the brats sit at room temperature for 20 minutes.

3. Transfer the brats to the smoker and cook until the skin of the sausage looks ready to pop, 1¼ to 1½ hours, depending on size. Serve hot, perhaps with Alabama Great White or Golden Mustard Barbecue Sauce.

SERVING SUGGESTION Don't wait for October for an Oktoberfest menu. Barbecue several varieties of sausage and buy loaves of hearty breads like pumpernickel and rye, several kinds of mustard, some garlicky dill pickles, and loads of German beer. Make up hefty bowls of Hot German Potato Salad (page 424) and Kraut Salad (page 428), and round out the celebration with Black Walnut Cake (page 460).

BBQ tip You can—and should—barbecue any kind of store-bought sausage. In addition to bratwurst, our biggest hits have included a robust Molinari Italian sausage and several varieties of Bruce Aidells's links, both from the San Francisco Bay area but distributed nationally. If you use precooked sausage, get something that was smoked originally, because it will need only about 30 minutes in your smoker—not long enough to absorb much smoke flavor.

Italian Sausage Torpedoes

These chubby sandwiches are modeled on ones that our friend Patty Karlovitz serves for special family occasions. She has the sausage shipped to New Mexico from her cousin Eugene's South Side Chicago meat market, which adds to their mystique, but any well-seasoned Italian link will work. SERVES UP TO 8

8 uncooked Italian sausage links, about 6 ounces each

Extra-virgin olive oil

2 large green Italian frying peppers or bell peppers

1 red bell pepper

1 large onion, halved

8 slices provolone (optional)

8 long crusty rolls

1. Prepare the smoker for barbecuing, bringing the temperature to 200°F to 220°F.

2. Rub the sausages and vegetables lightly with oil and let them sit at room temperature for 20 minutes.

3. Transfer the sausages and vegetables to the smoker. Cook the vegetables until tender, about 1 hour. Continue cooking the sausages until the skin of the sausage looks ready to pop, an additional 1¼ to 1½ hours, depending on size.

4. When cool enough to handle, slice the peppers and onion into thin strips, discarding loose skins and seeds but mixing the flavorful juices back into the vegetables. Keep warm. If using the cheese, place it on the rolls. When the sausages are ready, top the cheese in each roll with a hot sausage and a portion of the vegetable mixture and juices. Halve the sandwiches, if you wish, for easier eating. Serve hot.

GET YOUR "SAW DOGS" HERE

Saw's Soul Kitchen in Birmingham, Alabama, offers an extensive menu of barbecue, burgers, seafood, and daily specials listed on a floor-to-ceiling chalkboard. One of our favorite ideas is the hot dog bun filled with pulled pork and topped with mustard, caramelized onions, and coleslaw. You can also get the same meat with collard greens served over cheese grits.

BBQ Boudin

South Louisiana produces some of the country's best charcuterie. Among the varied specialties, the masterpiece may be boudin blanc, a Cajun pork and rice link sausage eaten at all hours of the day, from breakfast through dinner. Because the mixture is partially cooked before it goes into the casing and then poached briefly, a short stint in the smoker is all it needs to be ready to devour.

MAKES ABOUT 2 DOZEN LINKS, SERVING 12 OR MORE

FILLING

2 3/4-pound to 3-pound bone-in pork butt section

2 large yellow onions, chopped

2 tablespoons kosher salt or coarse sea salt, or more to taste

1 teaspoon dried thyme

1/4 to 1/2 pound fresh pork liver (optional)

2 plump garlic cloves, minced

6 cups freshly cooked rice, preferably well-seasoned and cooked in chicken stock

1 cup finely chopped scallions, green tops included

1 tablespoon freshly ground black pepper, or more to taste

1 1/2 teaspoons cayenne, or more to taste

1/2 cup cream or half-and-half

3 yards hog sausage casings

1. Cut the pork away from the bone into 4 or 5 relatively similar-sized chunks. Leave the fat on the meat. Place the pork and the bone in a large saucepan and cover by at least 2 inches with water. Add one-quarter of the chopped onions, 1 tablespoon of the salt, and the thyme. Bring the mixture to a boil, skimming off any foam. Reduce the heat to a simmer and cook until very tender, about 1 1/2 hours.

2. If you are using the liver, place it in another saucepan and cover it by at least 1 inch with water. Bring it to a boil, skimming off any foam. Reduce the heat to a simmer and cook for 1 hour. Drain the liver, discarding the water.

3. When the pork butt chunks are ready, remove them from the cooking liquid. Discard the bone, and strain and reserve the liquid. You will want 2 cups of liquid. If you have more, return the liquid to the pan and reduce it over high heat until you have 2 cups. If you have less than 2 cups, add enough water to measure the proper amount.

4. Working in batches, use a meat grinder (with a medium disk) or a food processor to grind or finely chop the pork (still with the fat), optional liver, remaining onions, and garlic. Transfer the mixture to a large bowl. Stir in 1 more tablespoon salt, the rice, scallions, black pepper, and cayenne. Pour in the cream and 1 cup of the cooking liquid and mix it in well. You want the filling to be moist but not runny. Add more or all of the cooking liquid as needed to get the proper consistency. To check the seasoning, cook up a tablespoon or so of the mixture in a small skillet. The final flavors will meld further, but now is the time to add more salt, pepper, or cayenne. Chill the filling for at least 1 hour and up to 1 day. (You can speed up the process by using the freezer, if you wish.)

5. Prepare the casings while the filling cools, soaking them in several changes of water over an hour or so. Run some water through each casing as well, to eliminate the remaining salt from the inside. (For more information about sausage casings and their stuffing, see the BBQ tips on pages 93 and 94.)

6. Leave the boudin filling in the refrigerator until just before you plan to stuff it into the casings. Using the stuffing attachment of a meat grinder or stand mixer, stuff the fillings into the casings. Work quickly to keep the fat from softening, which makes the mixture harder to stuff evenly. You should be able to make 1½ to 2 dozen sausages about 1 inch in diameter and 5 inches in length. With your fingers, twist the casings and, if you're the fastidious type, tie

off the individual sausages with kitchen twine. Cut between them. Prick any air bubbles with a needle. (You can proceed to the next step and smoke the boudin at this point, or cover and refrigerate it for up to another day.)

7. Poach the boudin. Bring a large pot of hot water to a simmer and add the boudin. Adjust the heat to keep the water at just a bare simmer, showing only an occasional breaking bubble. Cook for about 15 minutes. (Some or all of the boudin can be cooled briefly, then wrapped and refrigerated, for later use.)

8. Shortly before you plan to serve the boudin, prepare the smoker for barbecuing, bringing the temperature to 200°F to 220°F.

9. Place the boudin in a smoke-proof baking dish and cook in the smoker until the casings look ready to burst, about 30 minutes. Serve the boudin warm. Some people eat the boudin with the casing on. Most folks, however, squeeze the soft filling from the casing into their mouths—a casual, messy method that's perfectly effective.

PICK THOSE CHORDS, PICK THOSE PIGS

How did two New York bikers of Italian descent get around to opening a genuine honky-tonk barbecue joint in Syracuse and then in other cities? In *Dinosaur Bar-B-Que* (2001, Ten Speed Press), John Stage explains the story of the namesake restaurant. The Dinosaur kitchen knows its meat, boasting that the barbecue "is from pigs that made perfect hogs of themselves."

Cha-Cha Chorizo

A popular sausage throughout the Southwest, spicy chorizo is delicious smoked.

SERVES 4 TO 6

1¾ pounds pork butt, with fat, ground by your butcher or with a meat grinder at home

½ cup minced onion

6 garlic cloves, minced

1 jalapeño, minced

½ cup cider vinegar

Juice of 1 orange

3 tablespoons chili powder, preferably Gebhardt's

1½ teaspoons dried oregano, preferably Mexican

1½ teaspoons ground cumin

1 teaspoon table salt

½ teaspoon cayenne or ground chile de árbol

½ teaspoon canela (Mexican cinnamon) or other cinnamon

CHA-CHA MOP (OPTIONAL)

Juice of 1 orange

¼ cup cider vinegar

1½ teaspoons extra-virgin olive oil

1. At least the evening before you plan to smoke the sausages, mix the sausage ingredients in a large bowl. Refrigerate, covered, overnight or for a couple of days.

2. Prepare the smoker for barbecuing, bringing the temperature to 200°F to 220°F.

3. Form the sausage mixture into 8 patties. Let the patties sit at room temperature for about 15 minutes.

4. If you plan to baste the sausage patties (see page 45, "To Mop or Not"), mix the mop ingredients in a small saucepan and warm over low heat.

5. Transfer the patties to the smoker. Cook for about 1 hour, mopping once or twice in a wood-burning pit, or as appropriate in your style of smoker. The patties should be ready when they are richly browned and cooked through. Always err on the side of caution with the timing, though, and cut open one of the patties to check for doneness before eating any of them. Serve hot.

SERVING SUGGESTION Chorizo is a great breakfast sausage. It puts real zing in a simple dish like scrambled eggs. Serve it on the side or crumble the cooked sausage into the eggs.

PARTY TIME

Like to throw barbecue parties? You aren't alone, according to *Food & Wine* and *Bon Appétit*. In surveys in recent years, both magazines discovered that their readers—who presumably care about these things—ranked casual outdoor dinner parties as their favorite form of entertaining.

Danny Meyer, the most acclaimed restaurateur in New York—founder of beloved establishments such as Union Square Cafe and Gramercy Tavern—is now getting Manhattan to queue up for barbecue. It took him several years and multiple millions to open Blue Smoke, but the restaurant-cum–jazz club was an instant success, now cloned in baseball stadiums and airports. Best of all, the ribs taste just like those that Meyer grew up with in St. Louis.

BBQ Fatty

Nothing's simpler to smoke than a fatty, a rage among sausage-loving barbecuers. This is a basic rendition to illustrate the idea, but use your imagination to up the ante, perhaps stuffing it with cooked bacon, cheese, or sautéed onions and peppers, or dressing its body with interlaced bacon slices formed like a lattice pie crust. These additions make a fatty—well, really fatty. For other adornments check out bbqaddicts.com, an uplifting experience from Jason Day and Aaron Chronister.

SERVES 4 TO 6 PER SAUSAGE LOG

2 tablespoons Wild Willy's Number One-derful Rub (page 26), Southern Succor Dry Rub (page 27), or other favorite dry rub, per sausage log

1 or more 1-pound "logs" of breakfast sausage, such as Jimmy Dean Premium Pork Sage Sausage, very cold

1. Prepare the smoker for barbecuing, bringing the temperature to 200°F to 220°F.

2. Scatter the dry rub evenly on a baking sheet.

Roll the entire sausage log back and forth in the dry rub to coat it evenly. Place the sausage log in a smoke-proof dish or foil pan and let sit at room temperature for about 30 minutes.

3. Transfer the meat to the smoker and cook until the interior temperature reaches 160°F, 3 to 3¼ hours. Cut into thick rounds and serve.

Cajun Tasso

This porcine pleasure hails from the heart of Cajun country. Tasso is a seasoning pork, something like home-cured ham, used to flavor other dishes rather than eaten on its own. Try a chunk in your next pot of beans or collards, or chop it and add to gumbo, jambalaya, or soup. You can get fancy with it, too, using it to flavor crawfish and shrimp sautés or pasta sauces. Our thanks to Wayne Whitworth for the suggestion of making tasso at home. **MAKES ABOUT 2 1/2 POUNDS OF MEAT, PLENTY FOR A FEW POTS OF BEANS, SEVERAL JAMBALAYAS, AND GUMBO FOR A GANG**

1/2 pork butt, 3 1/2 to 4 pounds

CAJUN RAGIN' RUB
1/4 cup celery salt
1/4 cup freshly ground black pepper
1/4 cup ground white pepper
1/4 cup packed brown sugar
2 tablespoons garlic powder
1 to 1 1/2 tablespoons cayenne
1 tablespoon dried thyme
2 teaspoons dried sage

1. At least 3 hours before you plan to barbecue, cut the pork lengthwise (more or less) into strips about 1 inch in diameter. You'll have to work around the bone, which gets in the way of cutting the butt completely into long neat strips, but do the best you can. As you cut the strips, place them on a baking sheet.

2. Mix the dry rub ingredients thoroughly in a bowl. Pour the rub over the strips, and massage the spice mixture onto both sides of each strip. Place the meat in the refrigerator, uncovered, for 2 to 3 hours so that the spices dry somewhat onto the meat's surface. (The meat can sit in the spice mixture for a day or night, if you like, but uncover it for the last 2 or 3 hours if you can.)

3. Prepare the smoker for barbecuing, bringing the temperature to 200°F to 220°F.

4. Transfer the pork strips from the baking sheet to the smoker and cook until well-done and a bit dried out, well-browned but not burned looking, 3 to 3 1/2 hours. The tasso keeps for a week to 10 days in the refrigerator, but we usually freeze most of it to use over a couple of months.

Wood-Smoked Pork Belly

If you cure and cold-smoke pork belly, you get bacon. When hot-smoked, barbecue style, the succulent and unctuous meat fully cooks while soaking in smoke. You may want to serve this as an appetizer or turn it into a sandwich because of the richness of the meat. SERVES 8 OR MORE

SWEET MEAT RIB RUB

1/4 cup plus 2 tablespoons packed dark brown sugar

1 tablespoon dry mustard

1 tablespoon onion powder

1 tablespoon kosher salt or coarse sea salt

1 1/2 teaspoons freshly ground black pepper

1 1/2 teaspoons cayenne

3 1/2-pound to 4-pound uncooked section of pork belly, preferably with skin on and without rib bones

SOUTHERN SOP (OPTIONAL)

2 cups cider vinegar

1 cup water

3 tablespoons freshly ground black pepper

2 tablespoons kosher salt or coarse sea salt

1 tablespoon Worcestershire sauce

1 tablespoon paprika

1 tablespoon cayenne

1. Combine the rub ingredients in a small bowl. Pack the rub over the meaty side of the pork belly. If you plan to baste the meat (see page 45, "To Mop or Not"), reserve 1 tablespoon of the rub. Place in a large plastic bag and refrigerate, skin side down, for at least 4 hours and up to overnight.

2. Prepare the smoker for barbecuing, bringing the temperature to 200°F to 220°F.

3. If you plan to baste the meat, stir together the mop ingredients and reserved 1 tablespoon rub in a small saucepan and warm the mixture over low heat.

4. Place the pork belly, skin side up, in a large smoke-proof baking dish. Transfer it to the smoker and cook for about 3 hours, mopping twice in a wood-burning pit, or as appropriate in your style of smoker. The meat is ready when it is cooked to well-done, approximately 175°F to 180°F.

5. Let the meat sit at room temperature for 10 to 15 minutes. Slice off and discard the skin. Cut the meat into 1/2-inch-thick slices, or another size and shape as you wish. Serve hot. If you have leftovers, reheat the slices on a griddle or grill on both sides to crisp as well as heat through.

B.C. Canadian Bacon

We got this idea from friends in British Columbia, Canada, where they call this cut of pork "back bacon." Actually lean smoked pork loin, Canadian bacon is already cooked, but you can add an enormous boost to its flavor and texture with this technique. Cut leftovers into matchsticks and sprinkle over salads or pizzas.

SERVES 2 TO 4

1 pound chunk Canadian bacon

Vegetable oil

1 teaspoon Wild Willy's Number One-derful Rub (page 26), Southern Succor Rub (page 27), Cajun Ragin' Rub (page 29), or other savory seasoning blend

PINEAPPLE MOP (OPTIONAL)

1/2 cup chicken stock

1/2 cup pineapple juice

1 tablespoon vegetable oil

3/4 teaspoon dry mustard

1/4 teaspoon ground cloves

1. Prepare the smoker for barbecuing, bringing the temperature to 200°F to 220°F.

2. Rub the Canadian bacon lightly with oil and sprinkle it with rub. Let the meat sit at room temperature for 30 minutes.

3. If you plan to baste the meat (see page 45, "To Mop or Not"), stir together the mop ingredients in a small saucepan and warm the mixture over low heat.

4. Transfer the Canadian bacon to the smoker and cook for 1 to 1 1/4 hours, turning and mopping twice in a wood-burning pit, or as appropriate in your style of smoker.

5. Let the meat sit at room temperature for 5 to 10 minutes before slicing and serving.

SERVING SUGGESTION This home-smoked Canadian bacon is a natural for eggs Benedict. To add some extra punch, we like to substitute chile con queso or another spicy cheese sauce for the hollandaise.

WHAT ABOUT "MY BUTT'S ON FIRE?"

Say you're going to start a barbecue cook-off team. You need a name obviously, and maybe you're pondering something like "4 Men in Heat" or "Smokin' Joe and the Bar Be Dolls." It turns out that both of those names are taken, as you can discover at bbqteamnames.com, which lists thousands of monikers on hundreds of web pages. It's a hoot to read.

Martin Luther King, Jr., loved barbecue, particularly the pork ribs and sandwiches at Aleck's Barbecue Heaven in central Atlanta. Opened by Ernest Alexander in 1942, Aleck's was an important hangout for the early leaders of the civil rights movement. Part of the draw undoubtedly was the signature "Come Back" barbecue sauce, which is still bringing people in the door.

Triple Play Tube Steak

Bologna won't ever replace brisket in the hearts of many pitmasters, but barbecued versions are remarkably good, and certainly not just for kids. All you need to do is a quick score, slather, and smoke. SERVES 6 TO 8

2-pound chunk of bologna

Memphis Magic (page 374), Bar-B-Q Ranch Sauce (page 375), or other not-too-sweet, tomato-based barbecue sauce

1 tablespoon cider or white vinegar

1. Score the bologna ¼ inch deep with wide crisscross cuts. Thin ⅓ cup of the barbecue sauce with the vinegar. Cover the bologna thoroughly with the thinned sauce. Let the bologna sit at room temperature for 20 to 30 minutes.

2. Prepare the smoker for barbecuing, bringing the temperature to 200°F to 220°F.

3. Transfer the bologna to the smoker and cook for about 2 hours. The sauce will have caramelized on the bologna's surface. Serve sliced, hot or cold, with additional barbecue sauce.

SERVING SUGGESTION Make sandwiches out of the bologna, topped with barbecue sauce, Green Tomato Chowchow (page 436), and some chopped onions. If you liked bologna sandwiches as a kid, you'll relish this one.

Monday Night Ham Loaf

This is a superb way to use up barbecued ham left over from the weekend.

SERVES 6 TO 8

1 pound Ginger-Glazed Ham (page 80), Maple-Bourbon Ham (page 79), or other well-smoked fully cooked ham

3/4 pound ground pork

1 medium onion, chopped

1 cup cornbread crumbs or other bread crumbs

2 large eggs, beaten

1 cup milk

2 tablespoons yellow mustard

2 tablespoons Worcestershire sauce

1 1/2 tablespoons cider vinegar

1 tablespoon vegetable oil

1/4 teaspoon ground cloves

Pinch of ground ginger

Table salt to taste

MONDAY NIGHT GLAZE

2 tablespoons ginger preserves or jelly, or pure maple syrup

1 tablespoon pineapple or apple juice

1 teaspoon yellow mustard

1. Preheat the oven to 350°F. Process the ham in a food processor until minced fine, or grind the ham in a meat grinder. Transfer the ham to a bowl, add the remaining ingredients, and combine well.

2. Spoon the moist ham mixture into a loaf pan and smooth its surface. Bake the loaf for 45 minutes. While the loaf bakes, combine the glaze ingredients in a small bowl. Brush the loaf with the glaze. Continue baking for another 15 to 20 minutes, for a total cooking time of 60 to 65 minutes.

3. Remove the meat from the oven and let it sit for at least 10 minutes before cutting. Serve hot or cold. Leftovers keep for 3 to 4 days.

SERVING SUGGESTION For a hot-weather supper, start with Devil-May-Care Eggs (page 431), then serve the ham loaf with sides of Succotash Salad (page 425) and Hot and Spicy Buttermilk Potato Salad (page 423), and then Bourbon Peaches (page 439) to finish. Ham loaf also makes good mini sandwiches on split Sweet Potato Biscuits (page 411) or tiny wedges of Cracklin' Cornbread (page 408). Serve the sandwiches with ginger preserves or jelly, mango or peach chutney, or tangy mustard.

STILL SMOKING

Allen & Son BBQ remains a bastion of the old "Down East" barbecue style that's been popular in eastern North Carolina since the locals talked with British accents. Just outside Chapel Hill, the restaurant prides itself on the freshly homemade coleslaw that goes on a sandwich with the pork and also brags about its "addictive" hushpuppies.

Supper Spread

This is an all-American version of rillettes, the rich, savory potted French dish. Our recipe, using scrumptious barbecued pork shoulder, is modeled on one from Southern food authority Nathalie Dupree.

SERVES 2 AS A MAIN COURSE OR 4 TO 6 AS AN APPETIZER

1/4 cup unsalted butter

1 cup finely chopped smoked pork butt or picnic

1/2 cup water

2 garlic cloves, minced

1 teaspoon Worcestershire sauce

2 teaspoons minced fresh sage or 1 teaspoon dried sage

Tabasco or other hot pepper sauce to taste

Kosher salt or coarse sea salt and coarsely ground black pepper to taste

Crusty country-style white bread, toast triangles, or crackers

1. In a small heavy saucepan, melt the butter over low heat. Add the pork, water, garlic, and Worcestershire sauce. Barely simmer the mixture over very low heat until the liquid evaporates but the pork still looks moist, 15 to 20 minutes. The pork should be quite tender. Remove the pan from the heat and mix in the sage, Tabasco, and salt and pepper to taste. Spoon the mixture into a small crock, cover, and refrigerate at least until chilled, but preferably overnight.

2. Let the spread sit at room temperature for about 10 minutes before serving. Serve the spread with a crusty country-style white bread, toast triangles, or crackers.

SERVING SUGGESTION To complete an early winter supper, add South-of-the-Border Garlic Soup (page 286), a couple of varieties of pickles, and Southern Caesar Salad (page 416). Offer fresh pears to round out the meal.

Barbecue Spaghetti

This may never make it in Italy, but it's sure big in Memphis. SERVES 4

1 1/2 to 2 cups Memphis Magic (page 374) or other tomato-based barbecue sauce

1 1/2 cups pulled or shredded smoked pork butt or picnic

1 pound cooked spaghetti (or other sturdy pasta such as linguine or penne)

Chopped onion (optional), for garnish

Warm the barbecue sauce in a saucepan. Add the pork and heat through. Mix the sauce with the spaghetti and serve on a platter. Garnish with the onion if you wish.

BODACIOUS BEEF

SOME SOUTHERN PITMASTERS THINK TEXANS STARTED BARBECUING BEEF SIMPLY BECAUSE THEY COULDN'T TELL A STEER FROM A PIG. TEXANS, IN TURN, RECKON THAT ANYONE WHO PREFERS HOGS TO CATTLE DOESN'T KNOW THE DIFFERENCE BETWEEN A TROUGH AND A TABLE.

THE PORK AND BEEF BARBECUE TRADITIONS ARE ENTIRELY DIFFERENT ANIMALS IN ALL RESPECTS, INCLUDING ORIGINS. BRITISH COLONISTS BROUGHT PIGS TO THE

East Coast and adopted Native American cooking methods to create their style of barbecue, which was usually perfected by African American pitmasters. Long before these settlers moved west, Mexican ranchers and vaqueros, the earliest cowboys, introduced the Southwest to their specialty, *barbacoa de cabeza*. It's whole head barbecue, preferably made with a big bull's head that is smoked overnight in an underground pit.

Barbacoa de cabeza remained a chuck-wagon treat throughout the epic era of the cowboy, but the dish never had a chance in Dallas. German butchers in central Texas intervened around the beginning of the twentieth century to change the nature of beef barbecue. For them, sweetbreads, brains, and other parts of the head were too much of a delicacy to put in a pit. They took up barbecuing as a way to get rid of their worst cuts of beef, like brisket, sometimes a throwaway piece in the days before fast-food hamburgers. The thrifty butchers found that long, slow smoking tenderized even the toughest meat, turning a waste product into a hunk of heaven—not to mention a profitable sideline.

From small central Texas towns like Lockhart, Taylor, and Elgin, beef barbecue spread throughout the Southwest and Midwest. It met the pork barbecue tradition in Kansas City, one of the capitals of the 'Q,' and the two learned to live together in mutual respect on that neutral turf. Elsewhere, partisans may continue to clash on the merits of the meats, but anyone who tries both with an open mind will end up on the Kansas City side of the street. Even if pork ribs tickle you pink, you'll discover that the burnt ends of a brisket can't be beat.

A BASTION OF BURNT ENDS

Hayward Spears, another guy from Hope, Arkansas, makes some of the best burnt ends in Kansas City. His suburban restaurant, Hayward's, isn't too slack on other kinds of meat either, cooking 10 tons or so of barbecue a week. If you want some of the barbecue between bread, the large sandwiches are only a buck more than the regular size.

Braggin' Rights Brisket

The medieval alchemists, who sought to turn base metals into gold, should have tried barbecuing a brisket on a wood-burning pit. The transformation of the meat is on the same magnitude of magic—and much more successful. If you're cooking on a charcoal or electric smoker, skip to the recipe for Dallas Dandy Brisket.

SERVES 12 TO 18

WILD WILLY'S NUMBER ONE-DERFUL RUB

3/4 cup paprika

1/4 cup freshly ground black pepper

1/4 cup kosher salt or coarse sea salt

1/4 cup sugar

2 tablespoons chili powder

2 tablespoons garlic powder

2 tablespoons onion powder

2 teaspoons cayenne

8-pound to 12-pound packer-trimmed beef brisket

BASIC BEER MOP

12 ounces beer

1/2 cup cider vinegar

1/2 cup water

1/4 cup vegetable oil

1/2 medium onion, chopped or sliced in thin rings

2 garlic cloves, minced

1 tablespoon Worcestershire sauce

Peppery Sweet Onion Sauce (page 378), Struttin' Sauce (page 369), Bar-B-Q Ranch Sauce (page 375), or other tomato-based barbecue sauce (optional)

1. The night before you plan to barbecue, combine the rub ingredients in a small bowl. Apply the rub evenly to the brisket, massaging it into every little pore, reserving 1 tablespoon of the rub. Place the brisket in a plastic bag and refrigerate it overnight.

2. Remove the brisket from the refrigerator and let it sit at room temperature for 45 minutes.

3. Prepare the smoker for barbecuing, bringing the temperature to 200°F to 220°F.

4. In a saucepan, mix the mop ingredients with the reserved 1 tablespoon rub and warm over low heat.

5. Transfer the brisket to the coolest part of the smoker, fat side up, so the juices will help baste the meat. Cook the brisket until well-done and tender, 1 to 1 1/4 hours per pound. Every hour or so, baste the blackening hunk with the mop.

6. When the meat is cooked, remove it from the smoker and let it sit at room temperature for 20 minutes. Then cut the fatty top section away from the leaner bottom portion. An easily identifiable layer of fat separates the two areas. Trim the excess fat from both pieces and slice them thinly against the grain. Watch what you're doing because the grain changes direction. Sauce is considered very optional on brisket's home turf. If you wish, serve your favorite tomato-based barbecue sauce on the side.

SERVING SUGGESTION For a rousing ranch barbecue, start with Can't Wait Queso (page 340) and Chicken from Hell (page 359), served with an iced tub of beer and a gargantuan pitcher of Sunny Sweet Tea (page 484). Accompany the brisket with Creamy Coleslaw (page 390), Cowpoke Pintos (page 397), San Antonio Cactus and Corn Salad (page 421), and Cracklin' Cornbread (page 408). To finish, what else but Texas Peach Cobbler (page 452)?

BBQ tip The best barbecued brisket is heavily smoked and significantly shrunk during the cooking process. The only way to succeed completely is with a wood-burning pit or similar homemade smoker. If you have the right equipment, be sure to start with a packer-trimmed brisket, the whole cut with a thick layer of fat on one side. You may need to contact your butcher a few days ahead to get what you want. The alchemy works all the better as the meat quality increases. If you can get a highly marbled Wagyu brisket, for instance, it can be worth the extra expense. Whatever the source of the brisket, do not cut it in half or in smaller pieces and expect to reduce the cooking time proportionately. The meat retains its density unless you slice off the fatty top section to get the "flat cut" used in the Dallas Dandy Brisket recipe below.

BBQ tip Traditional barbecue meats are cooked well-done (180°F to 200°F). However rare you may like some naturally tender meat, you'll enjoy beef brisket, pork shoulder, ribs, and similar cuts the most when they are thoroughly cooked. It's almost impossible to get them too done, which gives you a fair range of flexibility for timing how long to leave them in your smoker.

Dallas Dandy Brisket

Even if you have a wood-burning pit, you may not want to fire it up for a full day every time you want some brisket. This is the best alternative style we've found, and it works great in a water smoker or charcoal grill. You won't get a full measure of the old-time barbecued brisket flavor, but you'll still have plenty to boast about.

SERVES 6 TO 8

DALLAS DANDY RUB

2 tablespoons Smoky Salt (page 29) or hickory-flavored salt

2 tablespoons packed brown sugar

2 tablespoons paprika

2 tablespoons chili powder

2 tablespoons freshly ground black pepper

DALLAS DANDY MARINADE

12 ounces beer

1 medium onion, chopped

1/2 cup cider or white vinegar

1/4 cup vegetable oil

2 canned chipotle chiles plus 2 tablespoons adobo sauce

2 tablespoons pure liquid smoke

4-pound fully trimmed brisket section (sometimes called the flat cut)

Smoked Onion Sauce (page 383), Peppery Sweet Onion Sauce (page 378), Bar-B-Q Ranch Sauce (page 375), Struttin' Sauce (page 369), or other tomato-based barbecue sauce (optional)

1. The night before you plan to barbecue, stir together the dry rub ingredients in a small bowl. Combine 2 tablespoons of the rub with the marinade ingredients in a blender and puree. Place the brisket in a plastic bag and pour the marinade over it. Refrigerate the brisket overnight.

2. Drain and discard the marinade. Pat the brisket down with all but 2 tablespoons of the remaining rub, coating the slab well. Let the brisket sit at room temperature for about 45 minutes.

3. Prepare the smoker for barbecuing, bringing the temperature to 200°F to 220°F.

4. Transfer the brisket to the smoker and cook for 3 hours. Place the meat on a sheet of heavy-duty foil, sprinkle it with the remaining 2 tablespoons rub, and close the foil tightly. Cook until well-done and tender, another 1 1/2 to 2 hours.

5. Open the foil and let the brisket sit at room temperature for 15 minutes. Remove the foil. Trim any excess fat and slice the brisket thinly against the grain, changing direction as the grain changes. If you wish, serve your choice of tomato-based barbecue sauce on the side.

SERVING SUGGESTION For a summer supper, round out the meal with Burstin' with Black-Eyed Peas Salad (page 419) and Boarding House Macaroni Salad (page 422). No dessert beats The Best Cure for a Southern Summer (page 469), unless perhaps it's the watermelon version of Ice-Sicles (page 467).

BBQ tip Chipotle chiles, which are smoked jalapeños, contribute their smoldering heat and smokiness to many great barbecue dishes. They can be found dried, but we often prefer the canned variety for its flavorful adobo sauce, a heady concoction of vinegar, tomato, onions, spices, and smoke. *Muy sabrosa.*

Burnt Ends

A Kansas City specialty, the burnt ends of a barbecued brisket are fit for a royal feast. Barbecue novices may shy away from these extra-crusty, extra-chewy little nuggets, but aficionados clamor for them. Any pit-smoked brisket has plenty of blackened surface to cut into ends, but we prefer to use the fatty top portion, or point, sliced off in one piece and cooked again. If you don't want to take the time for this on the same day you barbecue initially, freeze the meat and put it back on the pit when you fire up again. SERVES 4 TO 6

1 fully barbecued fatty top section Braggin' Rights Brisket (page 111)

Struttin' Sauce (page 369), Bar-B-Q Ranch Sauce (page 375), or other tomato-based barbecue sauce (optional)

1. Prepare the smoker for barbecuing, bringing the temperature to 200°F to 220°F.

2. Transfer the brisket section to the smoker and cook it for 3 to 4 hours, depending on its size. Let the brisket sit at room temperature for 10 minutes and then slice or shred it. After you break through the coal-like crust, the meat will pull apart into succulent shreds with chewy, deep-flavored ends. Savor at once, with your favorite tomato-based barbecue sauce on the side if you wish.

BBQ tip You should seldom trim the fat from meat before you barbecue it. The fat is a natural basting agent that helps keep the meat moist and flavorful, particularly when it's on the top side of the cut while it's cooking. Much of the fat melts away in your smoker—just check the water pan or reservoir—and the rest can be trimmed before serving.

BBQ tip The layer of pink, or smoke ring, you find just under the surface of most slow-smoked meat is not an indication of undercooking. When the pink runs from the outside in, as it does in barbecue, it results from the smoking process and becomes more distinct as the meat gets well-done. When the pink runs from the center out, as in a rare steak, the meat is cooked less thoroughly than possible. Barbecue authorities often judge smoked food initially by the depth of the smoke ring, hoping to find something heftier than a thin red line.

Salpicón

The pride of El Paso, Texas, and the adjoining town of Juarez, Mexico, a salpicón typically combines a mélange of colorful vegetables with baked or boiled brisket in a lively vinaigrette. Ours pairs the mixture instead with smoked meat. The hearty salad can serve as a main dish or, when accompanied by tortilla chips for dipping, as an appetizer. We'd like to dedicate this recipe to the memory of our friend and fellow cookbook author, Michael McLaughlin, who loved smoked brisket and spicy dishes as much as we do. *Vaya con dios.* SERVES 12 TO 14

SALPICÓN DRESSING

7-ounce can chipotle chiles in adobo sauce

1 cup extra-virgin olive oil

2/3 cup freshly squeezed lime juice

1/4 cup cider vinegar

2 garlic cloves, minced

Kosher salt and coarse sea salt and coarsely ground black pepper to taste

SALPICÓN SALAD

3 1/2 pounds shredded smoked beef brisket, such as Braggin' Rights Brisket (page 111), Burnt Ends (page 115), or Dallas Dandy Brisket (page 113)

4 red-ripe Roma or other plum tomatoes, diced

2 ripe avocados, preferably Haas, peeled, pitted, and diced

1 large red bell pepper, seeded and diced

1 medium red onion, diced

6 ounces Monterey Jack cheese, shredded

2/3 cup chopped fresh cilantro

6 medium radishes, grated

1 head romaine, shredded

1. If you're not a chile-head, start with half of the can of chipotle chiles. Combine all the dressing ingredients in a blender or food processor and process until well combined.

2. In a large bowl, combine the brisket with up to three-quarters of the dressing. Cover and refrigerate for at least 2 hours, or overnight.

3. Remove the meat from the refrigerator and let it sit at room temperature for about 30 minutes. Add the remaining ingredients to the brisket and toss well. Drizzle on more dressing as you wish, keeping in mind it will increase the salad's heat level. Serve immediately.

SERVING SUGGESTION Salpicón shines as the centerpiece of a fiesta meal. Accompany it with Blue Corn Muffins (page 412), Santa Fe Capirotada (page 464), and Turquoise Margaritas (page 477).

Brisket Hash

When you barbecue a brisket, you're likely to have leftovers unless you've invited a small town to dinner. We once hosted a breakfast barbecue just to serve this dish to 40 friends. **SERVES 4 TO 6**

2 tablespoons vegetable oil

1 tablespoon unsalted butter

2 1/2 cups diced potatoes, preferably unpeeled

1 1/2 cups diced onions

1 cup diced red bell pepper

1 to 2 pickled jalapeños, minced

4 cups shredded smoked brisket, such as Braggin' Rights Brisket (page 111), Burnt Ends (page 115), or Dallas Dandy Brisket (page 113)

3/4 cup beef stock

1 1/2 tablespoons yellow mustard

1 tablespoon ketchup

1 teaspoon coarsely ground black pepper

Kosher salt or coarse sea salt to taste

In a heavy skillet, warm the oil and butter together over medium heat. Add the potatoes, onions, bell pepper, and jalapeños and sauté for 10 minutes until the potatoes have begun to soften. Mix in the remaining ingredients. Cover and simmer for 10 minutes, stirring the mixture up from the bottom once after 6 or 7 minutes and patting it back down. Uncover the skillet and continue cooking for several minutes, until the liquid is absorbed and the mixture just begins to get crusty on the bottom. Serve hot.

SERVING SUGGESTION For a hearty breakfast, serve the hash with buttermilk biscuits with berry preserves and fresh fruit.

Deli-Cured Brisket

Don't bring this up in Fort Worth, but there are some non-Texan styles of brisket cookery that yield very good results. This version blends barbecue and deli traditions, introducing preparation techniques developed for corned beef and pastrami, two other great styles of cooked brisket. Like the previous recipe, we begin with a flat-cut brisket section, allowing you to get great results in just about any kind of smoker. Though harder to come by, because it's often ground, you can ask your butcher ahead for the fattier, more marbled point cut of the brisket, which makes a more succulent pastrami-type preparation. Serve this lightly smoked version on its own with dill pickles and a couple of good mustards, or piled high on sandwiches with horseradish on the side. **SERVES 6 TO 8**

BRINE

8 cups (2 quarts) water

1/2 cup kosher salt

6 tablespoons packed brown sugar

1/4 cup pickling spices

4-pound fully trimmed brisket section (sometimes called the flat cut), or a similar-size point cut

DELI RUB

6 tablespoons kosher salt or coarse sea salt

1/4 cup cracked black pepper

1/4 cup cracked coriander seeds

1/4 cup cracked mustard seeds

2 tablespoons garlic powder

DELI MOP

1 cup white vinegar

1 cup water

1. The night before you plan to barbecue, stir together the brine ingredients in a large bowl. Place the brisket in a plastic bag and pour the brine over it. Refrigerate the brisket overnight.

2. The next day, combine the dry rub ingredients in a small bowl. Drain and discard the brine. Pat the brisket down with all but 3 tablespoons of the rub, coating the slab heavily. Let the brisket sit at room temperature for about 45 minutes.

3. Prepare the smoker for barbecuing, bringing the temperature to 200°F to 220°F.

4. If you are going to baste the meat (see page 45, "To Mop or Not"), combine the vinegar, water, and remaining 3 tablespoons rub in a saucepan and warm over low heat.

5. Transfer the brisket to the smoker and cook for 3 hours, mopping at 45-minute intervals in a wood-burning pit or as appropriate in your style of smoker. Place the meat on a sheet of heavy-duty foil and close the foil tightly. Cook until well-done and tender, another 1 1/2 to 2 hours.

6. Open the foil and let the brisket sit at room temperature for 15 minutes. Remove the foil. Trim any excess fat and slice the brisket thinly against the grain, changing direction as the grain changes. Leftovers are good cold or reheated.

VARIATION: DELI-CURED BRISKET AND EGGS
For four breakfast eaters, whisk together 8 eggs with 2 tablespoons water and some salt and pepper. Thinly slice about 1 pound of the brisket and cook it in a skillet over medium heat until the meat leaves a thick film of fat in the bottom of the skillet. Pour the egg mixture over the meat and cook, lifting around the edges and tilting the skillet so the uncooked egg runs underneath, until the eggs just begin to set, 3 to 4 minutes. Nudge the mixture onto a platter and serve.

HOLY SMOKE

Dallas chef Dean Fearing, the kitchen star at Fearing's Restaurant, once said that in Texas, "Barbecue is God." Thinking about his comment a minute, he added, "or maybe it's just God's work."

BRISKET FRITO PIE For each person you plan to serve, first layer a big handful of Fritos (no, nothing else will do here) in a shallow bowl or plate. Spoon over about 1 cup of your favorite chili, with beans or without, as you prefer. Scatter up to 1 cup warm barbecued brisket shreds over it, then top with handfuls of grated mild cheddar and chopped iceberg or romaine lettuce. Garnish with chopped tomatoes and, if you like, chopped onions, and serve right away.

CRISPY BRISKET TACOS WITH JALAPEÑO RANCH DRESSING Stir about 1 table-spoon minced pickled jalapeño and a few grinds of black pepper into 1 cup ranch salad dressing and set aside. We like these with crispy taco shells. Sure, you could wimp out and buy some preformed shells, but if you went to the trouble to smoke a brisket, we think it deserves freshly made shells. To make a dozen tacos, first heat about half an inch of vegetable oil in a heavy skillet over medium-high heat. Have several thicknesses of paper towels nearby and also a baking rack arranged over some additional paper towels. Dunk each tortilla quickly in the hot oil, just long enough for it to turn limp, a few seconds for each. Lay the softened tortillas on the paper towels. Spoon about 2 tablespoons smoked brisket across the center of each tortilla. Fold up and secure the top with a toothpick. Return a couple of the filled tacos to the hot oil and fry for about 30 seconds per side, just until crisp. Drain well over the skillet, then set on the baking rack. Fry the remaining tacos. Remove the toothpicks and garnish as you wish. Then pass the ranch dressing and eat while piping hot.

SOFT BRISKET TACOS WITH CABBAGE-CILANTRO SLAW AND BARBECUE VINAIGRETTE Make the slaw by stirring together 2 tablespoons vegetable oil with 1 tablespoon white vinegar, $1/2$ teaspoon freshly ground black pepper, and a heaping $1/4$ teaspoon table salt. Add about $1/2$ teaspoon crushed red chile flakes, if you wish, then mix in $11/2$ cups shredded green cabbage, 1 tablespoon minced onion, and a good handful of minced fresh cilantro leaves. Refrigerate briefly while preparing the sauce and the tacos. Make the vinaigrette by stirring together 1 tablespoon smoky barbecue sauce, 1 table-spoon cider or white vinegar, and $1/4$ cup vegetable oil. Season to taste with salt and pepper and a bit more oil if you wish. Warm a dozen corn tortillas in a steamer or wrapped in foil in a 300°F oven for 15 minutes or more. Layer 2 tortillas together, one on top of the other, to make 6 sturdy tacos. Spoon about 3 tablespoons warm shredded barbecued brisket or burnt ends down the center of each tortilla pair. With a slotted spoon, add a tablespoon or two of the slaw to each taco, then drizzle with a scant tablespoon of vinaigrette and serve immediately.

BRISKET DEVILED EGGS Peel 1 dozen hard-cooked eggs. Scoop the yolks out of the eggs into a bowl, mash them, and mix with 6 tablespoons mayonnaise, 1 tablespoon Dijon mustard, and table salt and black pepper to taste. If you wish, stir in a grating of fresh horseradish or some minced fresh chives. Spoon the mixture back into the eggs, keeping it rather flat. Top each with finely shredded warm barbecued brisket, about a teaspoon or two per egg half. Top, if you wish, with a few bits of fresh chives, a sliver of jalapeño or serrano, or a bit of red bell pepper. Serve immediately or chill before serving.

BRISKET NACHOS You can simply pile a bunch of favorite ingredients on top of tortilla chips and nuke them, or you can add a little finesse and make them that much better. Pick out a quantity of good-size unbroken chips from the bag. Top each individually with your chosen toppings, which should be, at the minimum, a good melting cheese or combo of cheeses such as mild cheddar and Monterey Jack, sliced fresh jalapeños or pickled jalapeño slices, and shreds of barbecued brisket. We like a smear of warm refried beans across each chip before the building upward begins. Arrange the nachos neatly on a baking sheet and cook in a 375°F oven until the cheese is melted, about 5 minutes. Transfer to a decorative platter and eat immediately, perhaps with some salsa on the side.

BRISKET TEXAS BOWL O' RED Well, you probably want to serve at least a couple of bowls o' red. Heat 2 teaspoons vegetable oil into a large saucepan, add about ¾ cup chopped onion and 1 or 2 minced garlic cloves, and cook until the onion is translucent. Stir in ¼ cup Texas-style chili powder, such as Gebhardt's, and, if you wish, some ground cumin. Pour in 2 cups water and simmer for about 15 minutes over medium heat. Mix in 2 cups barbecued brisket, pulled into small bite-size shreds, and simmer for another 15 minutes. Add salt and, if you would like more heat, a few shakes of ground cayenne. The liquid should be thick and not too soupy. Cook a bit longer if needed. Serve in bowls with a little chopped onion and a few shreds of mild cheddar or Colby cheese.

BRISKET-STUFFED BISKIT Start with homemade or good-quality store-bought biscuits, preferably about 3 inches across. If the biscuits are hot from the oven, simply split and butter them. If not quite so fresh, split, butter, and toast the insides of the biscuits on a griddle. Cover half of each warm biscuit with a thin slice of melting cheese such as mild cheddar, mozzarella, or pepper Jack. Scramble or fry (over-hard works best on a sandwich) the same number of eggs as you have biscuits. Place the warm eggs over the cheese, then top with warm barbecued brisket. A little spoonful of barbecue sauce (perhaps mixed with mayo) can be drizzled on, too. Arrange the tops on the biscuits and you're good to go.

BRISKET-STUFFED SPUD Bake russet potatoes or plump Yukon Golds by your favorite method until tender. Slit each potato across the top. Push in a bit from all sides to break and push up the potato flesh into a center mound. Add kosher salt or coarse sea salt and black pepper and a small pat of butter to each, then top with hot smoked brisket shreds, a scoop of sour cream, and sliced scallion tops or chives. Serve other toppings, too, if you wish.

BRISKET SHEPHERD'S PIE Make this in a bread pan or a deep baking dish, depending on the quantity of leftover smoked meat you have. You'll want at least 1 inch of fairly well-packed brisket. We like to simmer some pearl onions and carrot chunks in a little stock until they're soft, then add them in a layer over the brisket. Spoon a layer of creamy mashed potatoes over all, at least 1 inch deep. If you like, top with a good sprinkling of paprika or Wild Willy's Number One-derful Rub (page 26). Bake at 350°F until hot and bubbly. The baking time will vary by the size of your pie, but plan on at least 20 minutes. If you want to be decadent, scatter some shredded cheese over the hot mixture and crank the oven up to broil. Broil just long enough to melt the cheese and brown the potato topping in a few spots. Scoop down through all of the layers to serve.

Espresso-Rubbed Beef Medallions

Beef medallions, or filets mignons, are incomparably tender, but we believe they usually need a boost in the flavor department. This simple coffee-based rub perks the meat up perfectly. The beef's brief smoking time means that you can skip any mopping procedure in this recipe. Just add a bit of butter to the top of each medallion as it comes out of the smoker. A few splashes of Worcestershire sauce can be a welcome addition at the table. **SERVES 6**

ESPRESSO RUB

2 tablespoons ground espresso

2 tablespoons ground coffee

1 1/2 tablespoons ground pasilla or ancho chile

1 1/2 tablespoons kosher salt or coarse sea salt

1 1/2 teaspoons coarsely ground black pepper

1 teaspoon packed brown sugar

Six 7-ounce to 8-ounce beef tenderloin medallions (filets mignons), 1 1/4 to 1 1/2 inches thick

2 thick pats of butter, each sliced in 3 pieces

Worcestershire sauce (optional)

1. Mix the rub ingredients in a small bowl. Massage the rub into all sides of the beef medallions. Let sit at room temperature for 30 minutes.

2. Prepare the smoker for barbecuing, bringing the temperature to 200°F to 220°F.

3. In a heavy skillet, sear the meat quickly on all sides over high heat. Transfer the tenderloin medallions to the smoker and cook until the internal temperature reaches 125°F to 130°F, 45 to 60 minutes. Be careful not to overcook, since tenderloin is best rare to medium-rare.

4. Place a bit of butter on each medallion and serve immediately, with Worcestershire sauce on the side if you wish.

BBQ *tip* American grass-fed beef was about as common as a jackalope when we wrote the first edition of *Smoke & Spice*. These days it is widely available, thanks to concerns about the survival of small-scale sustainable agriculture and keeping antibiotics and growth hormones out of our food and off our plates. In comparison to feedlot-finished beef, the taste is less sweet, a bit more minerally, and truly beefy. Check for grass-fed beef at farmers' markets and stores specializing in natural foods.

Bona Fide Fajitas

In addition to *barbacoa de cabeza*, Mexican ranchers and vaqueros in the Southwest gave the world fajitas, another slow-starter. The diaphragm muscle of cattle, fajitas or skirt steak didn't win acceptance even in Texas until the last few decades. After the dish became trendy across the country, restaurants began misusing the Spanish term to refer to almost any kind of grilled meat rolled in a flour tortilla. The only true fajitas are made with beef skirt, and the best ones are still slow-smoked outdoors over a wood fire. If you want to be literal, this is a *taco de fajitas*, but most people know it simply by the name of the meat itself. SERVES 6 TO 8

FAJITAS MARINADE AND OPTIONAL MOP

12 ounces beer

3/4 cup vegetable oil

1/2 medium onion, chopped

Juice of 2 limes

4 garlic cloves, minced

1 bay leaf

2 tablespoons Worcestershire sauce

1 tablespoon chili powder

1 teaspoon freshly ground black pepper

1 teaspoon crushed chiltepins or chiles pequíns or Tabasco sauce

1 teaspoon ground cumin

2-pound to 3-pound whole beef skirt, trimmed of fat and membrane

PICO DE GALLO

4 red-ripe Roma or plum tomatoes, diced

1/2 red bell pepper, chopped

1/4 cup chopped fresh cilantro

1/4 cup chopped red onion

2 to 3 fresh serranos or 3 to 4 fresh jalapeños, minced

Juice of 1/2 lime

1/2 teaspoon table salt, or more to taste

2 to 4 tablespoons tomato juice (optional)

Warm flour tortillas
Lime wedges and cilantro sprigs, for garnish
Sour cream

1. The night before you plan to barbecue, combine the marinade ingredients in a blender and puree. Place the skirt steak in a plastic bag or shallow dish and pour the marinade over it. Refrigerate the skirt steak overnight, turning occasionally if needed to saturate the surface with the marinade.

2. Prepare the smoker for barbecuing, bringing the temperature to 200°F to 220°F.

3. Remove the skirt from the bag and drain it, reserving the marinade if you plan to baste the meat. Let the skirt sit at room temperature for 30 minutes.

4. Make the pico de gallo by combining all the ingredients except the tomato juice in a bowl. If you prefer a more liquid consistency, add some or all of the tomato juice. Refrigerate until serving time.

5. If you are using the mop (see page 45, "To Mop or Not"), boil the marinade in a saucepan over high heat for several minutes and then keep the mop warm over low heat.

6. Transfer the skirt to the smoker. Cook for approximately 1 hour, mopping every 20 minutes in a wood-burning pit, or as appropriate for your style of smoker.

7. If your smoker has a separate grill area for cooking directly over the fire, or if you have another grill handy, move the meat there and sear it for 1 to 2 minutes per side. This step adds a pleasant crispy exterior texture but isn't necessary for flavor. Alternatively, smoke the meat for about 15 minutes longer.

8. Let the skirt sit for 10 minutes and then slice thinly at a diagonal angle against the grain. Pile the meat and warm tortillas on a platter garnished with lime wedges and cilantro, and serve the pico de gallo and sour cream on the side.

SERVING SUGGESTION Drink Mexican Martinis (page 475) with the fajitas. *Muy sabroso.*

BBQ tip A red-orange, pea-shaped chile pod that grows wild in parts of the Southwest, chiltepins add serious zing to barbecue marinades. Their pointed-pod cousins, chiles pequins, pack similar firepower. If your market has neither, Tabasco or a similar hot sauce makes a good substitute.

HOLD THE LETTUCE ON MINE

Barbecue restaurants in California range from fancy to funky. In Beverly Hills, pricey ribs come with a selection from the salad bar. You're better off in Oakland, where you may get a side of collard greens. Our favorite spot—partially for the name—is Dr. Hogly Wogly's Tyler, Texas BBQ in Los Angeles. The hot links are terrific, but if you want endive, you better bring your own.

Simply Elegant Beef Tenderloin

Few main dishes dazzle guests like beef tenderloin. This is an easy but elegant version, flavored simply with garlic, salt, and pepper and then polished to perfection with a quick sear and a slow smoke. SERVES 6 OR MORE

ROASTED GARLIC MASH

1 whole head of garlic

1 tablespoon kosher salt or coarse sea salt

1 teaspoon extra-virgin olive oil or vegetable oil

2-pound beef tenderloin

1 to 2 tablespoons coarsely ground black pepper

1/2 teaspoon ground white pepper

1 1/2 cups beef stock

3 tablespoons olive oil or vegetable oil

1. Break the garlic head apart into individual cloves, but don't peel them. Place them in a cast-iron or other heavy skillet and dry-roast over medium heat until soft and brown, 6 to 8 minutes, shaking or stirring as needed to color evenly. Peel the garlic (a quick task once roasted) and transfer to a small bowl. Using the back of a large fork, mash the garlic lightly. Add the salt and oil and continue mashing until you have a rough puree.

2. If you plan to baste the beef tenderloin (see page 45, "To Mop or Not"), reserve 1 teaspoon of the garlic paste. Rub the beef with the remaining paste, massaging it into every little crevice, then combine the two peppers and pat them over the surface. Wrap tightly in plastic and let sit at room temperature for about 30 minutes.

3. If you are using the mop, combine the reserved 1 teaspoon garlic paste with the beef

stock and 2 tablespoons of the oil in a saucepan and warm over low heat.

4. Prepare the smoker for barbecuing, bringing the temperature to 200°F to 220°F.

5. In a heavy skillet, heat the remaining 1 tablespoon oil over high heat. Sear the tenderloin on all sides, about 30 seconds per side and each end. Transfer the tenderloin to the smoker and cook for 1 1/2 to 1 3/4 hours, mopping every 20 minutes in a wood-burning pit, or as appropriate for your style of smoker. Start checking the internal temperature after 1 hour of cooking. The meat is ready when the internal temperature reaches 120°F to 125°F. Be careful not to overcook, since tenderloin is best rare to medium-rare. Let the tenderloin rest for 10 minutes before carving, during which the meat temperature will rise by 5 to 10 degrees. Slice the tenderloin and serve.

BBQ tip For big tender meat cuts like tenderloins and rib roasts, which you want done rare or medium-rare, pull them off the fire well before they reach the final temperature of doneness, generally considered to be 125°F for rare and 130°F to 135°F for medium-rare. The meat will continue to cook as it sits, and its temperature will rise by 5 to 10 degrees, giving you the perfect doneness when it comes time to carve.

Drunk and Dirty Tenderloin

This one owes its inspiration to our old Kentucky home—the one in Bourbon County. It was there, in the same year that the country adopted the Constitution, that a Baptist preacher named Elijah Craig invented the wonderful American whiskey that flavors this tenderloin. We developed the recipe originally, like a couple of others in the chapter, for our *Texas Home Cooking* (1993, Harvard Common Press). Over the years, it has proved to be one of our most popular dishes, great for casual dinners and fancy affairs alike. **SERVES 6 OR MORE**

DRUNK AND DIRTY MARINADE

1 cup reduced-sodium soy sauce

1/2 cup water

1/2 cup bourbon or other sour-mash whiskey

1/4 cup Worcestershire sauce

2 tablespoons packed brown sugar

1/2 teaspoon ground ginger

4 garlic cloves, minced

2-pound beef tenderloin

2 tablespoons coarsely ground black pepper

1 teaspoon ground white pepper

1/4 cup vegetable oil

1. At least 4 hours and up to 12 hours before you plan to barbecue, combine the marinade ingredients in a large glass measuring cup. Place the tenderloin in a plastic bag or shallow dish and pour the marinade over the meat. Turn the meat occasionally if needed to saturate the surface with the marinade.

2. Prepare the smoker for barbecuing, bringing the temperature to 200°F to 220°F.

3. Remove the tenderloin from the bag and drain the marinade, reserving it. Cover the tenderloin thoroughly with the black pepper first, then the white pepper. Let the tenderloin sit for 30 minutes.

4. Pour half of the marinade into a saucepan and refrigerate it until the tenderloin is cooked. If you plan to baste the meat (see page 45, "To Mop or Not"), pour the other half of the marinade into another saucepan and stir in the oil. Bring this mop mixture to a boil over high heat and boil for several minutes. Keep the mop warm over low heat.

5. Warm a heavy skillet over high heat. Sear the meat on all sides, about 30 seconds per side and each end. Transfer the tenderloin to the smoker and cook for 1 1/2 to 1 3/4 hours, mopping every 20 minutes in a wood-burning pit, or as appropriate for your style of smoker. Start checking the internal temperature after 1 hour of cooking. The meat is ready when the internal temperature reaches 120°F to 125°F. Be careful not to overcook, since tenderloin is best rare to medium-rare. Let the meat rest 10 minutes before carving, during which the meat temperature will rise by 5 to 10 degrees.

6. To make the sauce, bring the reserved portion of marinade to a boil, and boil for several minutes, until the marinade is reduced by one-quarter. Slice the tenderloin and serve topped by spoonfuls of the sauce.

SERVING SUGGESTION When you need an impressive but homey menu, start with Smoked Olives (page 346) and Drop-Dead Trout Spread (page 353) with crackers or bread. Alongside the tenderloin, offer garlicky scalloped potatoes and spinach sautéed with baby tomatoes. Cranberry-Ginger Crumble (page 456) completes a memorable meal.

one of our most popular dishes, great for casual dinners and fancy affairs alike

A TRUE OUTPOST

Unless you're looking for a fine horse to buy, you've got to be intent on barbecue to get to Clark's Outpost in Tioga, Texas. In rich ranch country an hour north of Dallas, the sprawling roadhouse fills up in the evening with locals, lost tourists, and barbecue pilgrims. Definitely try the brisket for a main dish, and for a starter, get adventuresome with the calf fries (if you don't know, ask your daddy).

Tamarind Tenderloin

Snappy Pickapeppa sauce, a tamarind-based elixir, makes an easy yet complex flavoring for steaks and chops. Here it adds verve to a top cut of meat and the accompanying table sauce. SERVES 6 OR MORE

2-pound beef tenderloin

2 to 3 tablespoons Pickapeppa sauce

1½ cups beef stock

1 tablespoon vegetable oil

TENDERLOIN DRY RUB

1 teaspoon garlic powder

1 teaspoon kosher salt or coarse sea salt

½ teaspoon ground ginger

½ teaspoon ground allspice

½ teaspoon packed brown sugar

TAMARIND SAUCE

3-ounce package cream cheese, softened

6 tablespoons Pickapeppa sauce

3 tablespoons half-and-half

1 garlic clove, minced

Thinly sliced scallion rings

1. An hour or two before you plan to barbecue, rub the meat with the 2 tablespoons Pickapeppa sauce. Wrap the tenderloin in plastic and refrigerate for at least 30 minutes and up to 1½ hours.

2. If you plan to baste the meat (see page 45, "To Mop or Not"), combine the remaining 1 tablespoon Pickapeppa sauce with the beef stock and oil in a saucepan and warm over low heat.

3. Prepare the smoker for barbecuing, bringing the temperature to 200°F to 220°F.

4. In a small bowl, combine the dry rub ingredients. Remove the tenderloin from the refrigerator. Cover the tenderloin thoroughly with the dry rub and let it sit uncovered at room temperature for 30 minutes.

5. Warm a heavy skillet over high heat. Sear the meat on all sides, about 30 seconds per side and each end. Transfer the tenderloin to the smoker and cook about 1½ to 1¾ hours, mopping every 20 minutes in a wood-burning pit, or as appropriate for your style of smoker. Start checking the internal temperature after 1 hour of cooking. The meat is ready when the internal temperature reaches 120°F to 125°F. Be careful not to overcook, since tenderloin is best rare to medium-rare. Let the meat rest 10 minutes before carving, during which the meat temperature will rise by 5 to 10 degrees.

6. Combine the sauce ingredients in a small saucepan over low heat, cooking just until the cheese is melted. Slice the tenderloin and serve, topped by spoonfuls of the sauce and a sprinkling of scallions.

A Slab of Porterhouse

Nothing screams steak like a colossal porterhouse, a hefty slab that combines a full strip steak and filet mignon divided from each other by a T-shaped bone. Make sure to get this cut sliced *at least* 2 inches thick so that you get an optimum combo of heavily crusted surface and juicy, tender interior. If your butcher carries prime meat, pay the extra tariff for it in this case. This is the stuff of legends. No sauce allowed.

SERVES 3 OR MORE

1 porterhouse steak, cut 2 to 2¹/₂ inches thick

1 teaspoon Smoky Salt (page 29) or other smoked salt, or Maldon salt, or more to taste

1 teaspoon cracked black pepper

2 pats unsalted butter

1. Sprinkle the steak with the salt and pepper. Let sit at room temperature for 30 to 45 minutes.

2. Prepare the smoker for barbecuing, bringing the temperature to 200°F to 220°F.

3. Transfer the meat to the smoker and cook for 50 to 75 minutes, until the meat registers 120°F to 125°F (very rare).

4. Sear the meat over high direct heat, on a grill that is fired up and ready to go or in a heavy cast-iron skillet on the stovetop, until richly brown and crisp on both sides, about 2 minutes per side for medium-rare meat. Transfer to a cutting board, top with the butter, and let rest for about 10 minutes.

5. Slice the strip section away from the bone, as close to the bone as you can get. Then cut the tenderloin section away from the bone. To serve, carve the meat across the grain into portions about ¹/₂ inch thick. Serve immediately, with any pooling juices.

BBQ tip In many of our recipes for top-quality steaks and tenderloins, we recommend searing the meat in addition to smoking it. Tough cuts like brisket cook long enough to develop a crusty surface or bark, but that doesn't happen in the shorter barbecuing time needed for naturally tender cuts. Since these cuts are best with a contrasting crust, too, we sear them off before or after smoking them. Often, we recommend the searing first because it means that the more forgiving time process of smoking comes just before eating, allowing you to give it a few minutes more or less depending on whether everyone's assembled for the meal. With a couple of cuts—a prime single steak like this porterhouse or the Santa Maria Tri-Tip (page 146), which is also served fairly rare—we prefer the results with the searing done just before the meat is brought to the table. Feel free to experiment with this before-versus-after technique to develop a style that works for you. Either way, be sure you get a spirited sizzle when you sear.

Garlic-Scented Sirloin

This may not be the scent you want if you're feeling frisky, but the heap of garlic in this sirloin sure keeps the meat moist. SERVES 6

BASIC BLACK RUB

2 tablespoons freshly ground black pepper

1 tablespoon kosher salt or coarse sea salt

2-pound to 2¹/₂-pound boneless top sirloin steak, about 2 inches thick, cut with a pocket for stuffing, or two 1-pound to 1¹/₂-pound steaks of similar shape, about 1 inch thick

FILLING

1 whole head of garlic

1 tablespoon butter, preferably unsalted

¹/₈ teaspoon anchovy paste

¹/₂ cup sliced scallions

2 tablespoons dry red wine

SCENTED MOP (OPTIONAL)

¹/₂ cup dry red wine

¹/₂ cup red wine vinegar

¹/₂ cup water

2 tablespoons unsalted butter

2 garlic cloves, minced

1. An hour or two before you plan to barbecue, combine the dry rub ingredients in a small bowl. Rub the steak well with the mixture inside and out. Wrap the steak in plastic and refrigerate it.

2. Prepare the smoker for barbecuing, bringing the temperature to 200°F to 220°F.

3. About 20 minutes before barbecuing, remove the meat from the refrigerator and let it sit at room temperature.

4. To make the filling, break the garlic head apart into individual cloves, but don't peel them. Place them in a cast-iron or other heavy skillet and dry-roast over medium heat until soft and brown, 6 to 8 minutes, shaking or stirring as needed to color evenly. Peel the garlic (a quick task once roasted) and transfer to a small bowl.

5. In a small skillet, heat the butter with the anchovy paste. Add the garlic, mashing it with a fork to form a rough puree. Stir in the scallions and wine and cook for a minute or two, until the scallions are limp. Remove the pan from the heat and let the filling cool briefly. Spoon the filling into the pocket of the sirloin or, if you are using two individual steaks, layer the filling on one steak and top it with the other. It is not necessary (or desirable) to secure the pair with toothpicks as long as you handle the sirloin "sandwich" with care.

6. If you plan to baste the meat (see page 45, "To Mop or Not"), stir together the mop ingredients in a small saucepan and warm over low heat.

7. In a heavy skillet, sear the sirloin quickly on both sides over high heat. Transfer the meat to the smoker and cook for about 1³/₄ hours, depending upon your desired doneness. Mop every 30 minutes in a wood-burning pit, or as appropriate for your style of smoker. We prefer the meat when the internal temperature reaches 145°F to 150°F, or medium. Let the meat sit for 5 minutes and serve.

SERVING SUGGESTION Dinner could begin with Brined Bluepoints (page 264). Accompany the steak with a mixed vegetable salad, perhaps marinated green beans and carrots, and Blue Corn Muffins (page 412). Try a fruit dessert, such as spears of fresh pineapple topped with a little rum and brown sugar.

Soy-Glazed Flank Steak

Flank steaks make excellent barbecue, particularly when marinated. SERVES 6 TO 8

SOY MARINADE AND GLAZE

3/4 cup reduced-sodium soy sauce

1/3 cup Pickapeppa sauce

1/3 cup Worcestershire sauce

1/4 cup dry red wine

1/4 cup red wine vinegar

3 tablespoons packed brown sugar, or more to taste

1 1/2 tablespoons toasted sesame oil

2 garlic cloves, minced

2 flank steaks, about 1 1/4 pounds each

1. The night before you plan to barbecue, combine the marinade ingredients in a large glass measuring cup. Place the flank steaks in a plastic bag or shallow dish and pour the marinade over them. Refrigerate the steaks overnight.

2. Prepare the smoker for barbecuing, bringing the temperature to 200°F to 220°F.

3. Drain the steaks and reserve the marinade. Let the steaks sit at room temperature for 25 minutes.

4. In a heavy saucepan, bring the marinade to a boil and boil it until reduced by one-third, 5 to 10 minutes. Keep the mixture warm for glazing the meat.

5. Brush the glaze over the steaks and transfer them to the smoker. Brush the steaks with the glaze again after about 25 minutes. Cook for a total of 45 to 55 minutes, until the meat is rare to medium-rare, 125°F to 135°F.

6. Let the steaks rest for 5 minutes before slicing thinly across the grain. Serve the slices with additional glaze on the top or on the side.

BBQ tip Allowing food to come to cool room temperature before barbecuing promotes quick and even cooking, and with meat, fowl, and fish, it reduces the chance that a cold center will harbor bacteria. It's unsafe, however, to leave most food at room temperature for any longer than 1 hour. Always adjust the order of the recipe steps as necessary to prevent leaving your meat out for too long.

Carpetbag Steak

The carpetbag steak is an American classic that's disappearing quickly. Revive the idea tonight, plumping up a succulent steak with a stuffing of fresh briny oysters— the ultimate in surf 'n' turf eating. SERVES 2 TO 4

CREOLE RUB

1 tablespoon celery salt

1 1/2 teaspoons paprika

1 1/2 teaspoons freshly ground black pepper

1 1/2 teaspoons ground white pepper

1 1/2 teaspoons packed brown sugar

3/4 teaspoon garlic powder

3/4 teaspoon dried thyme

3/4 teaspoon cayenne

Two 12-ounce to 14-ounce New York sirloin strip steaks, cut with a pocket for stuffing

1/3 to 1/2 cup shucked oysters, with their liquor

CARPETBAG MOP (OPTIONAL)

1/2 cup water

1/2 cup beef stock or clam juice

2 tablespoons cider vinegar

1 tablespoon extra-virgin olive oil

1. An hour or two before you plan to barbecue, combine the dry rub ingredients in a small bowl. Rub the steaks well with the mixture inside and out, saving at least 1 teaspoon of the rub for the stuffing and 1 teaspoon for the mop. Wrap the steaks in plastic and refrigerate them.

2. Prepare the smoker for barbecuing, bringing the temperature to 200°F to 220°F.

3. About 20 minutes before barbecuing, remove the steaks from the refrigerator and let them sit at room temperature. Drain the oysters gently, reserving their liquor if you plan to baste the steaks. Toss the oysters with 1 teaspoon of the reserved rub and stuff half of the oysters into each steak.

4. If you are using the mop (see page 45, "To Mop or Not"), combine the oyster liquor with the mop ingredients and the remaining 1 teaspoon reserved rub in a small saucepan. Bring the mixture to a boil and then keep it warm over low heat.

5. In a heavy skillet, sear the meat quickly on both sides over high heat. Transfer the steaks to the smoker and cook for 45 to 60 minutes, depending upon your desired doneness. Mop twice in a wood-burning pit, or as appropriate for your style of smoker. We prefer the steaks when the internal temperature reaches 130°F to 135°F (medium-rare).

6. Let the steaks sit for 5 minutes and serve. Cut the steaks in half for more delicate appetites.

SERVING SUGGESTION Add baked beans, white rice, good bread with garlic-dill butter, and Candy Bar Cheesecake (page 461).

PJ's Spicy Pinwheel Steak

We got the idea for this stuffed round steak from Wayne Whitworth, founder of Pitt's & Spitt's pits. We named it for his delightful wife, PJ, who's as spicy and spirited as this steak. SERVES 4

1-pound top round steak

2 teaspoons Wild Willy's Number One-derful Rub (page 26), Cajun Ragin' Rub (page 29), or other savory seasoning blend

FILLING

3 tablespoons peanut oil

1/2 pound bulk chorizo or other spicy fresh sausage

2 tablespoons minced onion

2 garlic cloves, minced

1 1/2 cups cooked greens (collards, kale, and spinach are especially good)

1 large egg, lightly beaten

1 cup dry bread crumbs

1/2 cup grated Parmesan cheese

2 tablespoons dry mustard

Table salt and freshly ground black pepper to taste

STEAK MOP (OPTIONAL)

1 cup beer

1/2 cup water

2 tablespoons cider or white vinegar

1 tablespoon peanut oil

1. About 1 hour before you plan to barbecue, cut the steak into quarters and pound each quarter into a 1/4-inch-thick rectangle. Combine the dry rub ingredients in a small bowl and sprinkle the steaks with the spice mixture. Let the steaks sit at room temperature while you finish the preparations.

2. Prepare the smoker for barbecuing, bringing the temperature to 200°F to 220°F.

3. To make the filling, warm the oil in a heavy skillet over medium heat. Add the chorizo, onion, and garlic and sauté briefly until the chorizo is cooked through. Mix in the remaining filling ingredients. Spoon equal portions of the filling over each piece of steak. Roll up each piece of steak from one of its long sides, jelly-roll style. Make the rolls snug but leave some room for the filling to expand. Secure the rolls with toothpicks.

4. If you plan to baste the meat (see page 45, "To Mop or Not"), stir together the mop ingredients in a small saucepan and warm the mixture over low heat.

5. Transfer the rolls to the smoker and cook for 35 to 45 minutes. Mop once before closing the smoker and again after 25 minutes in a wood-burning pit, or as appropriate for your style of smoker. Serve immediately, sliced into pinwheels for the most attractive presentation. Remember to remove those toothpicks!

BBQ tip Oak is the best all-around wood for barbecuing beef. For additional flavor, we like to add some cherry wood or a little mesquite near the end of the cooking.

Cinderella Short Ribs

The fatty beef short rib, a cheap cut often made into stew meat, is always one of the ugliest things at a grocery store. A little slow-smoking does wonders for the appearance and sure makes it taste pretty. **SERVES 6**

WILD WILLY'S NUMBER ONE-DERFUL RUB

3/4 cup paprika

1/4 cup freshly ground black pepper

1/4 cup kosher salt or coarse sea salt

1/4 cup granulated sugar

2 tablespoons chili powder

2 tablespoons garlic powder

2 tablespoons onion powder

2 teaspoons cayenne

5 to 6 pounds bone-in beef short ribs, cut between the ribs

BASIC BEER MOP (OPTIONAL)

12 ounces beer

1/2 cup water

1/2 cup cider vinegar

1/4 cup vegetable oil

1/2 medium onion, chopped or sliced in thin rings

2 garlic cloves, minced

1 tablespoon Worcestershire sauce

CINDERELLA GLAZE AND SAUCE

1 1/2 cups ketchup

1 cup beer

3/4 cup cider vinegar

1/4 cup minced fresh cilantro

3 tablespoons packed brown sugar

2 tablespoons Worcestershire sauce

2 garlic cloves, minced

2 teaspoons ground cumin

1 1/2 teaspoons ground anise

1 1/2 teaspoons kosher salt or coarse sea salt

1 teaspoon Tabasco or other hot pepper sauce

1. The night before you plan to barbecue, combine the rub ingredients in a bowl. Apply about half of the rub evenly to the ribs. Place the ribs in a plastic bag and refrigerate them overnight.

2. Prepare the smoker for barbecuing, bringing the temperature to 200°F to 220°F.

3. Remove the ribs from the bag. Sprinkle them lightly but thoroughly with more rub, reserving 1 tablespoon. Let the ribs sit at room temperature for 30 minutes.

4. If you plan to baste the meat (see page 45, "To Mop or Not"), combine the mop ingredients with the reserved 1 tablespoon rub in a small saucepan and warm over low heat.

5. Transfer the meat to the smoker, fatty side up. Cook for 4 to 5 hours, depending on the size of the ribs, until well-done. Mop the meat once an hour until the last hour in a wood-burning pit, or as appropriate for your type of smoker.

6. While the ribs are barbecuing, mix the glaze ingredients in a saucepan and bring the liquid to a simmer. Reduce the heat to low and cook the mixture for 30 minutes, stirring frequently. Brush the ribs with the glaze once or twice during the last hour of cooking. Return the remaining sauce to the stove and simmer for an additional 15 minutes to thicken it.

7. Remove the ribs from the smoker and let them sit at room temperature for 10 minutes. Trim the fat from the meat. Serve with the reduced sauce on the side. If you have any extra sauce, pull out a spoon and finish it off.

BBQ *tip* Any tomato-based sauce, including a barbecue sauce, will burn on the surface of food if applied as a glaze before the last hour of cooking. In rare instances, that's desirable, but not as a general rule.

Korean Kalbi Short Ribs

We believe you can never have too many recipes for barbecued short ribs, so we've added several new ones to this edition. Few things are a better investment of time and money than short ribs—they soak up a world of flavors as well as they soak up smoke. It's much easier now to find true Korean seasonings than when we first updated *Smoke & Spice* a decade ago, and kalbi (sometimes spelled galbi), the country's signature dish, is also one of the country's best exports. Traditionally, kalbi is grilled rather than smoked, but the classic flavors of soy, sesame oil, sugar, and scallions mate in perfect harmony with this slower outdoor cooking technique, too. This dish typically calls for what are called flanken ribs, a cross cut from the chuck end of the short ribs that results in long strips of meat with just a small section of bone in each. It's a common cut in Asian markets. These cook up great in any kind of smoker and are the fastest of our short rib recipes to reach the table. **SERVES 6**

KOREAN KICK PASTE

1 1/2 cups *ganjang* (Korean soy sauce) or Japanese soy sauce such as Kikkoman

1/4 cup plus 2 tablespoons granulated sugar or packed light brown sugar

1/4 cup toasted sesame oil

6 to 8 garlic cloves

3 to 4 scallions, limp green tops discarded, chopped roughly

2 tablespoons *gochujang* (Korean red pepper paste) or sriracha (optional)

4 to 5 pounds flanken-cut beef short ribs

SHORT-RIBS MOP (OPTIONAL)

1 cup water

2 tablespoons *ganjang* (Korean soy sauce) or Japanese soy sauce such as Kikkoman

2 tablespoons rice vinegar or white vinegar

2 tablespoons vegetable oil

Toasted sesame seeds and sliced scallions, both green and white portions, and lettuce leaves

Additional *gochujang* or sriracha (optional)

1. The night before you plan to barbecue, combine the paste ingredients in a blender or food processor and process until a smooth, thick puree forms. Apply the paste evenly to the ribs, reserving 1 tablespoon of the mixture if you plan to baste the ribs. Place the ribs in a plastic bag and refrigerate them overnight.

2. Prepare the smoker for barbecuing, bringing the temperature to 200°F to 220°F.

3. Remove the ribs from the refrigerator. Let the ribs sit at room temperature for 30 minutes.

4. If you are using the mop (see page 45, "To Mop or Not"), combine the water, soy sauce, vinegar, oil, and reserved 1 tablespoon seasoning paste in a small saucepan and warm over low heat.

5. Transfer the meat to the smoker, stretching the strips of beef out to their full length. Cook for about 3 hours, depending on the size of the ribs, until well-done. Mop the meat once an hour in a wood-burning pit, or as appropriate for your type of smoker.

6. Remove the ribs from the smoker and pull the tender meat away from the bones. Arrange the meat on a platter, and top with sesame seeds and scallions. Serve hot, with lettuce leaves for wrapping bits of the meat and with chile paste or sauce if you like.

SERVING SUGGESTION Add steamy white rice and some kimchi, Korea's chile-fueled fermented cabbage, probably available from wherever you purchased the short ribs or readily made from one of the many recipes available online.

"THE BEST BBQ JOINT IN THE WORLD"

So said Daniel Vaughn, known on Twitter as @BBQSnob, about Franklin Barbecue in Austin just months after *Texas Monthly* hired the writer in 2013 as its first barbecue editor. Many people in Texas and elsewhere, of course, considered the judgment highly inflammatory, and the two of us, figuring to join this bandwagon, queued up for three hours (about the normal wait time) to try some of Aaron Franklin's meat. Well, by golly, BBQSnob seems to have a great snout for 'Q.' It was the best brisket we've ever tasted, and the pulled pork, ribs, sausage, and turkey were also near the top of their class. Opened as a food truck in 2009, and now housed in a brick-and-mortar shack, Franklin's joint is on the fast track to barbecue fame.

Pan-Asian Short Ribs

It may sound a bit similar to the previous recipe, but this is an entirely different although equally delicious way to flavor humble-looking short ribs. This type of short ribs comes out their very best in a wood-burning pit. SERVES 6

PAN-ASIAN PANDEMONIUM PASTE

1/2 cup roughly chopped scallions

2 walnut-size chunks fresh ginger, peeled

3 tablespoons freshly squeezed lime juice

2 tablespoons reduced-sodium soy sauce

1 tablespoon Asian fish sauce

1/2 to 1 tablespoon Asian chile garlic paste

5 to 6 pounds bone-in beef short ribs, cut between the ribs

SHORT-RIBS MOP (OPTIONAL)

1 cup water

2 tablespoons reduced-sodium soy sauce

2 tablespoons rice vinegar or white vinegar

2 tablespoons vegetable oil

Plum Good Slopping Sauce (page 387) (optional)

1. The night before you plan to barbecue, combine the paste ingredients in a blender or food processor and process until a smooth thick puree forms. Apply the paste evenly to the ribs, reserving 1 tablespoon of the mixture if you plan to baste the ribs. Place the ribs in a plastic bag and refrigerate them overnight.

2. Prepare the smoker for barbecuing, bringing the temperature to 200°F to 220°F.

3. Remove the ribs from the refrigerator. Let the ribs sit at room temperature for 30 minutes.

4. If you are using the mop (see page 45, "To Mop or Not"), combine the water, soy sauce, vinegar, oil, and reserved 1 tablespoon paste in a small saucepan and warm over low heat.

5. Transfer the meat to the smoker, fatty side up. Cook for 4 to 5 hours, depending on the size of the ribs, until well-done. Mop the meat once an hour until the last hour in a wood-burning pit, or as appropriate for your type of smoker. If you want to glaze the ribs with Plum Good Slopping Sauce, brush the ribs with it once or twice during the last hour of cooking.

6. Remove the ribs from the smoker and let them sit at room temperature for 10 minutes. Trim the fat from the meat and serve.

Dino Ribs

Dino ribs look like the rack of ribs that used to tip over Fred Flintstone's car at the drive-in restaurant in the TV show's opening credits. Some folks refer to them as jumbo beef ribs or hunks o' heaven. What they actually are is uncut beef short ribs, meaning you

have a hearty 3- or 4-bone segment with some fine meat over, under, and around. You need to get them from a real meat market or a place like Costco where they cut some of their own meat. Call ahead or talk to your butcher at least a few days before you plan to barbecue this atavistic and amazing delicacy. We smoke them in what is referred to among serious barbecuers as a 3-2-1 method. The ribs spend 3 hours in the smoker in regular fashion, then get wrapped in foil to steam as they cook to help tenderize the meat for the next 2 hours, and are then unwrapped and again cooked naked at the end for 1 hour to develop a crusty surface. It's a little fiddly but super for this beefy cut. SERVES 6

STOUT BEER MARINADE

12 ounces stout or other dark beer such as a porter

1 medium onion, sliced thin

3 tablespoons vegetable oil

3 tablespoons white or cider vinegar

2 tablespoons molasses

2 tablespoons mustard, preferably brown, Dijon, or honey-Dijon

1 teaspoon kosher salt or coarse sea salt

Two 3- to 4-bone racks of uncut beef short ribs, about 12 inches or more in length

1/4 cup beef stock or beer (if you're not using the mop)

1. The night before you plan to barbecue, whisk together the marinade ingredients in a medium-size bowl. Place the ribs in one or more plastic bags, pour the marinade over, and turn a few times to distribute evenly. Refrigerate overnight.

2. Prepare the smoker for barbecuing, bringing the temperature to 200°F to 220°F.

3. Remove the ribs from the refrigerator and drain them, reserving the marinade if you plan to baste the meat. Let the ribs sit at room temperature for about 45 minutes.

4. If you plan to mop the meat (see page 45, "To Mop or Not"), bring the marinade to a boil in a saucepan and boil for several minutes. Keep the mop warm over medium heat.

5. Transfer the ribs to the smoker, meaty side up. Cook for about 6 hours, total, until well-done. During the first 3 hours, mop every 45 minutes to 1 hour in a wood-burning pit, or as appropriate for your style of smoker. After 3 hours, remove the ribs from the smoker and lay each section on a sheet of heavy-duty aluminum foil. If using the mop, splash each rack with a couple of tablespoons of the liquid; if not, divide the stock or beer between the foil packages. Close up each foil package and return it to the smoker for 2 hours more. Unwrap the ribs, discard the foil, and return the ribs to the smoker. The beef will recede from the bones as it smokes. Cook for approximately 1 hour more, until well-done and somewhat crusted.

6. Remove the ribs from the smoker and let them sit for 10 to 15 minutes before carving between the bones to make individual rib-bone and meat portions. If you have 4-bone roasts, serve the six most uniform meaty ribs and save the remaining two for big eaters or the cook's treat later.

Classic Crusty Texas Short Ribs

A visit to the John Mueller Meat Company in Austin reminded us that, while short ribs take hearty flavors well, they are also one of the finest meats to come out of a wood-burning pit smoker with little enhancement besides smoke. If you want to switch up the seasoning, opt for the very basic Basic Black Rub (page 30). And, sometime, make a field trip to Austin and go stand in line to try John's version. **SERVES 6**

TRAIL DUST

1/2 cup Worcestershire powder

1/4 cup freshly ground black pepper

1 tablespoon kosher salt or coarse sea salt

5 to 6 pounds bone-in beef short ribs, cut between the ribs

BASIC BEER MOP (OPTIONAL)

12 ounces beer

1/2 cup water

1/2 cup cider vinegar

1/4 cup vegetable oil

1/2 medium onion, chopped or sliced in thin rings

2 garlic cloves, minced

1 tablespoon Worcestershire sauce

Peppery Sweet Onion Sauce (page 378) (very optional)

1. Combine the rub ingredients in a small bowl. Apply the rub evenly to the ribs, saving 1 tablespoon of the mixture for the optional mop. Let the ribs sit for 30 to 45 minutes.

2. Prepare the smoker for barbecuing, bringing the temperature to 200°F to 220°F.

3. If you are using the mop (see page 45, "To Mop or Not"), combine the mop ingredients with the reserved 1 tablespoon rub in a small saucepan and warm over low heat.

4. Transfer the meat to the smoker, fatty side up. Cook for 4 to 5 hours, depending on the size of the ribs, until well-done. Mop the meat once an hour until the last hour in a wood-burning pit, or as appropriate for your type of smoker.

5. Remove the ribs from the smoker and let them sit at room temperature for 10 minutes. Trim the fat from the meat and serve. Accompany with barbecue sauce if you wish.

THREE MEATS ARE BETTER THAN ONE

Just south of Kansas City, Snead's looks the part of a barbecue bastion, a plain, rural roadhouse café with an aging sign no taller than the trees. Try one of the magnificent log sandwiches, a long bun stuffed with a robust mixture of barbecued beef, ham, and turkey. It'll turn a city slicker into a lumberjack.

Standing Tall Prime Rib

Try to get a true prime rib roast for this memorable dish, meat that meets USDA standards for the highest-grade beef. The cut that most supermarkets sell as a prime rib is actually just a USDA choice rib roast, good meat but not superior. Whatever its grade, when you carve a prime rib, everyone is actually getting a rib-eye steak. Lucky guests. **SERVES 4**

STANDING TALL MARINADE AND OPTIONAL MOP
$1^1/3$ cups dry red wine
$1^1/3$ cups red wine vinegar
$1/3$ cup extra-virgin olive oil
4 teaspoons dried rosemary
4 garlic cloves, minced
2 teaspoons dried thyme

3-pound prime standing rib roast

BASIC BLACK RUB
2 tablespoons freshly ground black pepper
1 tablespoon kosher salt or coarse sea salt
Rosemary sprigs (optional), for garnish

1. The night before you plan to barbecue, combine the marinade ingredients in a large glass measuring cup. Place the roast in a plastic bag, pour the marinade over it, and refrigerate it overnight.

2. Prepare the smoker for barbecuing, bringing the temperature to 200°F to 220°F.

3. Remove the roast from the refrigerator and drain it, reserving the marinade if you plan to baste the meat. Combine the dry rub ingredients in a small bowl and rub the roast with the mixture. Let the roast sit at room temperature for 45 minutes to 1 hour.

4. If you are plan to mop the meat (see page 45, "To Mop or Not"), bring the marinade to a boil in a saucepan and boil for several minutes. Keep the mop warm over low heat. Transfer the roast to the smoker, fatty side up. Cook for about $2^1/2$ hours, mopping every 30 minutes in a wood-burning pit, or as appropriate for your style of smoker. Start checking the internal temperature after $1^1/2$ hours of cooking. The meat is ready when the internal temperature reaches 120°F to 125°F. Be careful not to overcook, since the roast is best rare to medium-rare. Let the meat rest for 10 to 15 minutes before carving, during which the meat temperature will rise by about 10 degrees. Serve immediately, garnished with the rosemary sprigs if you wish.

SERVING SUGGESTION Use this as the centerpiece for a special meal, such as Christmas Eve or New Year's Eve dinner. Creamy Catfish Spread (page 352) and 007 Shrimp (page 362) make good nibbles. Parmesan-topped baked potatoes, steamed broccoli with orange butter, Squash Relish (page 437), and Buttermilk Biscuits (page 410) with fruit preserves might round out the main course. For dessert, poach pears or other winter fruit in sugar syrup with a touch of vermouth.

Pit Pot Roast

Chuck roast benefits from long, slow cooking, such as the braising technique used in most oven-cooked pot roasts. Barbecuing provides similar low and slow heat, and infuses the meat with the heady aroma of wood smoke, as in this spicy version.

SERVES 6 TO 8

WILD WILLY'S NUMBER ONE-DERFUL RUB
3/4 cup paprika
1/4 cup freshly ground black pepper
1/4 cup kosher salt or coarse sea salt
1/4 cup sugar
2 tablespoons chili powder
2 tablespoons garlic powder
2 tablespoons onion powder
2 teaspoons cayenne

3 to 4 garlic cloves, slivered
1 to 2 pickled jalapeños, slivered
3-pound boneless shoulder chuck roast

PIT POT MOP (OPTIONAL)
2 cups beer
1/2 cup cider vinegar
1 medium onion, chopped
2 tablespoons vegetable oil
2 tablespoons pickling liquid from a jar or can of pickled jalapeños

10-ounce can diced tomatoes with green chiles, undrained
1/4 cup beef stock or beer (if you're not using the mop)

1. The night before you plan to barbecue, combine the dry rub ingredients in a small bowl. Insert the garlic and jalapeño slivers into openings in the meat's surface. Massage the meat well with the dry rub, place it in a plastic bag, and refrigerate it overnight.

2. Remove the roast from the refrigerator and let it sit at room temperature for 45 minutes.

3. Prepare the smoker for barbecuing, bringing the temperature to 200°F to 220°F.

4. If you plan to baste the meat (see page 45 "To Mop or Not"), stir together the mop ingredients in a small saucepan and warm over low heat.

5. Transfer the roast to the smoker and cook for 4 hours, mopping every 45 minutes in a wood-burning pit, or as appropriate for your style of smoker. Place the roast on a large sheet of heavy-duty aluminum foil and pour the tomatoes with their juices over the meat. Add 1/4 cup of the mop, beef stock, or beer. Seal the foil tightly and continue cooking the roast until the meat is falling-apart tender, about 3 more hours.

6. Remove the roast from the smoker, unseal the foil, and let the roast sit at room temperature for 15 minutes before serving.

VARIATION: CLASSIC COUNTRY POT ROAST Instead of Wild Willy's, use Trail Dust (page 31) or Basic Black Rub (page 30) for the meat initially. Replace the canned tomatoes and chiles with the same amount of plain canned tomatoes. Add to the foil packet of meat: 6 to

8 small whole red-skinned potatoes (halved if much larger than a couple of inches around), 3 to 4 carrots in 2-inch chunks, and 6 to 8 baby onions (stems cut off) or 1 large onion sliced into 8 wedges. Pour the mop or other liquid over as instructed and continue cooking in the same way as above.

BBQ tip Aluminum foil is a wonder wrap in barbecuing, useful in many ways. When you cover food with it during the cooking process, as with the Pit Pot Roast, the foil creates a little steam oven that keeps meat moist. In other situations it can prevent delicate items from getting too smoky. In either case, if the heat source for your cooker comes from something other than wood, you can stop adding wood at the time you wrap the meat.

DON'T TAKE YOUNG GRANDKIDS ON A HOT WEEKEND

We made that mistake on a Saturday visit to John Mueller Meat Co. in Austin in June 2013. The line to order from the food trailer was almost two hours long, the heat made it feel like the sky was on fire, and the kids couldn't enjoy the free beer being passed out to the adults. They got really grumpy until we finally got our meat and sides, and settled into a shady spot at one of the outdoor picnic tables. We sampled widely from the menu, and liked it all, but thought the beef ribs and the baked squash were spectacular. As the grandson of Louie Mueller of Taylor, Texas, John is carrying on the family tradition in a grand manner.

Santa Maria Tri-Tip

Barbecue from central California can be a touch controversial. In Santa Maria, beef is cooked in a cloud of red oak wood smoke. Despite the wood fire, many BBQ purists from elsewhere in the country think that the Santa Maria style is closer to grilling than true barbecuing because of an elevated cooking temperature and use of an open rather than closed smoker. Besides, the meat is declared done when it's still medium-rare, which might incline a Texas pitmaster to say that he's seen steers hurt worse than that get back up and run away. While outsiders continue debating the merits of the cooking, in Santa Maria they're guffawing and enjoying the heck out of their top sirloin or tri-tip, a boomerang-shaped muscle from the bottom sirloin. Typically, the meat gets a simple mixture of salt, garlic salt, and pepper sprinkled generously over it before cooking, and then it's sliced up and served with a mild tomato salsa on the plate. Santa Marians have ingenious grills that can be raised or lowered over the wood fire to sizzle their beef to perfection. Our directions here presume that you are lacking such a grill, and explain a technique that works if you're using some type of barbecue smoker. SERVES 6

SANTA MARIA SALSA

2 cups chopped ripe tomatoes

1 small white onion, chopped fine

1/2 cup chopped roasted mild green chiles, such as Anaheim or New Mexican (Ortega's canned mild green chiles are the usual in Santa Maria)

1 plump garlic clove, minced

1 tablespoon vegetable oil

1 tablespoon apple cider vinegar

Kosher salt or coarse sea salt

SANTA MARIA RUB

1 tablespoon kosher salt or coarse sea salt

1 tablespoon garlic salt

1 tablespoon coarsely ground black pepper

2 tri-tip steaks, about 2 1/2 pounds each

1. Stir the salsa ingredients together, with salt to taste, and refrigerate for at least 1 hour.

2. Prepare the smoker for barbecuing, bringing the temperature to 200°F to 220°F.

3. Combine the rub ingredients in a small bowl. Massage the meat well with the rub.

4. Transfer the meat to the smoker and cook until the meat registers 120°F to 125°F (very rare), 50 to 75 minutes.

5. Sear the meat over high direct heat, on a grill that has been fired up previously or in a heavy cast-iron skillet on the stovetop, until richly brown and crisp on both sides, about 2 1/2 min-

The Taylor, Texas, International Barbecue Cook-off started in the late 1970s in response to the legislature declaring chili the official state dish. Every August the local organizers prove to the politicos that 'Q' is still the queen of Lone Star cooking. Home to some venerable barbecue joints, the town of Taylor makes a perfect spot to sound off on the subject.

utes on each side for medium-rare meat. Transfer to a cutting board and let rest for about 10 minutes.

6. Slice each tri-tip in half at the triangle point. Then turn each section so that you can slice the meat across the grain. Serve right away with the salsa.

VARIATION: SANTA MARIA TOP SIRLOIN Many locals prefer this cut to the tri-tip, and it does have the benefit of being a bit more naturally tender. Start with a single 2-inch-thick slab of top sirloin, about 5 pounds. Season and cook in similar fashion, allowing a few minutes more to get the single piece of meat to very rare doneness on the smoker and a couple of additional minutes for the last-minute searing, too.

SERVING SUGGESTION: On its home turf, this meat will always share the plate with pin-quito beans, a diminutive pinto bean cousin. For authenticity you can order pinquitos on-line (ranchogordo.com), but simply prepared ranch-style beans such as Cowpoke Pintos (page 397) can be substituted if no Santa Marians are coming to dinner. Round out the plate with Boarding House Macaroni Salad (page 422) and garlic bread. The menu is held in such esteem in Santa Maria that the local Chamber of Commerce copyrighted it decades ago.

BBQ tip Select tri-tip steaks that are well marbled throughout. They should have an even, thin layer of fat over one side. Slash down through the fat, but not into the meat, before adding dry rub, a marinade, or other flavoring. The cut is commonly available in central California, but elsewhere you may need to order it ahead.

Southwest Stew on a Stick

An old favorite, beef stew, tastes as good in kebob form as in a bowl. You'll want to use a tender cut of beef, though, for the relatively short cooking period. Either metal or soaked wooden skewers can be used. The kebobs are finished with a beer and molasses glaze. **SERVES 6**

STEW RUB

2 teaspoons chili powder

1 1/2 teaspoons kosher salt or coarse sea salt, or more to taste

1 teaspoon dry mustard

3/4 teaspoon ground cumin

1/2 teaspoon cayenne

1/2 teaspoon freshly ground black pepper

2 pounds top sirloin, cut into 1-inch cubes

1 1/2 cups pearl onions, peeled and parboiled

6 carrots, cut into thick chunks and parboiled

STEW GLAZE

3/4 cup beer

3/4 cup beef stock

2 tablespoons tomato paste

2 tablespoons molasses

1/2 teaspoon chili powder

1. At least 2 hours and up to 4 hours before you plan to barbecue, combine the dry rub ingredients in a small bowl. Toss the meat cubes with the rub, spoon them into a large plastic bag, and refrigerate.

2. Prepare the smoker for barbecuing, bringing the temperature to 200°F to 220°F.

3. Remove the meat from the refrigerator and skewer pieces of meat alternately with the onions and carrots. Cover the kebobs loosely with plastic and let them sit at room temperature while you prepare the glaze.

4. In a saucepan, combine the glaze ingredients and simmer over medium heat for 20 minutes or until reduced by about one-third. Keep the glaze warm.

5. Brush the skewers with the glaze and transfer them to the smoker. Cook for 30 to 45 minutes, until your desired doneness, brushing the kebobs with glaze about 5 minutes before they are done. Serve hot, brushed again with the glaze if you wish.

JUST HIDE THE PLATES IN THE PIT

"Barbecuing is only incidentally cooking, and barbecuists avoid, as much as possible, confusing the two. Barbecue is play—serious, mind-concentrating, important, risk-running, even exhausting . . . anything, in fact, except a chore. In real barbecue there's no washing up." John Thorne, *Simple Cooking* newsletter, 1988

Starnes Barbecue in Paducah thrives on Kentucky contrariness. Though mutton is the best-known barbecue of choice in much of the western part of the state, pork and beef are the stars at Starnes. Even more ornery, the two-booth joint serves its delicious meat on toasted bread, an idea that takes just a bite to like.

High Plains Jerky

Jerky was one of the main meats of the West when drying food was a major means of preservation. This is a simulated barbecue version, developed for flavor rather than longevity. SERVES 6 TO 8 AS A SNACK

1 pound top round steak

JERKY MARINADE
1/2 cup Worcestershire sauce
1/2 cup reduced-sodium soy sauce
1/4 cup packed brown sugar
4 garlic cloves, minced
2 teaspoons freshly ground black pepper
2 teaspoons ground red chile, preferably New Mexican or ancho
1 teaspoon onion powder

1. About 2 hours before you plan to barbecue, place the meat in the freezer to make slicing it easier. After 30 to 40 minutes, remove the meat from the freezer and slice it as thin as you can with a good sharp knife. Trim the meat of all fat.

2. Combine the marinade ingredients in a large glass measuring cup. Place the meat in a plastic bag or shallow dish and pour the marinade over it. Marinate for about 1 hour.

3. Prepare the smoker for barbecuing, bringing the temperature to 200°F to 220°F.

4. Remove the meat from the refrigerator, drain it, and let it sit at room temperature for 10 to 15 minutes.

5. Transfer the meat to a sheet of heavy-duty foil, separating the pieces; do not seal up the foil. Place the foil with the meat in the coolest part of your smoker and cook until the meat begins to blacken, about 45 minutes. Wrap the foil loosely over the meat and continue barbecuing until well dried, another 1 to 1¼ hours.

6. Remove the jerky from the smoker and let it cool to room temperature before serving. Refrigerate any leftovers.

BBQ *tip* When you order logs for a barbecue pit, ask for the smallest ones the supplier has. The ideal size is 12 to 14 inches, but anything up to 16 inches will work fine in most fireboxes.

Humdinger Hamburgers

Want to claim the title for best burgers in the neighborhood? This is the way to one-up your friends down the block who brag about their grilled hamburgers. Smoking makes ground meat taste like tenderloin. SERVES 4

WILD WILLY'S NUMBER ONE-DERFUL RUB

3 tablespoons paprika

1 tablespoon freshly ground black pepper

1 tablespoon kosher salt or coarse sea salt

1 tablespoon sugar

1½ teaspoons chili powder

1½ teaspoons garlic power

1½ teaspoons onion powder

½ teaspoon cayenne

2 pounds freshly ground beef, avoiding the higher-priced leaner meat

½ medium onion, chopped

3 chopped roasted mild green chiles, preferably New Mexican, Anaheim, or poblano, fresh or frozen (optional) (see BBQ tip)

BASIC BEEF MOP (OPTIONAL)

¾ cup beer

½ cup water

¼ cup cider vinegar

2 tablespoons vegetable oil

¼ cup chopped onion

1 garlic clove, minced

1½ teaspoons Worcestershire sauce

1½ teaspoons Wild Willy's Number One-derful Rub

Sourdough bread, sliced

Mustard, mayonnaise, dill pickle slices, tomato slices, lettuce, and Bar-B-Q Ranch Sauce (page 375) (optional)

1. An hour or two before you plan to barbecue, combine the rub ingredients in a small bowl.

2. In another bowl, mix the ground beef, onion, and chiles with your hands. Form the mixture into 4 thick patties and apply the dry rub thoroughly to all surfaces, reserving 1½ teaspoons of the spice mixture if you're planning to baste. Cover the patties with plastic and refrigerate them.

3. Prepare the smoker for barbecuing, bringing the temperature to 200°F to 220°F.

4. Remove the patties from the refrigerator and let them sit at room temperature for 15 minutes.

5. If you plan to baste the meat (see page 45, "To Mop or Not"), stir the mop ingredients together with the reserved 1½ teaspoons rub in a small saucepan and warm over low heat.

6. Transfer the patties to the smoker and cook until done to at least medium, about 1 hour, mopping every 20 minutes in a wood-burning pit, or as appropriate for your style of smoker.

7. Serve the burgers between slices of sourdough bread. Try a bite before you reach for any of the optional toppings, all good but less than essential with the richly flavored meat.

SERVING SUGGESTION Make the Humdinger Hamburgers and The Humble Hot Dog (page 153) the stars of a fall picnic. Add some Devil-May-Care Eggs (page 431), California Crunch (page 417), Peanut Butter Cake (page 457), and a light, fruity red wine.

On the old California ranchos, beef head's barbecue was a special feast for the full family. In her delightful 1988 *California Rancho Cooking* (Olive Press, reissued later by Sasquatch Books), Jacqueline Higuera McMahan recounts how the men dug a pit and tended the fire overnight, women made tortillas and salsas, and the children stuffed mint, oregano, and rosemary into the bull's ears and mouth. When they dug up the head after hours of covered smoking, the chief cook got the eyes and the cheek meat, and the boys grabbed "the huge set of teeth so they could run off to frighten any squeamish young ladies on the sidelines."

VARIATION: JERK BURGERS We recommend enthusiastic tinkering with the basic burger, but if you're hesitant about it, try this to get you started. Replace Wild Willy's rub with Jamaican Jerk Rub (page 32). Skip the green chiles in the burgers themselves. We like a topping of mayonnaise mixed about half-and-half with Pickapeppa sauce or Jamaican jerk sauce, or our Jamaican Barbecue Sauce (page 383).

BBQ *tip* For the best ground beef for barbecuing, ask your butcher to twice grind a piece of chuck, top or bottom round, or rump, with enough fat to make up about 20 percent of the whole.

BBQ *tip* Some of our recipes call for fresh green chiles, such as New Mexican or Anaheim, which must be roasted first to blister the tough skin. You can roast them individually over a gas stove burner, the same way you toast marshmallows over a fire. Spear the chiles on a fork, place them near the flame, and heat them until the skins have blistered and darkened uniformly. If you're roasting several chiles, you might want to do it in an oven. Place a layer of pods on a baking sheet and broil them until all are dark, turning the chiles frequently. After roasting, place the hot chiles in a plastic bag to steam and cool. Peel the roasted pods if you want to use them immediately, or freeze them, which makes the peeling easier. Canned chiles make a poor substitute for a home-prepared version, whether you start with fresh or frozen.

Pimiento Cheese–Stuffed Bar-B-Burgers

For decades, Southerners had pimiento cheese pretty much to themselves. We couldn't be happier now that it's as common in Albuquerque as in Atlanta. You can use any store-bought version or whip up the one included here. A simple rub is all you need on the meat, with so much flavor happening from the inside out. SERVES 4

PIMIENTO CHEESE

3/4 pound medium or sharp cheddar cheese, grated

1/2 cup mayonnaise

3-ounce to 4-ounce jar roasted red peppers or pimientos, drained

1 1/2 tablespoons minced onion

Table salt (optional)

2 pounds freshly ground beef, avoiding the higher-priced leaner meat

BASIC BLACK RUB

3 tablespoons coarsely ground black pepper

1 1/2 tablespoons kosher salt or coarse sea salt

BASIC BEEF MOP (OPTIONAL)

3/4 cup beer

1/2 cup water

1/4 cup cider vinegar

2 tablespoons vegetable oil

1/4 medium onion, chopped

1 garlic clove, minced

1 1/2 teaspoons Worcestershire sauce

4 large sturdy hamburger buns or kaiser rolls, split and toasted

Mayonnaise, ketchup, tomato slices, lettuce, and Carolina Red (page 371) (optional)

1. Make the pimiento cheese at least 30 minutes and up to several days ahead of when you plan to cook and serve the burgers. In a food processor, pulse together the cheese, mayonnaise, red peppers, and onion until almost smooth. Taste and add salt if you wish. Cover and refrigerate while you fire up the smoker.

2. Prepare the smoker for barbecuing, bringing the temperature to 200°F to 220°F.

3. Combine the rub ingredients in a small bowl.

4. Form the ground beef into 8 thin patties. Spoon a mounded tablespoon of pimiento cheese on top of 4 patties. Top each with a remaining patty and pinch together the edges all the way around to seal the cheese inside. Flatten each lightly. Sprinkle the dry rub thoroughly on all surfaces, reserving at least 1 1/2 teaspoons of the spice mixture.

5. If you plan to baste the meat (see page 45, "To Mop or Not"), stir the mop ingredients to-

gether with the reserved 1½ teaspoons rub in a small saucepan and warm over low heat.

6. Transfer the patties to the smoker and cook for about 1 hour, or until done to at least medium, mopping every 20 minutes in a wood-burning pit, or as appropriate for your style of smoker.

7. Serve the burgers on toasted buns, with the condiments that you wish.

SERVING SUGGESTION Serve these for football tailgating (the recipe easily doubles or triples) with Smoked Tomato Bloody Marys (page 478) or some chilled local microbrews, a few finger food nibbles to start, Boarding House Macaroni Salad (page 422), and Green Tomato Chowchow (page 436). Finish with South Georgia Pound Cake (page 458) and fresh berries or fruit. Go team!

The Humble Hot Dog

Los Angeles Dodgers fans once raised a big stink and forced the ballpark to start grilling its Dodger Dogs again instead of steaming them. That's a step in the right direction, but the difference in taste is nothing compared to a smokin' dog.

SERVES AS MANY AS YOU WISH

All-beef hot dogs, probably lots of them, of a good brand, such as Vienna Beef, Hebrew National, or Boar's Head

Squishy white bread hot dog buns

Mustard

Chopped onions

Pickle relish

Barbecue sauce, maybe Golden Mustard Barbecue Sauce (page 371) or Struttin' Sauce (page 369)

1. Prepare the smoker for barbecuing, bringing the temperature to 200°F to 220°F.

2. Transfer the hot dogs to the smoker and cook until the skins look ready to burst, about 1 hour. Remove them from the smoker and serve immediately with all the trimmings.

Ain't Momma's Meatloaf

As with a hamburger, smoking can raise meatloaf from the mundane to the sublime. We like this version, but if you—or your momma—have a favorite recipe, it can be modified for barbecuing by making the meat mixture extra moist and by adding plenty of Worcestershire sauce, vinegar, or other sharp flavor to cut the richness of the smoke. **SERVES 5**

MEATLOAF

1 tablespoon vegetable oil

1/2 cup minced onion

1/2 green or red bell pepper, chopped fine

3 garlic cloves, minced

1 teaspoon freshly ground black pepper

1 teaspoon kosher salt or coarse sea salt

1/2 teaspoon ground cumin

11/4 pounds ground beef

3/4 pound ground pork

1 large egg, lightly beaten

11/2 cups dry bread crumbs

1/4 cup beef stock

3 tablespoons sour cream

2 tablespoons Worcestershire sauce

1 teaspoon Tabasco or other hot pepper sauce to taste

BASIC BEER MOP (OPTIONAL)

12 ounces beer

1/2 cup water

1/2 cup cider vinegar

1/4 cup vegetable oil

1/2 medium onion, chopped or sliced in thin rings

2 garlic cloves, minced

1 tablespoon Worcestershire sauce

1 tablespoon Wild Willy's Number One-derful Rub (page 26), Cajun Ragin' Rub (page 29), or other savory seasoning blend

Bar-B-Q Ranch Sauce (page 375), Creole Classic Barbecue Sauce (page 382), or other spicy tomato-based barbecue sauce

1. Prepare the smoker for barbecuing, bringing the temperature to 200°F to 220°F.

2. In a heavy skillet, warm the oil over medium heat. Add the onion, bell pepper, garlic, pepper, salt, and cumin, and sauté until the vegetables are softened. Spoon the vegetable mixture into a large bowl.

3. Add the remaining meatloaf ingredients to the bowl and mix well with your hands. Mound the meat mixture into a smoke-proof loaf pan.

4. If you plan to baste the meat (see page 45, "To Mop or Not"), stir the mop ingredients together in a small saucepan and warm the mixture over low heat.

5. Transfer the loaf to the smoker. Cook until the meat has shrunk away from the sides of the pan, about 45 minutes. Gently ease the meatloaf out of the pan and place directly onto the grate of the smoker. Continue cooking the meatloaf for an additional 11/2 hours, dabbing it every 30 minutes with the mop in a wood-burning pit, or

as appropriate for your style of smoker. When 30 minutes of cooking time remain, apply the barbecue sauce to the top of the meatloaf.

6. After removing the loaf from the smoker, allow it to sit at room temperature for 10 minutes before slicing and serve warm, or refrigerate for later use in sandwiches.

SERVING SUGGESTION No meatloaf is ever complete at our house without Mayme's Macaroni and Cheese (page 405) on the side and, usually, Country Collard Greens (page 400) as well. Dessert's not essential, but we'd never turn down 'Nana Pudding (page 463).

VARIATION: BUBBA'S MEATLOAF Leave out ½ cup of the bread crumbs. Crush a couple of fistfuls of pork rinds or Cheetos and add them to the raw meat mixture. Up the Worcestershire sauce by 1 additional tablespoon to balance the richness of the rinds or cheese snack with a bit more tang.

BBQ *tip* If you want to create a real mess for your spouse to clean up, try starting a meatloaf in a smoker directly on the smoker's grate. It isn't pretty. You can, however, for even bolder smoke flavor, form the loaf and place it directly on an oil-sprayed grill topper rack. Then you can easily remove the loaf from the smoker on the small rack, let it cool briefly, and then take it off the rack. It's a more tidy process using the pan recommended above, and you can even skip the step of removing the meat from the pan partway through the cooking process, but that allows the meat to soak up extra flavor from the fully circulating smoke, too.

KEEPING THE TORCH LIGHTED AT THE HALL OF FLAME

Jim Goode knows barbecue about as well as anyone in the world. He's got three great BBQ restaurants in Houston along with the Goode Company's Hall of Flame (goodecompany.com for information and orders). Visit the store in person for anything you need for barbecuing at home, and then hop over to Kirby Drive to eat at the funky (but very hip) original Goode Company restaurant.

LEAN AND MEAN MEATS

THE PEOPLE OF OWENSBORO, KENTUCKY, AND BRADY, TEXAS, DON'T BELIEVE THAT EITHER PORK OR BEEF IS ALL THAT SPECIAL AS BARBECUE MEAT. NEITHER DO THE GROWING NUMBER OF GAME FARMERS IN THE COUNTRY, OR SOME FOLKS WHO FAVOR FANCY FOOD.

IN OWENSBORO, BARBECUE MEANS MUTTON. IN OTHER PLACES, PITMASTERS USUALLY PREFER THEIR SHEEP YOUNG AND TENDER, PERHAPS IN THE FORM OF A SUCCULENT LEG of lamb. Upscale restaurant chefs from Hawaii to Houston cherish the local venison. Down around Brady, where they raise a lot of goats, you don't want to kid anyone about what goes on the grate. Barbecue, like love, is a many-splendored thing.

Almost Owensboro Mutton

We cheat a bit with this recipe, since mutton is seldom available commercially in most of the country. The closest substitute we've found is a shoulder roast from a full-grown "yearling" lamb, which comes out much like Owensboro's best when barbecued in this straightforward style. The flavor is distinctive but mild—definitely worth a try. You may need to order this cut from your butcher in advance. SERVES 6

MUTTON AND LAMB RUB

1/2 cup freshly ground black pepper

2 1/2 tablespoons packed brown sugar

2 tablespoons kosher salt or coarse sea salt

1 1/2 tablespoons garlic powder

1/2 teaspoon ground allspice

7-pound to 8-pound lamb shoulder roast, preferably from a "yearling" lamb

1/4 cup Worcestershire sauce

MUTTON AND LAMB MOP (OPTIONAL)

1 1/2 cups beer or beef stock

3/4 cup white vinegar

3/4 cup water

1/4 cup Worcestershire sauce

Black Sauce (page 378) or Moonlite and Moonshine (page 380) (optional)

1. The evening before you plan to barbecue, combine the rub ingredients in a small bowl. Coat the meat with the Worcestershire sauce and then massage it with two-thirds of the rub. Transfer the meat to a large plastic bag and refrigerate it overnight.

2. Prepare the smoker for barbecuing, bringing the temperature to 200°F to 220°F.

3. Remove the meat from the refrigerator and let it sit at room temperature for about 30 minutes.

4. If you plan to baste the meat (see page 45, "To Mop or Not"), mix the remaining rub with the other mop ingredients in a saucepan and warm over low heat.

5. Transfer the meat to the smoker, fatty side up. Cook for approximately 1½ hours per pound, basting the lamb with a mop about once an hour in a wood-burning pit, or as appropriate in your style of smoker. When ready, the meat should be well-done and tender, with an internal temperature of about 170°F.

6. Remove the meat from the smoker and let it sit for 15 minutes at room temperature. Serve pulled into shreds or chopped fine, accompanied by Black Sauce or Moonlite and Moonshine sauce if you wish.

Thirty-six years young in 2014, the International Bar-B-Q Festival in Owensboro, Kentucky, raises money for local churches and charities every May. Visitors and participants annually consume around 10 tons of barbecued mutton and 1,500 gallons of burgoo in two days of joyful gluttony.

SERVING SUGGESTION Mutton and lamb shoulder taste great chopped and served between a couple of pieces of rye bread with slices of dill pickle and onion—an Owensboro favorite. Top the sandwiches with a dose of spicy Moonlite and Moonshine sauce (page 380). Offer a side dish of Kentucky Burgoo (page 393) and finish the meal with Booker's Bourbon Mint Ice Cream (page 465).

BBQ tip With all the alarms raised in recent years about food safety, it pays to be careful in barbecuing. Keep raw meat separate from other food, and wash all cutting boards and knives after using them. If you carry raw meat to the smoker on a plate, don't put anything cooked back on the same plate. Boil all marinades vigorously if using them as the basis for a mop or sauce to be used later on cooked meat.

AN EARLY VIRGINIA BARBECUE

Charles Lanman visited and reported on a pre–Civil War barbecue in Virginia in a book called *Haw-Ho-Noo; or, Records of a Tourist.* "Finally, the pigs and lambs have all been roasted, and the feast is ready; whereupon there followeth as busy and satisfactory a scene as can well be imagined. . . . In due course, after the more substantial feature of the barbecue has been enjoyed, the musicians are summoned to their allotted places, and the entire party of ladies and gentlemen proceed to trip the light fantastic toe. The exercise continues for whole hours, and white-haired men and little girls are seen wending their way through the intricate mazes of the country dance and the Virginia reel."

Seva's Sassy Lamb Ribs

A masterful meat-cutter and all-around meat authority, Seva Dubuar, introduced us to these ribs. An expert on lamb, she markets the meat through her New Mexico–based company. The "Denver cut" Seva suggests for barbecuing comes from the middle ribs of a lamb breast. **SERVES 4**

SIMPLE CHINESE FIVE-SPICE MEDLEY
1/3 cup five-spice powder
1/3 cup packed brown sugar

4 Denver-cut slabs of lamb ribs, about 1 pound each
West Coast Wonder sauce (page 379) (optional)

1. At least 2 hours and preferably the night before you plan to barbecue, mix the rub ingredients in a small bowl. Rub the ribs liberally with about one-third of the spice mixture. Place the ribs in a plastic bag and refrigerate.

2. Prepare the smoker for barbecuing, bringing the temperature to 200°F to 220°F.

3. Remove the ribs from the refrigerator. Rub them thoroughly again with the spice mixture and let them sit at room temperature for 20 to 30 minutes.

4. Transfer the meat to the smoker. Cook for 3½ to 4 hours, turning and sprinkling the ribs with the remaining dry rub about halfway through the cooking time. When done, the ribs should have a thin coating of crispy spices on the surface and should pull apart easily.

5. Serve warm with West Coast Wonder sauce if you wish.

SERVING SUGGESTION Add a fruit salad topped with poppy seed dressing and Sweet Potatoes with Orange-Pecan Butter (page 281).

BBQ *tip* **The most important tip we can give you about meat is to find a high-quality butcher or meat-cutter. Look for a market that cuts and grinds to order, perhaps does some aging, and has people who take an interest in you and what you're cooking. We've always found that the people at a serious meat market are fascinated by barbecuing and eager to help. That's especially true if you sometimes take them a sample of your 'Q' later.**

A KENTUCKY CRAFTSMAN

In 1918, Charles "Pappy" Foreman gave up blacksmithing to start barbecuing mutton for the folks of Owensboro, Kentucky. Five generations later the Foreman family continues to serve some of the finest mutton in the country at Old Hickory Bar-B-Q, still located near the site of Pappy's original pit.

Martini Leg of Lamb

This gin-scented dish is an elegant lamb preparation, inspired by a creation of Jinx and Jefferson Morgan, great cooks, Caribbean hoteliers, and bons vivants.

SERVES 6 TO 8

MARTINI PASTE
1/2 medium onion, chopped
10 garlic cloves
Juice and zest of 1 lemon
3 tablespoons gin
2 teaspoons kosher salt or coarse sea salt
1/4 cup extra-virgin olive oil

5-pound to 6-pound leg of lamb

MARTINI MOP (OPTIONAL)
1 cup gin
1 cup beef stock
2/3 cup water
Juice of 1 lemon
2 tablespoons extra-virgin olive oil

1. The night before you plan to barbecue, prepare the paste. In a food processor, combine the onion, garlic, lemon juice and zest, gin, and salt and process to combine. Continue processing, pouring in the oil until a thin paste forms.

2. Generously spread the paste on the lamb. Place the lamb in a plastic bag and refrigerate it overnight.

3. Prepare the smoker for barbecuing, bringing the temperature to 200°F to 220°F.

4. Remove the meat from the refrigerator and let it sit at room temperature for about 30 minutes.

5. If you plan to baste the meat (see page 45, "To Mop or Not"), mix the mop ingredients in a saucepan and warm the mixture over low heat.

6. Transfer the lamb to the smoker. Cook for 35 to 40 minutes per pound, until the internal temperature of the meat is 145°F (rare to medium-rare). Baste the meat with the mop every 45 to 50 minutes in a wood-burning pit, or as appropriate for your style of smoker.

7. Remove the lamb from the smoker and let it sit for 10 minutes. Slice the lamb and serve it warm or chilled.

BBQ tip Leg of lamb is best when lightly smoked. We like to cook it in a water smoker, but charcoal grills and ovens work well, too. If you're using a wood-burning pit, wrap the lamb in foil after the first hour. If your smoker's heat source is something other than wood, you can stop adding wood to the fire at that point.

BBQ tip We often use coarse salt in barbecuing, as we do in both of our leg of lamb preparations. We use either additive-free kosher salt or sea salt. Both have mild flavors, so you can spread them on generously without overpowering a dish.

Luscious Leg of Lamb

A spinach and goat cheese stuffing might taste good even in a tennis ball, but the combo is always a sure bet inside a tender leg of lamb. SERVES 6 TO 8

LUSCIOUS PASTE

10 garlic cloves

2 teaspoons kosher salt or coarse sea salt

1 1/2 tablespoons extra-virgin olive oil

5-pound to 5 1/2-pound boned leg of lamb

FILLING

1 tablespoon extra-virgin olive oil

1/2 medium onion, chopped

2 garlic cloves, minced

1/3 cup pine nuts or chopped walnuts

1 1/2 pounds spinach, cooked, drained, and chopped

8 ounces mild goat cheese

1/3 cup chopped fresh parsley

1/4 cup dried currants or chopped raisins

1 teaspoon anchovy paste or 1/2 teaspoon kosher salt or coarse sea salt

LUSCIOUS MOP (OPTIONAL)

2 1/2 cups beef stock

1/2 cup red wine vinegar

2 tablespoons extra-virgin olive oil

1 teaspoon anchovy paste or 1/2 teaspoon kosher salt or coarse sea salt

1. The night before you plan to barbecue, prepare the paste. With a mortar and pestle, or in a mini food processor, crush or mince the garlic with the salt. Add the olive oil in a stream until a thick paste forms. Rub the paste very lightly over the lamb. Place the lamb in a plastic bag and refrigerate it overnight.

2. Prepare the smoker for barbecuing, bringing the temperature to 200°F to 220°F.

3. Remove the meat from the refrigerator and let it sit at room temperature for about 30 minutes.

4. To make the filling, warm the oil over medium heat in a small skillet. Add the onion and garlic and sauté until softened. Add the pine nuts and continue to cook for another minute or two. Spoon the mixture into a bowl. Add the spinach, cheese, parsley, currants, and anchovy paste and blend well. Spread the filling evenly over the lamb. Roll up the meat snugly from one of the long sides, totally enclosing the filling. Tie as needed with kitchen twine to secure.

5. If you plan to baste the meat (see page 45, "To Mop or Not"), mix the mop ingredients in a saucepan and warm the mixture over low heat.

6. Warm a heavy skillet over high heat and sear the lamb quickly on all sides. Transfer the lamb to the smoker. Cook for 35 to 40 minutes per pound, until the internal temperature of the meat is 145°F (rare to medium-rare). Baste the meat with the mop after 30 minutes and 1 hour in a wood-burning pit, or as appropriate for your style of smoker.

7. Remove the lamb from the smoker and let it sit for 10 minutes. Slice the lamb and serve it warm.

SERVING SUGGESTION Start off with Warm Mushroom Salad (page 309) and serve the lamb with steamed asparagus dressed with olive oil, garlic, and lemon.

Minted Chops

These lovely little chops will score you kudos from every one of your lucky diners.

SERVES 4

MUTTON AND LAMB RUB

1/4 cup freshly ground black pepper

2 1/2 tablespoons packed brown sugar

2 tablespoons kosher salt or coarse sea salt

1 1/2 tablespoons garlic powder

1 1/2 teaspoons ground allspice

Eight 5-ounce lamb loin chops, cut 1 inch thick

Garlic-flavored oil (see BBQ tip on page 211)

MINTED MOP AND/OR SAUCE

1 cup brewed mint tea made with 2 mint tea bags

1/4 cup mint jelly

4 teaspoons garlic-flavored oil

Mint sprigs, for garnish

1. Prepare the smoker for barbecuing, bringing the temperature to 200°F to 220°F.

2. An hour before you plan to barbecue, combine the rub ingredients in a small bowl. Coat the chops with a thin layer of oil and then massage them with the rub. Let them sit at room temperature for 30 minutes while you prepare the mop and/or sauce.

3. If you are going to baste the meat (see page 45, "To Mop or Not"), mix the mop ingredients in a saucepan over low heat, keeping the mop warm. If you intend to use the mixture only as a sauce, combine the same ingredients in a saucepan and bring the mixture to a simmer over medium-high heat. Reduce the mixture by half and then keep it warm over low heat.

4. Transfer the chops to the smoker. Cook them to your desired doneness; after 45 to 55 minutes the chops will be rare, with an internal temperature around 140°F. Baste the chops twice in a wood-burning pit, or as appropriate for your style of smoker.

5. If you have used the mop, bring the remaining liquid to a vigorous boil and reduce it by half. Serve the chops immediately, drizzled lightly with the reduced sauce and garnished with the mint.

SERVING SUGGESTION Serve the lamb with cinnamon-scented rice to soak up the mint sauce and meat juices. Vanilla ice cream topped with Brazen Rum-Raisin Sauce (page 469) makes a cooling finish.

Lamb Chops à la Greek Town

No lamb repertoire is complete without a Greek rendition. This one came to us by way of Chicago's Greek Town, a fun place to eat, if not exactly a barbecue bastion.

SERVES 4

GREEK TOWN MARINADE AND OPTIONAL MOP
1 cup olive oil (an inexpensive kind is fine)

1 cup freshly squeezed lemon juice

5 garlic cloves, minced

2 bay leaves, crumbled

1¹/₂ tablespoons minced fresh oregano or 2 teaspoons dried oregano

1 teaspoon kosher salt or coarse sea salt

Eight 5-ounce lamb loin chops, cut 1 inch thick

1 tablespoon Char Crust Original (optional; see BBQ tip)

Freshly ground black pepper

Lemon wedges and oregano sprigs (optional), for garnish

1. About 2 hours before you plan to barbecue, combine the marinade ingredients in a large glass measuring cup. Place the chops in a shallow dish big enough to hold them in a single layer, or in a large plastic bag. Pour the marinade over the chops and refrigerate them.

2. Prepare your smoker for barbecuing, bringing the temperature to 200°F to 220°F.

3. Remove the chops from the refrigerator and drain them, reserving the marinade if you plan to baste the meat. Dust the chops with Char Crust, if you wish, and a generous grinding of pepper. Let the chops sit at room temperature for 30 minutes.

4. If you are using the mop (see page 45, "To Mop or Not"), pour the marinade into a saucepan. Bring the mixture to a vigorous boil over high heat and boil for several minutes. Keep the mop warm over low heat.

5. Heat a heavy skillet over high heat. Sear the chops quickly on both sides. Transfer them to the smoker and cook to your desired doneness; after 45 to 55 minutes, the chops will be rare, with an internal temperature around 140°F. Baste the chops with the mop twice in a wood-burning pit, or as appropriate for your style of smoker. Serve immediately, garnished with lemon and oregano if you wish.

SERVING SUGGESTION Offer Smoked Olives (page 346) and cubes of feta cheese for openers. Serve Arty Rice Salad (page 429) on the side and Key Lime Pie (page 447) for dessert.

BBQ tip Char Crust, a smoky-flavored dry rub, hails from the Windy City, as does this recipe. Once available only to restaurants, it now appears in some supermarkets and can be mail-ordered from the Char Crust Company (charcrust.com). Developed for grilled steaks, the original rub and a host of new varieties enhance many meats.

Lamb Burgers with Berry Sauce

Americans used to enjoy grilled or skillet-cooked lamb burgers much more frequently in the past than today. We've taken this wonderful idea and modified it for smoke cooking, which makes the burgers even more succulent. The meat has always been a perfect foil for fruity-tangy sauces, such as this bright raspberry-mint version.

SERVES 6

LAMB BURGER RUB

2 teaspoons garlic powder

2 teaspoons onion powder

1 teaspoon freshly ground black pepper

1 teaspoon kosher salt or coarse sea salt

BERRY SAUCE

1¼ cups fresh mint leaves, chopped fine

7 tablespoons raspberry vinegar

3 tablespoons sugar

1 tablespoon freshly squeezed lemon juice

Kosher salt or coarse sea salt and freshly ground black pepper to taste

2 pounds ground lamb

3 tablespoons raspberry vinegar

3 scallions, sliced thin

2 garlic cloves, minced

Kosher salt or coarse sea salt and freshly ground black pepper to taste

8 ounces mild goat cheese

BURGER MOP (OPTIONAL)

½ cup raspberry vinegar

2 tablespoons extra-virgin olive oil

1. Prepare the smoker for barbecuing, bringing the temperature to 200°F to 220°F.

2. Combine the rub ingredients in a small bowl. In another bowl, combine the sauce ingredients, stirring until the sugar dissolves.

3. Mix the lamb, vinegar, scallions, garlic, salt, and pepper in a large bowl. Form the mixture into 12 thin patties. Slice the cheese into 6 equal portions and cover 6 of the patties with it. Top the cheese with another patty and seal the edges carefully. Sprinkle the burgers lightly with the rub and let them sit at room temperature for 20 to 30 minutes.

4. If you plan to baste the burgers (see page 45, "To Mop or Not"), combine the mop ingredients in a small saucepan and warm over low heat.

5. Transfer the burgers to the smoker. Cook until lightly browned and medium-rare, about 40 minutes, or to your desired doneness. Dab the burgers with the mop once or twice in a wood-burning pit, or as appropriate in your style of smoker. Serve the burgers hot, with the berry sauce spooned over them or on the side.

VARIATION: BLUE CHEESE LAMB BURGERS Replace the goat cheese with a tangy blue cheese, such as Maytag blue. Change the vinegar throughout the recipe from raspberry to white. In the sauce, replace about half of the mint with fresh flat-leaf parsley, and reduce the sugar to 1 tablespoon. Just as yummy.

INCLUDING OUR PRESIDENT?

Ronald Reagan invited "Honey" Monk to barbecue for world leaders at the 1983 Economic Summit. Owner of the Lexington Barbecue #1, Monk said the heads of state weren't as picky or as smart about barbecue as the folks back home in North Carolina.

Ground Lamb Pita Pockets

This is a different kind of lamb burger, kissed lovingly by the Mediterranean sun. The recipe calls for zatar, a Middle Eastern seasoning blend based on tangy dried sumac, but it isn't essential for good results if you have trouble finding it. SERVES 6

MIDDLE EASTERN DRY RUB

2 tablespoons paprika

1½ tablespoons zatar (optional)

1½ teaspoons ground cumin

1½ teaspoons kosher salt or coarse sea salt

1½ teaspoons freshly ground black pepper

1 teaspoon ground cinnamon

⅛ teaspoon cayenne

CUCUMBER-CILANTRO SAUCE

2 medium cucumbers, peeled, halved lengthwise, seeded, and sliced into thin half-moons

¾ cup plain yogurt

3 tablespoons minced fresh cilantro

Pinch or 2 of zatar (optional)

Dash of cayenne (optional)

Kosher salt or coarse sea salt to taste

2¼ pounds ground lamb

2 garlic cloves, minced

Kosher salt or coarse sea salt and freshly ground black pepper to taste

6 pita breads, sliced open on one side

Feta cheese crumbles (optional)

1. Prepare the smoker for barbecuing, bringing the temperature to 200°F to 220°F.

2. Combine the rub ingredients in a small bowl. In another bowl, combine the sauce ingredients.

3. Mix the lamb, garlic, salt, and pepper in a large bowl. Form the mixture into 6 broad patties. Sprinkle the burgers lightly with the rub and let them sit at room temperature for 20 to 30 minutes.

4. Transfer the burgers to the smoker. Cook until lightly browned and medium-rare, about 40 minutes, or to your desired doneness. Place the burgers inside the pita breads, drizzle with sauce, and serve hot.

Up and At 'Em Lamb Sausage

While good any time of day, these sausages make a hearty breakfast meal, perfect on mornings when you're firing up the pit for a long spell of smoking. After tossing on a beef brisket or pork shoulder, barbecue a few of these to fortify you for the day.

MAKES SIX 4-OUNCE PATTIES

Juice and zest of 1 orange

1½ pounds mildly seasoned bulk lamb sausage

SWEET SENSATION RUB

Zest of 1 orange, dried and crumbled (about 1½ teaspoons) (see BBQ tip on page 28)

1½ teaspoons ground cinnamon

1½ teaspoons paprika

1 teaspoon ground chipotle chile, preferably, or ½ teaspoon cayenne

1 teaspoon sugar

½ teaspoon ground coriander

½ teaspoon kosher salt or coarse sea salt

UP AND AT 'EM MOP (OPTIONAL)

6 tablespoons freshly squeezed orange juice

1 tablespoon sherry or cider vinegar

1 tablespoon vegetable oil

1. Prepare the smoker for barbecuing, bringing the temperature to 200°F to 220°F.

2. Mix the orange juice and zest into the sausage. Form the sausage into 6 thick patties. Combine the dry rub ingredients in a small bowl and sprinkle the patties lightly with the dry rub. Let the patties sit at room temperature for about 15 minutes.

3. If you plan to baste the sausages (see page 45, "To Mop or Not"), mix the mop ingredients in a small pan. Warm the mop liquid over low heat.

4. Transfer the patties to the smoker. Cook until the sausages are richly browned and cooked through, 50 to 60 minutes. Mop them every 20 minutes in a wood-burning pit, or as appropriate in your style of smoker. Serve hot.

SERVING SUGGESTION When you need an elegant breakfast, pair the sausage with a variation on eggs Sardou, a fancy concoction first popularized by Antoine's in New Orleans. Top poached eggs with artichoke hearts, ham, and as many anchovies as you can handle, and then spoon hollandaise sauce over the whole cholesterol-laden extravaganza. Serve with some fruit-filled muffins.

BBQ tip Kansas City's "Baron of Barbecue," Paul Kirk, teaches classes on the barbecue craft around the country. Check out his schedule at baron-of-bbq.com and don't miss him if he's in your area. One of the keys to his success, Kirk says, is taking notes on everything he does. As the Baron emphasizes, it's the only sure way you can learn from experience.

Veal Top Chops

Little can top veal chops in classiness. Serve this sage-infused version when you want to impress. SERVES 4

TOP CHOP SAGE PASTE

1 cup fresh sage leaves

4 garlic cloves

1/4 teaspoon kosher salt or coarse sea salt

2 tablespoons dry Marsala wine

Juice of 1 lemon

3 tablespoons extra-virgin olive oil

Four 8-ounce to 10-ounce thick-cut veal loin chops

4 slices bacon, cut into thirds

TOP CHOP MOP (OPTIONAL)

3/4 cup dry Marsala wine

3/4 cup water

Juice of 1 lemon

1 1/2 tablespoons extra-virgin olive oil

Lemon wedges and sage sprigs, for garnish

1. At least 2 hours and preferably 4 hours before you plan to barbecue, make the sage paste. Combine the sage, garlic, and salt in a food processor and process until the sage is minced. Add the Marsala and lemon juice and process briefly. Continue to process, adding the oil in a thin stream until a thick paste forms. Apply the paste thickly to the chops, wrap them in plastic, and refrigerate.

2. Prepare the smoker for barbecuing, bringing the temperature to 200°F to 220°F.

3. Remove the chops from the refrigerator and let them sit at room temperature for 20 minutes. Drape the top of each chop with 1 slice (3 pieces) of bacon.

4. If you plan to baste the meat (see page 45, "To Mop or Not"), stir together the mop ingredients in a small saucepan and warm the mixture over low heat.

5. Transfer the chops to the smoker. Cook for 1 1/4 to 1 1/2 hours, mopping every 20 to 30 minutes in a wood-burning pit, or as appropriate for your style of smoker. The chops are ready when the internal temperature reaches 150°F, or medium-rare. Be careful not to overcook them.

6. Remove the chops from the smoker, discard the bacon, and let the chops sit at room temperature for 5 minutes. Serve hot, garnished with lemon and sage.

BARBECUING JIM CROW

Racial integration of the South began at the barbecue pit. African Americans owned and operated many of the original Bar-B-Q joints, but the food attracted everyone in town, even when churches, schools, and other restaurants were strictly segregated.

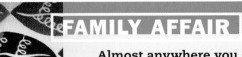
Almost anywhere you go in central Texas, it seems, there's a cafeteria-style Mikeska barbecue restaurant. Rudy has the one in Taylor, Mike took on Smithville, Jerry is over in Columbus, Maurice camps out in El Campo, and Louis and Clem share the turf in Temple. If the Czech-immigrant family gets any larger, they may make a move on Dallas.

Cherry Cumberland Veal Chops

An exceptionally lean meat, veal can dry out quickly when smoked unless you take care to keep it moist. In the previous veal chop recipe, the paste, mop, and bacon slices all contribute to that goal as well as adding flavor. In this version, the paste and fruity stuffing do double duty, too, accomplishing the same aims. These first appeared in another of our books, *Sublime Smoke* (1996, The Harvard Common Press). SERVES 4

VEAL GARLIC PASTE

1 whole head of garlic

1 tablespoon extra-virgin olive oil

1¼ teaspoons kosher salt or coarse sea salt

Four 8-ounce to 10-ounce thick-cut veal loin chops, cut with a pocket for stuffing

2 tablespoons dried cherries or cranberries

2 tablespoons minced onion

2 tablespoons port

1 ounce cream cheese, softened

1 tablespoon minced fresh parsley

CUMBERLAND SAUCE

Juice and zest from 1 medium orange

Juice and zest from ½ medium lemon

6 tablespoons port

6 tablespoons currant jelly or jam

2 tablespoons minced shallots

1 teaspoon Dijon mustard

Minced fresh parsley, for garnish

1. At least 2 hours and preferably 4 hours before you plan to barbecue, make the garlic paste. Break the garlic head apart into individual cloves, but don't peel them. Place them in a cast-iron or other heavy skillet and dry-roast over medium heat until soft and brown, 6 to 8 minutes, shaking or stirring as needed to color evenly. Peel the garlic (a quick task once roasted) and transfer to a small bowl. Mash the garlic together with the oil and salt. Set aside

1 tablespoon of the garlic paste. Apply the rest of the paste thickly to the chops, wrap them in plastic, and refrigerate.

2. In another bowl, make the filling, combining the reserved 1 tablespoon paste with the cherries, onion, port, cream cheese, and parsley.

3. Prepare the smoker for barbecuing, bringing the temperature to 200°F to 220°F.

4. Remove the chops from the refrigerator, stuff them with the filling, and let them sit, covered, at room temperature for 20 minutes.

5. Combine the sauce ingredients in a small saucepan and simmer over medium-low heat for 15 minutes. Remove the sauce from the heat, strain it, and reserve it at room temperature. (The sauce can be made several days in advance, if you wish, and refrigerated. Return it to room temperature before proceeding.)

6. Transfer the chops to the smoker. Cook until the internal temperature reaches 150°F (medium-rare), 1¼ to 1½ hours. Be careful not to overcook them.

7. Remove the chops from the smoker and let them sit at room temperature for 5 minutes. Serve hot, with the Cumberland sauce, topped with parsley.

I'LL TAKE THAT FORD IF YOU'LL THROW IN A SANDWICH ON THE SIDE

The way Roger Guin figured it, politicians threw a barbecue to attract crowds of people for a stump speech. Well, business was a little slow in his used car lot in Winfield, Alabama, so he built a pit on the side of the showroom and began serving barbecue. Guin brought in a few car buyers, but they were far outnumbered by the eaters. Nowadays the profit at Car-Lot BBQ comes from pork rather than pickups.

Stuffed Veal Roast

This veal sirloin roast stuffed full of sweet and savory treats makes a splendid special-occasion dish. The idea, though not the recipe, comes from the Kansas City Barbeque Society's *The Passion of Barbeque* (1992, Hyperion), a good source for inspiration. You may have to order the roast from your butcher in advance.

SERVES 4 TO 6

CHERYL'S CIDER SOAK (AND OPTIONAL MOP)

1 1/2 cups apple cider or juice

3/4 cup cider vinegar

1/2 medium onion, minced

3 tablespoons vegetable oil

1 1/2 tablespoons Worcestershire sauce

1 teaspoon ground cinnamon

1 teaspoon dried thyme

1 3/4-pound to 2-pound sirloin tip veal roast, about 2 inches thick, cut with a pocket for stuffing

FILLING

2 slices bacon, chopped

1/2 tart apple, such as Granny Smith, cored and chopped

2 tablespoons minced onion

1 garlic clove, minced

1/4 pound ground veal

1/4 cup dry bread crumbs

3 dried pitted dates, chopped

3 scallions, sliced

2 tablespoons minced fresh parsley

1/2 teaspoon dried rosemary, crushed

Pinch of ground cinnamon

Pinch of dried thyme

1. The night before you plan to barbecue, combine the soak ingredients in a large glass measuring cup. Place the roast in a plastic bag and pour the marinade over it, making sure some goes into the roast's pocket. Refrigerate the meat overnight.

2. Prepare the smoker for barbecuing, bringing the temperature to 200°F to 220°F.

3. Remove the roast from the refrigerator and drain the marinade, reserving it if you plan to baste the meat (see page 45, "To Mop or Not"). Let the roast sit for 30 minutes at room temperature while you prepare the filling.

4. In a skillet, fry the bacon over medium heat until browned and crispy. Remove the bacon with a slotted spoon, drain it, and place it in a medium-size bowl. Add the apple, onion, and garlic to the skillet and sauté until soft. Spoon the mixture into the bowl. Stir in the remaining filling ingredients and mix until well combined. Stuff the roast loosely with the filling.

5. If you are using the mop, heat the marinade in a small saucepan. Bring the mop mixture to a vigorous boil over high heat and boil for several minutes. Keep the mop warm over low heat.

6. Warm a heavy skillet over high heat. Sear the meat quickly on both sides. Transfer the roast to the smoker. Cook for 1¾ to 2 hours, mopping every 20 to 30 minutes in a wood-burning pit, or as appropriate for your style of smoker. The roast is best when the internal temperature reaches 145°F to 150°F (medium-rare).

7. Remove the roast from the smoker and let it sit at room temperature for 10 minutes. Slice the roast and serve.

SERVING SUGGESTION For an elegant dinner, nibble Curry Pecans (page 344) while sipping Mango-Lime Spritzers (page 483). Sit down to cups of creamy corn chowder and then pair the roast with spinach sautéed in olive oil. Small slices of South Georgia Pound Cake (page 458) topped with fresh strawberries make a tasty conclusion.

this roast stuffed full of sweet and savory treats makes a splendid special-occasion dish

A GRAND LOOK AT A GRAND TRADITION

Writer Lolis Eric Elie and photographer Frank Stewart decided to collaborate on *Smokestack Lightning* (1996, Farrar, Straus and Giroux) one day when they shared some barbecued ribs in North Carolina. They set out on a quest to look at American life and culture through the traditions of barbecue. Elie and Stewart succeeded admirably, serving up a heaping plateful of stories, observations, reflections, and evocative photos.

Southwestern Cabrito

A festive food throughout the Southwest, particularly in Spanish-speaking areas, cabrito is milk-fed kid slaughtered between the spring and late summer at an age of 30 to 40 days old and a weight of 10 to 15 pounds. If you lack a Latino market, you'll probably have to go directly to a farmer for the meat, but it's worth the trouble.

SERVES 8 TO 10

SAGE PASTE

3 cups fresh sage leaves

1 whole head of garlic, peeled

2 teaspoons kosher salt or coarse sea salt

2 cups olive oil (an inexpensive kind is fine)

1 cabrito, preferably 10 to 12 pounds, quartered

CABRITO MOP (OPTIONAL)

2 cups chicken or beef stock or beer

1 cup cider vinegar

1 cup olive oil (an inexpensive kind is fine)

1/4 cup chopped fresh sage

1/4 cup Worcestershire sauce

4 to 6 garlic cloves, minced

Sauce Olé (page 379) or Bar-B-Q Ranch Sauce (page 375) (optional)

1. The night before you plan to barbecue, prepare the paste in a food processor. First process the sage, garlic, and salt until the sage and the garlic are chopped fine. Add the olive oil in a slow stream, until a thick paste forms. Rub the paste over the cabrito, covering the meat evenly. Place the cabrito in a large plastic bag and refrigerate it overnight.

2. Prepare the smoker for barbecuing, bringing the temperature to 200°F to 220°F.

3. Remove the cabrito from the refrigerator and let it sit covered, at room temperature for 30 minutes.

4. If you plan to baste the meat (see page 45, "To Mop or Not"), mix the mop ingredients in a saucepan and warm the liquid over low heat.

5. Transfer the cabrito to the smoker. Cook the meat for about 1 hour per pound of weight for each quarter. The skinny forequarters will be done earlier than the meaty hindquarters, which usually take 4 to 5 hours, depending on size. In a wood-burning pit, turn the meat and drizzle the mop over it every 30 minutes. In other styles of smokers, baste as appropriate and turn the meat at the same time.

6. When the cabrito is done, remove it from the smoker and let it sit for 10 minutes at room temperature. Slice or shred the meat and serve with Sauce Olé or Bar-B-Q Ranch Sauce if you wish.

SERVING SUGGESTION On the side, offer Cowpoke Pintos (page 397), Smoky Corn on the Cob (page 288), and Mango and Avocado Salad (page 430). For dessert, Santa Fe Capirotada (page 464) caps the meal nicely.

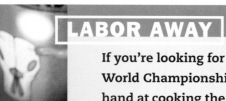
If you're looking for a special way to celebrate Labor Day weekend, head down to the World Championship BBQ Goat Cook-Off in Brady, Texas. You might want to try your hand at cooking the local goat in the main competition, or you can apply to be a judge for the Mystery Meat contest. In either case, be sure to chow down on the barbecue.

Curried Goat

After goats start eating grass, the flavor of the meat changes and the bony critters get tougher, requiring more complex and spicy preparations than you need with cabrito. This approach, popular in the Caribbean, works particularly well. Your meat market may not carry goat, but the butcher can probably direct you to a source.

SERVES 14 TO 16

CURRY PASTE

4 medium onions, chunked

1 whole head of garlic, peeled

1 to 2 fresh habanero or Scotch bonnet chiles or 4 to 5 fresh jalapeños, minced

3/4 cup curry powder

1 tablespoon kosher salt or coarse sea salt

1 cup vegetable oil

1 goat, preferably about 25 pounds, quartered

CURRY MOP (OPTIONAL)

2 cups chicken or beef stock or beer

2 cups cider vinegar

1 cup water

1 1/2 cups vegetable oil

2 tablespoons curry powder

Jamaican Barbecue Sauce (page 383) or South Florida Citrus Sauce (page 386) (optional)

1. The night before you plan to barbecue, prepare the paste in a food processor. First process the onions, garlic, habanero, curry, and salt until finely chopped. Then add the oil, processing until the mixture forms a thick paste. This can be done in two batches if needed.

2. Wearing rubber gloves, rub the paste over the goat, covering the meat evenly. Place the goat in a plastic bag and refrigerate it overnight.

3. Remove the goat from the refrigerator and let it sit, covered, at room temperature for 45 minutes.

4. Prepare the smoker for barbecuing, bringing the temperature to 200°F to 220°F.

5. If you plan to baste the meat (see page 45, "To Mop or Not"), mix the mop ingredients in a saucepan and warm the liquid over low heat.

6. Transfer the goat to the smoker. Cook for about 1¼ hours per pound of weight for each quarter. The forequarters will be done earlier than the hindquarters, which may take 10 hours or longer, depending on size. In a wood-burning pit, turn the meat and drizzle the mop over it every 30 minutes. In other styles of smokers, baste as appropriate and turn the meat at the same time.

7. When the meat is done, remove it from the smoker and allow it to sit for 15 minutes before serving. Slice or shred the meat and serve with Jamaican Barbecue Sauce or South Florida Citrus Sauce if you wish.

SERVING SUGGESTION We like to serve this with Sweet Sally's Sweet Potato Salad (page 426), Barbecued Rice (page 298), and some cooling cucumbers mixed with sour cream or yogurt. Dessert can be a platter of fresh fruits, such as mango, pineapple, and papaya slices, flavored with a touch of freshly squeezed lime juice.

BBQ tip Always wear rubber gloves when working with chiles as hot as the habanero and its Caribbean cousin, the Scotch bonnet. They make a jalapeño seem as mild as a jellybean. Even with less fiery chiles, either wear gloves or wash your hands thoroughly after handling them and before touching your eyes or other sensitive spots.

BEDDING DOWN

Despite its relative rarity today, goat was a common barbecue meat in many areas of the South just a generation or two ago. It was usually cooked over an underground pit, often on top of old bedsprings.

Journalists Alexander Sweet and John Knox described a Texas barbecue around 1880 in their book *On a Mexican Mustang through Texas*. "We arrived on the barbecue-grounds at about ten o'clock. More than two thousand people had already arrived, some from a distance of forty to fifty miles,—old gray-bearded pioneers, with their wives, in ox-wagons; young men, profuse in the matter of yellow-topped boots and jingling spurs, on horseback; fair maidens in calico, curls, and pearl-powder, some on horseback, others in wagons and buggies. . . . A deep trench, three hundred feet long, had been dug. This trench was filled from end to end with glowing coals; and suspended over them on horizontal poles were the carcasses of forty animals,—sheep, hogs, oxen, and deer,—roasting over the slow fire."

Down-on-the-Ranch Venison Pot Roast

Hearty and homey, this venison chuck roast makes a great centerpiece for a casual company dinner. Be sure to cook the roast long enough. Its fall-apart succulence will make you swoon. SERVES 6

DOWN-ON-THE-RANCH PASTE

1 medium onion, chunked

1 tablespoon yellow mustard

1 tablespoon Worcestershire sauce

1 tablespoon packed brown sugar

4 garlic cloves, minced

1 teaspoon kosher salt or coarse sea salt

1 teaspoon freshly ground black pepper

1/4 cup vegetable oil

3-pound venison chuck roast

DOWN-ON-THE-RANCH MOP (OPTIONAL)

1 cup beef stock or beer

1/2 cup water

1/4 cup cider vinegar, preferably unrefined

1/4 cup vegetable oil

14.5-ounce can whole tomatoes, undrained

1 tablespoon yellow mustard

1 tablespoon Worcestershire sauce

1. The night before you plan to barbecue, combine the paste ingredients in a food processor or blender until the onion is finely chopped and a thick puree forms. Slather the paste over the venison. Transfer the venison to a large plastic bag and refrigerate it overnight.

2. Before you begin to barbecue, take the roast from the refrigerator and let it sit, covered, at room temperature for 45 minutes.

3. Prepare the smoker for barbecuing, bringing the temperature to 200°F to 220°F.

4. If you plan to baste the meat (see page 45, "To Mop or Not"), stir together the mop ingredients in a small saucepan and warm over low heat.

5. Transfer the roast to the smoker and cook for 3 hours, mopping every 30 minutes in a wood-burning pit, or as appropriate for your style of smoker. Place the roast on a large sheet of heavy-duty aluminum foil and pour the tomatoes and their juice over the meat. Spoon the mustard and Worcestershire sauce over the tomatoes. Seal the foil tightly and continue cooking the roast until the meat is falling-apart tender, about 2 more hours.

6. Remove the roast from the smoker and let it sit at room temperature for 10 minutes before serving.

BBQ tip Wrapping the venison roast in foil partway through the cooking helps accomplish two things. It lets you seal in moisture and extra flavor, but it also helps shield the delicate meat from becoming too heavily infused with smoke in its lengthy cooking time. If the heat source for your smoker is something other than wood, you can stop adding wood when you wrap the venison in foil.

BATTER UP

The American Royal invitational cook-off each October deserves its reputation as the "World Series of Barbecue." Unlike the open competition held during the same event, all the contestants are winners of major cook-offs and participate strictly by invitation. To take the top prize, you've got to show premium skill barbecuing a range of meats.

Wine-Sopped Venison Scallops

These tender slices of venison get sloshed to perfection in a red wine marinade. Be careful not to overcook them. SERVES 6

RED WINE MARINADE

2 cups dry red wine

1/2 cup red wine vinegar

1/4 cup vegetable oil

1 1/2 tablespoons minced fresh sage leaves or 2 teaspoons dried sage

2 garlic cloves, minced

1 1/2 pounds venison scallops (from the loin or backstrap), cut against the grain in slices 1/3 inch thick

SOPPED SAUCE

1 cup beef stock

1/4 cup currant jelly

1/4 cup crème de cassis

1 medium onion, chopped

1 teaspoon minced fresh sage leaves or 1/2 teaspoon dried sage

1/4 teaspoon kosher salt or coarse sea salt, or more to taste

1 tablespoon unsalted butter

Kosher salt or coarse sea salt and freshly ground black pepper to taste

1 to 2 tablespoons vegetable oil

Sage sprigs (optional), for garnish

1. At least 2 hours and up to 3 hours before you plan to barbecue, combine the marinade ingredients in a food processor. Place the venison in a nonreactive dish or plastic bag and pour all but 1 cup of the marinade over it. Cover the venison and refrigerate it.

2. Prepare the smoker for barbecuing, bringing the temperature to 200°F to 220°F.

3. Combine the reserved 1 cup marinade, stock, jelly, crème de cassis, onion, sage, and salt in a heavy saucepan. Simmer over low heat until reduced by half, about 30 minutes. Whisk in the butter. Keep the sauce warm over low heat.

4. Drain the venison and sprinkle it with salt and pepper. In a heavy skillet, warm the oil over high heat until it almost smokes. Add the venison, a few scallops at a time, and sear it, a matter of just seconds. Repeat with the remaining meat.

5. Transfer the venison immediately to the smoker. Cook until the meat absorbs the smoke lightly but is still rare to medium-rare, 20 to 25 minutes.

6. Serve immediately with the sauce ladled over the venison. If desired, garnish with sage sprigs.

BBQ tip The lack of fat in venison calls for some adjustments in the way you normally cook meat. If your venison comes frozen, thaw it in a liquid compatible with the recipe, such as red wine or buttermilk. Don't expose cooked or uncooked venison to the air for long. Wrap the meat tightly in plastic while it marinates, and cover it with foil if the venison has to sit at all before serving. Eat venison as soon as possible after cooking. If you are serving prime cuts, such as backstrap scallops, finish everything because the meat doesn't reheat well.

Gamy Sausage

When you make sausage from venison, you need to blend it with a fattier meat, such as the wild boar or pork that we use here. SERVES 6 OR MORE

1 1/2 pounds ground venison

1 1/2 pounds ground wild boar or pork

1 small red bell pepper, seeded and chopped fine

1/4 cup dry red wine

1/4 cup grated Parmesan cheese

2 garlic cloves, minced

2 teaspoons dried oregano

2 teaspoons dried basil

2 teaspoons table salt

1 1/2 teaspoons fennel seeds

1 to 1 1/2 teaspoons crushed dried red chile of moderate heat, such as chile caribe, or a pinch of cayenne (optional)

2 yards hog sausage casings

Vegetable oil

1. At least the evening before you plan to barbecue, mix all of the ingredients except the casings and oil in a large bowl. Refrigerate, covered, overnight.

2. Prepare the casings, soaking them in several changes of water over several hours. (For more information about sausage casings and their stuffing, see the BBQ tips on pages 93 and 94.)

3. With the stuffing attachment of a meat grinder, stuff the cold sausage mixture into the casings, making 1-inch-thick links about 5 inches long. With your fingers, twist the casings and then tie off the individual sausages with kitchen twine. Cut between them. If you end up with any air bubbles, prick the casing in those spots with a needle. The sausage is ready to be smoked, but it can be refrigerated for several days or frozen for up to a month.

4. When you are ready to cook the sausage, prepare the smoker for barbecuing, bringing the temperature to 200°F to 220°F. Rub the sausages lightly with the oil.

5. Transfer the sausages to the smoker and cook until the skin of the sausage looks ready to pop, 2 to 2 1/4 hours. Always err on the side of caution with the timing and cut one of the sausages open to check for doneness before eating any of them. Serve hot.

SERVING SUGGESTION Make these sausages a part of a "mixed grill" by serving them with Hill Country Links (page 93) and Store-Bought Hot Brats (page 95). Add some good breads and a selection of hearty side dishes, such as Hot German Potato Salad (page 424), Kraut Salad (page 428), and Devil-May-Care Eggs (page 431). Finish off with The Best Cure for a Southern Summer (page 469).

BBQ tip If you need a good source for venison or wild boar meat, we recommend a south Texas outfit called Broken Arrow Ranch. It oversees the hunting and processing of deer, antelope, and wild boar on more than 100 Texas ranches. The Hill Country–based operation can be contacted online at brokenarrowranch.com.

Smoked Buffalo Steak

The American bison is making a comeback, especially in the Great Plains and West, where Native Americans are frequently involved in the animals' stewardship. The lean and beefy meat—not at all gamy—makes a great change of pace from more common meats. As with venison, the meat's leanness—a great reason for enjoying it—makes it worthy of a little extra care in preparation. SERVES 4 OR MORE

MUSTARD PASTE

2 tablespoons brown mustard

1 1/2 teaspoons vegetable oil

Kosher salt or coarse sea salt and freshly ground black pepper

Four 8-ounce rib eye, sirloin, or strip bison steaks, 3/4 to 1 inch thick

1 tablespoon vegetable oil

1. An hour or two before you plan to barbecue, combine the mustard paste ingredients and rub the mixture over the bison. Cover the meat and refrigerate it.

2. Prepare the smoker for barbecuing, bringing the temperature to 200°F to 220°F.

3. Let the meat sit, covered, at room temperature for 20 to 30 minutes.

4. In a heavy skillet, warm the oil over high heat until it almost smokes. Add the steaks, two at a time, and sear them on both sides, about 20 seconds per side. Repeat with the remaining meat.

5. Transfer the bison immediately to the smoker. Cook until the meat absorbs the smoke lightly but is still rare to medium-rare, 20 to 30 minutes. Serve immediately.

WALTZING OFF THE CALORIES

In the Old South, barbecues were often linked to fancy-dress balls. Scarlett O'Hara and Rhett Butler met at that kind of all-day party in *Gone with the Wind.* Slaves started the cooking the night before in big underground pits, and when Scarlett arrived in the morning, she "saw a haze of smoke hanging lazily in the tops of tall trees and smelled the mingled savory odors of burning hickory logs and roasting pork and mutton."

Buffalo Burgers with Roasted Garlic

Make a burger from lean but robust bison. To flavor it with roasted garlic, which is much milder when cooked than raw, roast the whole head in the oven ahead of putting these on the smoker. SERVES 6

1 whole head of garlic
Vegetable oil

BASIC BLACK RUB
2 tablespoons coarsely ground black pepper
1 tablespoon kosher salt or coarse sea salt

2 pounds ground bison
1/2 cup mayonnaise

BURGER MOP (OPTIONAL)
1/2 cup white vinegar
2 tablespoons vegetable olive oil

Yeast Buns (page 413) or other soft buns, toasted

1. Preheat the oven to 350°F.

2. Rub the garlic head lightly with vegetable oil and bake until softened, about 40 minutes. Squeeze the garlic cloves out of their skins into a small bowl and mash with a fork.

3. Meanwhile, prepare the smoker for barbecuing, bringing the temperature to 200°F to 220°F.

4. Combine the rub ingredients in a small bowl.

5. Mix the bison, 1 tablespoon of the rub, and half of the mashed roasted garlic in a large bowl. Form the mixture into 6 equal patties. Sprinkle the burgers with the remaining rub and let them sit at room temperature for 20 to 30 minutes. Combine the remaining mashed garlic with the mayonnaise and refrigerate until serving time.

6. If you plan to baste the burgers (see page 45, "To Mop or Not"), combine the mop ingredients in a small saucepan and warm over low heat.

7. Transfer the burgers to the smoker. Cook until lightly browned and medium-rare, about 40 minutes, or to your desired doneness. Dab the burgers with the mop once or twice in a wood-burning pit, or as appropriate in your style of smoker. Serve the burgers hot on toasted buns, with the garlic mayonnaise spooned over them.

DENVER DADDY

In Denver they name streets after their best pitmasters. The section of 34th Avenue outside the old location of Daddy Bruce's Bar-B-Q is now officially Bruce Randolph Avenue, in honor of the man who brought real barbecue to the city and also helped to feed the needy each Thanksgiving.

Ragin' Rabbit

A spicy Cajun-style coating keeps this rabbit hopping on your tongue. SERVES 5 TO 6

CAJUN RAGIN' RUB

1 tablespoon celery salt

1 tablespoon freshly ground black pepper

1 tablespoon ground white pepper

1 tablespoon packed brown sugar

1^1/$_2$ teaspoons garlic powder

^{1}/$_2$ to 1 teaspoon cayenne

^{3}/$_4$ teaspoon dried thyme

^{1}/$_2$ teaspoon dried sage

2 rabbits, about 2^1/$_2$ pounds each, quartered

1 tablespoon vegetable oil

1 tablespoon Creole mustard, such as Zatarain's

1. At least 2 hours and up to 3 hours before you plan to barbecue, combine the dry rub ingredients in a small bowl. Massage the meat lightly with the oil and mustard and sprinkle evenly with the dry rub. Place the meat in a shallow glass ovenproof or other smoke-proof dish, cover it, and refrigerate it.

2. Prepare the smoker for barbecuing, bringing the temperature to 200°F to 220°F.

3. Remove the rabbit from the refrigerator and let it sit in the dish, covered, at room temperature for 20 to 30 minutes. Cut a yard-long section of cheesecloth and dampen it thoroughly with water. Uncover the dish and drape the top of it loosely with several thicknesses of folded cheesecloth.

4. Transfer the cheesecloth-covered dish to the smoker. Cook for about 1^1/$_4$ hours, wetting down the cheesecloth with warm water a couple of times in a wood-burning pit, or with other styles of smokers, any time you raise the lid. The cheesecloth will brown but won't burn if it is kept moist. Remove the cheesecloth from the meat and discard it. Continue smoking until the meat is cooked through but still juicy, an additional 15 to 25 minutes. Serve the rabbit immediately.

SERVING SUGGESTION Lead off dinner with Smoked Spud Skins (page 284), hot from the smoker. Then serve the rabbit with lightly buttered noodles, Killed Salad (page 418), Squash Relish (page 437), and, for good measure, Peanut Butter Cake (page 457).

BBQ tip The function of the cheesecloth in the Ragin' Rabbit and other recipes is to keep lean meat moist during its slow smoking. You can skip the wrapping in smokers designed for moist cooking, such as water smokers and Cookshack ovens.

FOWL PLAY

BACKYARD COOKS HAVE HEAPED A LOT OF ABUSE ON POOR CHICKENS. WRINGING ONE'S NECK, AS OUR GRANDMOTHERS DID, ISN'T NEARLY AS NASTY AS WHAT SOME PEOPLE DO TO THE BIRDS OVER A HOT FIRE ON THE GRILL. A DINNER THAT SHOULD BE JUICY AND TASTY OFTEN COMES OUT AS DRY AS A SALT LICK. THE SLOW-SMOKING PROCESS OF REAL BARBECUE, IN CONTRAST, PRESERVES THE SUCCULENCE OF CHICKEN AND OTHER FOWL, WHILE ADDING NEW DIMENSIONS OF FLAVOR.

Chicken on a Throne

This established barbecue classic, also called "beer-can chicken," may be the best way of cooking a whole chicken ever invented in America. If you own a large smoker, and want to really delight your guests, arrange a row of these inside, with their legs crossed jauntily, or with one wing propped up in a salute. Your friends will talk about it for years. SERVES 5 TO 6

WILD WILLY'S NUMBER ONE-DERFUL RUB

6 tablespoons paprika

2 tablespoons freshly ground black pepper

2 tablespoons kosher salt or coarse sea salt

2 tablespoons sugar

1 tablespoon chili powder

1 tablespoon garlic powder

1 tablespoon onion powder

1 teaspoon cayenne

INJECTION LIQUID

12 ounces beer

1/4 cup vegetable oil

1/4 cup cider or white vinegar

Two 3 1/2-pound chickens, cleaned

THRONE MOP (OPTIONAL)

12 ounces beer

1 cup chicken stock

1/2 cup water

1/4 cup vegetable oil

Two 12-ounce cans beer (no bottles please)

1/2 medium onion, chopped

4 garlic cloves, minced

1/4 cup cider or white vinegar

Alabama Great White (page 385), Jalapeach Barbecue Sauce (page 384), Peppery Sweet Onion Sauce (page 378), or Old-Fashioned High-Cholesterol Great-Tasting Southern Sauce (page 372) (optional)

1. The night before you plan to barbecue, combine the rub ingredients in a small bowl. Set aside 2 tablespoons of the rub. In another bowl, mix the ingredients for the injection liquid with 2 teaspoons of the reserved rub.

2. With a kitchen syringe, inject about 1/2 cup of the injection liquid deep into the breast and legs of each chicken in several spots. Massage the chickens thoroughly, inside and out, with the remaining injection liquid, working it as far as possible under the skin without tearing the skin. Cover the chickens well with the greater amount of dry rub, again massaging inside and out and over and under the skin. Place the chickens in a plastic bag and refrigerate them.

3. Prepare the smoker for barbecuing, bringing the temperature to 200°F to 220°F.

4. Remove the chickens from the refrigerator and let them sit at room temperature for about 30 minutes.

5. While you wait, open the 2 beer cans and drink half—and only half—of each beer. With a can opener, remove the tops of the half-empty beer cans. If you are going to use the mop (see page 45, "To Mop or Not"), spoon 1 1/2 teaspoons

of the reserved rub into each can, saving the remaining 1 tablespoon for the mop. (If you are not using the mop, add 1 full tablespoon of the rub to each beer can.) Add half of the onion, garlic, and vinegar to each can. Insert the replenished beer cans into the cavities of the chickens, balancing the birds so that they rest upright with their legs bent forward. The cans should sit flat on the grill or on a cooking tray, holding the chickens at attention while their insides are steaming and their outsides are smoking.

6. If you are going to use the mop (see page 45, "To Mop or Not"), combine the ingredients with the remaining 1 tablespoon rub and keep the mixture warm over low heat.

7. Transfer the chickens to the smoker. Cook for 3½ to 4 hours, mopping every 30 minutes in a wood-burning pit, or as appropriate in your style of smoker. When the chickens are done, their legs will move freely and the internal temperature should be 180°F to 185°F.

8. Let the chickens sit for 5 to 10 minutes. Remove the skins, carve the chickens, and serve. Offer your choice of sauce on the side, if you wish, but be sure to try some of the savory bird unadorned before slathering on the sauce.

VARIATION: CHICKEN ON A POP CAN THRONE Use cans of root beer, Dr Pepper, or Cherry Dr Pepper to prop up your chickens, otherwise following the directions. The soft drinks give a slightly sweeter hint to the meat and are just as fun.

BBQ tip You should seldom remove the skin from chickens or other birds before barbecuing them. The skin keeps the meat moist and its fat acts as a natural basting agent. When there is skin on only a portion of the meat, as with a chicken breast, place that side up in your smoker. We remove the skin before serving, just as we trim any remaining layers of fat from other barbecue meats. It doesn't crisp up as it would with high-heat grilling and is generally a little oversmoked for most people's tastes. The one exception we've found is when chicken is cooked in a Big Green Egg or other kamado smoker, which produces poultry with moist meat and crackling crisp skin.

BELLO AND THE BIRD

Browsing the Web about barbecue one day, we found a site in the Netherlands that shows a homemade offset-firebox smoker and a few pictures of it in operation. Right there in the land of tulips, these guys are cooking Chicken on a Throne, presumably on a European beer can. The site described everything pretty thoroughly, but since it was in Dutch, we have no idea what it said. All we could decipher is that the smoker is called "Bello."

Mustard 'n' Lemon Chicken

If you want your chickens sober instead of steamy with beer, stuff their cavities with lemons and onions. The rub adds a tangy mustard taste. SERVES 5 TO 6

POULTRY PERFECT RUB

6 tablespoons paprika

2 tablespoons freshly ground black pepper

2 tablespoons celery salt

2 tablespoons sugar

1 tablespoon onion powder

1 tablespoon dry mustard

1 teaspoon cayenne

Zest of 1 to 2 lemons, dried and minced (see BBQ tip on page 28)

2 tablespoons unsalted butter

1 tablespoon Worcestershire sauce

Two 3 1/2-pound chickens, cleaned

1 medium onion, cut into thin wedges

1 lemon, cut into thin wedges

LEMON SPLASH (OPTIONAL)

1 1/2 cups chicken stock

1/2 cup freshly squeezed lemon juice

1/2 cup water

1/2 medium onion, chopped

1/2 cup unsalted butter

1 tablespoon Worcestershire sauce

1 tablespoon yellow mustard

Golden Mustard Barbecue Sauce (page 371) or Black Sauce (page 378) (optional)

1. The night before you plan to barbecue, combine the rub ingredients in a small bowl.

2. In a small saucepan, melt the butter and stir in the Worcestershire sauce. Massage the chickens thoroughly with the butter mixture, inside and out, working the mixture as far as possible under the skin without tearing it. Cover the chickens well with the dry rub, again massaging inside and out and over and under the skin. Reserve about one-third of the rub. Place the chickens in a plastic bag and refrigerate them.

3. Prepare the smoker for barbecuing, bringing the temperature to 200°F to 220°F.

4. Remove the chickens from the refrigerator and rub them again with the dry rub, reserving 2 teaspoons of the mixture if you plan to baste the birds. Let the chickens sit at room temperature for about 30 minutes, and then insert the onion and lemon slices into their cavities.

5. If you are going to use the Lemon Splash mop (see page 45, "To Mop or Not"), mix the ingredients with the reserved 2 teaspoons rub in a saucepan. Keep the mop warm over low heat.

6. Place the chickens in the smoker, breast down. Cook for 3 1/2 to 4 hours, basting the birds with the mop every 30 minutes in a wood-burning pit, or as appropriate in your style of smoker. Turn the birds breast side up about halfway through the cooking time. When the chickens are done, their legs will move freely and the internal temperature should be 180°F to 185°F.

7. Let the chickens sit for 5 to 10 minutes. Remove the lemons and onions from the cavities, remove the skins, carve the chicken, and serve. Offer Golden Mustard Barbecue Sauce or Black Sauce on the side if you wish.

SERVING SUGGESTION Accompany the chicken with your favorite fresh green vegetable and either Mayme's Macaroni and Cheese (page 405) or Boarding House Macaroni Salad (page 422). How about Becky's Pineapple Cake (page 459) for dessert?

I'LL TAKE A MUSTANG AND A BAG OF CHARCOAL

Henry Ford, who revolutionized the American automobile industry, also invented charcoal briquettes. He originally made his cars with lots of wood parts and ended up with a plant full of scraps. Ever the entrepreneur, Ford came up with the idea of charring the discards and compressing them into briquettes, a job he turned over to his brother-in-law, E. G. Kingsford. The new company sold the briquettes only at Ford dealers until the 1950s, when a surge of interest in outdoor cooking prompted grocery stores to start carrying them.

Birds of Paradise

This paradise comes from the Caribbean. The herb paste helps the chickens develop flavor while cooking, and the mojo sauce bathes them on the table. SERVES 5 TO 6

NAME-YOUR-HERB PASTE WITH MINT, PARSLEY, AND CILANTRO

1 1/2 cups fresh herb leaves (a combination of mint, flat-leaf parsley, and cilantro, about 1/2 cup each)

10 to 14 garlic cloves

1 teaspoon table salt

3/4 cup extra-virgin olive oil

Two 3 1/2-pound chickens, cleaned

MOJO MARINADE AND SAUCE (AND MOP)

3/4 cup freshly squeezed lime juice

3/4 cup freshly squeezed orange juice

2 tablespoons grated orange zest

3/4 cup extra-virgin olive oil

6 to 8 garlic cloves, minced

2 teaspoons ground cumin

2 teaspoons dried oregano

1 teaspoon kosher salt or coarse sea salt, or more to taste

1 cup water

1/3 cup chopped fresh cilantro

1. The night before you plan to barbecue, make the herb paste. Combine the herbs, garlic, and salt in a blender or food processor. Process until the herbs are finely chopped. Add the oil in a slow stream, mixing thoroughly.

2. Cover the chickens well with the paste, massaging inside and out and over and under the skin, working the mixture as far as possible under the skin without tearing it. Place the chickens in a plastic bag and refrigerate them.

3. Prepare the smoker for barbecuing, bringing the temperature to 200°F to 220°F.

4. Remove the chickens from the refrigerator and let them sit at room temperature for about 30 minutes.

5. If you are going to use the mop (see page 45, "To Mop or Not"), mix the mojo ingredients now, leaving out the water and cilantro. Reserve 1 1/2 cups of the mojo for the sauce and, for the mop, combine the remaining mojo with the water in a saucepan. Keep the mop warm over low heat.

6. Place the chickens in the smoker, breast down. Cook for 3 1/2 to 4 hours, basting the birds with the mop every 30 minutes in a wood-burning pit, or as appropriate in your style of smoker. Turn the birds breast side up about halfway through the cooking time. When the chickens are done, their legs will move freely and the internal temperature should be 180°F to 185 °F.

7. Let the chickens sit for 5 to 10 minutes.

8. Stir the cilantro into the reserved mojo sauce.

9. Remove the skins, carve the chickens, and serve, with mojo on the side.

SERVING SUGGESTION Set a festive table and put on some salsa music. Offer toasted thick shreds of dried coconut as a nibble. Accompany the chickens with fluffy white rice and Mango and Avocado Salad (page 430). Serve lively Mojito Sorbet (page 466) for dessert.

Fancy Chicken with Cheese

A creamy goat cheese under a chicken's skin helps to keep the meat moist and adds its own delightful flavor. Try this when you need to impress someone who looks down their nose at barbecue. SERVES 3

3½-pound chicken, cleaned

2 to 3 ounces fresh mild goat cheese

1 tablespoon prepared pesto

8 to 10 fresh basil leaves

FANCY MOP (OPTIONAL)

1 cup chicken stock

½ cup water

½ cup dry white wine

2 tablespoons extra-virgin olive oil

1 tablespoon prepared pesto

1. The night before you plan to barbecue, massage the chicken thoroughly with the cheese and pesto, inside and out, working them as far as possible under the skin without tearing it. Insert the basil leaves under the skin, placing them as evenly as possible over the chicken. If you wish, truss the chicken. Place the chicken in a plastic bag and refrigerate it overnight.

2. Prepare the smoker for barbecuing, bringing the temperature to 200°F to 220°F.

3. Remove the chicken from the refrigerator and let it sit at room temperature for about 30 minutes.

4. If you plan to baste the chicken (see page 45, "To Mop or Not"), mix the mop ingredients in a saucepan. Keep the mop warm over low heat.

5. Transfer the chicken to the smoker, breast down. Cook for 3½ to 4 hours, basting the chicken with the mop every 30 minutes in a wood-burning pit, or as appropriate for your style of smoker. Turn the bird breast side up about halfway through the cooking time. When the chicken is done, its legs will move freely and the internal temperature should be 180°F to 185°F.

6. Let the chicken sit for 5 to 10 minutes. Remove the skin, carve the chicken, and serve.

SERVING SUGGESTION Lead off by nibbling Smoked Olives (page 346). Accompany the chicken with pasta tossed with good olive oil and steamed zucchini, followed by Texas Peach Cobbler (page 452).

BBQ tip Perfectionists may want to truss stuffed whole chickens. Use kitchen twine, about a 3-foot length, and start by wrapping the ends of the legs together with the middle of the string. Crisscross the string back and forth under and around the birds and tie off when you get to the neck end. The birds will look a bit more shapely coming out of the smoker, but the extra step isn't needed for taste.

Chicken Oregano

Garlic always goes great with chicken and, as any Italian cook can tell you, it also makes a delicious seasoning duo with oregano. SERVES 6 TO 8

OREGANO MARINADE

2 cups olive oil (an inexpensive kind is fine)

1 cup freshly squeezed lemon juice

6 to 8 garlic cloves

2 teaspoons kosher salt or coarse sea salt

1/4 cup chopped fresh oregano or 2 tablespoons dried oregano

Eight 7-ounce to 8-ounce bone-in, skin-on chicken breasts

Oregano sprigs (optional), for garnish

1. At least 4 hours and up to 8 hours before you plan to barbecue, combine the marinade ingredients in a blender and puree. Loosen the skin of the chicken, and place the chicken in a shallow, nonreactive dish or plastic bag. Pour the marinade over the chicken and refrigerate it, turning once, if needed, to saturate the surface.

2. Prepare the smoker for barbecuing, bringing the temperature to 200°F to 220°F.

3. Remove the chicken from the refrigerator and drain the pieces. Let them sit at room temperature for about 20 minutes.

4. Transfer the chicken pieces to the smoker, skin sides up. Cook the chicken until it is cooked through and the juices run clear when a skewer is inserted into a breast, 50 to 60 minutes. Remove the chicken from the smoker and serve hot, garnished with oregano sprigs if you wish.

SERVING SUGGESTION Try this simple preparation with Sweet and Sour Cukes (page 420), roasted potatoes, and Lemon Pudding Ice Cream Pie (page 448).

VARIATION: CHICKEN TARRAGON Substitute tarragon vinegar for the lemon juice and fresh tarragon for the fresh oregano in the marinade. Garnish with tarragon sprigs.

Finger-Lickin' Fried Smoked Chicken

When eating out in Kansas City, it can be tough to decide between the world-class barbecue and the superlative fried chicken served at places like Stroud's. This technique, first suggested by Bobby Seale, is an at-home compromise between the two down-home dishes, one that bathes the birds in smoke before finishing them in a crunchy coating. SERVES 4

3½ to 4 pounds chicken parts

3 cups buttermilk

1½ tablespoons Tabasco or other hot pepper sauce

1½ cups all-purpose flour

2 to 3 teaspoons kosher salt or coarse sea salt

1 teaspoon freshly ground black pepper

1½ pounds (3 cups) solid shortening, preferably Crisco

3 tablespoons bacon drippings

1. At least 3 hours and up to 12 hours before you plan to barbecue, place the chicken in a shallow dish. Pour the buttermilk and Tabasco over the chicken. Turn the chicken in the buttermilk to coat it well. Cover the dish and refrigerate it.

2. Prepare the smoker for barbecuing, bringing the temperature to 200°F to 220°F.

3. Drain the chicken, reserving the marinade in the refrigerator. Allow the chicken to stand at room temperature for about 20 minutes.

4. Transfer the chicken to the smoker and cook for 35 to 45 minutes, long enough to give the bird some smoky flavor but only to cook it partially.

5. Return the chicken to the buttermilk bath. Pour the flour into a medium-size brown paper sack and sprinkle in the salt and pepper.

6. In a 10-inch to 12-inch cast-iron skillet, melt the shortening and bacon drippings over high heat. When small bubbles form on the surface, reduce the heat to medium-high. Drain each piece of the chicken, starting with the dark pieces, and drop them into the bag of seasoned flour. Shake well to coat.

7. Lower each piece gently into the skillet, skin side down. Arrange the chicken so that all pieces cook evenly. It's desirable that the pieces fit snugly together, although they shouldn't be sticking to each other. Reduce the heat to medium and cover the skillet. Fry the chicken for 10 to 11 minutes. Reduce the heat to medium-low, uncover the chicken, and turn it over. Fry it, uncovered, for another 10 to 11 minutes, wiping up any grease spatters on your stove as they occur. The chicken will be a rich mahogany brown and should be cooked through and tender inside. Cut into a test piece first, cooking an additional minute or two if needed. Remove the chicken, drain it, and serve it piping hot.

SERVING SUGGESTION For an old-fashioned Sunday dinner, add Country Collard Greens (page 400), Flash-Fried Okra (page 395), garlicky mashed potatoes and gravy, Sweet Potato Biscuits (page 411), Squash Relish (page 437), and loads of Sunny Sweet Tea (page 484). Finish off with Peanut Butter Cake (page 457).

"BARBECUE MAN"

Arthur Bryant became so legendary in barbecue circles that he rated an obituary in the *New York Times* titled simply, "Arthur Bryant, Barbecue Man." Raised in poverty in East Texas, he bought his famous Kansas City joint from his older brother, Charlie, in 1946. From then until his death in 1982, the "Barbecue Man" cooked almost daily on his white-tiled pits. Calvin Trillin called Arthur Bryant's the best restaurant in the world, but Bryant himself thought of his place as just the "House of Good Eats."

Quick Chick

Here's a great way to serve barbecued chicken on a weeknight when time is short. You don't want to fire up a log pit to cook Quick Chick, but it's great for stovetop smokers, electric-powered smokers, and other smokers that start up in a snap.

SERVES 4 TO 6

SPLIT-SECOND DRY RUB

1 tablespoon paprika

1 teaspoon kosher salt or coarse sea salt

1 teaspoon sugar

1/2 teaspoon freshly ground black pepper

1/2 teaspoon onion powder

Pinch of cayenne

6 boneless, skinless chicken breasts, pounded lightly

SPLIT-SECOND MOP

1 cup freshly squeezed orange juice

3 tablespoons unsalted butter

1 tablespoon Worcestershire sauce

Smoked Onion Sauce (page 383), South Florida Citrus Sauce (page 386), or Bour-B-Q Sauce (page 381) (optional)

1. Prepare the smoker for barbecuing, bringing the temperature to 200°F to 220°F.

2. Combine the rub ingredients in a small bowl. Rub the breasts with the mixture and let them sit at room temperature for about 20 minutes.

3. Combine the mop ingredients in a small saucepan, placing the pan over low heat to melt the butter. Keep the mop warm over low heat.

4. Drizzle the breasts with about one-third of the mop. Transfer the chicken to the smoker and cook for 25 to 30 minutes, or until cooked through. In a wood-burning pit, turn the breasts after 15 minutes and mop well again. With other smokers, don't worry about turning the breasts or mopping while cooking—just drizzle the breasts with more mop as soon as you remove them from the smoker. Serve immediately, with your choice of sauce if you wish.

SERVING SUGGESTION Accompany the chicken with cool Burstin' with Black-Eyed Peas Salad (page 419) and hot rice. Sweet Potato Pudding (page 462) makes a fitting finish if you have time to prepare it. Otherwise, offer a plate of fresh fruit.

VARIATION: DEVILED QUICK CHICK In place of the dry rub, make a paste of 2 tablespoons brown or Dijon mustard and 1 teaspoon each Worcestershire sauce, salt, and black pepper. Replace the orange juice in the mop with 1/2 cup water. We prefer Deviled Quick Chick without any sauce.

Chicken-Wrapped Apple Sausage

A revived interest in sausage in recent years has led to an explosion of new varieties, many leaner than the old favorites. We find Aidells's nationally distributed sausages among the best at balancing heartiness and healthiness. If you can't find an apple-laced chicken sausage, substitute any other made from chicken or turkey. SERVES 4

CHICKEN-APPLE MARINADE

1 cup apple juice

1/2 cup cider vinegar

2 tablespoons olive oil

2 tablespoons Wild Willy's Number One-derful Rub (page 26) or other savory seasoning blend to taste

4 teaspoons brown mustard

4 boneless, skinless chicken breasts, pounded thin

1 teaspoon olive oil

4 uncooked chicken-apple sausages, such as Aidells

1 1/2 teaspoons brown mustard

1/4 cup minced onion

Additional Wild Willy's Number One-derful Rub or other savory seasoning blend to taste

1 tart apple, cored and sliced thin

1/4 cup chicken stock

1. At least 2 hours and up to 3 hours before you plan to barbecue, combine the marinade ingredients in a large glass measuring cup. Place the chicken in a large plastic bag or shallow, nonreactive dish. Pour the marinade over the chicken and refrigerate it.

2. Prepare the smoker for barbecuing, bringing the temperature to 200°F to 220°F.

3. Remove the chicken from the refrigerator and let it sit at room temperature for about 20 minutes.

4. Warm the olive oil in a skillet over medium-low heat. Add the sausages and sauté until just cooked through. Remove the sausages from the skillet, saving the drippings. Cool the sausages briefly, and then rub them with the mustard.

5. Drain the chicken, reserving 1 cup of the marinade. Arrange a sausage on each chicken breast, sprinkling 1 to 2 teaspoons of the onion over each portion. Wrap the chicken around the sausage, securing each roll with toothpicks. It's not necessary to entirely encase the sausages, but make the rolls as attractive as possible. Sprinkle the tops of the rolls with dry rub.

6. Transfer the chicken to the smoker and cook until the chicken is cooked through and tender, about 25 minutes.

7. While the chicken smokes, add the apple and the remaining onion to the sausage pan drippings and sauté over medium heat until both begin to soften. Pour in the stock and the reserved 1 cup marinade and bring to a boil. Boil for at least 5 minutes, allowing most of the liquid to evaporate.

8. Remove the chicken from the smoker and arrange each chicken breast on a plate. Remove the toothpicks. Spoon equal portions of the apple mixture over the chicken and serve hot.

Thunder Thighs

Many dishes from the old South have their origins in Africa, and that's the source of the seasoning combination here, a thunderstorm of a mixture. SERVES 3 TO 4

THUNDER PASTE

1 small onion, chunked

1/3 cup freshly squeezed orange juice

2 tablespoons peanut oil

2 teaspoons ground anise

1 teaspoon turmeric

1 teaspoon curry powder

1 teaspoon kosher salt or coarse sea salt

1 teaspoon ground allspice

1/2 teaspoon ground cinnamon

8 bone-in, skin-on chicken thighs

THUNDER MOP (OPTIONAL)

1 cup chicken stock

1/2 cup freshly squeezed orange juice

1/4 cup water

1 tablespoon peanut oil

1/2 teaspoon curry powder

1. The night before you plan to barbecue, combine all the paste ingredients in a food processor or blender. Coat the thighs thickly with the paste, rubbing under and over the skin. Place the chicken in a plastic bag and refrigerate it overnight.

2. Prepare the smoker for barbecuing, bringing the temperature to 200°F to 220°F.

3. Remove the chicken from the refrigerator and let it sit at room temperature for about 15 minutes.

4. If you plan to baste the chicken (see page 45, "To Mop or Not"), combine the mop ingredients in a small saucepan and keep the mop warm over low heat.

5. Transfer the chicken to the smoker and cook for 1½ to 1¾ hours. Mop the thighs every 30 minutes in a wood-burning pit, or as appropriate for your style of smoker.

6. The chicken is done when it is very tender and the juices run clear when a skewer is inserted into a thigh. Serve the thighs immediately.

SERVING SUGGESTION Pair the thighs with Sweet Potatoes with Orange-Pecan Butter (page 281), Okra Pickles (page 432), and Cracklin' Cornbread (page 408). Sip creamy Plumb Loco Coco Punch (page 480) in place of dessert.

BBQ tip Some people use beer, wine, or other liquids in their water pan or reservoir, or they add slices of apples, onions, fresh or dried herbs, or other favorite foods. We usually don't notice much difference in taste, except when we're cooking in a water smoker, which produces more steam than other kinds of barbecue equipment do. If you have a lot of something, like a garden full of fresh rosemary, give it a try, but the effect usually seems very subtle for the price if you have to buy the ingredients.

Jammin' Jerk Chicken Thighs

Real Jamaican jerk is cooked over pimento wood, from the tree we know in the United States as allspice. You can get the wood from a source in Minnesota, pimentowood. com, which carries it in various forms. Alternatively, you can throw some whole allspice berries into the fire, about ¼ cup for something relatively quick-cooking like chicken parts. You can keep down their cost by buying them in bulk from a spice company such as penzeys.com. SERVES 4

JAMAICAN JERK RUB
6 tablespoons onion powder
6 tablespoons onion flakes
2 tablespoons ground allspice
2 tablespoons freshly ground black pepper
2 tablespoons cayenne
2 tablespoons sugar
1½ tablespoons dried thyme
1½ tablespoons ground cinnamon
1½ teaspoons ground nutmeg
¼ teaspoon ground habanero chile (optional)

8 bone-in, skin-on chicken thighs

JAMAICAN JERK MOP (OPTIONAL)
1 cup pineapple juice
¼ cup water

1. The night before you plan to barbecue, combine all the rub ingredients in a bowl, being careful to keep the incendiary habanero powder (if you are using it) off your bare hands and away from sensitive body parts. Coat the thighs with the paste, rubbing under and over the skin. Place the chicken in a plastic bag and refrigerate it overnight.

2. Prepare the smoker for barbecuing, bringing the temperature to 200°F to 220°F.

3. Remove the chicken from the refrigerator and let it sit at room temperature for about 15 minutes.

4. If you plan to baste the chicken (see page 45, "To Mop or Not"), combine the pineapple juice and water in a small saucepan and keep the mop warm over low heat.

5. Transfer the chicken thighs to the smoker and cook for 1½ to 1¾ hours. Mop the thighs every 30 minutes in a wood-burning pit, or as appropriate for your style of smoker.

6. The chicken is done when it is very tender and the juices run clear when a skewer is inserted into a thigh. Serve the thighs immediately.

SERVING SUGGESTION For a libation, start with Plumb Loco Coco Punch (page 480). Serve the chicken with Drunken Sweet Potatoes (page 282), white rice, and some collard or mustard greens. Finish with Mojito Sorbet (page 466).

Delectable Drumsticks

Yogurt, like buttermilk, is a miracle marinade, capable of tenderizing anything short of the calluses on a bureaucrat's butt. SERVES 2 TO 4

DELECTABLE MARINADE

1 cup plain yogurt

1 cup fresh mint leaves, chopped fine

1/4 cup bourbon or other sour-mash whiskey

8 chicken drumsticks

DELECTABLE MOP (OPTIONAL)

1/4 cup bourbon or other sour-mash whiskey

1/4 cup water

2 tablespoons vegetable oil

Lime-Mint Barbecue Sauce (page 385) (optional)

1. The night before you plan to barbecue, combine the marinade ingredients in a small bowl. Loosen the skin on the drumsticks and place them in a large plastic bag. Pour the marinade over the drumsticks and refrigerate overnight.

2. Prepare the smoker for barbecuing, bringing the temperature to 200°F to 220°F.

3. Remove the chicken from the refrigerator and drain it, reserving the marinade. Let the chicken sit at room temperature for about 15 minutes.

4. If you plan to baste the chicken (see page 45, "To Mop or Not"), combine the mop ingredients with the remaining marinade in a small saucepan and bring the mixture to a boil, boiling for several minutes. Keep the mop warm over low heat.

5. Transfer the chicken to the smoker. Cook until the drumsticks are very tender and the juices run clear when a skewer is inserted into one of them, 1 1/2 to 1 3/4 hours. Mop the chicken every 30 minutes in a wood-burning pit, or as appropriate in your style of smoker.

6. Remove the drumsticks from the smoker and serve them immediately, with a dish of Lime-Mint Barbecue Sauce for dipping if you wish.

SERVING SUGGESTION Accompany the drumsticks with white or brown rice, Zooks and Cilantro Sauce (page 294), and tangy Corn and Watermelon Pickle-lilli (page 438). Santa Fe Capirotada (page 464) makes an unusual dessert.

POLITICKING WITH THE 'Q'

Lyndon Johnson loved his barbecue. From the moment he took office as president, Johnson used barbecue parties to coddle political allies and cajole adversaries. His favorite pitmaster was Walter Jetton, who told about what he doled in the 1965 *LBJ Barbecue Cook Book* (Pocket Books).

Alabama Smoked Chicken Sandwich

Big Bob Gibson Bar-B-Q in Decatur, Alabama, serves an unusual barbecued chicken. After cooking, the chicken is dunked into a white barbecue sauce that dates back to Big Bob's early days, many decades ago. Nobody really remembers how or why the white sauce got started, but it's become as much a trademark of the place as the dancing pig sign. Don McLemore, the present-day honcho, says his grandfather, Big Bob, began the famous sauce as a simple mixture of mayonnaise, vinegar, and black pepper. Here's our own humble attempt to re-create this special treat in the backyard, starting with quick and easy chicken breasts. **SERVES 6**

SOUTHERN SUCCOR RUB

1 tablespoon freshly ground black pepper

1 tablespoon paprika

1 tablespoon turbinado sugar

1 1/2 teaspoons kosher salt or coarse sea salt

1/2 teaspoon dry mustard

1/4 teaspoon cayenne

6 boneless, skinless chicken breasts, pounded lightly

ALABAMA GREAT WHITE

1 cup mayonnaise (the real stuff—no Miracle Whip here)

2 tablespoons vinegar, preferably cider

1/4 cup plus 1 tablespoon water

1 tablespoon coarsely ground black pepper

3/4 teaspoon kosher salt or coarse sea salt

Pinch or two of onion powder

Pinch or two of cayenne

12 large slices toasted white bread

6 crisp lettuce leaves

Green Tomato Chowchow (page 436), bread-and-butter pickles, or other tangy relish

1. Prepare the smoker for barbecuing, bringing the temperature to 200°F to 220°F.

2. Combine the rub ingredients in a small bowl. Rub the breasts with the mixture and let them sit at room temperature for about 20 minutes.

3. Make the sauce, first whisking together the mayonnaise with about half of the vinegar. Add 1 tablespoon of the water and the seasonings and whisk until smooth. Spoon out 1/4 cup of the sauce and mix it with the remaining 1/4 cup water to use as a mop. The sauce and mop can sit at room temperature for some 30 minutes, but if either the cooking or eating gets delayed beyond that, refrigerate them, to be safe.

4. Drizzle the breasts with about one-third of the mop. Transfer the chicken to the smoker and cook until cooked through, 25 to 30 minutes. In a wood-burning pit, turn the breasts after 15 minutes and mop well again. With other smokers, don't worry about turning the breasts

or mopping while cooking—just drizzle the breasts with more mop as soon as you remove them from the smoker.

5. Assemble the sandwiches, slathering sauce on one side of all the bread slices. Arrange a lettuce leaf on each of six bread slices, then top each with a chicken breast and a hearty dollop of chowchow. Top each with a remaining bread slice, halve, and serve with the remaining sauce on the side.

VARIATION: PULLED CHICKEN SANDWICHES Pull the smoked chicken into shreds and toss with enough Alabama Great White sauce (page 204) or Apple City Apple Sauce (page 384) or other barbecue sauce to moisten. Spoon onto soft white buns such as Yeast Buns (page 413). Add Creamy Coleslaw (page 390) to the sandwiches, too.

Big Bob's famous sauce began as a simple mixture of mayonnaise, vinegar, and black pepper

KEEPING IT SIMPLE

In his delightful *American Taste* (1982, Arbor House), James Villas brags about the barbecue of his native North Carolina. The former *Town and Country* editor says that at any of the great joints in the state, "the scene's always about the same: a counter with short stools, plain wooden tables and chairs, paper napkins, plastic forks and iced-tea glasses, bottles of red-pepper vinegar, maybe a little country music on the spanking-new jukebox, and an inexpensive portrait of Jesus."

Smoked Chicken Sandwich with Summer Confetti

If the previous sandwich was country singer Tim McGraw, this would be Faith Hill— closely related, but this one's definitely prettier, with a more elegant appearance. It resembles a summer garden, with its bright bits of herbs, tomato, onion, and peppers. SERVES 6

CONFETTI PASTE

2 tablespoons extra-virgin olive oil

1 tablespoon brine from a jar of peperoncini peppers

1 tablespoon minced fresh basil

1 tablespoon minced fresh parsley

2 garlic cloves, minced

3/4 teaspoon kosher salt or coarse sea salt

6 boneless, skinless chicken breasts, pounded thin

SALAD TOPPING

1 small red-ripe tomato, chopped

2/3 cup chopped pimiento-stuffed green olives

1/3 cup minced red onion

2 to 3 tablespoons chopped peperoncini peppers

2 tablespoons minced fresh basil

2 tablespoons minced fresh parsley

2 tablespoons olive oil

1 teaspoon Dijon mustard

Pinch of kosher salt or coarse sea salt

6 slices provolone cheese

12 large slices sturdy sourdough bread or other good sandwich bread

1. At least 2 hours and up to the night before you plan to barbecue, combine the paste ingredients in a small bowl. Rub the paste thoroughly over the chicken, wrap it in plastic, and refrigerate for at least 1 hour.

2. While the chicken marinates, combine the salad topping ingredients in a bowl, cover the mixture, and refrigerate.

3. Prepare the smoker for barbecuing, bringing the temperature to 200°F to 220°F.

4. Transfer the chicken to the smoker and cook until cooked through, 25 to 30 minutes. Place a cheese slice on each breast and cook for another few minutes, until softened.

5. Assemble the sandwiches, arranging a chicken breast on each of six bread slices. Spoon equal portions of the salad topping over the chicken breasts. Top each with a remaining bread slice, halve, and serve.

VARIATION: SMOKED CHICKEN SALAD WITH SUMMER CONFETTI If you don't want something quite so filling, simply do away with the bread and the cheese. Slice the cooked chicken breasts and fan each one across a plate. Top with equal portions of the salad topping. Serve warm or lightly chilled.

Green Chile Chicken Soup

As mentioned several times, we often make extra smoked foods to have intentional leftovers for other dishes. This soulful soup is one of our favorite chicken leftover treats, so good you'll be tempted to fire up your smoker and make it from scratch. You can easily cook the chicken a day or two ahead of when you want to prepare the soup. SERVES 8

SOUTHWEST HEAT

2 tablespoons ground New Mexican red chile

2 tablespoons ground ancho chile

2 teaspoons kosher salt or coarse sea salt

2 teaspoons ground cumin

3/4 teaspoon dried oregano, preferably Mexican

Four to five 7-ounce to 8-ounce bone-in, skin-on chicken breasts

SOUP

2 tablespoons vegetable oil

1 1/2 medium onions, chopped

2 to 3 garlic cloves, minced

8 cups (2 quarts) chicken stock

14.5-ounce can stewed tomatoes, preferably a Mexican-flavored variety

1 cup chopped roasted mild green chiles, such as New Mexican or poblano, fresh or frozen (see BBQ tip on page 151)

1 1/2 teaspoons dried oregano

Kosher salt or coarse sea salt

Minced fresh cilantro and grated Monterey Jack cheese, for garnish

1. At least 2 hours before you plan to barbecue, and up to the night before, combine the dry rub ingredients in a small bowl. With your fingers, loosen the skin of the breasts and massage the chicken with the spice mixture, rubbing over and under the skin. Place the breasts in a plastic bag or covered container and refrigerate them for at least 1 1/2 hours.

2. Prepare the smoker for barbecuing, bringing the temperature to 200°F to 220°F.

3. Remove the chicken from the refrigerator and let it sit at room temperature for about 20 minutes.

4. Transfer the chicken pieces to the smoker, skin sides up. Cook the chicken until it is cooked through and the juices run clear when a skewer is inserted into a breast, 50 to 60 minutes.

5. While the chicken smokes, prepare the soup stock. Warm the oil in a large pot over high heat. Stir in the onions and garlic, and sauté until the onions are softened and browned on the edges. Frequently scrape up the vegetables from the bottom of the pan. Pour in the stock and add the tomatoes, chiles, oregano, and salt to taste. Bring to a boil, reduce the heat to a simmer, and cook until all the vegetables are tender, 25 to 30 minutes. (The stock can be prepared a day or two ahead to this point and refrigerated.)

6. When the chicken is cool enough to handle, shred the meat into bite-size chunks, discarding the skin and bones or saving them to make stock later.

7. Stir the chicken into the soup and continue simmering about 10 more minutes. Ladle the soup into bowls, top with cilantro and cheese, and serve hot.

we often make extra smoked foods to have intentional leftovers for other dishes

A SHARED PASSION

"[Barbecue] is America's very own slow food, hand-made and idiosyncratic. Like stock-car racing, oversweet iced tea, and the Baptist church, barbecue is an authentic emblem of the American South, especially the rural, working-class south. . . . Barbecue, like jazz, was one of the very few passions that southern blacks and whites shared during segregation. Today barbecue is one of the few passions shared by foodies and good ol' boys." R. W. Apple, Jr., in *Williams-Sonoma Taste*, Summer 2002

Worth-the-Wait Turkey

You may be talking gibberish yourself after a long, long day of barbecuing this bird, but your guests will be talking about the turkey for many more days to come.

SERVES 8 TO 10

INJECTION LIQUID
1/2 cup garlic-flavored oil (see BBQ tip)
1/2 cup beer
1/2 teaspoon cayenne

10-pound to 11-pound turkey

TURKEY PASTE
4 garlic cloves
1 tablespoon coarsely ground black pepper
1 tablespoon kosher salt or coarse sea salt
Pinch of cayenne
1 tablespoon garlic-flavored oil

TURKEY MOP (OPTIONAL)
2 cups turkey or chicken stock
1 cup beer
1 cup water
1/4 cup vegetable oil

Creole Classic Barbecue Sauce (page 382) or Struttin' Sauce (page 369) (optional)

1. The night before you plan to barbecue, combine the injection liquid ingredients in a small bowl. With a kitchen syringe, inject the mixture deep into the turkey in a half-dozen places, moving the needle around in each spot to shoot the liquid in several directions. Inject the greatest amount into the breast.

2. With a mortar and pestle or in a mini food processor, combine the paste ingredients, mashing the garlic with the pepper, salt, and cayenne. Add the oil to form a thick paste. Massage the turkey with the paste inside and out, working it as far as possible under the skin without tearing the skin. Place the turkey in a plastic bag and refrigerate it overnight.

3. Before you begin to barbecue, remove the turkey from the refrigerator and let it sit at room temperature for 45 minutes.

4. Prepare the smoker for barbecuing, bringing the temperature to 200°F to 220°F.

5. Cut a 4-foot to 5-foot length of cheesecloth and dampen it thoroughly with water. Wrap the bird in the cheesecloth and tie the ends.

6. Transfer the turkey to the smoker, breast side down (you should be able to feel through the cheesecloth), and cook for 1¼ to 1½ hours per pound, until the internal temperature reaches 180°F. Wet the cheesecloth down with more water at 30-minute intervals in a wood-burning pit, or as appropriate for your style of smoker.

7. After about 6 hours, remove the cheesecloth, snipping it with scissors if necessary, and discard it. When the cheesecloth is removed, baste the turkey for the remainder of its cooking time, if possible in your smoker (see page 45,

"To Mop or Not"). If you plan to baste, combine the mop ingredients in a saucepan and warm the mixture over low heat. Mop every 30 minutes in a wood-burning pit, or as appropriate for your style of smoker.

8. When the turkey is done, remove it from the smoker and allow it to sit for 15 minutes before carving. Serve with Creole Classic Barbecue Sauce or Struttin' Sauce if you wish.

SERVING SUGGESTION For a festive meal suitable for a holiday, start with Shrimp Rémoulade (page 262). Along with the bird, serve Candied Sweet Potatoes (page 399), Peabody-Style Stuffed Onions (page 276), cornbread dressing, and Buttermilk Biscuits (page 410). Load a relish tray with Green Tomato Chow-chow (page 436), Carolina Jerusalem Artichoke Pickles (page 434), Okra Pickles (page 432), and Bourbon Peaches (page 439), or make up a relish tray of store-bought favorites. Offer a scrumptious Black Walnut Cake (page 450) for dessert.

BBQ tip Injecting an oil mixture is a good way of adding internal moistness and flavor to lean meat. The amounts we recommend in recipes may seem large, but they don't make food greasy. Much of it cooks away.

BBQ tip To make your own garlic-flavored oil, mince a whole head of fresh garlic. Place it in a lidded jar and add enough oil to cover the garlic by a couple of inches. Refrigerate for at least a day before straining off the oil and using. Don't let it sit at room temperature for any length of time. Chilled, it will keep for weeks.

HENRY PERRY AND THE BRYANT BOYS

Henry Perry was our kind of pioneer, the founding father of Kansas City barbecue. Slapping together a living during the Depression, he started barbecuing ribs in an outdoor pit along the street, selling slabs wrapped in newspaper. Two Bryant brothers joined Perry in the business in 1931 and eventually turned the makeshift operation into the country's most famous 'Q' joint, Arthur Bryant's.

May it rest in shady peace since Shady Rest Pit-Bar-B-Que closed its doors in Owensboro, Kentucky. The pit in the name used to be worth a visit of its own. A splendid piece of barbecue sculpture, the huge, domed brick cooker puffed away majestically all day in the take-out area, where the walls were little more than layers of smoke.

Hot Times Jalapeño Turkey Breast

Spanish explorers celebrated a feast of thanksgiving near present-day El Paso back when our Pilgrim mothers and fathers were still boys and girls in England. That's all the excuse you need to add Southwestern flair to your next Thanksgiving meal.

SERVES 6 TO 8

INJECTION LIQUID

1/3 cup vegetable oil

1/3 cup pickling liquid from a jar or can of pickled jalapeños

1 teaspoon yellow mustard

5-pound to 7-pound turkey breast, boneless or bone-in, preferably skin-on

HOT TIMES RUB

2 tablespoons kosher salt or coarse sea salt

2 tablespoons packed brown sugar

2 teaspoons ground cinnamon

1/2 teaspoon dry mustard

1/2 teaspoon cayenne (optional)

HOT TIMES MOP (OPTIONAL)

2 cups chicken or turkey stock

1/4 cup vegetable oil

1/4 cup pickling liquid from a jar or can of pickled jalapeños

1/4 cup jalapeño jelly

Jalapeach Barbecue Sauce (page 384) or Bar-B-Q Ranch Sauce (page 375) (optional)

1. The night before you plan to barbecue, mix the injection liquid ingredients in a small bowl. With a kitchen syringe, inject all but about 2 tablespoons of the mixture deep into the turkey breast in a half-dozen places, moving the needle around in each spot to shoot the liquid in several directions. Using your fingers, massage the breast with the rest of the liquid, working it as far as possible under the skin without tearing the skin.

2. Stir together the rub ingredients in a small bowl. Massage the breast well with the mixture, again rubbing it over and under the skin. Place the breast in a plastic bag and refrigerate it overnight.

3. Prepare the smoker for barbecuing, bringing the temperature to 200°F to 220°F.

4. Remove the turkey breast from the refrigerator and let it sit at room temperature for about

30 minutes. Cut a 3-foot length of cheesecloth and dampen it thoroughly with water. Wrap the breast in the cheesecloth and tie the ends.

5. Transfer the breast to the smoker, skin side up (you should be able to feel through the cheesecloth), and cook for 1¼ to 1½ hours per pound, until the internal temperature reaches 180°F. Wet the cheesecloth down with more water at 30-minute intervals in a wood-burning pit, or as appropriate for your style of smoker.

6. After 4 hours, remove the cheesecloth, snipping it with scissors if necessary, and discard it. When the cheesecloth is removed, baste the turkey for the remainder of its cooking time, if possible in your smoker (see page 45, "To Mop or Not"). If you plan to baste, combine the mop ingredients in a saucepan and warm the mixture over low heat. Mop every 30 minutes in a wood-burning pit, or as appropriate for your style of smoker.

7. When the turkey is done, remove it from the smoker and allow it to sit for 10 minutes before carving. Serve with Jalapeach Barbecue Sauce or Bar-B-Q Ranch Sauce if you wish.

SERVING SUGGESTION For a different spin on a holiday meal, offer Little Devils (page 344) and Sangrita Marias (page 477) while everyone gathers. Sit down to Texas Terrine (page 364) for the first course. Accompany the turkey breast with Drunken Sweet Potatoes (page 282), San Antonio Cactus and Corn Salad (page 421), spinach sautéed with garlic, and Blue Corn Muffins (page 412). Prodigal Pecan Pie (page 442) makes a great ending.

VARIATION: GLAZED HOT TIMES JALAPEÑO TURKEY BREAST If you want a quick glaze for the turkey breast, heat together equal portions of jalapeño jelly and chicken stock. Spoon it over individual slices or offer it on the side.

Wildly Stuffed Turkey Breast

In the dozen-plus years since we developed this recipe, it's become a big-time favorite in Cheryl's family. Of course, it works well for Thanksgiving, but we also prepare it for other special fall and winter dinners. SERVES 6 TO 8

4¹/2-pound to 5¹/2-pound boneless turkey breast, preferably skin-on

¹/4 cup turkey or chicken stock

3 tablespoons vegetable oil

2 tablespoons frozen orange juice concentrate, thawed

WILD PASTE

3 garlic cloves, minced

2 tablespoons unsalted butter, softened

1 tablespoon frozen orange juice concentrate, thawed

1 tablespoon kosher salt or coarse sea salt

STUFFING

¹/3 cup dried cranberries

3 tablespoons frozen orange juice concentrate, thawed

¹/4 cup unsalted butter

¹/2 cup chopped red onion

2 garlic cloves, minced

2 cups cooked wild rice (or half wild rice and half brown rice)

¹/3 cup chopped pecan pieces

3 tablespoons minced fresh thyme or parsley

3 tablespoons turkey or chicken stock

Kosher salt or coarse sea salt

1. The night before you plan to barbecue the turkey, pound the meat if it's uneven in thickness. Mix the stock, oil, and orange juice concentrate in a small bowl. With a kitchen syringe, inject the mixture deep into the turkey breast in a half-dozen places, moving the needle around in each spot to shoot the liquid in several different directions.

2. Combine the paste ingredients in a small bowl. Using your fingers, spread the paste over the turkey breast. Place in a plastic bag and refrigerate overnight.

3. Prepare the smoker for barbecuing, bringing the temperature to 200°F to 220°F.

4. Remove the turkey breast from the refrigerator and let it sit at room temperature for about 30 minutes.

5. Make the stuffing for the turkey while it sits. Combine the cranberries with the orange juice concentrate in a small bowl. Melt the butter in a small skillet over medium heat. Add the onion and sauté it briefly until soft. Scrape the mixture into a bowl and add the remaining ingredients, including the cranberry–orange juice mixture. Spoon the stuffing compactly over the turkey and roll it up from one of the longer sides. Secure the roll with kitchen twine. Tie it snug but leave room for the filling to expand a bit while cooking.

6. Cut a 3-foot length of cheesecloth and dampen it thoroughly with water. Wrap the breast in the cheesecloth and tie the ends.

7. Transfer the turkey to the smoker. Plan to

cook it about 1¼ to 1½ hours per pound, until the internal temperature reaches 180°F. Wet the cheesecloth down with more hot water at 30-minute intervals in a wood-burning pit, or as appropriate for your style of smoker.

8. After about 3 hours, remove the cheesecloth, snipping it with scissors, and discard it. Continue smoking the turkey until done. When the turkey is cooked, remove it from the smoker and allow it to sit for 10 minutes before carving into thick slices.

BBQ tip You will likely need to call your butcher ahead to get a full boneless breast. If the breast turns out to be smaller than our suggested size, it will work fine, but you may have more stuffing than meat. Spoon any overflow into a baking dish, cover it, and warm it in a conventional oven or on the smoker, to serve along with the turkey breast.

SECRET TO A SANE HOLIDAY

Though we love to smoke our own turkeys, we admit to taking a shortcut sometimes when it's cold outside. Greenberg's in Tyler, Texas (gobblegobble.com, 903-595-0725), has almost 60 years of experience in smoking turkeys and has perfected the art. You won't find a better commercial holiday bird in the country, and they'll ship them anywhere.

In the past two decades, the number of barbecue cook-offs and festivals around the country has grown from a few dozen to many hundred. They are scattered from Florida to Alaska, from California to Massachusetts, and the prizes range from a ribbon up to thousands of dollars in cash in big national competitions.

Hot Browns

Louisville's grand old hotel, The Brown, developed the tasty "Hot Brown" sandwich, which we embellish here by using smoked turkey, preferably our own leftovers.

SERVES 2

CHEESE SAUCE

3 tablespoons unsalted butter

1 tablespoon minced onion

1½ tablespoons all-purpose flour

1 cup whole milk

1 teaspoon Worcestershire sauce

¼ teaspoon dry mustard

¼ teaspoon paprika

½ cup shredded mild or medium-sharp cheddar cheese (about 2 ounces)

Table salt to taste

4 slices good white bread

½ pound sliced or shredded smoked turkey breast, warmed

4 slices bacon, fried crisp

4 thin slices red-ripe tomato

1½ tablespoons grated Parmesan cheese

1. Preheat the oven to 350°F.

2. Start the cheese sauce by melting the but-

ter over medium heat in a heavy saucepan. Add the onion and sauté briefly until it is softened. Stir in the flour and continue stirring a minute or two. Add the milk, Worcestershire sauce, mustard, and paprika and heat until thickened, 3 to 5 minutes. Turn the heat down to low and sprinkle in the cheese, stirring to melt it evenly. Taste the sauce and add salt if needed. Keep the sauce warm in the top of a double boiler until you are ready to use it.

3. Toast the bread and cut each slice on the diagonal. Arrange the slices on two plates. Top each plate with half of the turkey and cheese sauce. Arrange the bacon slices, tomato, and sprinklings of Parmesan evenly over both. Pop the plates in the oven for 5 minutes. Serve immediately.

Two-Steppin' Turkey Legs

You'll be two-stepping yourself when you wrap your fist around one of these drumsticks and steer it into your mouth. SERVES 6

6 turkey drumsticks

3 tablespoons Worcestershire sauce

1 tablespoon vegetable oil

TWO-STEPPIN' LEG RUB

2 tablespoons kosher salt or coarse sea salt

1 tablespoon coarsely ground black pepper

1 tablespoon onion powder

1 tablespoon packed brown sugar

1/2 teaspoon cayenne

TWO-STEPPIN' LEG MOP (OPTIONAL)

1 cup white vinegar

1 tablespoon Worcestershire sauce

1 tablespoon vegetable oil

Black Sauce (page 378) (optional)

1. At least 4 hours before you plan to barbecue, and preferably the night before, loosen the skin on the turkey legs by running your fingers under it as far as possible without tearing the skin.

2. In a small bowl, combine the Worcestershire sauce and oil. In another small bowl, combine the dry rub spices. Coat your fingers with the wet mixture and rub it well over the legs, getting as much as you can under the skin. Then sprinkle on the dry seasonings liberally, again rubbing as much under the skin as possible. Reserve any remaining dry rub. Place the legs in a plastic bag and refrigerate for at least 4 hours, or overnight.

3. Prepare the smoker for barbecuing, bringing the temperature to 200°F to 220°F.

4. Remove the turkey legs from the refrigerator and let them sit at room temperature for about 30 minutes.

5. If you plan to baste the legs (see page 45, "To Mop or Not"), combine the mop ingredients with any remaining dry rub in a small saucepan and warm the mixture over low heat.

6. Transfer the turkey legs to the smoker. Cook until the legs are very tender and the juices run clear, 3 1/2 to 4 hours. Mop the legs at 45-minute intervals in a wood-burning pit, or as appropriate in your style of smoker. Serve the legs hot, to be eaten with your fingers. Brush on Black Sauce if you wish.

SERVING SUGGESTION Gobble the legs with down-home fare, such as Devil-May-Care Eggs (page 431), Sweet and Sour Cukes (page 420), and Buttermilk Onion Rings (page 401).

Quacker 'Q'

If you want to show off like a professional chef, dunk a duck in this marinade, similar to one created by James Beard, the master of American cooking. The Asian-accented marinade and plum finishing sauce will part your lips into a gorgeous smile.

SERVES 4 TO 6

Four to six 5-ounce duck breast halves

JAMES BEARD'S BASIC BARBECUE MARINADE

1/2 cup reduced-sodium soy sauce

1/2 cup dry sherry

1/2 cup strong brewed tea

2 tablespoons honey

2 tablespoons peanut oil

1 teaspoon freshly ground black pepper

1/2 teaspoon ground anise

1/2 teaspoon ground cloves

1 garlic clove, minced

Plum Good Slopping Sauce (page 387) (optional)

1. About 3 hours before you plan to barbecue, arrange a bamboo steamer over a saucepan of water and place the duck breasts in the steamer. Steam the breasts over medium-high heat for 20 minutes. Discard the greasy steaming liquid.

2. While the breasts steam, mix the marinade ingredients in a large glass measuring cup. Place the breasts in a shallow, nonreactive dish or plastic bag and pour the marinade over them. Refrigerate for 2 hours.

3. Prepare the smoker for barbecuing, bringing the temperature to 200°F to 220°F.

4. Remove the breasts from the refrigerator and drain, reserving the marinade if you plan to baste the meat (see page 45, "To Mop or Not"). To make the mop, bring the marinade to a vigorous boil over high heat in a heavy saucepan. Boil until reduced by about one-third.

5. Transfer the breasts to the smoker, skin sides up, and cook for 65 to 75 minutes. Mop the breasts immediately and at 30-minute intervals in a wood-burning pit, or as appropriate for your style of smoker. The breasts should be well-done, but still juicy, with some crispy caramelized edges.

6. Let the breasts sit for 5 minutes before slicing the meat on the diagonal. Serve hot or chilled, with Plum Good Slopping Sauce if you wish.

SERVING SUGGESTION Serve the duck with Wonderful Watermelon Pickles (page 435), Creamy Coleslaw (page 390), white or brown rice, and Wild Huckleberry Pie with Coconut Crumble (page 446).

VARIATION: QUACKER 'Q' WITH GREEN PEPPERCORN RUB Eliminate the marinade. Chop 3 tablespoons drained green peppercorns (the kind that come in little jars with brine) together with 1 tablespoon coarse salt and 2 teaspoons ground black pepper. This may be easiest in a mini food processor. Rub the mixture lightly over the duck breasts. No mop is necessary for keeping the breasts moist. Serve with the plum sauce.

BBQ tip When you barbecue fatty meats, the fat tends to melt away during the cooking process. This general rule doesn't apply to ducks, which shed their excess pounds more reluctantly than a Sumo wrestler. The time-tested method of steaming the birds first keeps you from having to tend the pit all night.

Duck Pastrami

A pastrami cure works great on a duck breast because of the density and sweetness of the meat. Leave on the skin during the cooking process to naturally baste the breasts. Unlike in some of our duck recipes, we skip the initial steaming step in favor of a lengthier soak over smoke. It results in a heartier pastrami-like flavor and texture. SERVES 4 TO 6

DELI-CIOUS RUB
3 tablespoons kosher salt or coarse sea salt
2 tablespoons cracked black pepper
2 tablespoons cracked coriander seeds
2 tablespoons cracked mustard seeds
1 tablespoon garlic powder
1 tablespoon packed light brown sugar

Four to six 5-ounce duck breast halves

DELI-CIOUS MOP (OPTIONAL)
1/2 cup white vinegar

Coarse mustard (optional)

1. The night before you plan to barbecue, combine the rub ingredients in a small bowl. If you plan to mop the duck breasts, set aside 1 tablespoon of the rub for the mop. Rub the duck breasts with the mixture, rubbing it under and over the skin, without tearing the skin.

2. Place the duck breasts in a shallow dish, skin sides up, and scatter any remaining rub over them. Cover with plastic and refrigerate overnight.

3. Prepare the smoker for barbecuing, bringing the temperature to 200°F to 220°F.

4. Remove the breasts from the refrigerator and pat them dry. If you plan to baste the duck (see page 45, "To Mop or Not"), combine the reserved 1 tablespoon rub with the vinegar and warm the mop over low heat.

5. Transfer the breasts to the smoker, skin sides up, and cook until nearly all the pink is gone from the meat, 1¼ to 1½ hours. (Check with a small knife cut in 1 breast.) Mop the breasts immediately and at 30-minute intervals in a wood-burning pit, or as appropriate for your style of smoker.

6. Let the breasts sit for 5 minutes before slicing them paper-thin on the diagonal. Serve hot or chilled, with a dollop of mustard if you wish.

Tea-Smoked Duck

When we wrote *Smoke & Spice* originally, we considered including this triumph of Chinese cooking but ultimately concluded that it would seem too exotic in a book that celebrated real American barbecue. So guess what dish people have asked us about more than any other in the ensuing years? Traditionally smoked in a large sealed wok, here is a version designed for an American smoker. **SERVES 4 TO 6**

DUCK PASTE

1/4 cup cracked Szechwan brown peppercorns

1/4 cup peeled and minced fresh ginger

Minced dried zest of 2 oranges or tangerines (see BBQ tip on page 28)

1 1/2 tablespoons kosher salt or coarse sea salt

1 tablespoon ground cinnamon

1 teaspoon Chinese five-spice powder

Two 4-pound to 4 1/2-pound ducks

5 tablespoons black or oolong tea leaves

12 cups (3 quarts) water

3 whole cinnamon sticks

Peel of 1 orange or tangerine in large sections

1 tablespoon Szechwan brown peppercorns

1 to 2 star anise (optional)

1. At least 10 hours and up to 24 hours before you plan to barbecue, combine the paste ingredients in a food processor or with a mortar and pestle. Rub the ducks with the paste thoroughly inside and out, and over and under the skin, being careful to avoid tearing the skin. Reserve 2 tablespoons of the paste if you plan to mop the ducks, and refrigerate it. Wrap the ducks in plastic and refrigerate them.

2. About 2 hours before you begin to barbecue, take the ducks from the refrigerator and let them sit at room temperature for 30 minutes. Prepare the tea for steaming the ducks. Place the tea leaves in a large heatproof bowl. Bring the water just to a boil, and pour it over the tea leaves. Let the mixture steep for 10 minutes. Pour the tea through a strainer into a large saucepan, reserving about 3 cups of the tea if you plan to mop the ducks. Place the leftover tea leaves in a disposable pie pan or other smoke-proof dish and add the cinnamon sticks, orange peel, peppercorns, and optional star anise. Set aside.

3. Arrange a bamboo steamer over the saucepan of tea and place the ducks in the steamer. (If one steamer isn't large enough for the two ducks, make a double batch of tea and use two saucepans and steamers.) Steam the ducks over medium-high heat for 1 1/2 hours. Discard the greasy steaming liquid.

4. If you plan to baste the ducks (see page 45, "To Mop or Not"), combine the reserved 2 tablespoons paste and 3 cups tea in a small saucepan and warm the mixture over low heat.

5. Prepare your smoker for barbecuing, bringing the temperature to 200°F to 220°F.

6. Place the pan of tea leaves and spices on your

smoker's lower grate or shelf. Place the ducks on the upper grate or shelf directly over the pan of spices. (If your smoker has a single grate, arrange the pan and the ducks alongside each other, with the pan closer to the heat source.) Cook for 4½ to 5 hours, mopping with the tea at 1-hour intervals in a wood-burning pit, or as appropriate for your style of smoker. The ducks will darken to a deep mahogany and their leg joints will move easily when done.

SERVING SUGGESTION Many Chinese cookbooks give recipes for scallion pancakes, which are delicious eaten warm with the duck. For a quick substitute, use thin flour tortillas or other "wrap" flatbread. Place a few slices of duck in the bread. Sprinkle with a few scallion rings, and spoon a bit of West Coast Wonder (page 379) barbecue sauce over. Roll up and savor.

VARIATION FOR LEFTOVERS: TEA-SMOKED DUCK WITH LONG-LIFE CHINESE NOODLES Reserve a cup or so of the duck from the first meal for this second dish. Reheat the duck and slice it (with skin) into matchsticks. Make a sauce by sautéing 2 garlic cloves in 1 tablespoon vegetable oil, then add ½ cup chicken stock, 2 tablespoons dry sherry, and 1 tablespoon each reduced-sodium soy sauce, Chinese oyster sauce, and toasted sesame oil. Cook 12 ounces thin egg noodles—leave those noodles long for a long and prosperous life!—and toss with the sauce and the duck. Add a few bright bits of vegetables, such as slivers of red bell pepper, snow peas, and scallions, and serve.

"SLOW DOWN, TAKE YOUR TIME. YOU'RE PROBABLY ONLY GOING BACK TO WORK."

That's one of Sparky's many sayings at Sparky's Roadside Barbecue, located in a modest storefront in downtown Miami, roadside to high-rise towers and a Metro station. Sparky, the nickname of both owners, offers a menu of barbecue basics plus a few curiosities like barbecued duck and a pulled pork variation on the popular Cubano sandwich.

Dandy Little Hens

We think Cornish game hens often look more appetizing than they taste, but in this case, the little birds burst with flavor. SERVES 4

DANDY DUNK

1½ cups tequila

1 cup freshly squeezed lime juice

¼ cup triple sec or other orange-flavored liqueur

¼ cup minced onion

¼ cup vegetable oil

2 tablespoons Worcestershire sauce

Pinch of cayenne or crushed chile de árbol

4 Cornish hens, 1¼ to 1½ pounds each

Kosher salt or coarse sea salt and freshly ground black pepper to taste

1 lime, sliced into 4 wedges

1 small orange, sliced

DANDY MOP (OPTIONAL)

2 tablespoons unsalted butter

1 tablespoon triple sec or other orange-flavored liqueur

Sauce Olé (page 379), South Florida Citrus Sauce (page 386), or Mango-Habanero Hellfire (page 387) (optional)

1. At least 4 hours and up to 12 hours before you plan to barbecue, combine the marinade ingredients in a large glass measuring cup. Place the game hens in a shallow, nonreactive dish or plastic bag, pour the marinade over them, and refrigerate. Turn the hens occasionally.

2. Prepare the smoker for barbecuing, bringing the temperature to 200°F to 220°F.

3. Remove the hens from the refrigerator. Drain the hens, reserving the marinade if you plan to baste them. Salt and pepper the birds lightly, stuff their cavities with the fruit, and let them sit at room temperature for about 20 minutes.

4. If you are going to use the mop (see page 45, "To Mop or Not"), bring the marinade to a vigorous boil over high heat in a small saucepan and boil for several minutes. Stir in the butter and triple sec and keep the mop warm over low heat.

5. Transfer the hens to the smoker, breast sides down, and cook for 2¼ to 2½ hours. Baste the birds with the mop every 30 minutes in a wood-burning pit, or as appropriate in your style of smoker. Turn the hens over about halfway through the cooking time. When the birds are done, their legs will move freely and the internal temperature should be 180°F to 185°F.

6. Let the hens sit for 5 to 10 minutes. Remove the skin and slice to serve. Pass a bowl of Sauce Olé, South Florida Citrus Sauce, or Mango-Habanero Hellfire if you wish.

SERVING SUGGESTION Start a summer meal by nibbling on Chicken's Little Livers (page 358) or guacamole and chips while sipping Firewater (page 475). Accompany the hens with Killed Salad (page 418) and Burstin' with Black-Eyed Peas Salad (page 419). A finale of Texas Peach Cobbler (page 452) should leave your guests smiling.

Kevin Bludso brought generations of Texas barbecue traditions west with him to create some reality cooking in the land of make-believe. His weekday lunch specials at Bludso's BBQ in Compton must be one of the best bargains in California. On Fridays, for example, a pork or chicken link sandwich with greens or mac and cheese costs $4, less than the hourly parking rate in most parts of the city.

Mushroom-Stuffed Quail

Another miniature fowl, quail has more inherent flavor than Cornish game hens, so it doesn't require as heavy a hand with the seasoning. SERVES 2 TO 4

1/4 cup dried mushrooms, such as morels or cèpes

1 cup warm water

4 quail

1 tablespoon extra-virgin olive oil

Table salt and freshly ground black pepper to taste

4 garlic cloves, slivered

2 bay leaves, halved

MUSHROOM MOP (OPTIONAL)

1/2 cup chicken stock

1 tablespoon extra-virgin olive oil

2 garlic cloves, minced

1. Prepare the smoker for barbecuing, bringing the temperature to 200°F to 220°F.

2. Combine the mushrooms and warm water in a small bowl and soak for 30 minutes.

3. Prepare the quail, cutting off their necks if necessary. Rub the quail with the oil inside and out, and then salt and pepper them liberally. Drain the mushrooms, reserving their liquid if you plan to baste the quail. Stuff each quail with the mushrooms, garlic, and bay leaves. Truss their tiny legs.

4. If you are going to use the mop (see page 45, "To Mop or Not"), pour the mushroom soaking liquid through a fine-mesh strainer into a small saucepan. Add the stock, oil, and garlic and warm the mop over low heat.

5. Transfer the quail to the smoker, breast sides down, and mop them every 20 to 30 minutes in a wood-burning pit, or as appropriate for your style of smoker. The quail are ready when they are well browned and their legs move easily at the joints, 1 1/2 to 2 hours. Serve the quail immediately, 1 or 2 to a portion.

Rosy Rosemary Quail

A bath in red wine turns these bantam birds a pleasant pink before they brown.

SERVES 4 TO 8

ROSEMARY MARINADE AND OPTIONAL MOP

3/4 cup dry red wine

3/4 cup red wine vinegar

3/4 cup extra-virgin olive oil

12 garlic cloves, minced

1 1/2 teaspoons crushed dried rosemary

8 quail, butterflied (see BBQ tip)

Kosher salt or coarse sea salt and freshly ground black pepper to taste

1. At least 3 hours and up to 4 hours before you plan to barbecue, combine the marinade ingredients in a large glass measuring cup. Arrange the quail in a shallow, nonreactive dish or plastic bag, pour the marinade over them, and refrigerate.

2. Prepare the smoker for barbecuing, bringing the temperature to 200°F to 220°F.

3. Drain the quail, reserving the marinade if you plan to baste the birds. Salt and pepper the quail lightly and let them sit at room temperature for about 20 minutes.

4. If you are going to use the mop (see page 45, "To Mop or Not"), bring the marinade to a vigorous boil and boil it for several minutes. Keep the mop warm over low heat.

5. Transfer the quail to the smoker, skin sides up, and cook until well browned and a little crispy, 1 1/2 to 2 hours. Mop every 30 minutes in a wood-burning pit, or as appropriate for your style of smoker. Serve the quail immediately.

SERVING SUGGESTION We usually offer Unholy Swiss Cheese (page 341) and more red wine for openers. With the quail, serve mixed greens dressed with vinaigrette and potato slices sautéed with garlic and thyme. Try a fruity dessert, such as Wild Huckleberry Pie with Coconut Crumble (page 446).

BBQ tip If your quail don't come butterflied, the little birds are easy to prepare yourself. Cut through the fragile breastbone, chop off the neck, and flatten as needed.

Fruited Pheasant

Farm-raised pheasants taste a lot like free-range chickens. This recipe makes the most of that flavor. SERVES 5 TO 6

PHEASANT MARINADE

4 cups cranberry-apple juice

1/2 cup balsamic vinegar

1/2 cup vegetable oil

6 garlic cloves, minced

1 tablespoon Worcestershire sauce

2 pheasants, 2 1/2 to 3 pounds each

2 teaspoons kosher salt or coarse sea salt

1 teaspoon freshly ground black pepper

PHEASANT MOP (OPTIONAL)

1/2 cup chicken stock

DRESSING

1/2 cup dried currants

1/2 cup cranberry-apple juice

3 tablespoons unsalted butter

1 medium onion, chopped

4 ounces mushrooms, sliced (wild varieties are especially nice)

1/2 cup chopped celery

1/2 cup pecan pieces

1/4 cup chopped fresh parsley

1/2 teaspoon dried marjoram

1/2 teaspoon dried thyme

1/2 cup raw wild rice cooked in chicken stock according to package directions

1/2 cup raw brown rice cooked in chicken stock according to package directions

1/2 cup chicken stock

Kosher salt or coarse sea salt to taste

Apple City Apple Sauce (page 384) (optional)

1. The night before you plan to barbecue, combine the marinade ingredients in a large glass measuring cup. Using your fingers, loosen the birds' skins, trying to avoid tearing them. Place the pheasants in a plastic bag and pour the marinade ingredients over the birds. Refrigerate them overnight, turning at least once, if needed, to soak the birds evenly.

2. Remove the pheasants from the refrigerator and drain them, reserving the marinade if you plan to baste the birds. Salt and pepper the pheasants inside and out, being sure to rub some under the skin. Let them sit at room temperature for 30 to 45 minutes.

3. Prepare the smoker for barbecuing, bringing the temperature to 200°F to 220°F.

4. If you are going to use the mop (see page 45, "To Mop or Not"), bring the marinade and stock to a vigorous boil in a large saucepan and boil for several minutes. Keep the mop warm over low heat.

5. Transfer the pheasants to the smoker, breast sides down. Cook for about 3 hours, mopping the birds every 30 minutes in a wood-burning pit, or as appropriate in your style of smoker.

6. While the pheasants cook, make the dressing. In a small bowl, combine the currants with the cranberry-apple juice and let them steep for about 15 minutes.

7. Warm the butter in a smoke-proof skillet. Add the onion, mushrooms, celery, and pecans. Sauté until the vegetables soften. Mix in the herbs, cooked rice, chicken stock, and currants (with any remaining liquid). Add salt, if needed. Cover the dressing with foil and refrigerate.

8. After the pheasants have smoked for about 2 hours, transfer the dressing skillet to the smoker. Continue smoking until the pheasants' internal temperatures measure 160°F. The juices will run pink if pierced. The dressing will be ready at the same time as the pheasant. If you want to add a smokier flavor to the dressing, uncover it during the last 15 minutes, adding a little water if the mixture appears dry.

9. Remove the pheasants from the smoker, tent them with foil, and let them sit for 10 minutes before carving. Accompany the sliced pheasants with the hot dressing and, if you wish, Apple City Apple Sauce.

SERVING SUGGESTION Munch on Curry Pecans (page 344) while waiting for the pheasant. Add a Southern Caesar Salad (page 416) and Cranberry-Ginger Crumble (page 456) topped with cranberry sorbet to round out the meal.

BBQ tip If you're cooking food in a smoker in a pan or skillet, try to find a container that won't discolor easily from the smoke, such as a cast-iron pot, or something that can be cleaned with relative ease, such as a Pyrex dish. Disposable foil pans are a good option, too. Other utensils may require a lot of scrubbing to remove the dark smoke color, particularly if you're barbecuing in a wood-burning pit.

SOMETHING ELSE TO MAKE MILWAUKEE FAMOUS

Milwaukee makes lots of beer, of course, so we figured there had to be some good barbecue, too. We found it at the Speed Queen, mainly at the time a take-out business with limited seating. The kitchen puts together plates and sandwiches that look like Sloppy Joes but taste like genuine 'Q.' Ask for "outside meat," the blackened exterior cuts often known farther south as "Mr. Brown."

DON'T GO TO TEXAS WITHOUT IT

Robb Walsh's *Legends of Texas Barbecue Cookbook* (2002, Chronicle Books) is the ultimate guide to its fascinating subject. Walsh entertains and enlightens at the same time, telling stories about the men behind the meat, offering time-honored recipes, giving good advice on where to eat, listing cook-offs to attend, and much more. All Texans need a copy, and so does any visitor who wants to venture into the soul of the state.

FISHING FOR COMPLIMENTS

BEFORE PORK SHOULDER, LONG BEFORE BRISKET, FISH WAS AMERICA'S FAVORITE BARBECUE FARE. WHEN SPANISH AND BRITISH EXPLORERS ARRIVED IN THE NEW WORLD CENTURIES AGO, THEY FOUND NATIVE AMERICANS SMOKING THEIR FOOD OVER WOOD FIRES. FROM THE CARIBBEAN ALL THE WAY OVER TO THE PACIFIC NORTHWEST, DIFFERENT TRIBES USED A SIMILAR METHOD OF COOKING THE CATCH OF THE DAY. THEY DIDN'T OFFER THE EUROPEANS TAKE-OUT FROM A "SANDY'S

Salmon Bar-B-Q" joint, but the natives did share their smoking secrets, and they even gave the newcomers the term *barbecue*.

Today, most smoked fish in markets and restaurants is smoke-cured rather than smoke-cooked in a barbecue manner, but both processes yield delicious results. As the original Americans knew long before Columbus or Sir Walter Raleigh, the fusion of flavors in fish and smoke is a natural bounty.

Kingly Salmon

For thousands of years before the arrival of Europeans, Native Americans in the Pacific Northwest perfected ways to cook salmon, their most abundant food. They boiled the fish in watertight baskets, steamed them in underground rock ovens, and, in one of their tastiest preparations, smoke-roasted split sides of the salmon over an alder wood fire. To preserve fish for the winter, the Indians smoked their catch until it was fully dehydrated, but during the season, they cooked it similar to this for immediate eating. A butterflied tail section from a Pacific king salmon offers royal flavor, but coho or silver salmon make regal meals, too. SERVES 8

KINGLY RUB

1/4 cup dried dill

1/4 cup packed brown sugar

2 teaspoons kosher salt or coarse sea salt

2 teaspoons freshly ground black pepper

3-pound to 3 1/2-pound salmon tail section, boned and butterflied

KINGLY MOP (OPTIONAL)

1 cup cider vinegar

1/4 cup vegetable oil

1. The night before you plan to barbecue, combine the rub ingredients in a small bowl. Open the salmon flat and massage it well with about two-thirds of the rub. Fold the salmon back into its original shape, place it in a plastic bag, and refrigerate it overnight.

2. Prepare the smoker for barbecuing, bringing the temperature to 180°F to 200°F.

3. Remove the salmon from the refrigerator and let it sit at room temperature for 30 minutes.

4. If you plan to baste the fish (see page 45, "To Mop or Not"), stir the remaining rub together with the mop ingredients in a small saucepan and warm the mixture over low heat.

5. Transfer the salmon to the smoker, skin side down, placing the fish as far from the fire as possible. Cook for 55 to 65 minutes, mopping it after 10 and 30 minutes in a wood-burning pit, or as appropriate for your style of smoker. The salmon should flake easily when done. Have a large spatula and a platter ready when taking the salmon off the smoker, because it can fall apart easily. Serve hot or chilled.

SERVING SUGGESTION Serve with Arty Rice Salad (page 429), Smoked Spud Skins (page 284), and some crusty bread. Rhubarb Crunch (page 451) would be wonderful for dessert.

BBQ tip Alder remains the best wood for smoking Pacific salmon. Alder chips are fairly common across the country, but you may have more difficulty finding the wood in chunks or logs. Fruit woods are the best substitute, particularly when mixed with smaller pieces of alder.

DON'T TRY IT ON THE MATTRESS

Chief cook Jim Ward designed and built the smoker for the Porky Pilots, an old-time barbecue contest team composed entirely of Federal Express pilots. The basic concept for the pit, Jim told us, came from the old Southern practice of barbecuing over a slow fire on discarded bedsprings, using a junked car hood for a cover. Back then, he says, when pitmasters didn't have thermometers, they could tell they were cooking at the right temperature if the flies stayed away from the meat.

Simply Superb Salmon

If you have access to superb fresh salmon, such as Alaskan Copper River salmon or other wild Pacific varieties, the best preparation is the simplest. The fish cost more than their farm-raised Atlantic cousins, but the difference in flavor may be even greater than the difference in cost. This is summer eating at its best and most elemental. SERVES 3 TO 4

1½-pound salmon fillet, preferably Copper River king or sockeye salmon

Kosher salt or coarse sea salt and freshly cracked black pepper

LEMON SPLASH

¾ cup chicken stock or fish stock

¼ cup freshly squeezed lemon juice

2 tablespoons chopped onion

¼ cup unsalted butter

1½ teaspoons Worcestershire sauce

1½ teaspoons yellow mustard

1 teaspoon Seafaring Seafood Rub (page 28) or ½ teaspoon more kosher salt or coarse sea salt

Lemon wedges (optional)

1. Prepare the smoker for barbecuing, bringing the temperature to 180°F to 200°F.

2. Remove the salmon from the refrigerator, sprinkle it rather boldly with salt and pepper, and let it sit, covered, at room temperature for 15 to 20 minutes.

3. Combine the mop ingredients in a saucepan and warm over low heat. Drizzle the salmon once with about one-third of the mop and transfer it to the smoker. Smoke it until just cooked through and flaky, 35 to 45 minutes for a fillet of about ½–inch thickness. In our experience, fillets of Copper River salmon tend to be thinner than many farm-raised. If your fish is thicker than ½ inch, simply add a few minutes to the cooking time. Mop once again after about 20 minutes in a wood-burning pit, or as appropriate for your style of smoker (see page 45, "To Mop or Not"). Have a large spatula and a platter ready for taking the salmon off the smoker, since it will be fragile when done. Drizzle a bit more mop over the fish as it comes off if you didn't during its cooking. Transfer the salmon to the serving platter. Serve warm or lightly chilled, garnished with lemon if you wish.

SERVING SUGGESTION Stretch the salmon to serve more folks by using it as an appetizer. Flake it into small chunks, arrange atop thin slices of pumpernickel, toasted white bread, or simple crackers. Add a bit of sour cream or crème fraîche, then crown with a dill sprig, a few pearls of salmon caviar, lemon zest, or tiny dices of red or yellow tomato.

BBQ tip Hot-smoked salmon differs substantially from cold-smoked lox or nova in its texture. Cold-smoked salmon has a silky, slick feel to it, where hot-smoked salmon is a bit drier, flakes easily, and is generally more permeated with smoke. We like either hot- or cold-smoked on a bagel, but prefer the hot-smoked variety for hashes, pastas, and other dishes where flaky chunks provide a more satisfactory texture.

with superb fresh salmon, such as Alaskan Copper River salmon or other wild Pacific varieties, the best preparation is the simplest

Sugar-and-Spice Brined Salmon

You can't open a food magazine these days without someone telling you to brine your pork, fish, chicken, you name it. While we think the idea—a heavily salted marinating liquid, sometimes with a sweetener added—has gotten a little overhyped, it serves an important role in many instances. Sometimes it's used to aid with preservation; other times it firms the texture of an ingredient or, as in this marinade, adds flavor interest to everyone's favorite fish. SERVES 4 OR MORE

SUGAR-AND-SPICE MARINADE

3/4 cup vodka

1/3 cup packed brown sugar

3 tablespoons kosher salt or coarse sea salt

2 tablespoons mixed pickling spice, bruised (see BBQ tip)

2 teaspoons dill seeds, bruised (see BBQ tip)

1 1/2-pound salmon fillet

1 cup water

Large bunch of fresh dill (optional)

1. At least 2 hours and up to 8 hours before you plan to smoke the fish, combine the marinade ingredients in a glass measuring cup. Place the salmon in a plastic bag or shallow dish, pour the marinade over it, and refrigerate it for at least 1 hour. Leave it longer to intensify the seasoning.

2. Prepare the smoker for barbecuing, bringing the temperature to 180°F to 200°F.

3. Remove the salmon from the refrigerator and drain it, reserving the marinade if you plan to baste the fish (see page 45, "To Mop or Not"). Leave any clinging spices on the surface of the salmon. Let the fish sit uncovered at room temperature for 15 to 20 minutes.

4. If you are using the marinade as a mop, stir the brine together with the water in a small saucepan and boil vigorously for a few minutes.

5. Transfer the salmon to the smoker, skin side down. Cook for 45 to 55 minutes, mopping it after 10 and 30 minutes in a wood-burning pit, or as appropriate for your style of smoker. Have a large spatula and a platter ready for taking the salmon off the smoker, since it will be fragile when done. We prefer to serve the salmon with some of the whole spices clinging to it. The fish can be eaten immediately or refrigerated and later served chilled. If you are using the fresh dill, arrange it on a serving platter. Top the dill with the salmon and serve.

BBQ tip Bruising the spices means to almost—but not quite—crush the whole spice seeds or pods. By pressing on the spices with a pestle or the side of a knife, you release the natural oils, making the seasonings more flavorful.

Tom Douglas's Sake-Cured Hot-Smoked Salmon

Our friend Tom helped define Pacific Northwest cuisine, which draws heartily on influences from around the Pacific Rim. He does amazing things with meat and local fish at his many popular Seattle restaurants. In this dish, smoking yields very rich Asian-accented little tidbits for a small lucky group. The recipe first appeared in *Tom Douglas' Seattle Kitchen* (2001, William Morrow). **SERVES 4 TO 8**

SAKE MARINADE

1 cup reduced-sodium soy sauce

1/2 cup water

1/4 cup sake

3/4 cup packed brown sugar

8 slices peeled fresh ginger "coins," 1/8 inch thick (see BBQ tip)

1 tablespoon chopped garlic

2 teaspoons kosher salt or coarse sea salt

1-pound salmon fillet, skinned and cut into 8 pieces

8 fresh sage leaves

1. The day before you plan to barbecue, whisk together the marinade ingredients in a large glass measuring cup, mixing until the sugar dissolves. Place the salmon in a nonreactive container and pour the marinade over it. Cover and refrigerate for at least 12 hours, turning occasionally if needed to totally submerge the fish.

2. Remove the salmon pieces from the marinade (reserving about 1/4 cup of it) and place the fish on a rack sprayed with oil set over a baking sheet. Refrigerate, uncovered, for the glaze to set, about 2 hours. Refrigerate the reserved marinade also.

3. Prepare the smoker for barbecuing, bringing the temperature to 180°F to 200°F.

4. Remove the salmon from the refrigerator and let it sit at room temperature for about 15 minutes. Arrange a sage leaf on top of each piece of salmon and brush with the reserved marinade.

5. Transfer the salmon to the smoker and smoke until just cooked through and flaky, 20 to 25 minutes. Serve the salmon pieces hot or chilled, one or two per guest.

SERVING SUGGESTION We like the salmon with something light, such as a salad of frisée (curly endive) or other greens, with sesame seeds or radish shreds for crunch, and a vinaigrette of sesame oil and rice vinegar.

BBQ tip The sake marinade, or cure, is a brine mixture, too, with most of the hallmark salt coming from soy sauce. The sake, garlic, and ginger all add a subtle flavor to the dish. To prepare the ginger "coins,"

Tom Douglas peels the fresh root, and then slices it across into thin rounds. In marinades, don't worry about getting off every bit of peel from the ginger since it will be discarded eventually.

Sweet and Hot Salmon Steaks

If you prefer salmon steaks to fillets, try them with a combination of spicy and sweet seasonings. SERVES 4

SWEET AND HOT MUSTARD PASTE

1/4 cup sweet hot mustard

1/4 cup minced onion

Juice of 1 large lemon

2 teaspoons minced fresh dill or sage or 1 teaspoon crumbled dried dill or sage

1 teaspoon kosher salt or coarse sea salt

Four 7-ounce to 8-ounce salmon steaks, about 1 inch thick

1. About 1½ hours before you plan to barbecue, combine the paste ingredients in a small bowl. Rub the salmon steaks thoroughly with the paste. Place the steaks in a shallow dish, cover with plastic, and refrigerate.

2. Prepare the smoker for barbecuing, bringing the temperature to 180°F to 200°F.

3. Remove the salmon from the refrigerator and let it sit at room temperature for 15 to 20 minutes.

4. Transfer the salmon steaks to the smoker and smoke them until just cooked through and flaky, 45 to 55 minutes. Have a large spatula and a platter ready for taking the salmon steaks off the smoker, since they will be fragile when done.

DON'T MISS THE BOAT

At the big Memphis in May barbecue championship in 1993, the Paddlewheel Porkers took the "People's Choice" award for the best 'Q.' You can't miss the group at a cook-off. They're the ones who are barbecuing and partying on the huge two-story replica of a Mississippi River paddleboat.

Jamaican Jerked Salmon

Jamaicans barbecue with "jerk" seasonings—assertive combinations of allspice, chiles, and other ingredients. Originally, jerking preserved meats like pork and chicken, but its popularity today stems from the spicy taste. The rub in this dish will dance on your tongue but won't scorch it, allowing the rich but subtle salmon flavor to shine through. SERVES 4

JAMAICAN JERK RUB

1 tablespoon onion powder

1 tablespoon dried onion flakes

1 teaspoon ground allspice

1 teaspoon freshly ground black pepper

1 teaspoon cayenne

1 teaspoon sugar

3/4 teaspoon dried thyme

3/4 teaspoon ground cinnamon

1/4 teaspoon ground nutmeg

Pinch of ground habanero chile (optional)

1 1/2-pound salmon fillet

JAMAICAN BARBECUE SAUCE

1 cup seafood stock

2 heaping tablespoons honey

1 tablespoon tamarind concentrate

1 tablespoon peeled and minced fresh ginger

1. About 1 1/2 hours before you plan to barbecue, combine the jerk seasoning ingredients in a small bowl. Rub the salmon thoroughly with a generous portion of the seasoning, reserving 1 tablespoon. Wrap the salmon in plastic and refrigerate it.

2. Prepare the smoker for barbecuing, bringing the temperature to 180°F to 200°F.

3. Remove the salmon from the refrigerator and let it sit at room temperature for 15 to 20 minutes.

4. Transfer the salmon to the smoker and smoke it until just cooked through and flaky, 45 to 55 minutes. Have a large spatula and a platter ready for taking the salmon off the smoker, since it will be fragile when done.

5. While the salmon cooks, make the sauce. Combine all of the ingredients with the reserved 1 tablespoon rub and bring to a boil over high heat. Reduce the heat and simmer until reduced by one-third, 5 to 10 minutes. Keep warm. In a wood-burning pit, brush the salmon with sauce after it has cooked for about 30 minutes. In other smokers, brush the salmon with the sauce as soon as it comes from the smoker. Serve the salmon with the remaining sauce served separately to spoon over individual portions of salmon.

SERVING SUGGESTION Accompany the elegant salmon with Scalloped Green Chile Potatoes (page 283) and Mango and Avocado Salad (page 430). Conclude with South Georgia Pound Cake (page 458), gilded if you like with lemon pudding or curd.

VARIATION: JAMAICAN JERKED SNAPPER Meaty snapper can also hold up well to jerk seasonings. Use a whole gutted red snapper, weighing in at 2½ to 3 pounds. Cut three slashes down to the bone on each side of the fish and then rub inside and out with the jerk rub. Smoke for about 15 minutes per pound.

BBQ *tip* The preferred temperature range for smoking fish is slightly lower than for meat. Generally, our recipes call for cooking fish and other seafood at a temperature of 180°F to 200°F. If your smoker is difficult to maintain in that range, it's no problem. Just subtract a little cooking time, generally up to 15 minutes for fish steaks, fillets, or even whole fish. Some experienced people like to hot-smoke fish at a temperature as low as 165°F. Be vigilant if you choose to go that low, and maintain the temperature consistently. If the mercury drops much lower, you can get into the temperature range where bacteria grow. The general idea behind the lower temperature is to get the seafood to absorb the maximum amount of smoke before it is cooked through.

Elemental Trout

The premier freshwater fish for barbecuing, trout relish a swim in the smoke. A couple of good recipes follow, which add layers of flavor. We start here with a basic, quick, and eminently flexible preparation. If you have access to wild-caught trout, it's much tastier than the farm-raised variety, the kind most of us have to accept routinely. SERVES 4

Four 8-ounce to 10-ounce trout, gutted and butterflied, or skin-on trout fillets

Olive or vegetable oil

Juice of 1 large lemon

Kosher salt or coarse sea salt and freshly ground black pepper

1. Prepare the smoker for barbecuing, bringing the temperature to 180°F to 200°F.

2. Remove the trout from the refrigerator and spray or rub with a thin coat of oil. Drizzle with lemon juice and sprinkle with salt and pepper. Let the trout sit at room temperature for 15 minutes.

3. Transfer the trout to a small grill rack. If working with whole trout, lay them open, like a book you are reading. Place the rack with the fish in the smoker. Cook the trout until opaque and easily flaked, 30 to 45 minutes depending on size. Serve immediately, or chill for later.

Stuffed Mountain Trout

In this preparation, the bacon does the work of a mop. SERVES 4

TROUT PASTE

4 garlic cloves

Juice of 1/2 lemon

1 teaspoon Worcestershire sauce

1 teaspoon freshly ground black pepper

1/2 teaspoon kosher salt or coarse sea salt

1 tablespoon vegetable oil

Four 8-ounce boned trout

8 slices bacon

5 tablespoons chopped onion

6 tablespoons chopped green bell pepper

6 tablespoons chopped celery

16 saltine crackers, crushed

6 tablespoons chopped pecans

1. About 1½ hours before you plan to barbecue, prepare the paste by mashing or chopping the garlic in a mortar and pestle or mini food processor. Mix in the lemon juice, Worcestershire sauce, pepper, and salt. Then blend in the oil to make a paste. Rub the trout inside and out with the paste. Wrap the trout in plastic and refrigerate for about 1 hour.

2. Prepare the smoker for barbecuing, bringing the temperature to 180°F to 200°F.

3. Remove the trout from the refrigerator and let them sit at room temperature for about 20 minutes.

4. In a heavy skillet, fry the bacon over medium heat, removing it from the skillet while still limp. Set the bacon slices aside. Add the onion, bell pepper, and celery to the bacon drippings and sauté briefly until softened. Remove the mixture from the heat and stir in the cracker crumbs and pecans. Stuff each trout with a portion of this filling. Wrap two slices of bacon around each fish, securing with toothpicks as needed.

5. Transfer the trout to the smoker. Cook until the bacon is brown and crisp, and the fish opaque and easily flaked, 40 to 50 minutes. Serve immediately.

BBQ tip Trout and catfish can take a heavier level of smoke flavor than most fish, making them particularly suitable for log-burning pits.

Mint Trout

Mint is mighty good with trout. Unlike most mops, the one in this recipe can be used in all kinds of smokers because it isn't applied during the cooking process. SERVES 4

MINT PASTE

3/4 cup fresh mint leaves

1/4 cup kosher salt or coarse sea salt

1/4 cup sugar

2 tablespoons coarsely ground black pepper

2 tablespoons freshly squeezed lemon juice

1 tablespoon vegetable oil

1 1/2 pounds trout fillets

MINT MOP

1 cup brewed mint tea made from 2 mint tea bags

Mint sprigs, for garnish

1. The night before you plan to barbecue, prepare the paste by combining the ingredients in a food processor and processing until pureed. Rub the trout fillets with a thick coating of the paste. Wrap the fillets in plastic and refrigerate them.

2. Prepare the smoker for barbecuing, bringing the temperature to 180°F to 200°F.

3. Remove the trout from the refrigerator and let them sit at room temperature for 15 minutes.

4. Transfer the trout, covered with the paste that clings to each fillet, to a small grill rack.

Drizzle each fillet with enough mint tea to moisten the coating well and place the fish in the smoker. Cook the trout until opaque and easily flaked, 30 to 45 minutes depending on the size of the fillets. Drizzle with additional mint tea and serve immediately, garnished with mint sprigs.

SERVING SUGGESTION Start with South-of-the-Border Garlic Soup (page 286). Pair the fish with Warm Mushroom Salad (page 309) and steamed asparagus served hot or cold. Finish off with sliced mangoes or papayas sprinkled with rum and lime juice. It's a great combo when you need to impress your boss or main squeeze.

BBQ *tip* Several recipes in this chapter suggest using a small grill rack to hold pieces of fish and seafood in a smoker. The mesh on the grate permits smoke to pass but prevents food from falling through. You'll find grill racks in barbecue stores, discount stores, and cookware stores, especially in the summer months.

New Yorkers used to barbecue turtles in the eighteenth century, according to food historians Waverley Root and Richard de Rochemont. No wonder they gave up on the 'Q,' at least until the recent emergence of several good barbecue restaurants in the city that serve traditional pork and beef dishes.

Smoked Trout Hash

Sometimes we think "heavenly hash" must have been coined specifically to describe hashes concocted with smoky trout or salmon. If you've only had the corned beef variety, you owe it to yourself to try this immediately. Poached eggs make a superlative topping, if you wish, at dinner as well as breakfast. SERVES 4

1¹/₂ tablespoons vegetable oil

1¹/₂ tablespoons unsalted butter

1 pound Yukon Gold or red-skinned waxy potatoes, peeled if you wish, and diced in ¹/₂-inch cubes

¹/₂ medium red onion, chopped

3 tablespoons half-and-half

2 teaspoons Dijon mustard

Kosher salt or coarse sea salt and freshly ground black pepper

1 recipe Elemental Trout (page 241), flaked

¹/₄ cup minced fresh dill

2 tablespoons minced fresh chives

Sour cream and capers (optional), for garnish

1. Warm the oil and butter in a large, heavy skillet over medium-low heat. Stir in the potatoes. Cover and cook for 10 minutes, adjusting the heat to hear just a light sizzle.

2. Uncover and turn the potatoes. Raise the heat to medium and cook until uniformly soft with some crisp brown spots, about 5 minutes.

Add the onion and pat the mixture back down. Cook until the onion is very soft and the mixture begins to stick in a few spots and brown on the bottom, about 5 minutes longer. Scrape up from the bottom, and then add the half-and-half, mustard, salt, and a generous grinding of pepper. Raise the heat to medium-high. Continue cooking until the liquid evaporates and the mixture begins to crisp and brown again, 5 to 8 minutes longer. Scrape up from the bottom and pat back down another time or two. Add the trout and the herbs and cook for a couple of minutes longer, until heated through. Serve hot, topped if you wish with a dollop of sour cream and a sprinkling of capers.

VARIATION: SMOKED SALMON HASH Replace the trout with about 1 pound hot-smoked salmon fillets or steaks, flaked. Reverse the proportions of dill and chives.

Peppered Catfish

Most Americans fry their catfish. This recipe will quickly disabuse you of that approach. Plan to make enough to save some for Katzen Dawgs (page 271) or Creamy Catfish Spread (page 352). SERVES 6

THREE-PEPPER CATFISH RUB

3 tablespoons coarsely ground black pepper

2 tablespoons kosher salt or coarse sea salt

1½ tablespoons coarsely ground white pepper

1 teaspoon onion powder

½ teaspoon cayenne

Six 8-ounce catfish fillets

CATFISH MOP (OPTIONAL)

2 cups seafood or chicken stock

½ cup vegetable oil

Juice of 3 limes

Golden Mustard Barbecue Sauce (page 371) (optional)

1. At least 2½ hours before you plan to barbecue, or preferably the night before, mix the rub ingredients in a small bowl. Cover the catfish lightly and evenly with the rub, reserving 2 tablespoons of the mixture if you plan to baste the fish. Place the fillets in a plastic bag and refrigerate them for 2 hours or overnight.

2. Prepare the smoker for barbecuing, bringing the temperature to 180°F to 200°F.

3. Remove the fillets from the refrigerator and let them sit at room temperature for 20 minutes.

4. If you are going to use the mop (see page 45, "To Mop or Not"), mix the ingredients with the reserved 2 tablespoons rub in a small saucepan and warm over low heat.

5. Place the catfish in the smoker on a small grill rack as far from the fire as possible. Cook the fish for approximately 1½ hours, dabbing the catfish with the mop every 20 minutes in a wood-burning pit, or as appropriate for your style of smoker. When cooked, the catfish will be opaque and firm, yet flaky. Serve warm. If desired, accompany the catfish with Golden Mustard Barbecue Sauce.

CATFISH TO GO

When you're yearning for smoked catfish and don't want to fix it yourself, contact Betty and Quentin Knussmann online at pickwickcatfishfarm.com in Counce, Tennessee. They raise the fish and smoke them over hickory. You won't find a better mail-order version. If you're in the vicinity, two hours east of Memphis, stop by the farm's restaurant for the catfish, some of Betty's hushpuppies, and barbecued ribs.

Flounder Surprise

This is a fancy "sandwich" of double-smoked salmon stuffed between two barbecued flounder fillets. Use leftovers from Kingly Salmon (page 232) or substitute a store-bought Pacific Northwest–style hot-smoked salmon. SERVES 4

1 1/2 to 1 3/4 pounds flounder or sole fillets

WILD WILLY'S NUMBER ONE-DERFUL RUB

3 tablespoons paprika

1 tablespoon freshly ground black pepper

1 tablespoon kosher salt or coarse sea salt

1 tablespoon sugar

1 1/2 teaspoons chili powder

1 1/2 teaspoons garlic powder

1 1/2 teaspoons onion powder

1/2 teaspoon cayenne

STUFFING

6 to 8 ounces hot-smoked salmon (see headnote)

1/2 cup dry bread crumbs

1/4 cup chopped celery

1/4 cup chopped onion

1 egg white, lightly beaten

1/4 teaspoon paprika

1 to 2 tablespoons milk

SURPRISE MOP (OPTIONAL)

1 cup seafood or chicken stock

3 tablespoons unsalted butter

Juice of 1 lemon

Lemon wedges (optional), for garnish

1. Prepare the smoker for barbecuing, bringing the temperature to 180°F to 200°F.

2. Cut the fillets into 8 equal portions. Mix the rub ingredients in a small bowl and rub the flounder portions evenly with the mixture. Let sit at room temperature for 15 to 20 minutes.

3. Place the smoked salmon in a food processor. Add the rest of the stuffing ingredients, except the milk, and process briefly. The stuffing should be thoroughly blended but not pureed to oblivion. Add as much of the milk as is needed to moisten the mixture without making it soupy. Spoon equal portions of the stuffing onto half of the fillets. Top each "stuffed" fillet with one of the remaining fillets.

4. If you plan to baste the fish (see page 45, "To Mop or Not"), combine the mop ingredients in a small saucepan and warm over low heat until the butter melts. Keep the mop warm over low heat.

5. Transfer the fillets to a small grill rack and place them in the smoker as far from the fire as possible. Cook until the flounder is opaque and flaky and the salmon heated through, 35 to 40 minutes. Mop twice during the cooking process in a wood-burning pit, or as appropriate for your style of smoker. Serve the fish with the lemon wedges if you wish.

BBQ tip To tell how much smoke flavor you're putting into food, simply check the amount of smoke being vented out of your barbecue equipment. If nothing is coming out, it's time to add more wood.

Rockfish with Old Bay Butter

The rockfish or striped bass is one of the mid- and upper-Atlantic coast conservation successes. After years of overfishing, an enforced moratorium and more intelligent management policies have put it back on the table again. Here we smoke whole fish, and then serve them with an Old Bay Seasoning–flavored butter. SERVES 6

3 small whole rockfish (striped bass), hybrid striped bass, other small bass, snapper, or other mild-flavored fish, about 2 pounds each, gutted and cleaned

Olive oil

Juice and zest of 2 lemons (reserve the zest for the butter below)

2 tablespoons Old Bay Seasoning

OLD BAY MOP (OPTIONAL)

Juice of 2 lemons

1/2 cup white vinegar

1/4 cup water

2 tablespoons extra-virgin olive oil

2 teaspoons Old Bay Seasoning

OLD BAY BUTTER

1/2 cup unsalted butter or Smoked Butter (page 373)

2 teaspoons Old Bay Seasoning, or more to taste

Lemon wedges and parsley sprigs, for garnish

1. Prepare the smoker for barbecuing, bringing the temperature to 180°F to 200°F.

2. Cut three deep diagonal slashes into both sides of the fish to promote even cooking and flavor absorption. Rub the fish inside and out with the oil and half of the lemon juice. Sprinkle sparingly with Old Bay Seasoning. Allow the fish to sit at room temperature for about 30 minutes.

3. If you plan to baste the fish (see page 45, "To Mop or Not"), mix the mop ingredients in a small saucepan. Warm the mop over low heat.

4. Transfer the fish to the smoker as far from the fire as possible. Cook until flaky and opaque, about 20 minutes per pound. Mop the fish early and once or twice more in a wood-burning pit, or as appropriate for your style of smoker.

5. While the fish cooks, melt the butter in a small skillet with the Old Bay Seasoning and reserved lemon zest. Keep warm.

6. Remove the fish from the smoker with a large spatula and transfer it to a decorative platter. Garnish the fish with lemons and parsley. To serve, remove the skin and cut through the fish, watching for its bones. Pass the sauce separately. Alternatively, skin the top side of the fish, spread a thick layer of the sauce over it, and serve.

BBQ tip Old Bay Seasoning is one of the best-selling commercial spice blends on the market. The distinctive mixture was created as a flavoring for Chesapeake Bay blue crabs but is now a staple for flavoring all kinds of seafood. Most supermarkets coast to coast carry it. If you substitute another seasoning, taste as you go, because many other similar blends are saltier than Old Bay.

Smoked Snapper Tostadas with Sangrita Sauce

Smoking snapper fillets is a snap, hardly allowing you enough time for a leisurely beer by the pit. This sauce is based on the Mexican drink sangrita—not to be confused with sangria—a tangy tomato-citrus chaser for tequila. SERVES 4

Four 8-ounce red snapper, sea bass, or other mild-flavored white fish fillets (or other more or less equal-size fillets that add up to 2 pounds)

1 tablespoon extra-virgin olive oil

Mexican hot sauce such as Cholula, or several teaspoons Southwest Heat or South-of-the-Border Smoky Heat (both on page 32)

SANGRITA SAUCE

6 tablespoons tomato juice

2 tablespoons freshly squeezed orange juice

2 tablespoons freshly squeezed lime juice

$1/2$ teaspoon grenadine syrup

Several dashes Mexican hot sauce, such as Cholula, or $1/4$ teaspoon Southwest Heat or South-of-the-Border Smoky Heat (both on page 32) or ground ancho chile

Table salt

Juice of 1 lime

1 fresh serrano or jalapeño chile, minced

2 scallions, with their green tops, minced

2 to 3 tablespoons minced fresh cilantro

8 crisp corn tostada shells (like flat taco shells)

1 to 2 ripe Hass avocados, peeled, pitted, and diced

1 large red-ripe tomato, chopped

1. Prepare the smoker for barbecuing, bringing the temperature to 180°F to 200°F.

2. Rub the snapper with the oil. Sprinkle with hot sauce or dry rub. Allow the fish to sit at room temperature for about 30 minutes.

3. Mix the sauce ingredients in a small bowl. If you plan to baste the fish (see page 45, "To Mop or Not"), set aside a few tablespoons of the sauce to use as the mop.

4. Transfer the snapper to the smoker as far from the fire as possible. Cook until the fillets are flaky and opaque, 25 to 30 minutes. Adjust the time a bit if your fillets are larger or smaller. Drizzle the mop lightly over the fillets after about 15 minutes in a wood-burning pit, or as appropriate for your style of smoker.

5. Remove the snapper from the smoker. When cool enough to handle, flake the fish into a medium-size bowl, discarding skin and bones. Toss the fish with the lime juice, chile, scallions, and cilantro. Spoon the snapper mixture evenly onto the tostada shells. Top with avocado and tomato. Serve two per person with the sauce, passed separately and drizzled over the tostadas.

Cuban Snapper

This is a new spin on a dish that's now common in south Florida, where red snapper is often poached or cooked in clay. SERVES 4 TO 6

3-pound to 3 1/2-pound gutted whole red snapper, sea bass, or other mild-flavored white fish

1 tablespoon extra-virgin olive oil

Juice of 2 lemons

Table salt and freshly ground black pepper to taste

STUFFING

1/2 cup dry bread crumbs

1/2 medium onion, chopped

3 tablespoons minced fresh flat-leaf parsley

1/4 teaspoon dried thyme

1/4 teaspoon dried oregano

1/4 teaspoon ground nutmeg

1/4 teaspoon cayenne or ground chile de árbol

CUBAN MOP (OPTIONAL)

1 cup fish or seafood stock

1/4 cup water

2 tablespoons extra-virgin olive oil

Juice of 1 lemon

AVOCADO SAUCE

2 ripe Hass avocados

Juice of 2 limes

2 tablespoons chopped onion

1 teaspoon table salt

Freshly ground black pepper to taste

3 to 4 tablespoons extra-virgin olive oil

Lemon and lime wedges and parsley sprigs, for garnish

1. Prepare the smoker for barbecuing, bringing the temperature to 180°F to 200°F.

2. Cut three deep diagonal slashes into both sides of the snapper to promote even cooking and flavor absorption. Rub the fish inside and out with the oil and half of the lemon juice, reserving the remaining lemon juice for the stuffing. Sprinkle sparingly with salt and liberally with pepper. Allow the fish to sit at room temperature for about 30 minutes.

3. In a bowl, mix the bread crumbs, onion, parsley, thyme, oregano, nutmeg, cayenne, and reserved lemon juice. Stuff the fish loosely. Place the fish on a greased grill rack or baking sheet.

4. If you plan to baste the fish (see page 45, "To Mop or Not"), mix the mop ingredients in a small saucepan. Warm the mop over low heat.

5. Transfer the snapper to the smoker as far from the fire as possible. Cook until flaky and opaque, about 20 minutes per pound. Mop the fish early and once or twice more in a wood-burning pit, or as appropriate for your style of smoker.

6. While the fish cooks, peel, pit, and chop the avocados. Combine them in a food processor with the lime juice, onion, salt, and pepper. With the processor running, add the oil in a steady stream, until the sauce has the consistency of thin mayonnaise. Spoon the sauce into a small bowl.

7. Remove the snapper from the smoker with a

large spatula and transfer it to a decorative platter. Garnish the snapper with lemons, limes, and parsley. To serve, remove the skin and cut through the fish, watching for its bones. Serve each portion with some of the stuffing and pass the sauce separately. Alternatively, skin the top side of the fish, spread a thick layer of the sauce over it, and serve.

SERVING SUGGESTION Snack first on Fiesta Salsa (page 349) and tortilla chips with Mexican Martinis (page 475). Accompany the snapper with a mixed green salad and tangy citrus vinaigrette, and top it off with 'Nana Pudding (page 463), dulce de leche ice cream, or fresh tropical fruit.

Tuna Caper

This tuna's Mediterranean flavors should tantalize. SERVES 4

OLIVE PASTE

1/4 cup chopped pitted black olives, preferably kalamata or niçoise

2 garlic cloves, halved

1/4 cup extra-virgin olive oil

2 tablespoons dry red wine

1 tablespoon capers

1 teaspoon dried thyme

4 tuna steaks, about 1 inch thick

1/4 teaspoon kosher salt or coarse sea salt

Lemon wedges and basil sprigs (optional), for garnish

1. Prepare the smoker for barbecuing, bringing the temperature to 180°F to 200°F.

2. In a food processor, process the paste ingredients to a thick puree. Rub the paste over the tuna steaks. Transfer the tuna to a plate and allow the steaks to sit at room temperature for about 20 minutes.

3. Heat a skillet over high heat and sprinkle in the salt. Add the tuna steaks and sear them quickly on both sides.

4. Transfer the steaks to the smoker. Cook the tuna to desired doneness, 20 to 25 minutes for medium-rare. Avoid overcooking the tuna. Serve hot, garnished with lemons and basil if you wish.

SERVING SUGGESTION Serve Unholy Swiss Cheese (page 341) to start. Accompany the tuna with steamed artichokes, a platter of red-ripe tomatoes and mozzarella dressed with olive oil, and crispy bread sticks. Offer Becky's Pineapple Cake (page 459) or a fruity sorbet for dessert. For a light meal, the tuna makes a great salad ingredient, used either hot or cold.

Kohala Tuna Steaks

In recent decades, Hawaiian chefs have created a sumptuous new regional cuisine, often featuring the local tuna. Here's a smoked version of a Big Island favorite.

SERVES 4

KOHALA MARINADE

6 tablespoons unsalted butter, melted

6 tablespoons toasted sesame oil

6 tablespoons rice vinegar

Juice of $1/2$ lemon

$1^1/2$ teaspoons peeled and minced fresh ginger

1 garlic clove, minced

1 crushed Thai, Hunan, or other tiny hot red chile

$1/2$ teaspoon dried thyme

4 tuna steaks, about 1 inch thick

$1/4$ teaspoon kosher salt or coarse sea salt

Reduced-sodium soy sauce

West Coast Wonder (page 379) (optional)

1. Prepare the smoker for barbecuing, bringing the temperature to 180°F to 200°F.

2. Mix the marinade ingredients in a large glass measuring cup. Place the tuna steaks in a shallow, nonreactive dish or a plastic bag and pour the marinade over the tuna. Allow the steaks to sit at room temperature for 20 to 30 minutes.

3. Heat a skillet over high heat and sprinkle in the salt. Drain the tuna steaks. Sear the steaks quickly on both sides.

4. Transfer the steaks to the smoker. Cook the tuna to desired doneness, 20 to 25 minutes for medium-rare. Avoid overcooking the tuna. Serve hot with soy sauce and, if you wish, a touch of West Coast Wonder barbecue sauce.

SERVING SUGGESTION Mix up a salad of thinly sliced snow peas, carrots, water chestnuts, and napa cabbage or bok choy tossed with a vinaigrette made with toasted sesame oil and rice vinegar. A creamy dessert works best, perhaps Lemon Pudding Ice Cream Pie (page 448).

BBQ tip Before you smoke meaty fish steaks, such as tuna and swordfish, it helps to sear them quickly over high heat to seal in their juices and add a light crust.

Soused Swordfish

If you have any leftovers, these swordfish will have a helluva hangover the next day.

SERVES 4

SOUSED MARINADE

3/4 cup bourbon or other sour-mash whiskey

3/4 cup seafood or chicken stock

1/4 cup vegetable oil

3 garlic cloves, minced

1 tablespoon green peppercorns, plus 1 teaspoon brine

Four 8-ounce to 10-ounce swordfish steaks

BASIC BLACK RUB

2 tablespoons coarsely ground black pepper

1 tablespoon kosher salt or coarse sea salt

1. At least 2 hours and up to 8 hours before you plan to barbecue, combine the marinade ingredients in a large glass measuring cup. Place the swordfish in a shallow, nonreactive pan or a plastic bag. Pour the marinade over the swordfish and refrigerate it for at least 1½ hours.

2. Prepare the smoker for barbecuing, bringing the temperature to 180°F to 200°F.

3. Drain the swordfish, reserving about 3/4 cup of the marinade. Combine the rub ingredients in a small bowl and sprinkle them lightly but evenly over both sides of the steaks. Let the swordfish sit at room temperature for 15 to 20 minutes.

4. In a small pan, bring the reserved 3/4 cup marinade to a vigorous boil over high heat and boil for several minutes. Keep the liquid warm over low heat.

5. Heat a heavy skillet over high heat. Place the steaks in the skillet, in batches if necessary, and sear quickly on both sides. Remove the steaks immediately, drizzle the hot marinade lightly over them, and transfer the steaks to the smoker. Cook until the fish is cooked through, 40 to 50 minutes. Serve the swordfish hot.

SERVING SUGGESTION When you need an uptown down-home meal, try these steaks with Barbecued Rice (page 298) and California Crunch salad (page 417). For dessert, we would opt for Long-on-Strawberries Shortcake (page 455).

BBQ tip Bourbon is a great marinade ingredient for barbecuing because of its smoky, sweet flavor. It works particularly well with red meat but also enhances some lighter fare, such as meaty swordfish.

Not long ago we read about a diet that we could learn to like—a barbecue version of a low-carb regimen. The creative genius behind the idea gave a sample day's menu that starts with three eggs and bacon for breakfast, a handful of smoked almonds for a midmorning snack, a beef brisket salad with a crumbled blue cheese dressing at lunch, smoked link sausage as an afternoon snack, and a smoked salmon fillet for dinner. He lost lots of pounds, he said, probably from laughing all day at Weight Watchers.

Sherried Grouper

Here's a more delicately inebriated fish, and one that's quick to prepare. SERVES 4

SHERRY MARINADE AND SAUCE

Juice of 2 oranges (about 2/3 cup)

Zest of 1 orange, minced

1/2 cup dry sherry

6 tablespoons peanut oil

1 tablespoon Creole mustard, such as Zatarain's

2 garlic cloves, minced

1/4 teaspoon table salt

1/4 teaspoon freshly ground black pepper

Four 6-ounce grouper, mahi-mahi, or other firm white fish fillets

Chopped fresh parsley, orange slices, and orange zest, for garnish

1. Prepare the smoker for barbecuing, bringing the temperature to 180°F to 200°F.

2. Combine the marinade ingredients in a large glass measuring cup. Lay the fillets in a single layer in a shallow, nonreactive dish or place them in a plastic bag. Pour the marinade over the fillets and let them sit at room temperature for about 30 minutes.

3. Drain the fillets, reserving the marinade. In a small pan, bring the marinade to a vigorous boil over high heat. Reduce the heat to simmer and cook for several minutes, until the marinade forms a thin sauce. Taste and adjust the seasoning, if needed. Keep the sauce warm over low heat.

4. Transfer the fillets to the smoker. Cook until the fish is opaque and flaky, 25 to 30 minutes. Spoon the sauce on a serving platter and top it with the fillets. Garnish the fish with a sprinkling of parsley and a scattering of orange slices and zest. Serve immediately.

California Dreamin' Fish Tacos

Some people dream of sunshine in Southern California. We dream of soft tacos overflowing with fish and salsa. The optional vegetable relish here adds another flavorful touch. SERVES 4 TO 6

Two 12-ounce to 14-ounce mahi-mahi, snapper, or other mild white fish fillets

1 cup Lawry's Mesquite Marinade with Lime Juice or other store-bought mesquite marinade

Juice of 1 lime

TOMATILLO SALSA

3 teaspoons extra-virgin olive oil

1 small red or sweet onion, chopped

1 pound fresh tomatillos, husked and chopped, or 2 cups canned tomatillos, drained

2 canned chipotle chiles in adobe, minced, or more to taste

1 tablespoon white vinegar

1 teaspoon dried oregano, preferably Mexican

1/2 cup chopped fresh cilantro

Table salt and freshly ground black pepper to taste

VEGETABLE RELISH (OPTIONAL)

3 tablespoons extra-virgin olive oil

1/2 pound jicama, peeled and cut into matchsticks

1 small red onion or sweet onion, chopped

1 small red pepper, seeded and cut into matchsticks

1 small zucchini, cut into matchsticks

1 roasted green chile (optional), preferably New Mexican or poblano, fresh or frozen, seeded and cut into matchsticks (see BBQ tip on page 151)

6 squash blossoms (optional), cut into matchsticks

1/3 cup chopped fresh cilantro

Warm flour tortillas, preferably no larger than 6 inches in diameter

Lime wedges, for garnish

1. Prepare the smoker for barbecuing, bringing the temperature to 180°F to 200°F.

2. Place the mahi-mahi fillets in a nonreactive, shallow dish. Pour the marinade over the fish, add the lime juice, and let the fish sit at room temperature for 30 minutes.

3. While the fish marinates, warm 1½ teaspoons of the oil in a heavy skillet over medium heat. Add the onion and sauté until softened. Spoon the onion into a bowl. Warm the remaining 1½ teaspoons of the oil in the same skillet over medium-high heat. Add the tomatillos and sauté until lightly browned. Place the tomatillos in the bowl with the onion. Stir in the chipotles, vinegar, and oregano, and refrigerate.

4. Remove the mahi-mahi from the marinade, draining as little of the liquid as possible. Spoon some of the remaining marinade over the fish and place the fillets in the smoker. Cook the mahi-mahi until opaque and easily flaked, 45 to 55 minutes.

5. Remove the fish from the smoker. Let it cool for a couple of minutes while you finish the salsa, stirring in the cilantro and adding salt and pepper to taste. Transfer the salsa to a decorative bowl. Flake the fish into bite-size chunks and mound it on one side of a large platter. Cover it with foil.

6. Prepare the vegetable relish, if you wish. In a skillet, warm the oil over medium heat. Add the jicama, red onion, red pepper, zucchini, and chile and sauté until the vegetables are crisp-tender. Stir in the squash blossoms and cilantro and heat through. Spoon the vegetable relish onto the other half of the platter.

7. Serve immediately with the tortillas and lime wedges. For each taco, spoon some of the fish into a tortilla, along with a spoonful of the vegetable relish. Top with salsa and, if you wish, a squeeze of lime juice. Fold the tortilla in half and devour.

BBQ tip Our recipes rarely call for commercial marinades, but we're happy to make an exception for Lawry's Mesquite Marinade with Lime Juice in the fish tacos. The sauce works great with many smoked fish dishes. It saves time but doesn't sacrifice flavor in the process. If the tomatillo salsa preparation seems lengthy to you, simply pick up your favorite at the store when you're purchasing the marinade.

soft tacos overflow with fish and salsa, and the optional vegetable relish adds a flavorful touch

When we first wrote *Smoke & Spice*, almost every reader who wasn't from California seemed to think fish tacos were on the same level of weird as barbecued boots. In just two decades, the idea has swept across the country as a hot food trend, fueled largely by quick-service, prepared-to-order eateries that specialize in fish tacos. Even our small hometown of Santa Fe has one of the restaurants, a great place called Bumble Bee's Baja Grill, run by a cowboy turned cook named Bumble Bee Bob Weil.

Jalapeño-Lime Shrimp

Dean Fearing, a fearless Dallas chef, inspired this fiery Southwestern shrimp treat. It's as classic a combo as Carolina pork and vinegar. SERVES 4

JALAPEÑO-LIME MARINADE

1/3 cup pickled jalapeño slices

1/4 cup pickling liquid from a jar or can of pickled jalapeños

Juice of 2 limes

1/4 cup corn oil

3 tablespoons minced fresh cilantro

4 scallions, sliced

3 garlic cloves, halved

1 teaspoon kosher salt or coarse sea salt

1 pound peeled large shrimp (24 to 30 shrimp), preferably with tails left on

JALAPEÑO-LIME MOP

1/2 cup seafood or chicken stock

Juice of 1 lime

Slices of fresh red jalapeño or other red chile (optional), for garnish

1. Puree the marinade ingredients in a food processor or blender. Place the shrimp in a shallow, nonreactive dish or plastic bag. Pour the marinade over the shrimp and let the shrimp marinate at room temperature for 30 to 40 minutes.

2. Prepare the smoker for barbecuing, bringing the temperature to 180°F to 200°F.

3. Drain the shrimp from the marinade, pouring the marinade into a saucepan. Add the stock and additional lime juice to the remaining marinade for the mop. Bring the liquid to a vigorous boil over high heat and boil for several minutes. Keep the mop warm over low heat.

4. Place the shrimp on a small grill rack and baste liberally with the mop. Transfer the shrimp to the smoker and place as far from the fire as possible. The shrimp should cook in approximately 25 minutes, but watch them carefully. They are ready when opaque, slightly firm, and lightly pink on the exterior. Remove the shrimp from the smoker and mop them heavily again. Place the shrimp on a platter, scatter the red jalapeños over them, if you wish, and serve.

BBQ tip Shrimp dishes work particularly well in stovetop smokers, making them great winter treats when it's too cold to barbecue outside.

Cajun Shrimp with Worcestershire Butter and French Bread

We serve these smokin' shrimp on toasted bread that soaks up all their luscious buttery juices. SERVES 4 OR MORE

1 pound peeled large shrimp (24 to 30 shrimp), preferably with tails left on

6 tablespoons unsalted butter, cut into 8 pats

2 tablespoons Worcestershire sauce

2 teaspoons Cajun or Creole seasoning or Cajun Ragin' Rub (page 29)

1 teaspoon freshly squeezed lemon juice

1-pound loaf soft French bread, halved crosswise and then lengthwise (to make 4 long pieces), toasted

1. Prepare the smoker for barbecuing, bringing the temperature to 180°F to 200°F.

2. Place the shrimp in a smoke-proof dish or foil pan large enough to hold them in a single layer. Scatter the butter, Worcestershire sauce, and seasoning over and around the shrimp.

3. Transfer the shrimp to the smoker as far from the fire as possible. The shrimp should cook in approximately 25 minutes, but watch them carefully and stir at least once. They are ready when opaque, slightly firm, and lightly pink on the exterior. Stir the lemon juice into the shrimp mixture.

4. Arrange a piece of toasted French bread on each plate. Spoon the shrimp and butter sauce over the bread. Serve hot.

THE BIG PIG JIG

The American Bus Association has twice selected the annual Big Pig Jig in Vienna, Georgia, as one of the Top 100 Events in North America. Attendees who don't want to participate in the big barbecue cook-off can compete in the golf tournament or the sidewalk-art contest. Even people who aren't feeling competitive have a wide choice of spectator activities, including an arts and crafts fair, a fun parade, and evening concerts.

Smoked Shrimp and Scallop Platter

Serve this as a main-dish platter for up to four to share, or make it an appetizer for a lucky group. If you can afford more scallops, buy them. They'll all disappear.

SERVES UP TO 4

1 pound medium to large shrimp

3/4 to 1 pound sea scallops

3 tablespoons extra-virgin olive oil

Juice and zest of 1 lemon (reserve the zest and 3/4 teaspoon of the juice for the mayo below)

BASIC BLACK RUB

2 tablespoons coarsely ground black pepper

1 tablespoon kosher salt or coarse sea salt

LEMON-SAFFRON MAYO

2 pinches of crumbled saffron threads

1 cup mayonnaise (not a low-fat variety)

2 tablespoons extra-virgin olive oil

1 to 2 garlic cloves, minced

Minced fresh parsley or snipped chives

1. Prepare the smoker for barbecuing, bringing the temperature to 180°F to 200°F.

2. Peel the shrimp, leaving their tails on. If any of the scallops is much larger than an inch, halve it. In a bowl, toss the shrimp and scallops with the oil, all but 3/4 teaspoon of the lemon juice, and dry rub. Let the shellfish marinate at room temperature for 15 to 20 minutes.

3. Make the mayonnaise while the shellfish marinate. Combine the saffron with the reserved lemon zest and 3/4 teaspoon juice in the bottom of a small bowl and let sit for 5 minutes. Whisk in the mayonnaise, oil, and garlic. Cover and refrigerate ready to use.

4. Arrange the shrimp and scallops on a small grill rack or baking sheet and transfer to the smoker. Smoke as far from the fire as possible until just cooked through and opaque. Check after 20 minutes for doneness, and remove any shrimp and scallops that are cooked through. Continue cooking if needed, for up to 10 more minutes. Serve warm or chilled. Arrange the shrimp and scallops on a decorative platter with the sauce. Sprinkle parsley over and serve. If the neighbors aren't watching, eat with your fingers.

EUREKA!

The immodest sign out front says it all at Bubba's barbecue joint in Eureka Springs, Arkansas: "It may not look famous, but it is." Who cares what for?

Shrimp Rémoulade

Rémoulade sauce, a Louisiana marvel, is usually served on boiled shrimp. A touch of smoke in the shellfish enhances all the flavors. SERVES 4 TO 6

1 1/2 pounds peeled medium shrimp, preferably with tails on

SHRIMP MARINADE

3 tablespoons extra-virgin olive oil

Juice of 1 lemon

2 teaspoons Cajun or Creole seasoning or Cajun Ragin' Rub (page 29)

RÉMOULADE SAUCE

1/3 cup extra-virgin olive oil

2 large celery ribs, chopped

4 scallions, chopped

2 tablespoons Creole mustard, such as Zatarain's

2 tablespoons ketchup

1 tablespoon freshly squeezed lemon juice

1 tablespoon capers

1 tablespoon chopped fresh cilantro

2 to 3 teaspoons Tabasco or other hot pepper sauce

1 teaspoon prepared horseradish, or more to taste

1 teaspoon paprika

1/2 teaspoon Cajun or Creole seasoning or Cajun Ragin' Rub (page 29)

1/2 teaspoon table salt, or more to taste

Lettuce leaves, for garnish

1. Prepare the smoker for barbecuing, bringing the temperature to 180°F to 200°F.

2. In a bowl, toss the shrimp with the marinade ingredients. Let the shrimp marinate at room temperature for 15 to 20 minutes.

3. While the shrimp marinate, place all the sauce ingredients in a blender or food processor and puree until smooth. Refrigerate until ready to use.

4. Transfer the shrimp to the smoker and smoke them until just cooked through and lightly fragrant, 15 to 20 minutes. They are ready when opaque, slightly firm, and lightly pink on the exterior. Combine the shrimp with the sauce in a serving dish and chill for 1 to 2 hours. Garnish the dish with the lettuce just before serving.

VARIATION: ZYDECO SHRIMP RÉMOULADE Zippier than a zydeco tune, this version introduces even more smoke flavor to the dish by smoking tomatoes for the rémoulade sauce along with the shrimp. Put 2 large plum tomatoes beside the shrimp in the smoker and cook them the same amount of time. Delay making the sauce until everything is done. Then substitute the tomatoes for the ketchup in the sauce, pureeing them skins and all.

SERVING SUGGESTION Serve as an appetizer preceding Cajun Country Ribs (page 77) or Creole Crown Roast (page 91), or as a light main dish accompanied by Peppery 'Pups (page 406).

The word *barbecue* comes from the Spanish *barbacoa*, the term early explorers in the New World applied to the wood frame Caribbean natives used in their smoke cooking. The Spanish word is probably an adaptation of an Indian word.

Eye-Popping Oysters

We've seen these peppery oysters bring jubilation to the most jaded of palates. Crack the peppercorns with a mortar and pestle or use coarsely ground black pepper.

MAKES 1 DOZEN

EYE-POPPING MARINADE AND MOP

1/2 cup bottled clam juice

3 tablespoons freshly squeezed lemon juice

3 tablespoons extra-virgin olive oil

1 tablespoon freshly cracked black pepper

3 to 4 garlic cloves, minced

1 dozen oysters, shucked, bottom shells and brine reserved

About a dozen ice cubes

Lemon wedges and freshly cracked black pepper, for garnish

1. Combine the clam juice, lemon juice, oil, pepper, garlic, and any oyster brine in a large glass measuring cup. Place the oysters in a small bowl or plastic bag. Pour the marinade over the oysters and refrigerate for about 45 minutes.

2. Prepare the smoker for barbecuing, bringing the temperature to 180°F to 200°F.

3. Drain the oysters, reserving the marinade for the mop. Arrange each oyster on a half-shell. Bring the marinade to a vigorous boil and boil for several minutes. Reduce the heat and keep the mop warm.

4. Put the ice cubes in a small smoke-proof baking pan or deep pie pan. Place the oysters on the half-shell on a small grill rack and place the rack over the ice-filled baking pan.

5. Place the oysters over ice in the smoker as far from the fire as possible. Cook for about 40 minutes, drizzling with the mop once or twice in a wood-burning pit, or as appropriate for your style of smoker. The oysters are done when slightly firm but still plump and juicy. Swab them with the mop when they come off the smoker. Serve the oysters warm with lemon wedges and more pepper.

SERVING SUGGESTION Serve as many oysters as you can afford—don't worry, you'll never have any left—with Hand Salad (page 420) and a lot of Cracklin' Cornbread (page 408).

Brined Bluepoints

In contrast to the previous recipe, these firm-textured oysters should dry out during their cooking. Atlantic bluepoints work great this way, but another cold-water oyster can be substituted. The oysters are best smoked a day ahead of serving, and their preparation can be spread over two days. They take a bit of fiddling, but the result is worth the time. MAKES 12 TO 18 OYSTERS

BROWN SUGAR BRINE

3/4 cup water

1/4 cup kosher salt or coarse sea salt

3 tablespoons minced onion

3 tablespoons packed brown sugar

1 teaspoon ground oregano

12 to 18 shucked plump oysters

BROWN SUGAR RUB

1/4 cup kosher salt or coarse sea salt

2 tablespoons packed brown sugar

1 teaspoon onion powder

1/2 teaspoon ground oregano

Extra-virgin olive oil

1. At least 4 hours before you plan to barbecue, mix the brine ingredients in a large nonreactive bowl, stirring to dissolve. Add the oysters to the liquid and place a plate over them to keep them submerged. Marinate the oysters at room temperature for about 30 minutes.

2. Rinse the oysters and pat them dry. Transfer them to a platter lined with several thicknesses of paper towels. Allow the oysters to air-dry for 1 hour, changing the towels if they become soaked with liquid given off by the oysters.

3. Combine the rub ingredients in a small bowl.

Dunk each oyster lightly in the mixture.

4. Line the platter with a new batch of paper towels. Return the oysters to the platter. Allow them to air-dry for 1 more hour. Rinse the oysters again and pat them dry. Change the paper toweling on the platter and return the oysters to the platter. Allow the oysters to air-dry for 1 more hour. The oysters should have a glossy-looking surface. (The oysters can be covered and refrigerated overnight at this point. Bring them back to room temperature before proceeding.)

5. Prepare the smoker for barbecuing, bringing the temperature to 180°F to 200°F.

6. Transfer the oysters to a small grill rack and place them in the smoker as far from the fire as possible. Cook them until somewhat shrunken and dried, yet short of shriveled and toughened, 45 to 55 minutes. Place the oysters in a small bowl and cover them with the oil. Refrigerate overnight or for up to 2 days. Serve at room temperature.

SERVING SUGGESTION We prefer the oysters as an appetizer, accompanied by bread or crackers.

A Honey of a Lobster Tail

Honey enhances the already sweet flavor of a juicy Maine lobster tail. In this dish, the smoke is deliciously subtle and light. SERVES 4

A HONEY OF A MARINADE AND OPTIONAL MOP

2 cups seafood stock

1 cup dry white wine

1/2 cup honey

1/4 cup extra-virgin olive oil

2 tablespoons white vinegar

2 tablespoons kosher salt or coarse sea salt

2 bay leaves

2 teaspoons dried thyme

Four 6-ounce to 7-ounce Maine lobster tails

1. An hour or two before you plan to barbecue, mix the marinade ingredients in a saucepan and bring to a boil over high heat. Stir, if needed, to dissolve the honey and salt. Remove the pan from the heat and let the mixture cool to room temperature.

2. Immerse the lobster tails in the cooled marinade and refrigerate them for 1 hour.

3. Prepare your smoker for barbecuing, bringing the temperature to 180°F to 200°F.

4. Drain the lobster, reserving the marinade if you plan to baste the tails (see page 45, "To Mop or Not"). To make the mop, bring the marinade back to a vigorous boil over high heat and boil for several minutes. Keep the liquid warm over low heat.

5. Transfer the lobster tails to the smoker, placing the lobster as far from the heat as possible. Smoke until just cooked through and tender, 35 to 40 minutes. Mop once or twice in a wood-burning pit, or as appropriate for your style of smoker. Serve the lobster warm or chilled.

SERVING SUGGESTION Start a special dinner with 007 Shrimp (page 362). Add a green salad with a citrus vinaigrette and Maque Choux Peppers (page 292). For a delectable finale, top angel food cake with fresh fruit. To use the lobster in a luscious salad, slice chilled lobster and combine it with mixed greens tossed with a honey-based dressing.

BBQ tip For barbecuing on a covered grill, we like to use a combination of wood chips and chunks. The chips produce more initial smoke, but the chunks last much longer. Be sure to replenish the wood as the vented smoke dies out, which may be as often as every 30 minutes if you're using chips alone.

Jungle Prince Scallops

A Hawaiian Thai specialty, jungle prince curry tastes as intriguing as it sounds.

SERVES 4

1 pound bay scallops

Clam juice or seafood stock (optional)

2 tablespoons peanut oil

2 garlic cloves, minced

1 tablespoon chopped fresh lemongrass

2 teaspoons peeled and minced fresh ginger

2 teaspoons Thai green curry paste, or more to taste

1 cup canned unsweetened coconut milk (not cream of coconut)

1 tablespoon Asian fish sauce or 2 tablespoons reduced-sodium soy sauce

1 cup shredded bok choy or napa cabbage

1/2 cup chopped fresh basil

1. Prepare the smoker for barbecuing, bringing the temperature to 180°F to 200°F.

2. If the scallops aren't moist and plump, soak them for about 10 minutes in enough clam juice or seafood stock to cover.

3. Arrange the scallops on a small grill rack or baking sheet. Smoke as far from the fire as possible until just barely cooked through and opaque, 10 to 15 minutes. Remove the scallops from the smoker.

4. Warm the oil in a skillet over medium heat. Stir in the garlic, lemongrass, ginger, and curry paste and cook for 2 to 3 minutes. Pour in the coconut milk and fish sauce and simmer until reduced by about one-third. Stir in the bok choy and cook for an additional 2 to 3 minutes. Mix in the scallops and the basil, remove from the heat, and serve immediately.

SERVING SUGGESTION Serve over white rice. Add a cool dessert such as Booker's Bourbon Mint Ice Cream (page 465) or Mojito Sorbet (page 466).

FOLLOWING IN THE FOOTSTEPS

George Bush the Elder likes the barbecue at Otto's in Houston, which loves to publicize its connection to the ex-president. Bush can also barbecue for himself, on a Pitt's & Spitt's pit that he brought home from Camp David. His son George W. favors the 'Q' at Cooper's in the hill country town of Llano, where you order your barbecue at outside pits and bring the meat inside to pay for it, sauce it, and dress it with side dishes.

Scallop and Snapper Ceviche

The citrus juice in traditional ceviche chemically "cooks" the seafood. In this version, we finish the process with smoke, adding another contrasting flavor.

SERVES 2 AS A MAIN COURSE OR 4 AS AN APPETIZER

2 oranges, peeled and sectioned

1/2 pound red snapper, yellowtail snapper, or other firm-fleshed white fish, cut into bite-size chunks

1/2 pound scallops (small bay scallops can be used as is, larger sea scallops should be halved)

1/3 cup freshly squeezed lime juice

1 ripe Hass avocado, peeled, pitted, and cubed

1 Roma or other plum tomato, chopped

1/4 cup finely diced red bell pepper

1/4 cup finely diced red onion

1 to 2 fresh serranos or 1 fresh jalapeño, minced

1 to 2 tablespoons extra-virgin olive oil

1/4 teaspoon kosher salt or coarse sea salt

Diced yellow tomato or yellow bell pepper (optional), for more color

Lime wedges, for garnish

1. Squeeze enough orange sections to make 2 tablespoons of juice. Cut the remaining sections in halves or thirds and reserve.

2. Marinate the snapper and scallops in the lime and orange juices in a nonreactive bowl for 30 to 40 minutes.

3. While the seafood "cooks," prepare the smoker for barbecuing, bringing the temperature to 180°F to 200°F.

4. Drain the seafood and arrange it on a small grill rack or in a pie pan. Cook it as far from the fire as possible until warmed through, about 15 minutes. Taste one morsel. If the smoke hasn't yet gently soaked into the snapper and scallops, allow a few more minutes. Be careful to avoid drying out the seafood.

5. Lightly mix the fish with the orange sections and remaining ingredients in a medium-size bowl. Refrigerate for up to 30 minutes. Serve in parfait glasses, margarita glasses, or glass bowls to show off the ceviche's colors. Garnish with the limes.

SERVING SUGGESTION For a weekend lunch, serve the ceviche with Sweet Potato Biscuits (page 411) and finish with Santa Fe Capirotada (page 464).

If you haven't come across John T. Edge's *Southern Belly* (2000, Hill Street Press), go get a copy. The subtitle tells it straight in claiming that the book is "The Ultimate Food Lover's Companion to the South." Edge ambles with wit and passion through the real, down-to-earth culinary delights of ten states, focusing in particular on good local restaurants and barbecue joints.

Cookin' Clams

Contrary to some claims, the New England clambake was not the first form of barbecue in the country. A traditional clambake uses a wood fire in a pit for cooking, like barbecue, but the clams are steamed with moisture from seaweed rather than smoked. If you would really rather have barbecue, just leave out the wet seaweed.

SERVES 6

4 to 5 dozen fresh clams, in their shells, cleaned in several changes of cold water

Melted garlic butter, Smoked Butter (page 373), or Old-Fashioned High-Cholesterol Great-Tasting Southern Sauce (page 372) (optional)

1. Prepare the smoker for barbecuing, bringing the temperature to 180°F to 200°F.

2. Discard any clams that aren't tightly closed. Arrange the clams in a single layer on a small grill rack or baking sheet. Depending on the size of your smoker and cooking implements, this may require cooking in more than one batch. Place the clams as far from the fire as possible. Cook them until the shells pop open, 10 to 15 minutes. Discard any clams that don't open within several minutes of the rest of the batch.

3. Serve the clams immediately, with garlic butter, Smoked Butter, or Old-Fashioned High-Cholesterol Great-Tasting Southern Sauce if you wish.

SERVING SUGGESTION For a Fourth of July feast, complement the clams with Smoky Corn on the Cob (page 288), Creamy Coleslaw (page 390), and onions and red-skinned potatoes boiled with generous spoonfuls of Wild Willy's Number One-derful Rub (page 26). Have at least two fruit desserts on hand, perhaps Long-on-Strawberries Shortcake (page 455) and Wild Huckleberry Pie with Coconut Crumble (page 446).

Smoked Mussels with Dill Mayonnaise

Despite an abundance of mussels in Atlantic and Pacific coastal waters, Americans have never eaten them to the extent that Europeans have for generations. They can be scrumptious, particularly, we think, in this preparation. SERVES 4

DILL MAYONNAISE

1 cup mayonnaise

2 tablespoons extra-virgin olive oil

2 tablespoons minced fresh dill, preferably, or 1 tablespoon dried dill

1/4 teaspoon freshly squeezed lemon juice or white vinegar

MUSSEL MOP

1/2 cup bottled clam juice

2 tablespoons freshly squeezed lemon juice

2 tablespoons extra-virgin olive oil

4 to 5 dozen mussels in their shells

Dill sprigs (optional), for garnish

1. Whisk together the mayonnaise ingredients in a small bowl. Cover and refrigerate.

2. Combine the mop ingredients in a small bowl.

3. Prepare the smoker for barbecuing, bringing the temperature to 180°F to 200°F.

4. Place the mussels in a shallow smoke-proof dish large enough to hold them in a single layer, more or less.

5. Place the mussels in the smoker as far from the fire as possible. Plan on a total cooking time of 25 to 30 minutes. If you plan to baste the mussels (see page 45, "To Mop or Not"), drizzle some of the mop into the mussels that have opened after 15 to 20 minutes. The mussels are done when all have opened and they are still plump and juicy. Drizzle the mop over all the mussels when they come off the smoker. Serve the mussels in large shallow bowls accompanied by the mayonnaise and garnished, if you like, with dill. Pop them from the shells with a fork, dunk into the mayonnaise, and savor.

RAIN OR SHINE

A barbecue competition team composed entirely of post office employees, the U.S. Porkmasters converted a mail jeep into their contest cooker. They put a charcoal oven under the hood and a smoker in the rear—vented, of course, through the exhaust pipe. You could always count on them to deliver the 'Q.'

Crab in Garlic Cream

This one is richer than the Rockefeller clan. Serve the crab over spinach fettuccine or other noodles, or spooned into golden puff pastry shells.

SERVES 4 AS A MAIN COURSE OR 6 AS AN APPETIZER

GARLIC CREAM

1 tablespoon unsalted butter

3 garlic cloves, minced

1 tablespoon minced onion

1 cup heavy cream

12-ounce can evaporated milk

1/2 teaspoon kosher salt or coarse sea salt, or more to taste

1/2 teaspoon ground white pepper

1 1/2 pounds king crab legs

8 ounces seafood sausage, preferably a link style

Vegetable oil

1. Prepare the smoker for barbecuing, bringing the temperature to 180°F to 200°F.

2. In a large saucepan, melt the butter over medium heat. Add the garlic and onion and sauté until softened. Add the cream and milk and stir in the salt and pepper. Simmer until reduced by one-third. Keep the sauce warm.

3. Crack the crab legs at the joints and in several other spots. Oil the legs and the seafood sausage. Place the sausage on the smoker. After the sausage has cooked for about 45 minutes, add the crab to the smoker. Cook both for another 15 minutes. The sausage should be cooked through but still succulent, and the exposed crabmeat should flake easily. Both should have a gentle but distinct smoke taste.

4. Remove the crab from the shells and slice the sausage into thin rounds. Mix both with the garlic cream and heat through if needed. Serve hot.

CLEVER COOKS

Barbecue contest teams compete against one another on all levels, including their names. Some of the winners over the years include Pork, Sweat & Beers (Cordova, Tennessee), ZZ Chop (Irving, Texas), Sow Luau (Memphis), Great Boars of Fire (Cobden, Illinois), Pork Forkers (Columbus, Mississippi), and Hazardous Waist (Collierville, Tennessee).

Katzen Dawgs

The name is clever and so is the idea—smoked catfish hushpuppies that are superb for appetizers or a main course. Offer a tip of your gimme cap to John Wysor, from the Spoon River Charcuterie in Charlotte, North Carolina, for concocting the original recipe, and another nod to Donna Ellis at Cookshack for making it available. Use your own smoked catfish, which can be cooked up to a couple of days in advance, or buy some from the store. **SERVES 4 AS A MAIN DISH OR 6 TO 8 AS AN APPETIZER**

3/4 pound smoked catfish (such as Peppered Catfish, page 246)

1/2 cup buttermilk

1/2 cup minced onion

2 tablespoons minced scallion tops

2 large eggs, lightly beaten

1 tablespoon melted bacon drippings or butter

1 tablespoon freshly squeezed lemon juice

1 teaspoon Tabasco or other hot pepper sauce, or more to taste

3/4 cup yellow cornmeal, preferably stone-ground

1/4 cup all-purpose flour

1 tablespoon baking powder

1/2 teaspoon baking soda

1/2 teaspoon freshly ground black pepper

1/4 teaspoon table salt

Vegetable oil for deep-frying

Tartar sauce or Creole Classic Barbecue Sauce (page 382) (optional)

1. Remove the bones from the catfish, if necessary, and chop the fish coarsely. In a bowl, mix the fish, buttermilk, onion, scallions, eggs, bacon drippings, lemon juice, and Tabasco.

2. Combine the cornmeal, flour, baking powder, baking soda, pepper, and salt in a large bowl. Pour the fish mixture into the dry ingredients. Stir just to blend.

3. In a deep, heavy skillet, heat 3 inches of oil to 365°F. Drop heaping tablespoons of the batter into the oil, a few at a time. Don't overcrowd. The hushpuppies will rise to the surface as they cook, so turn them if they are browning unevenly. Fry until golden brown on all sides, about 3 minutes. Drain. Serve immediately with tartar sauce or Creole Classic Barbecue Sauce if you wish.

SERVING SUGGESTION For supper, match the Dawgs with Sweet and Sour Cukes (page 420) and 'Nana Nut Salad (page 430). When you want a hearty appetizer, serve the Dawgs as finger food, like Caribbean accras (cod fritters), accompanied by icy drinks such as Cham-gria (page 483), Apricoritas (page 476), or Derby Day Mint Juleps (page 473).

GARDEN OF EATIN'

FOR SOME BARBECUE PURISTS, FISH STRETCHES THE LIMITS OF THE 'Q.' VEGETABLES JUST GO BEYOND THE BOUNDS. YOU START PUTTING SQUASH IN A PIT AND THEY'LL BE DANCING IN THE HOG TROUGH WITH EXASPERATION.

SO LET 'EM. THE FACT IS, SOME VEGETABLES AND EVEN FRUITS TASTE GREAT SMOKED. IT MAY BE A WHILE BEFORE YOU FIND A YAM BARBECUE FESTIVAL, OR AN AUTHENTIC BAR-B-Q JOINT FEATURING PIT-SMOKED APPLES, BUT GOOD pitmasters should always be ready to take some liberties in the privacy of their backyard. Try these delicious dishes and they'll probably spark some other licentious ideas.

Vidalias 'n' Georgia BBQ Sauce

Almost the size of footballs, Georgia's famous Vidalia onions are available only in the late spring and early summer, just in time to kick off the barbecue season. When slathered with a mustardy sauce from the same state, smoked Vidalias and other sweet onions become golden orbs of succulence. SERVES 6 AS A SIDE DISH

3 Vidalia or other large sweet onions
Vegetable oil
Golden Mustard Barbecue Sauce (page 371) or other mustard-based barbecue sauce

1. Prepare the smoker for barbecuing, bringing the temperature to 200°F to 220°F.

2. Slice each onion in half through the root and peel the outer layer. Cut down to, but not through, the base of each onion half in crisscross directions to make an onion "flower." Rub or spray a thin coat of oil over the onions and wrap each half in foil.

3. Transfer the onions to the smoker and cook for 30 to 35 minutes. Remove the foil or peel it back to form a flat base and brush the onions with a thick coating of barbecue sauce. Continue cooking until the onion is tender, 35 to 45 minutes more. Remove the onions from the smoker and brush with additional barbecue sauce before serving.

SERVING SUGGESTION Try these with traditional barbecued pork, such as The Renowned Mr. Brown (page 51), Perfect Picnic (page 53), or Going Whole Hog (page 58). They'd be a proud accompaniment to Ginger-Glazed Ham (page 80), too.

VARIATION: POP-TOP VIDALIAS Instead of topping the onions with a mustard-based barbecue sauce, substitute Pop Mop (page 47) using Dr Pepper, Cherry Dr Pepper, RC Cola, or Coke. It does double duty as a mop and sauce, and you'll end up with a sweet caramelized flavor.

BBQ tip If you want to experiment with vegetables, keep a couple of general principles in mind. Usually you coat vegetables with oil before putting them in the smoker, to keep them from drying out. You can do this by hand or by spritzing them with a spray oil. That may be all you do, because simple preparations are often the best. You may want to play creatively with dry rubs, pastes, marinades, or mops, but you are less likely to need them than when you barbecue meat.

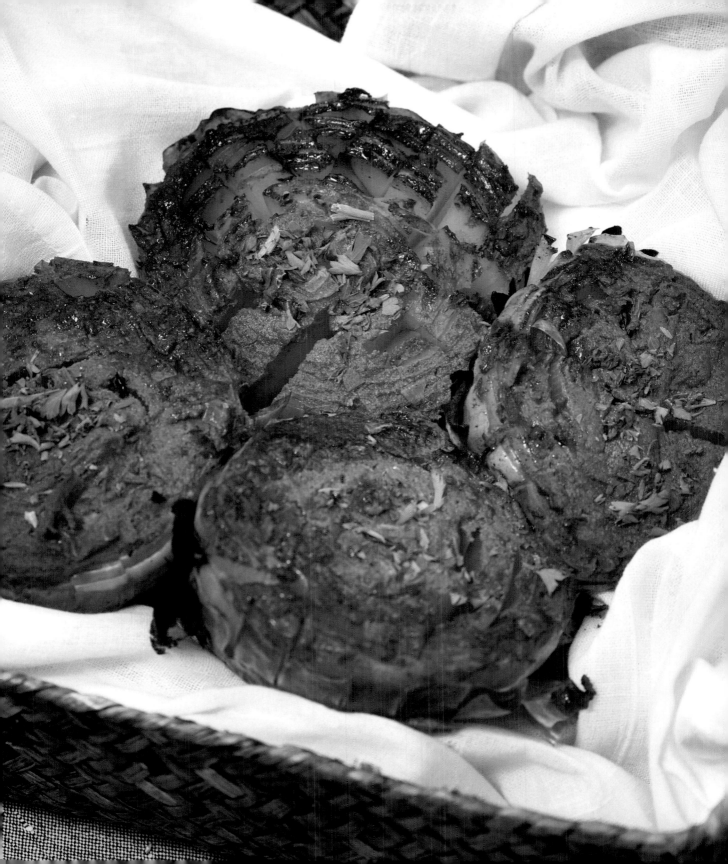

Peabody-Style Stuffed Onions

Best known for the ducks that parade and swim in its lobby, the Peabody Hotel in Memphis has also earned kudos for its stuffed onions. If the kitchen smoked them—the dish, not the ducks—the onions might rival the quackers in acclaim.

SERVES 4 AS A MAIN COURSE OR 8 AS A SIDE DISH

4 medium onions

Vegetable oil

1 tablespoon unsalted butter

2 garlic cloves, minced

12 ounces fresh spinach, chopped

1½ cups cooked rice

1 cup ground ham (leftovers from Ginger-Glazed Ham, page 80, or Maple-Bourbon Ham, page 79, are especially flavorful)

1 cup dry cornbread crumbs or other bread crumbs

6 tablespoons grated Romano or Parmesan cheese, plus additional for sprinkling over the onions

½ teaspoon dried sage

¼ teaspoon dried thyme

Table salt and freshly ground black pepper to taste

¾ cup chicken stock

1 large egg, lightly beaten

1. Prepare the smoker for barbecuing, bringing the temperature to 200°F to 220°F.

2. Slice the ends off the onions and cut them in half horizontally, but don't remove the skins. Carefully scoop out the centers of the onion halves with a melon baller or spoon, leaving a shell about ⅓ inch to ½ inch thick. Do not discard the centers. Coat the onions with oil.

3. Transfer the onions to the smoker and cook until softened but not yet tender, 30 to 35 minutes.

4. While the onions are cooking, prepare the stuffing. Chop half of the onion center pieces and set them aside. Save the other half for another use.

5. In a skillet, warm the butter over medium heat. Add the chopped onion and the garlic and sauté for 1 to 2 minutes. Stir in the spinach and cook until limp, adding a tablespoon of water if the mixture begins to stick. Stir in the rice, ham, bread crumbs, cheese, sage, thyme, salt, and pepper, and add as much of the stock as needed to bind the mixture together. It should be moist but not soupy. Mix in the egg.

6. Remove the onions from the smoker and, when cool enough to handle, peel them. Spoon the stuffing into the onions and sprinkle a bit of Romano or Parmesan over the top of each. Return the onions to the smoker and cook them until they are tender and the stuffing is lightly browned, an additional 20 to 25 minutes. Serve hot.

SERVING SUGGESTION These make a good lunch entrée accompanied by a fruit salad, perhaps Mango and Avocado Salad (page 430). Serve slices of South Georgia Pound Cake (page 458) for dessert and, if you like, Booker's Bourbon Mint Ice Cream (page 465).

Better-Than-French Onion Soup

This gutsy, deeply flavored soup is a gem. It's particularly splendid when you make its beef stock with barbecued brisket trimmings. Smoke the onions ahead if you like, for easier preparation. SERVES 4 AS A MAIN COURSE OR 6 AS AN APPETIZER

4 medium onions, unpeeled

Vegetable oil

6 cups beef stock, preferably homemade

1/4 cup dry red wine

1 tablespoon Memphis Magic (page 374) or other not-too-sweet tomato-based barbecue sauce

1 teaspoon dried thyme

Kosher salt or coarse sea salt to taste

1/4 teaspoon freshly ground black pepper

4 slices crusty country-style white bread

1 cup shredded Gruyère cheese

1. About 3 hours before you plan to eat the soup, prepare the smoker for barbecuing, bringing the temperature to 200°F to 220°F.

2. Rub the onions with a thin coating of oil and place them in the smoker. Cook until the skins are well browned and the onions feel soft, about 1½ hours. When the onions are cool enough to handle, peel them and slice them thin.

3. Place the onions in a saucepan and add the stock, wine, barbecue sauce, thyme, salt, and pepper. Simmer the soup for 45 minutes.

4. Preheat the broiler. Toast the bread.

5. Spoon the hot soup into four ovenproof bowls. Top each portion of soup with a piece of toast and some of the cheese. Broil briefly until the cheese is melted. Serve immediately.

BBQ tip Homemade stock makes an enormous difference in the flavor of soups, and it's simple to prepare. Start by saving trimmings and bones from raw or cooked poultry and beef—separate from each other, for their different stocks—and collect carrot peels, celery tops, and onion skins together to use in both stocks. Stash the ingredients in the freezer in plastic bags until you've got several pounds. To make a stock, put the ingredients into a stockpot or large saucepan with a little garlic, a few peppercorns, and, if you have it, some parsley. Don't add salt, which can make it difficult to control the saltiness of dishes that use the stock. Cover everything with twice as much water, bring the pot to a boil, and then reduce the heat to low. Simmer slowly for several hours. Leave the pot uncovered, evaporating the liquid and intensifying the taste. We usually cook the stock until about one-third of the original liquid remains, but you can reduce it further for greater richness and simpler storage. When the stock is ready, strain it and freeze it in multiple batches, for easy use later as needed.

Smoked Onion Rings

These are basic yet scrumptious, a perfect stovetop-smoker side dish for a winter evening. For a more festive appearance, sprinkle the onion rings with chopped chives, parsley, or other compatible herbs after cooking, or drizzle with your favorite barbecue sauce. **SERVES 4 TO 6 AS A SIDE DISH**

2 large onions, sliced into 1/3-inch-thick rings
2 tablespoons vegetable oil
2 tablespoons balsamic vinegar or pepper vinegar
Table salt and freshly ground black pepper

1. If you want to keep the onions in neat concentric rings, run a soaked bamboo skewer through each slice. Arrange the onions in a shallow dish. Whisk together the oil and vinegar and splash over the onions. Turn the slices as needed to coat both sides lightly. Sprinkle with salt and pepper.

2. Prepare the smoker for barbecuing, bringing the temperature to 200°F to 220°F. Skewered onions can go directly onto the cooking grate. Otherwise, arrange the slices on a small grill rack or shallow smoke-proof pan. Cook until tender, 20 to 30 minutes. Serve warm.

BARBECUE STEWS FROM THE PAST

A magazine article in 1895 described a noontime barbecue meal from that period. The writer said that even if you weren't hungry yet at that hour, "You begin to be so when you sniff the savory odors from afar. There is something indescribably delicious about meat cooked in this way, and, delicious, too, are the other things that go with it. There is a succulent stew made of corn, tomatoes, ochra [sic], onions, carrots, green peppers, and meat boiled to shreds, which forms an important part in the barbecue menu; and another stew is made of the tongues, heads, and feet of pigs whose carcasses have been roasted. This is good, but very rich."

American jazz and barbecue grew up together in the Kansas City ghettos of the 1920s and 1930s. African American pacesetters, from Charlie Parker to Charlie Bryant, nourished both, often at the same speakeasies and clubs.

Bar-B-Q'ed Cabbage Head

OK, we know it sounds weird. However, versions of this dish have become almost as popular as jalapeño poppers at BBQ competitions. They won't replace pork and brisket at the center of the plate, but wedges of the cabbage may be nestled nearby.

SERVES 4 TO 6

1 medium to large cabbage head, about 2½ pounds

4 slices bacon, chopped

1 medium onion, chopped

1 tablespoon cider or white vinegar or beer, if you happen to have one open

1 teaspoon Wild Willy's Number One-derful Rub (page 26) or 3/4 teaspoon garlic salt plus 1/4 teaspoon freshly ground black pepper

1/4 cup tomato- or mustard-based barbecue sauce, such as Struttin' Sauce (page 369) or Golden Mustard Barbecue Sauce (page 371)

1. Pull off any loose outer leaves from the cabbage. Par-cook the whole cabbage in a large pan of salted water over medium heat for about 15 minutes to soften it. Drain the cabbage and turn it core side up. Make a little foil collar for the cabbage to sit on, tearing off about a foot-long piece of heavy-duty foil, then crumpling it into a ring that will hold the cabbage upright. Cut out the core, cutting down about 3 inches into the cabbage and making an opening on the surface 2 to 3 inches across. Pop the core out with a knife and discard it.

2. Prepare the smoker for barbecuing, bringing the temperature to 200°F to 220°F.

3. Cook the bacon in a medium-size skillet over medium heat. After the bacon has softened and begun to render fat, add the onion to the pan and sauté until the onion is translucent and the bacon is crisp, about 5 minutes more. Remove the bacon-onion mixture with a slotted spoon and reserve both the mixture and the bacon drippings.

4. Pour the vinegar into the cabbage's empty cavity. Then sprinkle the cavity with the rub, add the barbecue sauce, and pack in the bacon-onion mixture. Rub the outside of the cabbage with the bacon drippings.

5. Place the cabbage on its foil ring in the smoker. Cook until the cabbage is fully tender (check with a bamboo skewer), 45 to 60 minutes. Pull any burned or dried-out leaves off the cabbage. Slice the cabbage down through the top into 4 or 6 wedges and serve.

Sweet Potatoes with Orange-Pecan Butter

Like onions, sweet potatoes have a natural affinity for smoke. The deep caramel flavor needs no garnish, but we like to gild the lily with the addition of a simple butter sauce. SERVES 4 AS A MAIN OR SIDE DISH

4 small sweet potatoes

Vegetable oil

ORANGE-PECAN BUTTER

4 to 6 tablespoons unsalted butter

1 teaspoon honey

Juice and zest of 1 orange

2 tablespoons chopped pecans

1/4 teaspoon dry mustard

Kosher salt or coarse sea salt and freshly ground black pepper to taste

1. Prepare the smoker for barbecuing, bringing the temperature to 200°F to 220°F.

2. Scrub the potatoes well, prick them in several spots, and rub a light film of oil over them. Transfer the potatoes to the smoker and cook them until they are soft, about 2 hours. The po-tatoes can sit for 15 minutes before serving, or you can wrap them in foil to keep them warm for up to an hour.

3. While the potatoes cook, melt the butter and honey together in a small saucepan over low heat. Stir in the remaining ingredients. Reheat the butter, if necessary, just before serving.

4. To serve, slit open the top of each of the sweet potatoes and drizzle with the orange-pecan butter. Serve hot.

BBQ *tip* **Try Candied Sweet Potatoes (page 399) or any favorite sweet potato recipe using smoked spuds. They add a delicious depth to the flavor of many dishes.**

A SWEET VEGGIE FINALE

Southern Arizona is better known for cactus than ribs, but Jack's Original Barbecue in Tucson has been serving an authentic version of its specialty since the 1950s. The restaurant offers it all, from peppery links to blackened brisket. For vegetable lovers, there's sweet potato pie for dessert.

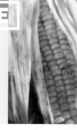

Two renowned Texas pitmasters died in the 1990s, but both mentored enough younger cooks to keep their influence alive for many years. Sonny Bryan attracted all of Dallas to his Smokehouse shack for three decades. You never knew who you would see eating one of the magnificent brisket sandwiches in his parking lot, dribbling sauce on anything from overalls to designer dresses. "Stubbs" Stubblefield, of Lubbock fame, became the caterer of choice for West Texas musicians and artists. When Jo Harvey and Terry Allen celebrated a big wedding anniversary in Santa Fe, they trucked Stubbs and his pit hundreds of miles to cook the 'Q' and join the fun. Both men made memories.

Drunken Sweet Potatoes

Tipsy from tequila, these potatoes enhance any Southwest barbecue spread.

SERVES 4 AS A SIDE DISH

¹/₄ cup unsalted butter

1¹/₄ pounds grated sweet potato (from about 1 large sweet potato)

2¹/₂ tablespoons packed brown sugar

¹/₄ teaspoon table salt

¹/₄ cup tequila

Juice of 2 limes

1. Prepare the smoker for barbecuing, bringing the temperature to 200°F to 220°F.

2. In a cast-iron skillet or smoke-proof baking dish, melt the butter. Stir in the sweet potatoes and then pat the potatoes down into a thick, even layer. Sprinkle the brown sugar and the salt over the potatoes.

3. Transfer the potatoes to the smoker and cook for 1 hour. Stir in 3 tablespoons of the tequila and half of the lime juice, pat the potatoes back down again, and continue cooking the potatoes until they are quite tender but crisped a bit around the edges, 50 to 60 minutes. Remove the potatoes from the smoker and stir in the remaining tequila and lime juice. Serve warm.

SERVING SUGGESTION Pair the potatoes with Bona Fide Fajitas (page 124) and Texas Peach Cobbler (page 452).

Scalloped Green Chile Potatoes

A touch of smoke and a kiss of green chile wake up sleepy scalloped potatoes. Use fresh, thawed frozen, or jarred chiles, because the canned version is pretty drowsy itself. SERVES 4 AS A MAIN DISH OR 6 AS A SIDE DISH

3 baking potatoes

Vegetable oil

3/4 cup chopped roasted green chiles, preferably New Mexican, Anaheim, or poblano, preferably fresh or frozen (see BBQ tip on page 151)

3/4 cup grated Monterey Jack cheese (about 3 ounces)

1/3 cup chopped red onion

1 cup half-and-half

Kosher salt or coarse sea salt and freshly ground black pepper to taste

Nutmeg to taste

1. Prepare the smoker for barbecuing, bringing the temperature to 200°F to 220°F.

2. Peel the potatoes and cut them into 1-inch chunks. Coat each chunk with oil.

3. Place the potatoes on a small grill rack, transfer them to the smoker, and smoke until they are partially cooked and well perfumed with smoke, 50 to 75 minutes. When the potatoes are cool enough to handle, slice them thinly.

4. Preheat the oven to 350°F and grease a 9 x 13-inch baking dish. Layer one-third of the potatoes with about one-third of the chiles, cheese, onion, half-and-half, salt, and pepper. Repeat the layers until all the ingredients are used. Dust liberally with nutmeg.

5. Bake, covered, for 40 minutes. Uncover the dish and bake for an additional 10 minutes, or until the potatoes are meltingly tender. Serve warm.

McPIG

The country's first drive-in restaurant sold barbecue to newly mobile Americans in the early years of the automobile. Opened in 1921 in Dallas, Texas, the Pig Stand expanded into a national chain by the next decade. Waiters with white shirts and black bow ties ran to meet approaching cars and tried to jump on the running board before they stopped, giving rise to the term *carhop*.

Smoked Spud Skins

As potatoes themselves do, the skins step lively after a barbecue bath.

SERVES 4 TO 6 AS AN APPETIZER

8 baking potatoes, scrubbed

Butter or olive oil

1 to 2 tablespoons Wild Willy's Number One-derful Rub (page 26), Cajun Ragin' Rub (page 29), or other savory seasoning blend

3/4 cup grated Monterey Jack or cheddar cheese (about 3 ounces)

Sliced scallions, for garnish

Alabama Great White (page 385), Peppery Sweet Onion Sauce (page 378), Sauce Olé (page 379), or Creole Classic Barbecue Sauce (page 382) (optional)

1. Bake or boil the potatoes until tender. Then cut in halves or quarters and scoop out to leave a shell 1/4 inch to 1/2 inch thick. (Reserve the scooped-out portions for mashed potatoes or another use.)

2. Prepare the smoker for barbecuing, bringing the temperature to 200°F to 220°F.

3. Rub the potato skins with a thin coat of butter or oil. Sprinkle the skins, inside and out, with the rub or other dry spice mixture.

4. Transfer the skins to the smoker and cook until they are browned and crispy, 55 to 65 minutes. Sprinkle the cheese over the skins and cook for an additional couple of minutes, until the cheese melts. Top with the scallions. Serve piping hot, with Alabama Great White, Peppery Sweet Onion Sauce, Sauce Olé, or Creole Classic Barbecue Sauce if you wish.

Simple 'Shrooms

Mushrooms make one of the most impressive smoked vegetables to serve sliced as a side dish without further embellishment. SERVES 4 AS A SIDE DISH

16 to 18 large button mushrooms or 8 portobello mushroom caps, sliced 1/3 inch thick

Olive oil

Kosher salt or coarse sea salt and freshly ground black pepper

1. Prepare the smoker for barbecuing, bringing the temperature to 200°F to 220°F.

2. Brush the mushroom slices with enough oil to coat, then sprinkle them generously with salt and pepper. Arrange the mushrooms on a small grill rack or a piece of heavy-duty foil.

3. Place the mushrooms in the smoker and cook until they ooze liquid and are cooked through and tender, 20 to 25 minutes. Serve warm.

SERVING SUGGESTION Top a steak or burger with the mushrooms, toss them with a warm spinach salad, or chop them to use as an omelet or calzone filling.

"Food like barbecue and chili remains an embarrassment to people who want to think of themselves as living in a big-league city that is sophisticated enough to have an array of Continental restaurants—Continental restaurants that are modeled, an unwary traveler can discover, on the continent of Antarctica, where everything starts out frozen. . . . [These city dwellers are] afflicted with a disease of the American provinces I have managed to isolate and identify as rubaphobia—not the fear of rubes but the fear of being thought of as a rube." Calvin Trillin, *Alice, Let's Eat* (1978, Random House).

'Bello Burger

This is a smoked adaptation of one of our favorite grilled veggie sandwiches, hearty enough to satisfy most avowed carnivores. SERVES 4 AS A MAIN DISH

4 portobello mushroom caps (stems reserved for another purpose), each about 5 inches in diameter

Olive oil

Kosher salt or coarse sea salt to taste

4 thin slices provolone cheese, each large enough to cover a mushroom cap, at room temperature

1/3 cup mayonnaise

3 tablespoons prepared pesto

4 red-ripe tomato slices

4 large squares focaccia bread, split and toasted, or 4 large crusty rolls, split

1. Prepare the smoker for barbecuing, bringing the temperature to 200°F to 220°F.

2. Brush the mushrooms lightly with oil and sprinkle them with salt.

3. Place the mushrooms in the smoker and cook until they ooze liquid and are cooked through, 20 to 25 minutes. Cover the mushrooms with cheese shortly before removing them from the smoker.

4. Stir together the mayonnaise and pesto and spread the mixture over the bread slices. Place a tomato on four of the slices, then top with a mushroom and the remaining pieces of bread. Serve hot.

SERVING SUGGESTION Serve the burgers with Smoked Spud Skins (page 284) for a casual chow-down, or dress them up a bit with Southern Caesar Salad (page 416).

Barbecuers with bicycles might want to enter the Tour de Pig at the Lexington [North Carolina] Barbecue Festival, held each October. If that doesn't wear you out, you can also compete in the Hawg Run, enter the golf tournament, or try to win the occasional cheerleading competition by coming up with an exciting new way to root for barbecue.

South-of-the-Border Garlic Soup

Some of the finest Mexican dishes are soups that feature *ajo*, or garlic. We drew on that tradition in developing this preparation, where the garlic is mellowed dramatically by smoking. SERVES 4 AS A MAIN DISH OR 6 AS AN APPETIZER

2 whole heads of garlic

1½ tablespoons vegetable oil, plus more to coat the garlic

1 medium onion, sliced thin

1 medium tomato, chopped

8 cups (2 quarts) chicken stock, preferably homemade

1 to 2 dried chipotle chiles

Juice of 1 lime

1 ripe Hass avocado, peeled, pitted, and cubed

1 tablespoon minced fresh cilantro, or more to taste

2 corn tortillas, cut into matchsticks

Lime slices, for garnish

1. Prepare the smoker for barbecuing, bringing the temperature to 200°F to 220°F.

2. Rub the unpeeled garlic bulbs with a thin coating of oil and transfer them to the smoker. Cook the garlic until the peel is well browned and the cloves feel quite soft, about 1 hour. When the garlic is cool enough to handle, peel all the cloves and reserve them.

3. Heat 1 tablespoon of the oil in a large sauce-pan over medium-low heat. Add the onion to the oil and sauté until it's softened and lightly colored. Spoon the mixture into a blender and add the tomato and reserved garlic. Puree.

4. Add the remaining ½ tablespoon oil to the saucepan and heat it over medium-high heat. Pour in the blender mixture and sauté it until it begins to dry out and the tomato darkens a shade or two. Add the chicken stock and the chipotle and reduce the heat to medium. Simmer the mixture for 25 to 30 minutes, remove it from the heat, and add the lime juice.

5. Divide the avocado, cilantro, and tortillas among individual bowls and pour the hot soup over them. Garnish each bowl with a slice of lime and serve.

SERVING SUGGESTION For a light supper, pair the soup with Can't Wait Queso (page 340). Shake up a batch of Mexican Martinis (page 475), too.

Bronzed Artichokes

This two-step preparation yields exceptionally tender artichokes. You can do the smoking several days in advance of the steaming and serving.

SERVES 2 AS A MAIN DISH OR 4 AS AN APPETIZER OR SIDE DISH

2 medium artichokes

Juice of 1 lemon

2 teaspoons olive oil

Golden Mustard Barbecue Sauce (page 371) or vinaigrette dressing (optional)

1. At least 3 hours before you plan to eat the artichokes, trim them, cutting off all tough leaf tips. Spread the leaves slightly. Place the artichokes in a bowl and add the lemon juice and olive oil. Pour enough water over the artichokes to submerge them. Soak the artichokes for at least 30 minutes and up to 2 hours.

2. Prepare the smoker for barbecuing, bringing the temperature to 200°F to 220°F.

3. Drain the artichokes. Place the artichokes in the smoker and cook until the leaves are deeply bronzed and have loosened somewhat, 1½ to 1¾ hours.

4. Remove the artichokes from the smoker and steam them over boiling water until very tender, 25 to 30 minutes. The artichokes can be eaten warm or chilled. Serve whole, accompanied by Golden Mustard Barbecue sauce or vinaigrette dressing if you wish.

A SERIOUS PIG PASSION

Roving food writers Jane and Michael Stern vividly remember their first visit to D & H Bar-B-Que in Manning, South Carolina. As they say in their wonderful *Roadfood* (1992, HarperCollins), "It was here, twenty years ago, that we detoured from writing a book about truck drivers and ate some of our first genuine southern barbecue. Since then we have spent our life looking for good food, barbecue foremost among our targets; and the hunger inspired by that first real Carolina pig-out has kept us on the road for a million miles."

Smoky Corn on the Cob

Putting bacon in the husk adds resonant flavor to slow-smoked corn.

SERVES 6 AS A SIDE DISH

6 ears of corn, with husks

Kosher salt or coarse sea salt and freshly ground black pepper to taste

6 slices bacon

Old-Fashioned High-Cholesterol Great-Tasting Southern Sauce (page 372), Garlic-Herb Butter (page 47), or melted butter (optional)

1. Pull back the corn husks just enough to remove the silks. Place the corn in a large bowl and cover it with cold water. Soak the corn for at least 30 minutes and up to 2 hours. Drain the corn.

2. Prepare the smoker for barbecuing, bringing the temperature to 200°F to 220°F.

3. Salt and pepper the corn and wrap a piece of bacon around each ear. Rearrange the husks in their original position. Tear 1 or 2 husks into strips and use them to tie around the top of the ears to hold the husks in place.

4. Place the corn in the smoker and cook until tender, 1 to 1¼ hours. Remove the corn from the smoker and discard the husks and bacon. Serve hot, with a sauce or butter if you like.

VARIATION: NAKED CORN ON THE COB Instead of wrapping the corn in bacon, try slathering the corn in extra-virgin olive oil, pumpkin seed oil, or garlic-flavored oil. All add great taste, too.

FROM BORSCHT TO BARBECUE

The showmanship awards at the Memphis in May cook-off are always great fun. One year we attended, the AutoZone barbecue team staged an elaborate skit about Boris Borscht, a Russian ballet dancer who gets fed up with the food at home and sets out to find real flavor. Boris samples and rejects the cooking of France, Italy, and Mexico. Discouraged, he pins his last hopes on Memphis, where he blows his tutu eating barbecue. Too fat to dance any longer, he starts a new life as Boris Barbecue, "the 'Q' man."

Black-Eyed Pea Cakes

Almost anything flat and porous, from hamburgers to vegetable cakes, is well suited to barbecue. SERVES 2 TO 3 AS A MAIN DISH OR 4 TO 6 AS A SIDE DISH

CAKES

2 cups cooked or canned black-eyed peas, well-drained

1/2 cup saltine-style cracker crumbs

2 tablespoons minced red bell pepper

2 tablespoons minced onion

1 garlic clove, minced

1 tablespoon minced fresh parsley

1 egg yolk

2 teaspoons minced pickled jalapeño

2 teaspoons mayonnaise

1 teaspoon yellow mustard

Approximately 1/2 cup saltine-style cracker crumbs

1 tablespoon unsalted butter

1 tablespoon vegetable oil

Golden Mustard Barbecue Sauce (page 371) or Carolina Red (page 371)

1. To make the cakes, puree 1 cup of the peas in a food processor. Place the pureed peas and the remaining whole peas in a bowl and add the remaining cake ingredients. Refrigerate the mixture for at least 1 hour, and up to 24 hours.

2. Prepare the smoker for barbecuing, bringing the temperature to 200°F to 220°F. Grease a smoke-proof baking dish.

3. Remove the cake mixture from the refrigerator. It should be moist, but stiff enough to form loose cakes. Place the additional cracker crumbs on a small plate. Make 6 to 8 cakes, dipping each in the cracker crumbs and coating well.

4. Warm the butter and oil in a skillet over medium-high heat. Fry the cakes for about 30 seconds per side, just long enough to crisp their surfaces.

5. Transfer the cakes to the smoker and cook until they are firm and heated through, 20 to 30 minutes. Remove the cakes from the smoker and serve hot, with Golden Mustard Barbecue Sauce or Carolina Red if you wish.

SERVING SUGGESTION The cakes make a satisfying main dish enhanced by a side of Sweet and Sour Cukes (page 420). You'll still have room for Black Walnut Cake (page 460) afterward.

Down-Home Ratatouille

We realized that ratatouille had been adopted as American fare a couple of decades ago when a cowboy café in Cheyenne, Wyoming, offered it to us as the vegetable of the day. We knew the dish still had some territory to cover, though, because the waiter called it "rat tool." SERVES 4 AS A MAIN DISH OR 6 AS A SIDE DISH

1 whole medium eggplant, sliced thick (do not peel)

2 leeks, halved

1 green bell pepper

1 red bell pepper

1 medium onion, sliced thick

3 tablespoons extra-virgin olive oil

2 garlic cloves, minced

3/4 cup canned crushed tomatoes

1/2 cup chicken stock

1/4 cup slivered cracked green Greek olives or other green olives with character

1. Prepare the smoker for barbecuing, bringing the temperature to 200°F to 220°F.

2. Rub the eggplant, leeks, bell peppers, and onion with 2 tablespoons of the olive oil. Place the vegetables in the smoker as far from the heat as possible. Cook until the vegetables are crisp-tender, 35 to 45 minutes. Remove the vegetables from the smoker and, when cool enough to handle, chop into bite-size pieces.

3. In a heavy skillet, heat the remaining 1 tablespoon oil over medium heat. Add the garlic and sauté for 1 minute. Stir in the smoked vegetables and any accumulated juice. Add the tomatoes and chicken stock and simmer the mixture until it's very thick and the vegetables are tender. Stir in the olives and heat through. Serve warm.

VARIATION: RATATOUILLE SOUP Puree leftovers with chicken stock and half-and-half in equal parts, using just enough liquid to meld the mixture into a thick potage.

BBQ *tip* Not all vegetables mate with serious smoke as well as the ones we've included in this chapter. Perhaps the biggest surprise to us was eggplant, because it grills wonderfully. It works in this ratatouille because it doesn't cook fully in the smoker, and is later mixed with other vegetables and flavorings. Other veggies that don't smoke well include turnips, broccoli, Brussels sprouts, and asparagus. That still leaves a load of options from your farmers' market or produce department.

Maque Choux Peppers

An assertive Cajun corn dish, maque choux dances a *fais do-do* on the tongue when combined with crimson peppers. **SERVES 4 AS A MAIN DISH**

4 medium red bell peppers

3 tablespoons unsalted butter

2 tablespoons vegetable oil

2 cups corn kernels, fresh or frozen

1 medium onion, chopped

1/2 medium green bell pepper, seeded and chopped

1/2 teaspoon ground white pepper

Kosher salt or coarse sea salt to taste

1 cup chicken stock

1/4 cup cream or half-and-half

Several healthy splashes of Tabasco or other hot pepper sauce

2 cups dry cornbread crumbs or other bread crumbs

1 egg white, beaten

1. Slice off the tops of the red bell peppers about 1/2 inch down from the stems. Remove the seeds and cores from the peppers. If any won't stand upright, slice a little off the bottom, being careful not to cut into the pepper's cavity. Reserve the peppers and their tops.

2. Melt the butter and oil in a medium-size skillet. Add the corn, onion, and green bell pepper and sauté over medium heat until fragrant. Add the white pepper and salt. Cover the pan and cook for about 10 minutes. Remove the lid, add the stock, cream, and Tabasco, and continue cooking, uncovered, until about half of the liquid has evaporated. Remove the filling from the heat and mix in the cornbread crumbs and egg white.

3. Prepare the smoker for barbecuing, bringing the temperature to 200°F to 220°F.

4. Grease a smoke-proof baking dish that can hold the peppers snugly upright.

5. Stuff each red bell pepper with a portion of the filling. Replace the tops of the peppers and secure with toothpicks. Arrange the peppers in the prepared dish.

6. Transfer the peppers to the smoker. Cook until they are tender but still hold their shape, 65 to 75 minutes. Remove the toothpicks and serve the peppers warm.

SERVING SUGGESTION The peppers make a hearty meatless main dish, accompanied by Buttermilk Biscuits (page 410) and a simple green salad. Finish with Peanutty Pie (page 445).

VARIATION: MEATY STUFFED PEPPERS Replace the oil and the corn with 2 cups ground pork.

BBQ tip Before you begin barbecuing, take a close look at your cooking grate. If you forgot to clean it the last time you used the smoker, scrape the grate thoroughly with a wire brush. Then always spray the surface with a vegetable oil cooking spray to prevent food from sticking to the grate.

Hominy and Summer Squash Nuggets

Here's one example of how barbecue cooking can transform a familiar casserole dish into a new delight. Experiment with other favorite recipes.

SERVES 4 TO 6 AS A SIDE DISH

2 tablespoons vegetable oil

1/2 medium onion, chopped

1 pound yellow squash, diced

2 tablespoons diced red bell pepper or pimiento

1 to 2 pickled jalapeños, minced

1/4 teaspoon dried oregano, preferably Mexican

2 tablespoons milk

1 3/4 cups canned hominy, drained

3 tablespoons sour cream

1/2 cup grated jalapeño Jack or sharp cheddar cheese (2 ounces)

3 to 4 tablespoons crushed corn or tortilla chips

1. Prepare the smoker for barbecuing, bringing the temperature to 200°F to 220°F. Grease a smoke-proof baking dish.

2. In a skillet, warm the oil over medium heat. Add the onion and sauté until it is well softened but not browned. Mix in the squash, bell pepper, jalapeño, and oregano, and continue cooking until the vegetables are limp. Add the milk, reduce the heat slightly, and cover the pan.

Simmer the mixture until the squash is very soft, 15 to 20 minutes. Remove the pan from the heat and stir in the hominy and sour cream.

3. Layer half of the vegetable mixture in the prepared baking dish and sprinkle it with half of the cheese. Top with the remaining mixture and cheese. Sprinkle the crushed corn chips over the top. Transfer the dish to the smoker and cook until the mixture is hot, bubbly, and lightly smoky, 40 to 50 minutes. Serve immediately.

BBQ tip It's just as important to keep the inside of your smoker clean as it is the cooking grate. A good scrub after each use ensures efficient operation and prevents residue from a previous barbecue from flavoring your next meal. Empty out ashes from the firebox and liquids left in a water pan or reservoir.

Zooks and Cilantro Sauce

If you have a garden, it probably overproduces zucchini around the height of the barbecue season. We use some of the largess this way.

SERVES 4 AS A MAIN DISH OR 8 AS A SIDE DISH

Four 6-ounce to 8-ounce zucchini

Olive or vegetable oil

Wild Willy's Number One-derful Rub (page 26) or other savory seasoning blend (optional)

SAUCE

1 cup chopped fresh cilantro

1/2 cup chopped fresh parsley

2 scallions, chopped

1 garlic clove, minced

1/2 cup chicken or vegetable stock

1/4 cup half-and-half

Juice of 1 lime

Kosher salt or coarse sea salt and freshly ground black pepper to taste

1. Prepare the smoker for barbecuing, bringing the temperature to 200°F to 220°F.

2. Rub the zucchini liberally with the oil. Sprinkle with the dry rub if you wish.

3. Place the zucchini in the smoker and cook until tender, about 1 hour.

4. While the zucchini cooks, combine the cilantro, parsley, scallions, and garlic in a food processor and process until smooth. Add the stock and half-and-half and process again until combined.

5. Pour the sauce mixture into a saucepan. Cook it over medium-low heat for about 10 minutes, reducing the liquid by one-quarter. Don't boil the sauce or it will lose the fresh cilantro punch. Remove the sauce from the heat, add the lime juice and salt and pepper to taste, and reserve.

6. When the zucchini are ready, slice each vegetable in half horizontally. Transfer the zucchini to a serving platter and spoon the sauce over. Serve warm.

EARLY BARBECUE POETRY

Robert Francis Astrop penned an ode to barbecue in his 1835 book, *Original Poems*:

Ye who love good eating, just go to a 'Cue

Ye'll find and enjoy it there, I warrant you.

Who ever went there and ne'er got enough?

Who ever went there and found the meat tough?

Who ever went there and came mad away?

Who ever went there, *and kept steady all day?*

New Mexico may not be in the South, but it does enjoy true Southern 'Q' at Mr. Powdrell's Barbeque House in Albuquerque. The Powdrell family, pitmasters for generations, left Louisiana during the Great Depression to seek a better life farther west. The current clan landed in Albuquerque decades ago and has been smoking ever since. If you go, ask if they are serving a side dish of roasted chiles, sometimes available and always popular locally with barbecue.

Cinnamon-Scented Acorn Squash

This is the essence of fall distilled into one aromatic package.

SERVES 4 AS A SIDE DISH

1 good-size acorn squash

1 teaspoon vegetable oil

CINNAMON BUTTER

4 to 6 tablespoons unsalted butter

2 teaspoons packed brown sugar

1 teaspoon ground canela (Mexican cinnamon) or other cinnamon

1/2 teaspoon ground red chiles, preferably New Mexican or ancho, or chili powder

2 tablespoons chopped walnuts, for garnish

1. Prepare the smoker for barbecuing, bringing the temperature to 200°F to 220°F.

2. Cut the squash in half but don't remove the seeds (they help to keep it moist while cooking).

Rub the oil over the cut surfaces of the squash and on the outside.

3. Place the squash halves in the smoker, cut sides down, and cook until tender, about 2 hours.

4. While the squash cooks, melt the butter in a small pan and stir in the sugar, canela, and chile. Keep the butter warm until needed.

5. Scrape the seeds out of the squash halves and cut each half in half. Spoon some of the melted cinnamon butter over each piece of squash and top with a sprinkling of chopped walnuts. Serve hot.

Sausage and Wild Rice Butternut Squash

If you want to win serious meat-eaters over to squash barbecue, tantalize them with a little pork, too. SERVES 4 AS A MAIN DISH OR 6 AS A SIDE DISH

1 small butternut squash (under 2 pounds)
Vegetable oil

DRESSING
2 tablespoons dried currants
Juice of 1/2 orange
1 tablespoon Worcestershire sauce
1/4 pound bulk breakfast-style sausage
1/2 medium onion, chopped
1 celery rib, chopped
1 cup cooked wild rice
2 teaspoons minced fresh sage or 1 teaspoon dried sage
Pinch of nutmeg
Table salt and freshly ground black pepper to taste

Black Sauce (page 378; optional)

1. Prepare the smoker for barbecuing, bringing the temperature to 200°F to 220°F.

2. Cut the squash in half but don't remove the seeds (they help to keep it moist while cooking). Rub the oil over the cut surfaces of the squash and on the outside.

3. Place the squash halves in the smoker, cut sides down, and cook until the squash is softened but not yet tender, about 1½ hours.

4. While the squash cooks, combine the currants with the orange juice and Worcestershire in a small bowl and let them steep. Fry the sausage in a heavy skillet, adding the onion and celery after some of the fat has been rendered. Sauté until the sausage is cooked through and the vegetables softened. Mix in the currants with any remaining liquid and the rest of the dressing ingredients.

5. Remove the squash from the smoker and, as soon as the halves are cool enough to handle, scrape the seeds out of each half. Slice each piece in half again for main-dish servings, in thirds for side-dish portions. Mound the hot dressing over the squash and serve, with Black Sauce if you wish.

Cheese-Stuffed Tomatoes

These summer beauties brighten even a sunny day.

SERVES 6 AS A LIGHT MAIN DISH OR SIDE DISH

6 ripe medium tomatoes

1 cup grated Gouda or Monterey Jack cheese

1 cup rye bread cubes

1/2 teaspoon caraway seeds

Paprika to taste

1. Slice the tops off the tomatoes and, with a spoon, scoop out the seeds and pulp, leaving a thick shell. Turn the tomatoes upside down to drain for 5 minutes.

2. Prepare the smoker for barbecuing, bringing the temperature to 200°F to 220°F.

3. Mix the cheese, bread, and caraway. Stuff the mixture into each of the tomatoes and top each with a liberal dusting of paprika.

4. Transfer the tomatoes to the smoker and cook until the cheese is melted and the tomatoes are warmed through, 20 to 30 minutes. Remove the tomatoes from the smoker and serve immediately.

SERVING SUGGESTION Serve these alongside mixed sausages and spicy brown mustard.

DELTA BARBECUE AND BLUES

Abe Davis, a Lebanese immigrant, started selling his barbecue in 1924 at a streetside stand in Clarksdale, Mississippi, in the heart of the Delta country. Abe's still thrives in a new, modern building, and the cooks still prepare their pork sandwiches in their own distinctive way, smoking the meat first and then grilling it for a crusty finish. The business is at the intersection of U.S. highways 61 and 49, touted locally as the spot blues maestro Robert Johnson sang about in "Cross Road Blues."

Barbecued Rice

Baking vegetable-flecked rice in a smoker absorbs an enticing hint of the outdoors.

SERVES 6 AS A SIDE DISH

1 cup uncooked white rice

1 small green bell pepper, seeded and chopped

2 celery ribs, chopped

1 small onion, chopped

2 tablespoons Worcestershire sauce

1/4 teaspoon freshly ground black pepper

Table salt to taste

2 1/2 cups chicken or beef stock

1 cup canned French-fried onions (optional)

1. Prepare the smoker for barbecuing, bringing the temperature to 200°F to 220°F.

2. In a smoke-proof dish, combine the rice with the bell pepper, celery, onion, Worcestershire sauce, pepper, and salt. Pour the stock over the rice and cover the dish with foil.

3. Place the dish in the smoker and cook for about 1 1/2 hours, until most of the liquid is absorbed. Uncover the rice and cook until the rice is tender and all the liquid is absorbed, another 15 to 25 minutes.

4. Serve immediately, or cover again and keep warm for up to 1 hour. Stir in the fried onions just before serving if you wish.

SERVING SUGGESTION We like to serve this rice alongside enchiladas or tacos. Try Mojito Sorbet (page 466) for dessert.

THE GLOBALIZATION OF BBQ

The Memphis in May World Championship Barbecue Cooking Contest brags of being the biggest event of its kind in the country. Since the first cook-off in 1978, the annual affair has attracted teams from all corners of the globe, including Ireland, France, Estonia, Thailand, and New Zealand. Former senator Bob Kerrey of Nebraska took a shot at the title once and Al Gore has competed regularly.

Garlic Cheese Grits

This is an old Southern favorite, reworked for the smoker. SERVES 6 AS A SIDE DISH

5 cups water

1 cup grits (not instant)

1 teaspoon kosher salt or coarse sea salt

2 tablespoons unsalted butter

1/2 medium onion, minced

4 garlic cloves, minced

2 cups grated sharp cheddar cheese (about 8 ounces)

2 large eggs, lightly beaten

1 teaspoon paprika

1/4 teaspoon Tabasco or other hot pepper sauce

1. Prepare the smoker for barbecuing, bringing the temperature to 200°F to 220°F. Grease a 9 x 11-inch smoke-proof pan.

2. In a large saucepan (grits will expand in volume during the cooking), bring the water to a boil. Sprinkle in the salt and then the grits, a handful at a time, stirring constantly. Reduce the heat to a simmer and cook until thickened and soft in texture, about 20 minutes. Stir the grits occasionally as they cook.

3. In a small skillet, warm the butter over medium heat. When it is melted, add the onion and garlic and cook until they are well softened. Remove from the heat.

4. Remove the grits from the heat and stir in the onion-garlic mixture, cheese, eggs, paprika, and Tabasco. Pour the grits into the prepared pan.

5. Place the grits in the smoker and cook until the mixture is lightly firm and somewhat browned, 1½ to 1¾ hours. Remove the grits from the smoker and let sit at room temperature for at least 5 minutes. Cut into squares or wedges and serve warm or at room temperature.

SERVING SUGGESTION Top the grits with Warm Mushroom Salad (page 309) or Down-Home Ratatouille (page 291) and serve with mixed greens. For heartier appetites, use the grits as a base for pulled-pork leftovers tossed with your favorite tomato-flavored barbecue sauce; serve with Creamy Coleslaw (page 390) or Lexington Red Slaw (page 391) on the side.

Peaches Keen

Some fruits are delicious smoked, particularly peaches, pineapples, bananas, and apples. We usually cook bananas and apples whole, but prefer peaches and pineapples cut into pieces first. In this case, peaches are halved and flavored with a fruity vinegar. SERVES 6 AS SIDE DISH OR DESSERT

6 ripe but firm peaches, halved and pitted, but with peel left on

Oil, preferably walnut

2 tablespoons raspberry or other fruit vinegar, or more to taste

Crème fraîche or mascarpone cheese (optional), thinned with a bit of milk

1. Prepare the smoker for barbecuing, bringing the temperature to 200°F to 220°F.

2. Rub the peaches liberally with the oil.

3. Spoon a teaspoon of vinegar into the cavity of each peach half and transfer them to the smoker. Cook until the peaches are heated through and softened, 35 to 45 minutes. Remove them from the smoker and serve warm, with a bit more vinegar, if you wish, or little dabs of crème fraîche.

Prosciutto-Wrapped Peaches

Another peachy treat, and meaty as well.

SERVES 6 AS SIDE DISH OR MORE AS AN APPETIZER

6 ripe but firm peaches, quartered and pitted, but with peel left on

Oil, preferably extra-virgin olive

1 dozen paper-thin slices of prosciutto

Balsamic vinegar syrup (optional)

1. Prepare the smoker for barbecuing, bringing the temperature to 200°F to 220°F.

2. Rub the peaches liberally with the oil.

3. Cut the prosciutto slices in half down the center. Wrap each peach quarter in a half-slice of prosciutto. Generally, the meat will stick to itself, but you can secure each tidbit with a toothpick if you wish.

4. Cook until the peaches are heated through and softened and the prosciutto has crisped in a few spots, 25 to 35 minutes.

5. Serve hot, perhaps with a drizzle of vinegar syrup.

For a Portland, Maine, perspective on barbecue, check out the witty and wise *Uncle Billy's Downeast Barbeque Book* (1991, Dancing Bear Books). Uncle Billy's nephew Jonny—also known as Jonathan St. Laurent, classically trained as a French chef—developed the menu and wrote the book.

Smokin' Waldorf

New York's Waldorf-Astoria Hotel not only created the original Waldorf salad but invented room service to deliver it. Here's a twist, using smoked apples and the tang of lime juice. You can smoke the fruit a day ahead of the salad's preparation if you wish. SERVES 2 AS A MAIN DISH OR 4 AS A SIDE DISH

2 apples, unpeeled

Oil, preferably walnut

2 celery ribs, chopped

2/3 cup raisins

2/3 cup chopped walnuts

1/3 cup mayonnaise

1/3 cup plain yogurt

Juice of 2 limes

1 to 2 teaspoons sugar

Lettuce leaves (optional), for garnish

1. Prepare the smoker for barbecuing, bringing the temperature to 200°F to 220°F.

2. Coat the apples liberally with the oil and place them in the smoker. Cook until the apples are deeply browned and softened, about 1 hour.

Remove from the smoker and set aside until cool enough to handle. Peel the apples and slice them into bite-size chunks. Combine the apples in a bowl with the celery, raisins, and walnuts.

3. In a large glass measuring cup, combine the mayonnaise, yogurt, lime juice, and sugar. Pour over the apple mixture. Mix well, cover, and refrigerate for at least 30 minutes.

4. Serve cool, on top of lettuce leaves if you wish.

SERVING SUGGESTION The salad is filling enough for a main course at lunch. Try it with Blue Corn Muffins (page 412).

Barbecue is a Southern specialty even in a northern city like Chicago. The biggest concentration of Bar-B-Q joints is on the tough South Side, where even Al Capone wouldn't take a casual stroll. Stalwart rib lovers head to Lem's, a venerable neighborhood institution. The food's clearly the attraction because the most notable architectural accents are the bars on the windows.

Perky Pineapple Relish

Lime, mint, and chile help give this chunky relish a hint of the Southeast—Asia, that is. To speed up the preparation, you can often find already-peeled fresh pineapples with their juice in supermarket produce sections.

MAKES ABOUT 3 CUPS, ENOUGH FOR 4 TO 6 SIDE-DISH SERVINGS

1 medium whole pineapple, peeled and cut lengthwise into spears about 1 inch thick at their widest side (any juice reserved)

1/2 medium red onion, minced

2 tablespoons freshly squeezed lime juice

1/2 teaspoon reduced-sodium soy sauce or Asian fish sauce

2 tablespoons minced fresh mint

1/8 teaspoon crushed red chile flakes, or more to taste

1 teaspoon sugar (optional)

1. Prepare the smoker for barbecuing, bringing the temperature to 200°F to 220°F.

2. Place the pineapple spears in the smoker and cook for 40 to 50 minutes, until lightly smoky and soft. Remove from the smoker and set aside until cool enough to handle. Cut into small, even chunks, and transfer to a bowl. Stir in the remaining ingredients, adding sugar at the end if needed to balance the flavors. Chill for at least 30 minutes before serving.

SERVING SUGGESTION Serve the relish alongside grilled or smoked chicken or pork chops or tenderloin, or over rice or couscous.

Barbecued Bananas

You just might go bananas over these. SERVES 4 AS A SIDE DISH OR DESSERT

4 bananas, unpeeled

Vegetable oil

Brown sugar and ground cinnamon *or* caramel sauce (optional), for garnish

1. Prepare the smoker for barbecuing, bringing the temperature to 200°F to 220°F.

2. Rub the bananas with a thin coating of oil.

3. Place the bananas in the smoker and cook until the bananas are deeply browned and soft, 50 to 60 minutes. Remove from the smoker and set aside until cool enough to handle. Peel the bananas and slice them. Serve them warm, topped with a simple sprinkling of brown sugar and cinnamon or spoonfuls of your favorite caramel sauce.

BBQ *tip* Weather can affect not only whether you barbecue but also how you do it. A hot sun increases the cooking temperature inside a smoker and a cold, cloudy day decreases it, requiring adjustments in the amount of fuel used or the time allowed for cooking. Wind is also a factor because of the air circulation inside most smokers. On a blustery day, you have to watch the vents and other draft controls carefully to prevent the wind from causing major fluctuations in the cooking temperature.

PLEASE DON'T GNAW ON THE BONES

One of the biggest barbecue events of the year, Kansas City's American Royal cooking contest, got off to a slow start in 1979, when it drew 25 competitors and maybe 2,000 spectators. Today the event is so large that the judges alone number around 1,000, some of whom are assigned to present and past non-barbecue categories such as side dishes and bone art.

SMOKE-SCENTED SALADS, PASTAS, AND PIZZAS

I T MAKES NO SENSE TO US TO SPEND HOURS BAR-

BECUING FOR JUST ONE MEAL. YOU MIGHT AS WELL

BUY SOCKS ONE AT A TIME. WITH HARDLY ANY MORE

EXPENDITURE OF EFFORT, TIME, OR BEER, YOU CAN EASILY

SMOKE FOOD FOR SEVERAL MEALS AT ONCE. THERE MAY

NOT BE ANY FREE LUNCHES ON EARTH, BUT THIS TWO-FOR

COMES CLOSE.

TYPICALLY, WHEN WE FIRE UP OUR BIG BARBECUE PIT,

WE COOK ENOUGH PORK BUTT, BEEF BRISKET, AND OTHER

freezer-friendly goodies to last us for months of sandwiches, salads, hashes, pastas, and the like—and that's what's left after an initial feeding frenzy with friends. Even when we're barbecuing in an outdoor smoker with a smaller capacity, we fill it with sausages, fish fillets, peppers, and other tuck-away items for deliberate leftovers in the days ahead. We don't usually bother with additional ingredients when we're stovetop smoking inside, but that's because the cooking is so simple and quick, you can do it every day. We give instructions for making everything from scratch in case you want to prepare the dish on the day of a meal, but we usually try to work ahead of the curve ourselves.

This chapter covers some of the dishes we make with the extra food, each suitable for serving as a main course. Other possibilities such as sandwiches appear frequently in other chapters. Consider all the options as little light bulbs popping up over your head, inspirations to combine all sorts of ingredients in ways of your own. If you're going to earn your stripes as a pitmaster, you need to learn to love your leftovers.

FAMOUS HOT-GUT SAUSAGE

In 1995, the Texas legislature officially proclaimed the little town of Elgin as the "Sausage Capital" of the state. The burg's Southside Market established the local reputation beginning in 1882, when the founding butcher started delivering his "hot gut" sausage door to door. Insurance companies forced the business out of its original sawdust-floored location into a new building, but the Market still sells its own spectacular barbecued sausage, as spicy and juicy as any you'll find. For online mail order, go to southsidemarket.com.

Calico Pepper Salad

On a long day of barbecuing, nothing is better for lunch than this colorful salad. Like many other dishes in the chapter, it also makes a fine supper prepared in a stovetop smoker. SERVES 4

3 large bell peppers, preferably 1 each of red, yellow, and green

1 fresh green chile, preferably New Mexican, Anaheim, or poblano (optional)

1 fresh jalapeño or 1 to 2 fresh serranos

1 small onion, unpeeled

3 garlic cloves, unpeeled

1 tablespoon vegetable oil

1 tablespoon garlic-flavored oil (see BBQ tip, page 211)

1 tablespoon minced fresh cilantro

1/2 teaspoon ground cumin

Dashes of red wine vinegar

Table salt

1. Prepare the smoker for barbecuing, bringing the temperature to 200°F to 220°F.

2. Rub the bell peppers, green chile, jalapeño, onion, and garlic with enough vegetable oil to coat their surfaces lightly.

3. Transfer the vegetables to the smoker, as far from the heat as possible. Cook until they are well softened, 25 to 30 minutes for the garlic and 65 to 75 minutes for everything else. Remove each of the vegetables as it is done.

4. Place the bell peppers, the green chile, and the jalapeño in a plastic bag to steam. Chop the garlic and onion finely and transfer them to a bowl. Remove the peppers from the bag and pull the skin off of each. Slice the bell peppers and green chile into thin ribbons (discarding the seeds) and add them to the garlic and onion. Mince the jalapeño (discarding the seeds) and add about half of it to the bowl.

5. Stir in the garlic-flavored oil, cilantro, cumin, and a bit of vinegar and salt, and taste. Add more jalapeño or the other seasonings as desired. Serve warm or chilled.

SERVING SUGGESTION Pair this with spaghetti tossed with olive oil, garlic, and fresh chopped tomatoes. Round out the meal with Parmesan-topped crusty bread.

Smoldering Vegetable Antipasto Platter

Here's a versatile way to show off your prowess with barbecued vegetables. Serve the platter hot or chilled, use it as a light main dish or a starter for a party, and feel free to vary the mix of veggies and herbs. Experiment with other sauces, too, but do use fresh herbs rather than dried in any that feature the herbs as a main flavor.

SERVES 6 TO 8

SALSA VERDE

1/2 cup chopped fresh parsley

1/4 cup chopped shallots

2 tablespoons chopped fresh mint

2 teaspoons chopped fresh rosemary

1 cup extra-virgin olive oil

1 to 2 tablespoons freshly squeezed lemon juice

1 to 2 tablespoons chopped capers

1/2 teaspoon anchovy paste (optional)

Kosher salt or coarse sea salt and freshly ground black pepper to taste

1 medium to large red bell pepper

1 medium to large yellow bell pepper

1 large red onion, halved but unpeeled

1 medium zucchini

6 small red-ripe Roma or other plum tomatoes, halved vertically

Extra-virgin olive oil

Kosher salt or coarse sea salt

Shavings of fresh Parmesan cheese (made with a vegetable peeler) (optional)

Herb sprigs, for garnish

1. Prepare your smoker for barbecuing, bringing the temperature to 200°F to 220°F.

2. Mix the sauce ingredients in a small bowl and reserve at room temperature.

3. Prepare the vegetables by coating all of them with olive oil and sprinkling them with salt.

4. Transfer the vegetables to the smoker and cook the tomatoes for about 30 minutes, then remove them. Continue smoking the other vegetables until soft, about 30 more minutes. Slice the peppers into rings or long slices, as you wish, discarding seeds and veins. Remove any papery skins from the onion halves and slice into thin rings. Cut the zucchini into thin rings or long slices.

5. Arrange the vegetables on a large, pretty platter. Drizzle about half of the sauce lightly over the vegetables. Top with a few curls of Parmesan cheese if you like, and tuck in some herb sprigs. Serve at room temperature, or chilled, with the remaining sauce.

VARIATION: SMOLDERING VEGETABLE PASTA Chop the smoked vegetables, toss with a chunky pasta like penne or rigatoni, and mix in enough of the salsa verde to moisten the mixture. Serve warm or at room temperature.

BBQ *tip* When making antipasto combinations, or other smoked vegetable dishes, keep in mind that their outdoorsy character is usually enhanced by a bit of an acid—

vinegar, lemon juice, salsa, capers—as a tangy counterpoint. It can be added before, during, or after cooking.

Warm Mushroom Salad

Great ideas travel faster than gossip at a church picnic. Pat Wilson of the Camerons stovetop smoker company passed this on to us after picking it up from Allen Frey, a Vermont restaurateur. SERVES 4 TO 6

12 ounces portobello mushrooms, stemmed

Kosher salt or coarse sea salt

DRESSING

3/4 cup chopped Roma or other plum tomatoes, or canned crushed tomatoes

1/3 cup extra-virgin olive oil

1 tablespoon balsamic vinegar

1 tablespoon chopped fresh basil

1 tablespoon minced fresh parsley

3 garlic cloves, minced

2 scallions, sliced

Table salt and coarsely ground black pepper to taste

Lettuce leaves, for garnish

1. Prepare the smoker for barbecuing, bringing the temperature to 200°F to 220°F.

2. Slice the mushroom caps into large bite-size pieces and salt them lightly. Arrange the mushrooms on a small grill rack or a piece of heavy-duty foil.

3. Place the mushrooms in the smoker and cook until they ooze liquid and are cooked through, 15 to 20 minutes.

4. While the mushrooms cook, mix the dressing ingredients in a medium-size bowl. Add the smoked mushrooms and mix again lightly. Mound on the lettuce leaves and serve warm.

VARIATION: SOUTHWESTERN MUSHROOM-CORN SALAD Switch the oil in the dressing to corn or another milder oil, and the vinegar to sherry vinegar. Add 1/4 to 1/2 teaspoon ground cumin or chili powder if you like. Replace the basil and parsley with the same amount of fresh cilantro. Mix in 1/2 cup cooked corn kernels with the mushrooms.

BBQ *tip* Stovetop smokers cook at a higher temperature than you ordinarily want for barbecue, but they still impart plenty of smoke flavor to porous foods such as vegetables and fish. If you're cooking chicken in this style of smoker, remove the skin and cut the meat into thick strips. For a steak or a similar cut of red meat, smoke it for 15 to 20 minutes and then finish it with high heat over a grill or in a skillet.

Curried Turkey Salad

Both of us love this sweet-tangy hot-cool explosion of flavors. If you don't have turkey leftovers for this, or a way to smoke the turkey quickly and easily, you should even consider sneaking in a good supermarket version. SERVES 6

1 tablespoon curry powder

1/2 teaspoon kosher salt or coarse sea salt

Three 7-ounce to 8-ounce boneless turkey breast fillet sections

1 cup minced red onion

1/3 cup flaked coconut

1/3 cup chopped dried apricots or yellow raisins

CURRIED SALAD DRESSING

1/2 cup mayonnaise

1/4 cup plain yogurt, or additional mayonnaise

2 tablespoons honey

1 tablespoon freshly squeezed lemon juice

1 1/2 teaspoons curry powder

3/4 cup salted roasted cashews

Mixed salad greens, for garnish

1. At least 3 hours and up to the night before you plan to serve the salad, mix the curry powder with the salt. Rub the mixture on the turkey breast sections, cover, and refrigerate for at least 1 hour.

2. Prepare your smoker for barbecuing, bringing the temperature to 200°F to 220°F.

3. Remove the turkey from the refrigerator and let it sit at room temperature for 30 minutes.

4. Transfer the turkey to the smoker. Smoke until cooked through, with clear juices when a skewer is inserted, about 50 to 60 minutes.

5. When the turkey is cool enough to handle, pull the meat into shreds or cut it into bite-size chunks. Discard the skin and bones or, better yet, save them for stock. Combine the turkey in a large bowl with the onion, coconut, and dried fruit.

6. In a small bowl, stir together the mayonnaise, yogurt, honey, lemon juice, and curry powder. Mix the dressing into the turkey mixture. Refrigerate the salad for at least 1 hour and up to overnight. Shortly before serving time, add the cashews to the salad.

7. Mound the salad on a bed of greens and serve chilled.

Chicken Salad with Sizzling Salsa Vinaigrette

If this zippy salad could sing, it would choose a mariachi tune. SERVES 4

4 boneless, skinless chicken breast halves, pounded to 1/2-inch thickness

Extra-virgin olive oil

Juice of 2 limes

Kosher salt or coarse sea salt

SIZZLING SALSA VINAIGRETTE

1/4 cup plus 2 tablespoons of your favorite spicy salsa

1/4 cup plus 2 tablespoons extra-virgin olive oil

2 to 3 tablespoons white vinegar

Kosher salt or coarse sea salt to taste

1/4 cup minced mild onion

1/4 cup chopped celery

3 tablespoons minced fresh cilantro

Romaine or other crisp lettuce, shredded

Tortilla chips (optional)

1. Rub the breasts with enough oil to coat well, then spoon the lime juice over them and let them sit at room temperature for about 20 minutes.

2. Prepare the smoker for barbecuing, bringing the temperature to 200°F to 220°F.

3. Whisk together the vinaigrette ingredients in a small bowl, adding vinegar to taste, and then salt if needed. If you want to baste the chicken (see page 45, "To Mop or Not"), set aside several tablespoons of the dressing for that purpose.

4. Drain the chicken and salt it lightly. Transfer the chicken to the smoker and cook until cooked through, 25 to 30 minutes. In a wood-burning pit, turn the breasts after 15 minutes and mop with the reserved dressing. With other smokers, don't worry about turning the breasts or mopping while cooking. When done, set the breasts aside briefly, until cool enough to handle, then tear into bite-size shreds. (The chicken can be prepared to this point a day ahead, covered, and refrigerated.)

5. Combine the chicken in a bowl with the onion, celery, and cilantro. Add as much of the vinaigrette as needed to bind the salad. Pile the salad on romaine, garnish with chips around the edges, if you wish, and serve.

BBQ tip The kind of sawdust or chips you use in a stovetop smoker makes a noticeable difference in the level of smoky flavor you get. Use alder for the lightest touch and pecan or mesquite for the heaviest dose.

Though there's a touch of heresy in the notion, some fine pitmasters use more charcoal than wood in barbecuing pork. In Memphis in particular, many people seem to prefer their pork with just a hint of smoke, supplementing that flavor with a robust sauce. Emily Payne and her daughter-in-law Flora serve their sandwiches that way at Payne's and so does Frank Vernon's family at the equally good Bar-B-Q Shop.

Chicken Salad Supreme

This salad is a veritable feast of fruit and poultry. Smoke the chicken as described in the previous recipe if you wish to prepare it from scratch for the dish. SERVES 4 TO 6

DRESSING

1/3 cup honey

1/4 cup white vinegar

2 tablespoons freshly squeezed lemon juice

1 tablespoon poppy seeds

1 teaspoon dry mustard

1 teaspoon grated onion

1/2 teaspoon table salt

1 cup vegetable oil

1 1/2 pounds chilled smoked chicken, chunked

3/4 cup diced cantaloupe

3/4 cup diced honeydew melon

1/2 cup sliced scallions

1/2 teaspoon minced lemon zest

1/2 cup sliced almonds, toasted

Lettuce leaves

Fresh strawberries and lemon wedges, for garnish

1. In a food processor, briefly process the dressing ingredients, except the oil, until combined.

Pour in the oil and continue processing until you have a thick dressing.

2. In a medium-size bowl, mix the chicken, melons, scallions, and lemon zest with about two-thirds of the dressing. Refrigerate if desired.

3. Stir the almonds into the salad shortly before serving. Mound the salad on the lettuce leaves and garnish with strawberries and lemons. Spoon additional dressing over the top if you wish.

SERVING SUGGESTION Impress your mom when she comes to visit. Serve Bronzed Artichokes (page 287) first, followed by this salad and Sweet Potato Biscuits (page 411). She'll be dazzled.

Port-Glazed Duck Salad

This little gem of a salad requires a few steps, but they are easy and can be spread over a couple of days if you wish. SERVES 4 TO 6

Four 5-ounce skin-on duck breast halves

1 cup port

1/2 cup cider vinegar or red wine vinegar

2 tablespoons Dijon mustard

PORT SAUCE

Juice and zest of 1 orange

Juice and zest of 1/2 lemon

7 tablespoons port

7 tablespoons cherry jelly or jam

2 tablespoons minced shallots

1 teaspoon Dijon mustard

SALAD

1/2 small red cabbage, shredded

2 tablespoons sherry vinegar

1/4 teaspoon table salt, or more to taste

1. At least 4 hours and up to the night before you plan to serve the salad, arrange a bamboo steamer over a saucepan of water and place the duck breasts in the steamer. Steam the breasts over medium-high heat for 20 minutes. Discard the greasy steaming liquid.

2. While the breasts steam, prepare a marinade, mixing the port, vinegar, and mustard in a plastic bag or shallow, nonreactive dish.

3. Remove the breasts from the steamer and let them cool briefly to room temperature. Add the breasts to the marinade and refrigerate for at least 2 hours.

4. In a small saucepan, combine the sauce ingredients and simmer over medium-low heat for 15 minutes. Remove the sauce from the heat and strain it. Divide the sauce equally between two bowls and reserve both in the refrigerator.

5. Prepare the smoker for barbecuing, bringing the temperature to 200°F to 220°F.

6. Remove the duck from the refrigerator and let it sit at room temperature for 30 minutes. Remove one bowl of sauce from the refrigerator.

7. Drain the breasts and put them in the smoker, skin sides up. Using one bowl of sauce, brush the breasts with a little of it twice while cooking. Discard any leftover sauce. Cook the duck until it's well-done and smoky but still moist, 65 to 75 minutes. Cool the duck to room temperature and then refrigerate for at least 1 hour and up to overnight.

8. In a bowl, combine the cabbage, vinegar, and salt with 2 teaspoons of the sauce from the second bowl. Refrigerate the mixture until you are ready to serve the duck.

9. Arrange equal portions of the cabbage on individual plates. Slice the duck breasts thin and arrange fanned slices of the meat over the cabbage. Drizzle the remaining sauce over the meat before serving, or reserve some to pass on the side if you wish.

Smoked Albacore–Potato Salad

A West Coast favorite for smoking, albacore brims with fish oils that flavor it richly. We use it more frequently for smoking than the more delicate yellowfin tuna. SERVES 4

ROASTED GARLIC MASH

1 whole head of garlic

1 tablespoon kosher salt or coarse sea salt

1 teaspoon extra-virgin olive oil or vegetable oil

10-ounce albacore steak or other tuna steak

White wine vinegar

DILL VINAIGRETTE

1/2 cup extra-virgin olive oil

2 tablespoons white wine vinegar

2 to 3 tablespoons minced fresh dill

2 teaspoons Dijon mustard

Kosher salt or coarse sea salt and freshly ground black pepper to taste

1 1/2 pounds small potatoes, halved or neatly chunked if larger than bite-size, steamed until tender, and cooled to room temperature

4 lightly packed cups crisp greens, like shredded romaine

Briny black or green olives

1. Break the garlic head apart into individual cloves, but don't peel them. Place them in a cast-iron or other heavy skillet and dry-roast over medium heat until soft and brown, 6 to 8 minutes, shaking or stirring as needed to color evenly. Peel the garlic (a quick task once roasted) and transfer to a small bowl. Using the back of a large fork, mash the garlic lightly. Add the salt and oil and continue mashing until you have a rough puree.

2. Prepare the smoker for barbecuing, bringing the temperature to 180°F to 200°F.

3. Place the albacore steak in a shallow, nonreactive dish and rub it with the mash. Cover the steak and allow it to sit at room temperature for 20 to 30 minutes.

4. Heat a skillet over high heat with a thin film of oil. Sear the steak quickly on both sides. Give the steak a healthy splash of vinegar, in place of a mop.

5. Transfer the steak to the smoker. Cook the tuna to the desired doneness, 20 to 25 minutes for medium-rare. Avoid overcooking the tuna. When cool enough to handle, cut into thin slices or bite-size pieces.

6. Place the potatoes in a large bowl. In a small bowl, whisk together the vinaigrette ingredients and toss about two-thirds of it with the potatoes. Arrange the greens on a platter and top with the potatoes and then the tuna. Drizzle the remaining vinaigrette over the tuna and greens. Tuck olives in and around, and serve.

VARIATION: FLANK STEAK–POTATO SALAD Substitute simply seasoned smoked flank steak for the albacore, and leave the dill out of the dressing.

North Woods Whitefish Salad

If you like smoked Great Lakes whitefish from the deli, as almost everyone does, you'll really relish your own home-smoked version. SERVES 4

WHITEFISH BRINE

1/2 cup kosher salt

1/4 cup packed brown sugar

2 teaspoons freshly ground black pepper

1 1/2 cups water

1 1/2-pound chunk whitefish, sablefish, sea bass, or pike

SALAD

1/2 cup mayonnaise

6 tablespoons sour cream

1 medium celery rib, chopped fine

2 tablespoons minced dill pickle

2 tablespoons minced red onion

1/2 teaspoon prepared horseradish

Freshly ground black pepper to taste

Watercress or mixed greens (optional)

1. Prepare the brine, stirring together the salt, sugar, and pepper in a medium-size bowl, then pouring in the water. Stir to dissolve. Place the whitefish in a zipper-top plastic bag and pour the brine over the fish. Refrigerate it for at least 2 hours and up to 8 hours. (The saltiness and sweetness will become more pronounced the longer the fish marinates in the brine.)

2. Drain the fish and let it sit, uncovered, at room temperature for 15 to 30 minutes.

3. Prepare your smoker for barbecuing, bringing the temperature to 180°F to 200°F. Place the fish on the cooking grate as far from the fire as possible. Cook until the fish flakes throughout, 40 to 50 minutes.

4. When cool enough to handle, flake the fish into a bowl, discarding the skin and the many bones. Stir in the salad ingredients. Chill for at least 1 hour and up to a couple of days. Serve mounded onto plates, surrounded by watercress if you wish.

VARIATION: NORTH WOODS WHITEFISH SALAD PLATTER Make a hearty deli platter for a lazy Sunday by arranging the salad with store-bought lox or Nova, bagels, rye bread, tomato and onion slices, lemon chunks, capers, and dill sprigs, if available. If you need dessert, rugalach cookies are just the ticket.

Chunky Trout Salad

Our favorite freshwater fish for smoking, trout struts its stuff in this simple salad, enlivened by a tangy horseradish vinaigrette and colorful bits of fruit. SERVES 4

DRESSING

$1/4$ cup extra-virgin olive oil

$1/4$ cup vegetable oil

$2^1/2$ tablespoons white wine vinegar

2 tablespoons minced shallots

1 teaspoon prepared horseradish

$1/2$ teaspoon Dijon mustard

$1/4$ teaspoon Worcestershire sauce

$3/4$ teaspoon kosher salt or coarse sea salt

Pinch of ground white pepper

Four 8-ounce butterflied boned trout

7 to 8 cups mixed salad greens

1 small red-skinned apple, cut into bite-size chunks

$3/4$ cup halved seedless grapes (green, red, or a combination)

$1/2$ cup chopped pecans, toasted, or chile-coated pecans

2 tablespoons minced shallots

Freshly ground black pepper to taste

1. About 2 hours before you plan to smoke the trout, combine the dressing ingredients in a blender and puree until smooth.

2. Place the trout, lying open, in a shallow, nonreactive dish. Drizzle each fish with about 1 tablespoon of the dressing. Cover the trout and refrigerate for about $1^1/2$ hours. Refrigerate the remaining dressing as well.

3. Prepare your smoker for barbecuing, bringing the temperature to 200°F to 220°F.

4. Remove the trout from the refrigerator and let them sit, covered, at room temperature for 15 to 20 minutes.

5. Transfer the fish to the smoker, skin side down. Cook the trout until opaque and easily flaked, 35 to 45 minutes. When the fish is cool enough to handle, break it into uniform chunks or chill it in the refrigerator for at least 1 hour if you wish to serve it cold.

6. Toss the greens with enough dressing to coat the leaves lightly. Arrange the greens evenly among four plates. Place equal portions of the trout over the greens. Top the salad with a scattering of apples, grapes, pecans, shallots, and pepper, drizzle with any remaining dressing, and serve.

Spicy Asian Flank Steak Salad

This is a salad a carnivore can love. SERVES 4

PAN-ASIAN PANDEMONIUM

1/2 cup roughly chopped scallions

2 walnut-size chunks fresh ginger, peeled

3 tablespoons freshly squeezed lime juice

2 tablespoons reduced-sodium soy sauce

1 tablespoon Asian fish sauce

1/2 to 1 tablespoon Asian chile garlic paste

1 flank steak, about 1 1/4 pounds

LIME-SOY MOP (OPTIONAL)

1/2 cup water

2 tablespoons freshly squeezed lime juice

2 tablespoons reduced-sodium soy sauce

5 cups mixed greens

2 medium carrots, shredded

1/2 cup lightly packed fresh mint leaves

1/4 cup lightly packed fresh cilantro leaves

QUICK THAI DRESSING

2 tablespoons freshly squeezed lime juice

1 tablespoon Asian fish sauce

1 1/2 teaspoons sugar

1. The night before you plan to barbecue, place the Pan-Asian seasoning paste ingredients in a blender or food processor and process until a smooth, thick puree is formed. If you plan to baste the meat (see page 45, "To Mop or Not"), set aside 2 tablespoons of the paste for the mop.

Rub the flank steak with the remaining paste. Place the flank steak in a plastic bag or shallow dish and refrigerate overnight.

2. Prepare the smoker for barbecuing, bringing the temperature to 200°F to 220°F.

3. Remove the steak from the refrigerator and let it sit at room temperature for 25 minutes.

4. If you are using the mop, combine the 2 tablespoons reserved seasoning paste with the water, lime juice, and soy sauce in a small saucepan over low heat.

5. Transfer the steak to the smoker. Mop once before closing the smoker and again after 25 to 30 minutes in a wood-burning pit, or as appropriate for your style of smoker. Cook for a total of 45 to 55 minutes, until the meat is rare to medium-rare. Let the steak rest for 5 or 10 minutes before cutting.

6. While the steak is resting, combine the greens, carrots, mint, and cilantro on a platter. Stir together the dressing ingredients and toss with the greens mixture. Slice the steak thinly across the grain, arrange over the greens mixture, and serve.

A Blast of a BLT Salad

When tomatoes are ripe and juicy in late summer, and you've got good smokehouse bacon in the fridge, few foods match a BLT in bold flavor. This salad is in the limited competition. SERVES 4

1 large mild onion, unpeeled

Vegetable oil

6 slices smoky slab bacon

2 large thick slices French or sourdough bread, in 1/2-inch cubes

6 tablespoons mayonnaise

2 tablespoons buttermilk or plain yogurt

1 teaspoon good quality lemon-pepper seasoning

Kosher salt or coarse sea salt and freshly cracked black pepper (optional)

5 cups torn iceberg lettuce, well chilled

2 medium red-ripe tomatoes, chopped in 1/2-inch cubes

1. Prepare the smoker for barbecuing, bringing the temperature to 200°F to 220°F.

2. Slice the onion in half and rub or spray a thin coat of oil over the halves.

3. Transfer the onion to the smoker and cook until tender, 45 to 55 minutes. Remove the onion halves from the smoker and chop them neatly in small bite-size bits. (The onion can be smoked a day or two ahead, covered and refrigerated until you need it.)

4. Slice the bacon into 1-inch pieces and fry in a large, heavy skillet over medium heat until crisp. Remove with a slotted spoon. Pour off the bacon drippings as needed until just a thick coating remains in the skillet. Stir in the bread cubes, coating them evenly with the drippings, and sauté them over medium heat until lightly browned and crisp. Reserve the bread cubes.

5. For the dressing, stir together the mayonnaise, buttermilk, and lemon-pepper seasoning. Taste, and add salt and pepper if needed.

6. Toss about 1/4 cup of the dressing with the lettuce and the smoked onion and arrange it on a platter. Top with the tomatoes, bread cubes, and bacon and toss again lightly. Serve immediately, with the remaining dressing on the side.

READ ALL ABOUT IT

Published in Douglas, Georgia, the *National Barbecue News* (barbecuenews.com) is a newspaper-style monthly that covers the whole country. Readers get news and views on cook-offs, recipes, restaurants, smokers, and more, including a few barbecue jokes.

Black-Eyed Pea and Ham Macaroni Salad

Got a potluck dinner coming up? Impress your friends with this. SERVES 4

12-ounce fully cooked ham steak, about 1/2 inch thick

1 teaspoon yellow mustard

1 tablespoon packed brown sugar or Sweet Sensation (page 30)

Freshly cracked black pepper to taste

12 ounces small shell macaroni, cooked al dente

11/2 to 2 cups fresh-cooked or canned black-eyed peas, drained

3/4 cup chopped celery

1/2 cup chopped sweet or other mild onion

1/2 cup chopped red bell pepper

6 tablespoons corn oil, preferably refined, or vegetable oil

3 tablespoons cider vinegar

A few splashes of pepper vinegar or Tabasco or other hot sauce

1/4 cup minced fresh parsley

1. Prepare the smoker for barbecuing, bringing the temperature to 200°F to 220°F.

2. Rub the ham steak with the mustard, and then with brown sugar and pepper. Let it sit at room temperature for 20 to 30 minutes.

3. Transfer the ham to the smoker. Cook until the sugar has melted onto the surface and the ham is heated through and well perfumed with smoke, 25 to 35 minutes.

4. In a large bowl, stir together the macaroni, black-eyed peas, celery, onion, and bell pepper. When the ham steak is ready, cut it into 1/4-inch cubes, discarding fat and any bone. Add the ham to the macaroni mixture.

5. In a small bowl, whisk together the oil, cider vinegar, and a little pepper vinegar and pour over the salad. Toss to combine. Chill for 30 minutes or up to overnight. Stir the parsley into the salad shortly before serving.

BBQ tip With fully cooked meats, like Canadian bacon or ham steak, you're just adding extra flavor with the smoke. The process goes quickly when the cuts are thin and small, eliminating any need for basting.

NO PITFALLS HERE

One of the best pits in Virginia is called a "pitt" because the sign painter couldn't spell. You may wonder at first if the same fellow painted the orange and yellow building at Pierce's Pitt Bar-B-Que in Lightfoot, but after one of the succulent pork sandwiches, you'll be an empathetic shade of Day-Glo yourself.

The late Gary Wells, one of the founders of the Kansas City Barbeque Society, always insisted that no one should take the organization too seriously. His intent was having fun. You would know people were getting overly earnest, he once said, when membership was noted in obituaries.

Smoky Summer Spaghetti

With their deeply flavored resonance, smoked ingredients often combine wonderfully with pasta. For this simple but soulful vegetable spaghetti, the tomato and bell pepper can be smoked in about the time it takes to get the noodles ready.

SERVES 4 OR MORE

2 large red-ripe tomatoes, halved

2 red bell peppers, halved and seeded

1/4 cup extra-virgin olive oil

1 pound spaghetti or bucatini

1 1/2 tablespoons freshly squeezed lemon juice

1 small bread slice

3/4 teaspoon kosher salt or coarse sea salt, or more to taste

Crushed red chile flakes (optional)

Several tablespoons minced fresh herbs, such as basil, flat-leaf parsley, oregano, thyme, or a combination

Several tablespoons freshly grated Pecorino Romano or Parmesan cheese

1. Prepare the smoker for barbecuing, bringing the temperature to 200°F to 220°F.

2. Rub the tomatoes and bell peppers with enough of the oil to coat their surfaces lightly. Place the tomatoes and peppers in a smoke-proof dish, or make a little tray for them out of doubled heavy-duty aluminum foil.

3. Transfer the vegetables to the smoker. Cook until they are softened but the bell peppers still have a bit of toothsome bite, 20 to 25 minutes.

4. While the vegetables smoke, heat a large pot of salted water for the pasta and cook it according to the package directions.

5. When the vegetables are ready, plop them into a blender, add the remaining oil, the lemon juice, and the bread, and puree. Stir in the salt and chile flakes if you wish. Toss with the pasta in a large bowl, and scatter herbs and cheese over. Serve warm or at room temperature.

VARIATION: FAUX BOLOGNESE SPAGHETTI For a heartier rendition, add 1/2 pound or more browned ground pork, or a mixture of ground pork and bulk Italian sausage, to the vegetable sauce before serving.

Robust Chicken-Thyme Ravioli

Stuffing pasta with your own mix of lightly smoked chicken and fresh herbs will blow away any version you can buy ready-made. Plus, it's easy to make your own ravioli from wonton wrappers available in nearly every supermarket today. SERVES 4

ROASTED GARLIC MASH

1 whole head of garlic

1 tablespoon kosher salt or coarse sea salt

1 teaspoon extra-virgin olive oil or vegetable oil

Two 5-ounce to 6-ounce boneless, skinless chicken breast halves, pounded lightly

RAVIOLI SAUCE

2 tablespoons extra-virgin olive oil

1/2 cup chicken stock

1 tablespoon minced fresh thyme or lemon thyme

1/2 teaspoon kosher salt or coarse sea salt

3/4 cup ricotta cheese

1/4 cup chicken stock

1/4 cup coarsely chopped walnuts

1/4 cup grated Pecorino Romano cheese

2 tablespoons heavy cream

1 tablespoon minced fresh thyme or lemon thyme

Kosher salt or coarse sea salt to taste

32 wonton wrappers

Grated Pecorino Romano cheese and toasted walnut pieces or halves, for garnish

Thyme or lemon thyme sprigs (optional), for garnish

1. Break the garlic head apart into individual cloves, but don't peel them. Place them in a cast-iron or other heavy skillet and dry-roast over medium heat until soft and brown, 6 to 8 minutes, shaking or stirring as needed to color evenly. Peel the garlic (a quick task once roasted) and transfer to a small bowl. Using the back of a large fork, mash the garlic lightly. Add the salt and oil and continue mashing until you have a rough puree. Reserve 1 teaspoon of the paste for the sauce. Coat the chicken breasts with the remaining paste, wrap them in plastic, and let them sit at room temperature for 20 minutes.

2. Prepare your smoker for barbecuing, bringing the temperature to 200°F to 220°F.

3. Transfer the chicken to the smoker and cook it until firm and the juices run clear, 30 to 35 minutes.

4. While the chicken cooks, make the sauce. Heat the oil in a small skillet over medium heat. Add the remaining sauce ingredients and the reserved 1 teaspoon paste and simmer the mixture for several minutes to combine the flavors. Reserve the sauce.

5. When the chicken is cool enough to handle, tear each breast into several pieces and place it in a food processor. Pulse lightly, until the chicken is in fine shreds. You should have about 1½ cups of chicken.

6. Transfer the chicken to a bowl and mix in the ricotta cheese, chicken stock, walnuts, cheese, cream, thyme, and salt.

7. Spoon 2 tablespoons of filling onto a won-ton wrapper. Wet the edges of that wrapper and those of a second wrapper. Top the filling with the second wrapper and press down firmly all around the edges to make a tight seal. If available, use a ravioli crimper or other dough trimmer to help seal the edges. Set the ravioli on a platter to partially dry while you form the remaining ravioli. You should end up with about 16 large ravioli. (They can be cooked immediately or made a day ahead and refrigerated.)

8. Heat several quarts of salted water in a large saucepan. When the water comes to a rolling boil, gently slide in the ravioli. Cook just 3 to 5 minutes, until the dough is tender and no longer gummy. Drain the ravioli and transfer them to individual plates or shallow bowls.

9. Quickly reheat the sauce and spoon it over the ravioli. Garnish each serving with a sprinkling of cheese and walnuts and, if you wish, a thyme sprig. Serve hot.

it's easy to make your own ravioli from wonton wrappers available in nearly every supermarket

AMAZING GRACE

For many years barbecue, beer, and blues formed a soulful trio at Kansas City's Grand Emporium, which occupied a building that had housed various taverns, a poker room, and a brothel since 1912. It was the only place in the country twice honored by the Blues Foundation as the "Best Blues Club in America." "Amazing" Grace Harris cooked the 'Q' and served it nightly with some of the hottest licks in town.

Smoke Stickers

Our favorite way to use barbecued poultry leftovers is in Asian pot stickers. Restaurants usually serve them as an appetizer, but we often have them as a light main course with a salad, perhaps Asian Vegetable Slaw (page 428).

SERVES 2 AS A MAIN COURSE OR 4 OR MORE AS AN APPETIZER

SIMPLE CHINESE FIVE-SPICE MEDLEY

2 tablespoons five-spice powder

2 tablespoons packed brown sugar

Two 5-ounce boneless, skinless chicken breast halves, pounded lightly

1/2 cup rice vinegar or white vinegar

SMOKE-STICKER SAUCE

1/2 teaspoon cornstarch

3/4 cup chicken stock

2 tablespoons dry sherry

2 teaspoons reduced-sodium soy sauce

1 teaspoon hoisin sauce or Hoisin BBQ Sauce (page 386)

1 teaspoon rice vinegar or white vinegar

1/2 cup chopped bok choy, napa cabbage, or spinach

2 scallions, chopped

2 teaspoons peeled and minced fresh ginger

1 garlic clove, minced

1 tablespoon reduced-sodium soy sauce

1/4 to 1/2 teaspoon Asian chile garlic paste

1 large egg white

2 dozen wonton wrappers, preferably round

2 tablespoons peanut oil

Thin sliced scallion rings (optional)

1. Prepare the smoker for barbecuing, bringing the temperature to 200°F to 220°F.

2. Combine the rub ingredients in a small bowl. Rub the breasts with the mixture, reserving 1 tablespoon for the sauce, and let them sit at room temperature for about 20 minutes.

3. Drizzle the breasts with about one-third of the vinegar. Transfer the chicken to the smoker and cook until cooked through, 25 to 30 minutes. In a wood-burning pit, turn the breasts after 15 minutes and mop again with more vinegar. With other smokers, don't worry about turning the breasts or mopping while cooking—just drizzle the breasts with more vinegar as soon as you remove them from the smoker.

4. While the chicken smokes, prepare the sauce. In a medium-size bowl, combine the cornstarch with 1 tablespoon of the stock. When combined, stir in the sherry, soy sauce, hoisin sauce, vinegar, and reserved 1 tablespoon rub, and set aside.

5. When cool enough to handle, pull the chicken into large shreds and transfer to a food processor. Add the bok choy, scallions, ginger, garlic, soy sauce, chile garlic paste, and egg white. Process until well combined. (The filling can be made a day ahead to this point, covered, and chilled. Return it to room temperature before proceeding.)

6. Place a heaping teaspoon of the filling in the center of a wonton wrapper, moisten the edges, and seal it in a half-moon shape. (Square wrappers can be folded into triangles.) Repeat with the remaining filling and wrappers.

7. Warm the oil in a large skillet over high heat. When very hot, add the pot stickers and fry them until the bottoms are deep golden brown (don't flip them), about 2 minutes. Give the sauce a stir and pour it over the pot stickers. Immediately cover the skillet and reduce the heat to medium-low. Cook for 2 more minutes, then uncover again and raise the heat to high.

Cook until the sauce is thick and clings to the pot stickers, another minute or two. Serve immediately, sprinkled with the scallion rings if you wish.

BBQ tip If you're also a big fan of pot stickers, invest in an inexpensive dumpling press, available in many cookstores and Asian markets. We're not usually enamored of gadgets, but this one earns its keep.

NO COOKING IN THE FOUNTAIN

Americans are moving outdoors. We used to live in our houses, but now one of the biggest trends in home design is the "outdoor room." We're amazed when we attend the annual trade show of the Hearth, Patio & Barbecue Association with everything that's available to furnish and accessorize a patio. The options range from pool tables to flaming fountains.

Priest Stranglers with Sausage and Sage

Italians have memorable names for many dishes and ingredients. One that certainly makes the cut is "priest stranglers," the common name for a pasta known more formally as strozzapreti. The long, toothsome, twisted shape makes it difficult to eat and talk at the same time without choking, foiling preachers and lecturers of all kinds. **SERVES 4 OR MORE**

4 uncooked Italian sausage links, approximately 4 ounces each

3 tablespoons extra-virgin olive oil, plus additional for coating the sausages

12 ounces strozzapreti or penne or rotini pasta

1 to 2 tablespoons minced fresh sage

Table salt to taste

1/4 cup grated Parmesan or Pecorino Romano cheese

Sage sprigs (optional)

1. Prepare your smoker for barbecuing, bringing the temperature to 200°F to 220°F.

2. Coat the sausages with oil and transfer them to the smoker. Smoke until cooked through and still juicy, 1 to 1¼ hours.

3. Shortly before you expect the sausage to be done, cook the strozzapreti according to the package directions. Drain the pasta, reserving several tablespoons of the cooking water. Transfer the pasta to a large bowl. Toss it with the oil and sage. Slice the sausage into thin rounds and add to the pasta. Add salt if necessary and stir in some of the reserved pasta water if the mixture seems dry. Scatter the cheese over the top, garnish with sage sprigs if you wish, and serve.

VARIATION: PRIEST STRANGLERS WITH SAUSAGE, SAGE, TOMATOES, AND CREAM Oil 2 or 3 Roma or other plum tomatoes and place them in the smoker with the sausage. Remove them when they are tender, with split skins, 25 to 30 minutes. When cool enough to handle, peel and chop them, and add them and 2 tablespoons heavy cream to the warm pasta and sausage when ready. Some sautéed mushrooms can be a nice addition, too, if you like.

The little Texas town of Meridian (population 1,500) hosts one of the country's biggest invitational cook-offs, the National Championship Barbecue Cook-Off. To qualify for the August contest, you must win or place in another major competition during the previous year. Virtually everyone in Meridian, as well as folks nearby, gets involved in the preparations and activities, which also include a car show and a carnival.

Linguine and Smoked Clams

This is as easy as life gets. Clams go into the smoker whole and simply yawn open when they're ready to eat. Mix them with a simple sauce and hot linguine and ring the dinner bell. SERVES 4 TO 5

32 medium-size fresh littleneck or cherrystone clams, in their shells, cleaned in several changes of cold water

SAUCE

2/3 cup extra-virgin olive oil

5 garlic cloves, minced

2 medium shallots, minced

1/2 to 1 teaspoon crushed red chile flakes

1 cup dry white wine

1/2 cup clam juice or seafood stock

1/2 cup minced flat-leaf parsley

Kosher salt or coarse sea salt and freshly ground black pepper to taste

1 pound linguine, cooked al dente

1/2 cup peas, fresh or thawed frozen

1. Prepare your smoker for barbecuing, bringing the temperature to 180°F to 200°F.

2. Make the sauce, first warming the oil in the skillet over low heat. Add the garlic and shallots and sauté slowly until the garlic turns pale gold. Add the chile flakes, wine, and clam juice and simmer until the liquid reduces by one-third. Add the parsley, salt, and pepper and remove from the heat.

3. Discard any clams that aren't tightly closed. Arrange the clams in a single layer on a small grill rack, grill basket, or shallow foil pan. Cook the clams until the shells pop open, 15 to 20 minutes. Discard any clams that don't open within several minutes of the rest of the batch.

4. Toss together the hot linguine, clams, and any juices, and peas. Serve right away in shallow pasta bowls.

Salmon and Basil Lasagna

If your image of lasagna is a heavy dish of cheese, meat, and red sauce, try this version for a surprise. Splendidly extravagant for special occasions, the dish stacks layers of salmon with wide ribbons of pasta and a creamy basil-laced cheese sauce. We developed the idea originally for our book *Sublime Smoke* (1996, The Harvard Common Press), and it has remained a personal favorite ever since. SERVES 4

12-ounce salmon fillet

Extra-virgin olive oil

1 tablespoon minced fresh basil

1/2 teaspoon kosher salt or coarse sea salt

LASAGNA SAUCE

1 tablespoon extra-virgin olive oil

1 tablespoon minced shallot

2 garlic cloves, minced

1 cup heavy cream

1/2 cup sour cream

1/8 teaspoon kosher salt or coarse sea salt

1/8 teaspoon ground white pepper

LASAGNA

4 lasagna noodles

1/4 cup minced fresh basil

1/3 cup freshly grated Parmesan cheese

1. Coat the salmon with oil. Sprinkle the flesh side of the fish with the basil and salt. Cover the fillet and let it sit at room temperature for 30 minutes.

2. Prepare your smoker for barbecuing, bringing the temperature to 180°F to 200°F.

3. Transfer the salmon to the smoker and smoke until just cooked through, 30 to 40 minutes.

4. While the salmon smokes, make the sauce.

Warm the oil in a small heavy saucepan over medium heat. Add the shallot and garlic and sauté them until soft but not browned. Stir in the rest of the sauce ingredients and adjust the heat to allow the mixture to simmer steadily. Cook the sauce, stirring frequently, until reduced by one-third. Keep the sauce warm.

5. Cook the lasagna noodles according to the package directions. Drain the noodles, cut them into thirds, and reserve.

6. Flake the salmon into bite-size chunks. (The salmon can be smoked a day in advance and refrigerated. Reheat it before proceeding.)

7. To assemble the lasagna, spoon about 1 tablespoon of the sauce on each plate. You will need 12 pasta strips altogether, so pick out the dozen most attractive. Lay a strip over the sauce on each plate and top with about 1 ounce of the salmon. Spoon sauce thinly over the fish and scatter about 1 teaspoon each of the basil and cheese over the sauce. Repeat with a second layer. For the top layer of the lasagna, again layer the pasta strip followed by the salmon. Top with equal portions of the remaining sauce, basil, and cheese. Serve hot.

Just About Perfect Pizza Crusts

This is the crust we recommend for the pizzas that follow. It's our favorite style—thin, crunchy, and full of flavor even before you put on toppings. Make a few extras for the freezer if you wish. MAKES 2 THIN 10- TO 11-INCH PIZZA CRUSTS

1 envelope active dry yeast (about 2½ teaspoons)
½ teaspoon sugar
2/3 cup lukewarm water, 105°F to 115°F
Approximately 2 cups bread flour
¼ cup stone-ground cornmeal
1½ teaspoons kosher salt or coarse sea salt
2 tablespoons extra-virgin olive oil

1. Combine the yeast and sugar with the water in a small bowl and let sit for a few minutes until foamy. With a heavy-duty mixer or in a food processor, mix the yeast with a scant 2 cups flour and the rest of the ingredients for several minutes, until the dough becomes smooth and elastic.

2. Transfer the dough to a floured pastry board or counter and knead at least 2 more minutes, adding in another tablespoon or two of flour if needed to get a mass that is no longer sticky. Dough on the dry side is a bit more challenging to work with, but it yields a crisper crust. Form the dough into a ball, place it in a greased bowl, and cover with a damp cloth. Set the dough in a warm, draft-free spot and let it rise until doubled in size, about 1 hour. Punch down the dough on the floured pastry board and let it rest for 10 minutes. Roll out the dough into two thin disks, about ⅛ inch thick and 10 to 11 inches in diameter, stretching and prodding it with your fingers, too. (A lip around the border isn't necessary on the dough because our pizza toppings tend to be light mixtures without much liquid.)

3. The dough is ready to use at this point, but also can be saved for later in the refrigerator or freezer. The crusts can be stacked on a baking sheet covered with waxed paper, with more waxed paper layered between the crusts. Do the same if you plan to refrigerate or freeze the crusts. If freezing, first chill the crusts on the baking sheet for about 30 minutes to firm the dough, then wrap the crusts and freeze. Bring the crusts back to room temperature before proceeding.

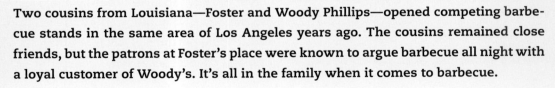

ALL IN THE FAMILY

Two cousins from Louisiana—Foster and Woody Phillips—opened competing barbecue stands in the same area of Los Angeles years ago. The cousins remained close friends, but the patrons at Foster's place were known to argue barbecue all night with a loyal customer of Woody's. It's all in the family when it comes to barbecue.

White Pizza with Vegetable Confetti

A white pizza has no tomatoes or sauce, but it's still full of spunk when dressed well. If you want to embellish it further, try chunks of hot-smoked salmon and a sprinkling of chives. **MAKES 2 THIN-CRUSTED 10- TO 11-INCH PIZZAS**

1/2 each of a medium-size red bell pepper, yellow bell pepper, and green bell pepper

1 small red onion, halved

Extra-virgin olive oil

CHEESE TOPPING

1 1/2 cups grated mozzarella cheese, at room temperature

3/4 cup freshly grated Parmesan cheese, at room temperature

2 garlic cloves, minced

3 tablespoons minced fresh basil or 1 1/2 tablespoons dried basil

1 teaspoon dried oregano

1/2 to 1 teaspoon crushed red chile flakes

Just About Perfect Pizza Crusts (page 330)

1. Prepare the smoker for barbecuing, bringing the temperature to 200°F to 220°F.

2. Rub the bell pepper and onion halves with enough oil to coat their surfaces lightly.

3. Transfer the vegetables to the smoker, as far from the heat as possible. Cook until they are well softened, 35 to 45 minutes. Remove each of the vegetables as it is done.

4. Place the bell peppers in a plastic bag to steam. Chop the onion finely and reserve. Re-move the peppers from the bag, pull the skin off of each, and dice them. Keep the toppings at room temperature, or bag and refrigerate for later use.

5. Preheat the oven to 500°F. Use a pizza stone, if available, placing it in the oven before you begin to heat it.

6. Stir together the cheese topping ingredients.

7. If not using a pizza stone and peel, place the dough rounds on greased pizza pans or baking sheets. Brush about 1 tablespoon oil over each crust. Top with vegetable bits and then the cheese mixture. Bake until the crust is crisp with a few browned edges and the cheese is melted, 10 to 12 minutes. Slice the pizzas into wedges and serve immediately.

BBQ tip Most of our pizza recipes in this chapter make two pizzas, medium to large in diameter but thin in crust and light on toppings. A hungry person can eat one by itself for a full meal, but they will go further when other dishes are being served.

TAYLOR-MADE BARBECUE

Louie Mueller's in Taylor, Texas, looks and smells barbecue. Almost a century old now, the barn-like building features a huge brick pit with a two-story chimney poking out of the ceiling. You line up at the pit, place your order, and carry your 'Q,' wrapped in butcher paper, to a table. Dining room renovations have spoiled some of the old atmosphere, but you certainly won't mistake this place for a fast-food joint.

Smoked Duck Pizza

This fancy pizza also works best without tomatoes. Don't let the fig preserves put you off. This is really good. MAKES 2 THIN-CRUSTED 10- TO 11-INCH PIZZAS

Two 4-ounce to 5-ounce boneless, skinless duck breast halves

Extra-virgin olive oil

Kosher salt or coarse sea salt and freshly ground black pepper to taste

CHEESE TOPPING

1/2 cup grated mozzarella cheese, at room temperature

1/2 cup crumbled creamy fresh goat cheese, at room temperature

1/2 cup freshly grated Parmesan cheese, at room temperature

1 garlic clove, minced

1/2 teaspoon crushed red chile flakes

Just About Perfect Pizza Crusts (page 330)

1/4 cup fig preserves

1. Prepare the smoker for barbecuing, bringing the temperature to 200°F to 220°F.

2. Coat the duck breasts lightly with oil, sprinkle with salt and pepper, and let sit at room temperature for 25 to 30 minutes.

3. Transfer the breasts to the smoker and cook until the duck is rare to medium-rare, 25 to 35 minutes. When done, slice thinly across the grain, or cover and chill unsliced for later use.

4. Preheat the oven to 500°F. Use a pizza stone, if available, placing it in the oven before you begin to heat it.

5. Stir together the cheese topping ingredients.

6. If not using a pizza stone and peel, place the dough rounds on greased pizza pans or baking sheets. Brush about 1 tablespoon oil over each crust. Top with the duck breast slices and then the cheese mixture. Dot with the fig preserves. Bake until the crust is crisp with a few browned edges and the cheese is melted, 10 to 12 minutes. Slice the pizzas into wedges and serve immediately.

Smoked Sausage Pizza

It almost sounds too simple, but get a good, spicy sausage and you'll end up with a marvelous pizza. If you want more on top, consider the addition of smoked mussels or clams. We use sliced fresh tomatoes on the pizza instead of a customary tomato sauce, which tends to undercut the flavor of many smoked ingredients.

MAKES 2 THIN-CRUSTED 10- TO 11-INCH PIZZAS

2 uncooked Italian sausages, about 4 ounces each

Extra-virgin olive oil

CHEESE TOPPING

3/4 cup grated mozzarella cheese, at room temperature

1/2 cup freshly grated Parmesan cheese, at room temperature

1 garlic clove, minced

2 tablespoons minced fresh basil or 1 tablespoon dried basil

1/2 teaspoon dried oregano

1/2 teaspoon crushed red chile flakes

Just About Perfect Pizza Crusts (page 330)

3 small red-ripe Roma or other plum tomatoes, sliced thin

Handful or two of sliced green or black olives (optional)

1. Prepare the smoker for barbecuing, bringing the temperature to 200°F to 220°F.

2. Coat the sausages with oil and transfer them to the smoker. Smoke until cooked through and still juicy, 1 to 1¼ hours. Slice into thin rounds. Keep warm, or bag and refrigerate for later use.

3. Preheat the oven to 500°F. Use a pizza stone, if available, placing it in the oven before you begin to heat it.

4. Stir together the cheese topping ingredients.

5. If not using a pizza stone and peel, place the dough rounds on greased pizza pans or baking sheets. Brush about 1 tablespoon oil over each crust. Top with sausage, tomatoes, and, if you wish, olives, and then the cheese mixture. Bake until the crust is crisp with a few browned edges and the cheese is melted, 10 to 12 minutes. Slice the pizzas into wedges and serve immediately.

BBQ tip The popular Big Green Egg (biggreenegg.com) smoker/grill now offers pizza stones in whole rounds and half-moon styles to emulate a hearth oven. If you own one of these, you can bake oven-type pizzas and calzones outdoors instead of heating up your kitchen.

Wild Mushroom Calzone

Wild mushrooms taste better, but even tame little old button mushrooms will work in this calzone, which is simply a pizza with the crust folded over. Add some sautéed leeks or onions, or chopped marinated artichoke hearts, if you like.

MAKES 2 LARGE CALZONES

12 ounces wild mushrooms or other mushrooms, sliced thickly

Extra-virgin olive oil

Kosher salt or coarse sea salt

CHEESE FILLING

1 cup ricotta

1 cup grated mozzarella cheese, at room temperature

1/4 cup freshly grated Parmesan cheese, at room temperature

2 small red-ripe tomatoes, chopped

1 garlic clove, minced

1 to 2 tablespoons minced fresh parsley or basil

1/2 teaspoon dried oregano

Pinch of crushed red chile flakes, or more to taste

Just About Perfect Pizza Crusts (page 330)

1. Prepare the smoker for barbecuing, bringing the temperature to 200°F to 220°F.

2. Rub the mushrooms with enough oil to coat their surfaces, and salt them lightly. Arrange the mushrooms on a small grill rack or a piece of heavy-duty foil.

3. Transfer them to the smoker and cook until they ooze liquid and are soft, 15 to 20 minutes. Keep the mushrooms warm, or bag and refrigerate for later use.

4. Preheat the oven to 425°F. Use a pizza stone, if available, placing it in the oven before you begin to heat it.

5. Stir together the cheese filling ingredients.

6. If not using a pizza stone and peel, place the dough rounds on greased pizza pans or baking sheets. Spoon half of the filling over each crust, covering just half of each and leaving a 1/2-inch edge all around. Divide the mushrooms between the two calzones, sprinkling them evenly over the cheese filling. Fold the uncovered side of the dough over the filled portion. Pull the bottom edge up just over the top edge and crimp the edge neatly and tightly. Cut a 1-inch slit in the top of each calzone. Bake until medium-brown and crisp, 25 to 30 minutes. Cool for 5 minutes before slicing into the molten cheese filling. Eat with a knife and fork.

SERVING SUGGESTION Pizza parties aren't just for kids. Even generally reserved grownups like mixing and matching and munching. Prepare crusts and various toppings ahead, and buy some pizza sauce that you jazz up with a handful of fresh herbs. Then let everyone at it. With some ice-cold beer, a few bottles of wine, and a big salad, you're set for the evening.

Deep-Dish Smoked Mozzarella Pizza

Making the most of home-smoked mozzarella, this Chicago-style deep-dish pizza is absolutely addictive. If you're a pepperoni fan, it's a good addition here.

MAKES 1 THICK-CRUSTED 10- TO 11-INCH PIZZA

PIZZA SAUCE

14.5-ounce can plum tomatoes, undrained

3 tablespoons extra-virgin olive oil

2 tablespoons dried basil

1 garlic clove, minced

1/2 teaspoon dried oregano

1/4 teaspoon table salt

1/4 to 1/2 teaspoon crushed red chile flakes

CHEESE TOPPING

1 1/2 cups grated mozzarella cheese, softened

1/4 cup freshly grated Parmesan cheese, softened

Just About Perfect Pizza Crusts (page 330)

1. Prepare the smoker for barbecuing, bringing the temperature to 200°F to 220°F.

2. Preheat the oven to 425°F.

3. Combine the sauce ingredients in a small saucepan. Cook over medium heat, breaking up the tomatoes with a spoon, until thickened, about 15 minutes. Let the sauce cool briefly.

4. Stir together the cheese topping ingredients.

5. Coat an 8- to 9-inch cast-iron skillet or other smoke-proof skillet with oil. Press the pizza crust dough rounds together and then arrange the dough in the skillet, forming a thick lip about 1-inch high around the edge. Spoon the sauce into the crust and bake until crisp with a few browned edges, 25 to 30 minutes.

6. Sprinkle the cheese thickly over the pizza. Transfer the skillet to the smoker. Cook until the cheese is completely melted, 15 to 20 minutes. Slice the pizza into wedges and eat immediately, with a knife and fork.

BBQ tip Not only does the smoke perfume the mozzarella in this pizza, but it also gives the whole pizza more of the wood-scented character of Neapolitan pizzas baked in wood-fueled ovens.

Easy Mexican Tortilla Pizza

Unlike our more conventional pizzas, this tortilla pizza can be simply heated through in the smoker and served immediately, without ever having to step back into your kitchen. Add a side of Fiesta Salsa (page 349), if you like, and bring on the Turquoise Margaritas (page 477). **MAKES 2 MEDIUM TORTILLA PIZZAS**

2 uncooked chorizo sausages, approximately 4 ounces each

2 fresh mild green chiles, such as New Mexican, Anaheim, or poblano

Vegetable or extra-virgin olive oil

CHEESE TOPPING

1 cup grated mozzarella or asadero cheese, at room temperature

1/2 cup freshly grated Parmesan cheese, at room temperature

1 garlic clove, minced

1/4 teaspoon dried oregano

1 small red-ripe Roma or other plum tomato, chopped

2 large thin flour tortillas, at room temperature

1. Prepare the smoker for barbecuing, bringing the temperature to 200°F to 220°F.

2. Coat the sausages and chiles with oil and transfer them to the smoker. Smoke until cooked through and still juicy, about 1 hour. Keep the smoker on if you plan to make the pizzas shortly. Place the chiles in a plastic bag to steam. When cool enough to handle, remove from the bag and pull the skin off of each. Slice into thin ribbons, discarding the seeds. Slice the sausage into thin rounds.

3. Stir together the cheese topping ingredients and scatter over the tortillas.

4. Arrange the sausage rounds and chile strips evenly over the cheese. Place on a foil-covered baking sheet and cook in the smoker until the cheese is melted and the tortillas are chewy and a bit crisp in spots, about 10 minutes. (If you want a crisper crust, transfer the tortillas to the grill or griddle over your smoker's firebox, or to a griddle or skillet on the stove, and cook over high heat for several more minutes.) Slice the pizzas into wedges and serve immediately.

VARIATION: EASY MEXICAN TORTILLA PIZZA WITH MUSHROOMS, BACON, AND ADOBO Smoke the mushrooms as for Wild Mushroom Calzone (page 334). Replace the chorizo and green chile toppings with the smoked mushrooms, 2 to 3 crumbled crisp-cooked bacon slices, and a few drizzles of the adobo sauce from a can of chipotle chiles.

One of the most legendary Bar-B-Q joints in the country, Leonard's in Memphis got its start in 1922 when Leonard Heuberger opened a small stand and delivered barbecue by bicycle. Heuberger usually gets the credit for inventing the Memphis barbecue sandwich—pork, coleslaw, and red sauce served in a bun—and the Leonard's of today still features a fine version of the original.

this tortilla pizza can be simply heated through in the smoker and served immediately, without ever having to step back into your kitchen

WHILE YOU WAIT

WHEN YOU'VE GOT HUNGRY FOLKS STANDING AROUND THE FIRE, AND DINNER WON'T BE DONE FOR A SPELL, POP ONE OF THESE DISHES IN YOUR SMOKER. THEY MAKE A SUPER SNACK OR LIGHT MEAL ANY TIME OF THE DAY, BUT THEY'RE PARTICULARLY GOOD AS LATE AFTER-NOON APPETIZERS WITH YOUR FAVORITE LIBATION.

MANY OF THE DISHES WE SUGGEST ARE SMOKED VERSIONS OF POPULAR APPETIZERS USUALLY PREPARED IN other ways. Try your hand at the same game, figuring out which of your personal favorites might benefit from some smoke flavor, and then doing a little experimentation with the idea. As in other facets of barbecuing, you may be amazed by the ease of success.

Can't Wait Queso

Few things are simpler, or tastier, than a melted cheese starter. This is the barbecue version of a Mexican and Tex-Mex favorite, *queso fundido*, a baked white cheese.

SERVES 2 TO 8, DEPENDING ON HUNGER LEVELS

12-ounce chunk medium cheddar cheese or half cheddar and half Monterey Jack

1 to 2 teaspoons Southwest Heat (page 32), Cajun Ragin' Rub (page 29), Wild Willy's Number One-derful Rub (page 26), or other savory seasoning blend

1 to 2 pickled or fresh jalapeños, sliced

Warm flour tortillas

1. Prepare the smoker for barbecuing, bringing the temperature to 200°F to 220°F.

2. Place the cheese in a small smoke-proof baking dish. Sprinkle it with the rub and the jalapeños. Place the cheese in the smoker as far from the fire as possible. Cook until the cheese melts through, about 1¼ hours. (Avoid overcooking because the cheese becomes rubbery.) Serve immediately, spooning the melted cheese onto the warm flour tortillas. Cut the tortillas in quarters to make them more manageable to eat as finger food.

VARIATION: MEXICAN QUESO FUNDIDO Mexican cheeses are becoming much more widely available today across the country. If you have access to Chihuahua, asadero, or Oaxaca, grate them into the baking dish in place of the cheddar or Jack and sprinkle 2 to 4 ounces crumbled fried chorizo on top. Smoke until the cheese melts through, about 30 minutes. Sprinkle scallions on top and serve on warm flour tortillas.

BBQ tip For convenience's sake, we've featured in this chapter appetizers that you can cook with other food in spare space in your smoker, but each is also tasty enough to do on its own. If you have equipment that's easy to start and use—such as a stovetop smoker, electric water smoker, or Cookshack oven—these recipes remain a breeze, and they can add a lot of smoky flavor to a non-barbecue meal.

Unholy Swiss Cheese

In the Alps, melted raclette cheese is a warming snack after a winter afternoon of skiing. This smoked version is worth savoring any time of the year. If you can't find raclette, substitute Gruyère for a similar flavor.

SERVES 2 TO 8, DEPENDING ON HUNGER LEVELS

12-ounce chunk raclette cheese

1 tablespoon Dijon mustard, preferably country-style

1 1/2 to 2 pounds boiled new potatoes or other small potatoes

Cornichons or other sour pickles and additional Dijon mustard

1. Prepare the smoker for barbecuing, bringing the temperature to 200°F to 220°F.

2. Place the cheese in a small smoke-proof baking dish. Smear the mustard over it. Place the cheese in the smoker as far from the fire as possible. Cook until the cheese melts through, about 1 1/4 hours. (Avoid overcooking, because the cheese becomes rubbery.)

3. Serve immediately on the potatoes, which can be halved, if needed, for easier eating. Accompany the cheese with the cornichons and more mustard.

SERVING SUGGESTION If you add a hearty loaf of bread, a green salad, and a bottle of red wine, you've got the makings for a satisfying Sunday night supper.

DUTCH TREAT

In Holland, the local Gouda cheese is sometimes smoked and sprinkled with cumin seeds. When we do it in the smoker, as another European variation on the melted cheese theme, we use a tablespoon of cumin seeds plus a tablespoon of minced onion. Peter Noom, a Dutch friend who loves barbecue, gave us the idea.

Nachos Blancos

Gooey with molten strings of mild cheese and punctuated with spicy toppings, an authentic nacho bears little resemblance to the popular ballpark variety awash in an ugly orange sauce. Smoking the nachos adds an extra dimension to the snack, making grocery-store tortilla chips taste of fresh-roasted corn. SERVES 4 TO 6

Approximately 36 large tortilla chips

2 cups grated Monterey Jack cheese (8 ounces)

1/3 pound sliced bacon or chorizo (optional), fried and crumbled

1 medium red onion, chopped

4 to 6 fresh or pickled serranos or jalapeños, seeded and minced

Sour cream

Sauce Olé (page 379; optional)

1. Prepare the smoker for barbecuing, bringing the temperature to 200°F to 220°F.

2. Arrange the tortilla chips on a foil-covered baking sheet or smoke-proof platter. Scatter the cheese, meat (if you wish), onion, and chiles over the chips.

3. Place the nachos in the smoker. Cook until the cheese is well melted, 10 to 20 minutes. Serve immediately with sour cream and, if you wish, Sauce Olé.

Smoked Mushroom Quesadillas

We eat quesadillas frequently—as both appetizers and light meals—so one day we just popped a couple in the pit and discovered a new treat for ourselves and friends. If you prefer, switch out the corn tortillas for their flour cousins, or add a handful of lightly cooked corn kernels to the smoked mushrooms. MAKES 4 SMALL QUESADILLAS

8 ounces mushrooms, such as white or brown button or portobello caps

Kosher salt or coarse sea salt

8 ounces asadero, Monterey Jack, pepper Jack, or cheddar cheese, or a combination, grated

1 minced canned chipotle chile in adobo sauce or 1 sliced or minced fresh or pickled jalapeño or serrano (optional)

8 corn tortillas

Vegetable oil spray

Fiesta Salsa (page 349) or other salsa

1. Prepare the smoker for barbecuing, bringing the temperature to 200°F to 220°F.

2. Slice the mushrooms into large bite-size

pieces and salt them lightly. Arrange the mushrooms on a small grill rack or a piece of heavy-duty foil.

3. Place the mushrooms in the smoker and cook until they ooze liquid and are soft, 15 to 20 minutes.

4. Scatter the cheese and optional chile over 4 of the tortillas, then top with the mushrooms. Arrange the remaining tortillas on top of the mushrooms. Spray the top tortillas lightly with oil. Place on a foil-covered baking sheet and cook in the smoker until the cheese is melted and the tortillas are chewy and a bit crisp in spots, 25 to 35 minutes. (One or more of the top tortillas may curl up a little, even with the spritz of oil. If so, simply flip those quesadillas over before cutting.) Slice into wedges and serve immediately, with salsa.

Bacon-Wrapped Jalapeños

When Cheryl was a teenager in Illinois a couple of generations ago, she didn't know there was any particular heat difference in various kinds of fresh chiles. She read about a chile rellenos dish in a cookbook, made with somewhat mild New Mexican or Anaheim pods. She couldn't find those chiles in the store so bought instead incendiary jalapeños. The batter-dipped and fried chiles turned out to be a disastrous main dish, but her family still kids her about having invented the jalapeño popper. Here's a more intentional attempt at a simpler form of the popper. If you want to surprise your guests in a slightly tamer way than Cheryl did, add a little hot- or cold-smoked salmon to the cheese filling. SERVES 6 OR MORE AS AN APPETIZER

8 ounces cream cheese, softened

1 cup shredded mild cheddar

18 medium-size fresh jalapeños, halved lengthwise, seeds and stems removed

12 ounces thinly sliced bacon

1. Prepare the smoker for barbecuing, bringing the temperature to 200°F to 220°F.

2. Combine the cream cheese and cheddar in a small bowl. Spoon the mixture into the jalapeño halves, mounding it just a bit in the center.

3. Cut the bacon slices in half horizontally and wrap a half-slice lengthwise around each pepper half. Secure with a toothpick. Arrange the jalapeños in a shallow smoke-proof dish or in a piece of heavy-duty foil molded into a small tray.

4. Place the dish in the smoker and cook until the bacon has browned and crisped and the cheese is gooey, about 30 minutes. Enjoy right away as finger food.

Curry Pecans

The "smoked" nuts you get on commercial airlines usually rely on liquid smoke or hickory-flavored salt for their flavor. There's a world of difference in the real thing.

MAKES 2 CUPS

CURRY MARINADE
Juice of 2 medium oranges
1½ teaspoons curry powder
1½ teaspoons Worcestershire sauce
1 teaspoon sugar
1 garlic clove, minced
½ teaspoon kosher salt or coarse sea salt, or more to taste

2 cups pecan halves

1. Combine the marinade ingredients in a non-reactive bowl. Add the pecans and allow them to sit at room temperature for about 1 hour.

2. Prepare the smoker for barbecuing, bringing the temperature to 200°F to 220°F.

3. Drain the nuts. Transfer them to a piece of greased heavy-duty foil or a greased foil baking pan just large enough to hold the nuts in a single layer and place the nuts in the smoker. Cook the pecans until they are crisp and lightly smoked, 50 to 60 minutes. Serve immediately or keep in a covered jar for several days.

BBQ tip Although the ideal temperature for barbecuing food is between 180°F and 220°F, don't panic if the temperature drifts up to 250°F or down to 160°F. A little time in an extreme range won't hurt most food, but start making adjustments as quickly as possible to get back to the right level.

Little Devils

A Southwest favorite, these nuts are spicy but not as hot as you might guess from the amount of Tabasco used. The smoking process tames some of the sauce's fiery potency. MAKES 2 CUPS

2 cups raw peanuts
½ cup (yes, *cup*) Tabasco or other hot pepper sauce
Peanut oil
Table salt to taste

1. Combine the peanuts with the Tabasco in a small bowl. Let the nuts sit in the sauce for about 30 minutes.

2. Prepare the smoker for barbecuing, bringing the temperature to 200°F to 220°F.

3. Select a smoke-proof dish that will hold the peanuts in a single layer. Thickly coat the dish with the oil. Stir in the peanuts and sprinkle with salt.

4. Place the peanuts in the smoker and cook until the peanuts are well browned and dry, 50 to 60 minutes. Check the nuts toward the end of the cooking time to avoid burning.

5. Transfer the peanuts to absorbent paper to cool. Serve immediately or keep in a covered jar for several days.

SERVING SUGGESTION For a cocktail party with Southwestern flair, serve the Little Devils along with Fiesta Salsa (page 349) and chips, Nachos Blancos (page 342), garlicky guacamole, jicama slices with lime juice, carrot slices marinated in jalapeño pepper pickling liquid, and Turquoise Margaritas (page 477) or Apricoritas (page 476).

VARIATION: DEVILISH PISTACHIOS Substitute 2 cups unshelled pistachio nuts for the peanuts and green Tabasco for the regular.

Smoked Rosemary Walnuts

Sugar and spice, and much better than nice. MAKES 2 CUPS

2 tablespoons unsalted butter

1½ tablespoons packed brown sugar

1½ to 2 teaspoons lightly crushed dried rosemary

¼ teaspoon garlic powder

2 cups (about ½ pound) walnut halves

¾ teaspoon kosher salt or coarse sea salt, or more to taste

1. Prepare the smoker for barbecuing, bringing the temperature to 200°F to 220°F.

2. In a skillet, melt the butter with the sugar,

rosemary, and garlic powder. Stir in the walnuts and coat well. Stir in the salt, tasting as you add it.

3. Transfer the nuts to a shallow smoke-proof dish or piece of heavy-duty foil molded into a small tray. Place the nuts in the smoker and cook until dried and fragrant, about 30 minutes. Transfer the walnuts to absorbent paper to cool. Serve immediately or keep in a covered jar for several days.

Bar-B-Q'ed Potato Chips

We find commercial "barbecue" chips just ghastly. Here's a way to add the real spirit of the outdoors. Serve with Three-Onion Dip (page 351) if you like.

SERVES AS MANY AS YOU LIKE

Any size bag of potato chips, preferably sturdy ridged or hand-cut chips

Chili powder

1. Prepare the smoker for barbecuing, bringing the temperature to 200°F to 220°F.

2. Arrange the chips in a shallow smoke-proof dish or in a piece of heavy-duty foil molded into a small tray. Sprinkle with chili powder. Place in the smoker and cook until the chips are warm throughout and have taken on a light but identifiable smoke flavor, 5 to 15 minutes. Serve immediately.

Smoked Olives

While black and green olives are staples on American relish trays, you rarely see them baked, a common preparation in the Mediterranean region. We take the cooking a step further, adding a light taste of smoke. MAKES 2 CUPS

1 cup black olives with character, such as Greek kalamata or atalanti, drained lightly

1 cup green olives with character, such as Greek cracked, drained lightly

2 tablespoons extra-virgin olive oil

2 tablespoons dry white wine

2 garlic cloves, minced

3/4 teaspoon dried oregano

Freshly ground black pepper to taste

1. Prepare the smoker for barbecuing, bringing the temperature to 200°F to 220°F.

2. Arrange the olives densely in a shallow small smoke-proof dish or in a piece of heavy-duty foil molded into a small tray. Add the remaining ingredients.

3. Place the olives in the smoker and cook until the olives absorb half of the liquid and take on a light but identifiable smoke flavor, 55 to 65 minutes. Serve immediately or let sit for several hours to develop the flavor further. Refrigerate any leftovers.

Mouthwatering Watermelon Morsels

This is as simple as it is scrumptious, at least if you've got a supply of watermelon pickles on hand. You can find the pickled rinds in Southern supermarkets, or you can make your own (see page 435). **MAKES A BUNCH**

Watermelon rind pickles
Bacon slices, cut in thirds

1. Prepare the smoker for barbecuing, bringing the temperature to 200°F to 220°F.

2. Wrap each watermelon rind pickle in a piece of bacon and secure with toothpicks. Transfer the tidbits to the smoker and cook them until the bacon is brown and crisp, 35 to 45 minutes. Serve hot.

SERVING SUGGESTION For a summer afternoon get-together with a Southern theme, serve these along with Greens-Stuffed Mushrooms (page 356), Sweet Potato Biscuits (page 411) with ham or turkey slices, Squash Relish (page 437), Okra Pickles (page 432), and Peanutty Pie (page 445) made into individual tarts. Accompany the spread with Derby Day Mint Juleps (page 473) and Sunny Sweet Tea (page 484).

Bronzed Garlic

This is our kind of bread spread. **SERVES 4 TO 6**

2 large whole heads of garlic
Extra-virgin olive oil
Crusty country-style white bread

1. Prepare the smoker for barbecuing, bringing the temperature to 200°F to 220°F.

2. Coat the garlic heads well with oil. Place the garlic in the smoker and cook it until browned and well softened, 40 to 50 minutes.

3. Pull any loose browned skin from the garlic.

Slice a thin layer off the top of each head, just deep enough to expose the tops of the individual cloves.

4. Serve hot accompanied by the bread. To eat, break off the cloves and squeeze the softened garlic onto chunks or slices of bread.

SERVING SUGGESTION Use leftover smoked garlic as a spread on sandwiches or mix it into mayonnaise.

Fiesta Salsa

Smoky salsas rival barbecue sauces in possibilities. Here's a classic to get you started. MAKES ABOUT 1½ CUPS

1 pound red-ripe tomatoes (2 to 3 medium)

2 teaspoons extra-virgin olive oil

¼ cup chopped red onion

2 to 3 garlic cloves, minced

2 canned chipotle chiles, minced, plus 2 teaspoons adobo sauce, or more to taste

Juice of 1 lime

Table salt to taste

2 to 3 tablespoons chopped fresh cilantro

Tortilla chips or corn or flour tortillas

1. Prepare the smoker for barbecuing, bringing the temperature to 200°F to 220°F.

2. Coat the tomatoes with 1 teaspoon of the oil. Transfer the tomatoes to the smoker. Cook them until they are very soft and the skins are ready to split, 45 to 55 minutes. Set the tomatoes aside until cool enough to handle. Coarsely chop the tomatoes with their peels.

3. Transfer the tomatoes, peels, and any juice to a blender. Add the remaining 1 teaspoon oil, onion, garlic, chipotles and adobo sauce, and lime juice and puree. Pour into a small serving bowl, add salt to taste, and refrigerate for at least 45 minutes.

4. Stir in the cilantro just before serving. Serve with tortilla chips or tortillas.

BBQ tip You can create smoked salsas from many combinations of vegetables—or even fruits—by keeping in mind a couple of key principles. For contrasting flavors, avoid smoking everything you plan to throw into the mix. Add a little more lime or other acid than you do in traditional recipes, to balance the assertive smoke taste.

BIG DADDY'S THRONE

Despite growing into a small chain, the original Dreamland Bar-B-Que in Tuscaloosa, Alabama, hasn't changed much since Big Daddy John Bishop and his wife, Lilly, opened for business in 1958. The meat of choice is still succulent ribs, the only thing served at first, but other options now include pork, sausage, and chicken. When Big Daddy passed away in 1997, his daughter Jeannette, the new proprietor, moved her father's large redwood chair from its old location outside by the barbecue pit to a prominent spot inside. Some say he still presides as always from his perch on high.

The Ridgewood in Bluff City, Tennessee, has gotten its share of good press in the last couple of decades, since Jane and Michael Stern anointed its barbecue as the best in the country. The restaurant serves its luscious pork East Tennessee style, with slices piled on big buns and slathered with a thick, tasty ketchup-based sauce. The beef also wins raves, and we've never come across a contrary word about the beans and slaw either.

Better-Than-Store-Bought Bacon-Horseradish Dip

Tired of sneaking into supermarkets to buy that ersatz version of bacon-horseradish dip with fake bacon, pseudo sour cream, and enough preservatives to keep Keith Richards young another half-century? MAKES ABOUT 1 1/2 CUPS

1 cup sour cream

1 tablespoon plus 1 teaspoon prepared horseradish

1 1/2-inch-thick slice from a medium onion

Vegetable oil

3 to 4 slices bacon, chopped

2 ounces fresh mild goat cheese, softened

Potato chips or carrot sticks

1. Prepare the smoker for barbecuing, bringing the temperature to 200°F to 220°F.

2. Spoon the sour cream and 1 tablespoon of the horseradish into a smoke-proof baking dish. Rub the onion slice with oil. Place the sour cream and onion in the smoker side by side and cook for 30 to 40 minutes. The sour cream should be runny but not separated, and the onion well softened but not cooked through.

3. While the sour cream and onion cook, fry the bacon in a small skillet. Drain the bacon.

4. Stir the cheese into the sour cream until well combined. Chop the onion and crumble the bacon. Mix into the sour cream. Add as much of the remaining 1 teaspoon horseradish as desired. The smoked horseradish will mellow in flavor, and any added at the end creates a pleasantly pungent bite. Chill for at least 30 minutes for best flavor. Serve with potato chips or carrot sticks.

Bean, Beer, and Bacon Dip

Canned beans have never tasted better. MAKES ABOUT 2¹/₂ CUPS

15-ounce can refried beans

¹/₂ cup beer

4 slices crisp-fried bacon, crumbled

¹/₂ cup grated pepper Jack or Monterey Jack cheese

¹/₄ to ¹/₂ cup of your favorite tomato-based salsa

Table salt (optional)

Tortilla chips or corn chips

1. Prepare the smoker for barbecuing, bringing the temperature to 200°F to 220°F.

2. Stir together the beans, beer, bacon, and cheese in a smoke-proof dish. Place in the smoker and cook until heated through and lightly infused with smoke, about 30 minutes. Add the salsa, checking the heat level before you commit yourself to all of it. Stir in a little salt if needed. Serve warm with chips.

VARIATION: JUST PLAIN DELICIOUS BEAN DIP
The smoked beans give the dip its biggest flavor boost, so if you're out of some of the other ingredients, or just prefer the purist approach, simply smoke the beans alone and add salsa at the end.

Three-Onion Dip

This is almost more onion than dip. Delicious with chips, crackers, raw vegetables, or spooned over a baked potato or potato skins. MAKES ABOUT 2¹/₂ CUPS

1 medium onion, chopped

3 large shallots, chopped

6 scallions, green and white parts chopped separately

2 tablespoons vegetable oil

1¹/₂ cups sour cream

Few drops Worcestershire sauce

Table salt (optional)

Potato chips, crackers, or raw vegetable slices

1. Prepare the smoker for barbecuing, bringing the temperature to 200°F to 220°F.

2. Mix the onion, shallots, and white portions of the scallions with the oil and pour into a shallow, smoke-proof dish or shallow tray made of doubled heavy-duty foil. Place in the smoker and smoke until the onions are tender, 50 to 60 minutes. Mix with the sour cream, Worcestershire sauce, and green scallion tops. Add salt if you wish. Chill for at least 1 hour for best flavor. Serve with chips, crackers, or vegetables.

Smoked Clam Dip

An adaptation of an old classic, made ready for revival. MAKES ABOUT 1½ CUPS

1 pound fresh clams in their shells, preferably medium-size cherrystones or littlenecks, cleaned in several changes of cold water

¾ cup sour cream

1½ tablespoons minced fresh chives

1½ tablespoons minced onion

¼ teaspoon Worcestershire sauce

Pinch of cayenne

Kosher salt or coarse sea salt

Potato chips or crackers

1. Prepare the smoker for barbecuing, bringing the temperature to 200°F to 220°F.

2. Discard any clams that aren't tightly closed. Arrange the clams in a single layer on a small grill rack, grill basket, or piece of doubled heavy-duty foil and place them in the smoker. The shells will pop open within about 15 minutes, signaling that the clams are cooked, but smoke them about 5 more minutes to make them a bit more fragrant. Don't let them turn to leather, though. Discard any clams that haven't opened within several minutes of the rest. Transfer the clams from the smoker carefully, to avoid losing the clam juice that will be puddled in the bottom shells.

3. When cool enough to handle, pour the clam juice into a medium-size bowl. Pop the clams from their shells with a fork or small knife. Mince the clams. Add them to the bowl, along with the remaining ingredients, and stir to combine.

4. Refrigerate for at least 1 hour for best flavor. Serve with chips or crackers.

BBQ tip Clams are among a handful of shellfish we typically smoke in the shell. They stay moist but still take on the enticing aroma of woodsmoke.

Creamy Catfish Spread

Any time we smoke catfish we save some for this spread, one of the tastiest appetizers you can pop between your lips. MAKES ABOUT 2 CUPS

8 ounces Peppered Catfish (page 246) or store-bought smoked catfish

4 ounces cream cheese, softened

2 tablespoons unsalted butter

1 to 1½ tablespoons milk

2 teaspoons minced onion

1½ teaspoons brandy

1 teaspoon freshly squeezed lemon juice

¼ teaspoon Tabasco or other hot pepper sauce

Table salt and freshly ground black pepper to taste

Cucumber rounds, crackers, or crusty country-style white bread

1. Flake the catfish, discarding any skin and bones.

2. Combine the fish and remaining spread ingredients in a food processor and process until well mixed. Pack the spread into a small serving bowl and refrigerate, covered, for at least 30 minutes.

3. Serve with cucumber rounds, crackers, or bread.

Drop-Dead Trout Spread

Of all the recipes in the first edition of *Smoke & Spice*, this is probably the one most requested by family and friends. It'll be an instant hit at your house, too.

MAKES ABOUT 2 CUPS

HORSERADISH PASTE
2 teaspoons freshly squeezed lemon juice
$1/2$ teaspoon prepared horseradish
$1/2$ teaspoon kosher salt or coarse sea salt
$1/2$ teaspoon freshly ground black pepper

8-ounce whole trout, with or without head, or 8 ounces trout fillets
3-ounce package cream cheese, softened
3 tablespoons minced onion
3 tablespoons pecan pieces, toasted
1 tablespoon freshly squeezed lemon juice
$1^1/2$ teaspoons Creole mustard, such as Zatarain's
1 teaspoon white wine Worcestershire sauce or $3/4$ teaspoon regular Worcestershire sauce
Several drops Tabasco or other hot pepper sauce
Additional kosher salt or coarse sea salt (optional)
Zucchini rounds, crackers, or bread sticks

1. Prepare the smoker for barbecuing, bringing the temperature to 200°F to 220°F.

2. In a small bowl, combine the paste ingredients. Rub the trout inside and out with the paste and let the fish sit at room temperature for 20 to 30 minutes.

3. Transfer the trout to the smoker. Cook the fish until it's opaque and flakes easily, 35 to 45 minutes. Allow the trout to cool for at least 15 minutes.

4. Flake the fish, discarding any skin and bones. Place the fish and the cream cheese, onion, pecans, lemon juice, mustard, Worcestershire, Tabasco, and, if you like, salt in a food processor and process until well mixed. Pack the spread into a small serving bowl and refrigerate, covered, for at least 30 minutes.

5. Serve with zucchini rounds, crackers, or bread sticks.

BBQ tip We always throw a couple of onions on the smoker whenever we're barbecuing. The smoke mellows their pungency but heightens their taste. Use them as a substitute for raw onion in this or any other recipe.

Bluefish Mousse

Though a little lighter and more delicate in texture than the previous two smoked fish spreads, this mixture still packs plenty of flavor. The oils in Atlantic bluefish make it a natural for smoking, but you can also use whitefish, cod, or mahi-mahi. Whip it together a day ahead of serving if you wish. MAKES ABOUT 2 CUPS

8-ounce to 10-ounce bluefish fillet

1½ to 2 tablespoons Seafaring Seafood Rub (page 28) or store-bought seafood dry rub

2 lemon wedges

2 tablespoons freshly squeezed lemon juice

1 envelope unflavored gelatin

2 garlic cloves

2 tablespoons chopped fresh dill or 1 tablespoon dried dill

⅓ cup boiling water

1 cup heavy cream

⅓ cup mayonnaise

Several dashes Tabasco or other hot pepper sauce

Kosher salt or coarse sea salt, or more Seafaring Seafood Rub (page 28) or other dry rub used above (optional)

Lettuce leaves

Dill sprigs (optional)

Toasted baguette slices or crackers

1. Prepare the smoker for barbecuing, bringing the temperature to 200°F to 220°F.

2. Rub the fish fillet well with the dry rub and let sit at room temperature for 20 minutes. Squeeze one of the lemon wedges over the fish and transfer the fish to the smoker.

3. Smoke until done throughout, 35 to 45 min-utes. Squeeze the other lemon wedge over the fish as it comes out of the smoker. When cool enough to handle, break the fish into small chunks, discarding any skin and bones.

4. Pour the lemon juice into a food processor, sprinkle the gelatin over it, and let it sit for about 5 minutes so the gelatin can soften. Add the garlic, dill, and boiling water and process until the gelatin dissolves, about 30 seconds. Add the cream, mayonnaise, and Tabasco and process again until smooth. Taste and add salt or a bit more rub if the mixture needs more sea-soning. The mousse should taste somewhat as-sertive now since it will be served cold.

5. Add the fish to the processor and pulse to combine. Mix the mousse well but stop short of pureeing it. Spoon into a greased 2-cup mold or bowl, and refrigerate until set, at least 2 hours.

6. Line a platter with lettuce. Unmold the mousse, first dipping the bottom of the mold into hot water for just a couple of seconds. In-vert onto the platter, garnish with dill, if de-sired, and serve with baguette slices or crack-ers.

Heavenly Hearts

Artichoke hearts with cheese and mayonnaise make a divine spread. SERVES 4 TO 6

14-ounce can artichoke hearts, drained

1 cup mayonnaise

3/4 cup grated Parmesan or Romano cheese

1 teaspoon white or cider vinegar

1/2 teaspoon dried basil

1 garlic clove, minced

1/4 cup fresh bread crumbs

Melba toasts, crackers, or crusty country-style white bread

1. Prepare the smoker for barbecuing, bringing the temperature to 200°F to 220°F.

2. Slice the artichoke hearts into quarters.

3. In a shallow, smoke-proof dish, mix the artichokes with the mayonnaise, cheese, vinegar, basil, and garlic. Top the mixture with the bread crumbs.

4. Transfer the dish to the smoker and cook the artichoke mixture until the cheese and mayonnaise are melted together, 25 to 35 minutes. Serve immediately on Melba toasts, crackers, or crusty country-style white bread.

Mozzarella Toasts

These luscious little finger snacks gain much of their flavor from fresh mozzarella, the kind that comes in containers with water. For extra accents, minced fresh sage, thyme, parsley, or oregano would always be welcome. MAKES 1 1/2 DOZEN

12 small 1/2-inch-thick slices of French bread, preferably from a crusty baguette

Extra-virgin olive oil

8 ounces fresh mozzarella, sliced thin

1 1/2 to 2 tablespoons small capers

Crushed red chile flakes

1. Prepare the smoker for barbecuing, bringing the temperature to 200°F to 220°F.

2. Brush each bread slice on one side with olive oil. Top each bread slice with mozzarella to cover it, then a sprinkling of capers and chile flakes. Place carefully directly on the smoker's cooking rack and cook until the bread has toasted lightly and the cheese is melted, 15 to 20 minutes. Serve immediately.

In Henderson, Kentucky, they mix their meat with music at the W. C. Handy Blues and Barbecue Festival in June. Two dozen or so singers and bands perform over the weeklong celebration. Between concerts and feasting, you can enroll your kids in an art camp, attend a zydeco dance workshop, or buy a carry-away breakfast treat at a church bake sale.

Greens-Stuffed Mushrooms

Southerners have always loved greens with smoked food, a pairing that reaches a peak of perfection in this appetizer. SERVES 4 TO 6

12 to 16 large white mushrooms

2 tablespoons unsalted butter

2 tablespoons vegetable oil

1/4 cup chopped onion

2 tablespoons minced red bell pepper

2 garlic cloves, minced

12 ounces mustard greens or kale, chopped fine

1/2 cup chicken stock

1 teaspoon yellow mustard

Table salt and freshly ground black pepper to taste

4 ounces cream cheese, softened

6 tablespoons dry bread crumbs

Pecorino Romano or Parmesan cheese, grated

1. Prepare the smoker for barbecuing, bringing the temperature to 200°F to 220°F.

2. Stem the mushrooms and hollow out the caps. Chop the stems and trimmings and reserve.

3. Warm the butter and oil in a skillet. Add the mushroom caps and sauté over medium-low heat for 2 to 3 minutes, turning frequently. Remove the partially cooked mushroom caps from the pan and set them aside. Add the mushroom stems and trimmings, onion, bell pepper, garlic, and greens to the skillet. Sauté the mixture for 2 to 3 minutes. Mix in the stock, mustard, salt, and pepper and simmer, covered, for about 5 minutes. Remove the pan from the heat. Immediately stir in the cream cheese, followed by the bread crumbs.

4. Stuff the mushroom caps, mounding the filling high. Sprinkle with the Romano cheese.

5. Place the mushrooms on a small grill rack or baking sheet and transfer them to the smoker. Cook them until the filling browns on top and the mushrooms are tender, 20 to 30 minutes. Serve hot.

SERVING SUGGESTION The mushrooms make a good side dish, too, especially with pork.

Wild Wings

When in doubt, wing it. MAKES 3 DOZEN PIECES

WILD WINGS SAUCE

1 cup beer

Juice of 1 lime

1/4 cup molasses

1/4 cup creamy peanut butter

1/4 cup Worcestershire sauce

1 1/2 tablespoons chili powder

1/2 teaspoon dry mustard

1/4 teaspoon ground anise

1/4 teaspoon table salt

18 chicken wings

1. Combine the sauce ingredients in a large, heavy pan. Simmer over medium heat until reduced by about one-third, 15 to 20 minutes. The sauce can be made a day or two ahead.

2. Prepare the smoker for barbecuing, bringing the temperature to 200°F to 220°F. Grease a large smoke-proof baking pan or dish.

3. With a cleaver or butcher knife, remove the chicken wing tips (save them to make stock). Then cut each wing in half at the joint.

4. Transfer the wing sections and the sauce to the baking dish. Place the dish in the smoker and cook the chicken for 1 1/4 to 1 1/2 hours, stirring the wings once or twice. The chicken should be cooked through and tender, and the sauce reduced to a thick glaze. Serve hot.

VARIATION: **WING DING** You can flavor wings in so many ways. Use Korean Kick (page 42), Pop Mop (page 47), or Vaunted Vinegar Sauce (page 370) in place of the sauce here.

BBQ tip For other quick off-the-pit nibbles, try smoked sliced link sausage accompanied by a stout mustard and Bar-B-Q Ranch Sauce (page 375), smoked bite-size cubes of chicken with Jamaican Barbecue Sauce (page 383), or smoked shrimp skewered with jalapeño-stuffed or onion-stuffed green olives. Another good starter is a block of cream cheese covered with Lime-Mint Barbecue Sauce (page 385) and served with crackers.

A HEAP OF RIBS

If you're looking for saucy ribs in Memphis, head for Gridley's. It used to be a chain operation with several look-alike locations, but the business has scaled back to a single strip-mall restaurant. The menu offers everything from barbecue burritos to onion rings, but the ribs are the showstopper.

Chicken's Little Livers

These bantam tidbits make a marvelous mouthful. MAKES 1 DOZEN

FRUITY MARINADE AND MOP

1/4 cup raspberry vinegar or other fruit vinegar

1/4 cup chicken stock

1/4 cup vegetable oil

1/2 small onion, chopped

1 garlic clove, minced

1/4 teaspoon ground ginger

1/4 teaspoon table salt

1/4 teaspoon freshly ground black pepper

12 chicken livers, trimmed of any membrane

4 slices bacon, cut into thirds

1. At least 1 hour and up to 2½ hours before you plan to barbecue, combine the marinade ingredients in a large glass measuring cup. Place the chicken livers in a shallow, nonreactive bowl. Pour the marinade over the livers and marinate for up to 2 hours in the refrigerator.

2. Prepare the smoker for barbecuing, bringing the temperature to 200°F to 220°F.

3. Drain the livers, reserving the marinade. Wrap each liver in a piece of bacon and secure with a toothpick. Bring the marinade to a vigorous boil and keep it warm over low heat to use as a mop.

4. Place the livers on a small grill rack, mopping them liberally before placing them in the smoker. Cook until the bacon is crisp, 35 to 45 minutes. Apply the mop once or twice during the cooking process if you are using a wood-burning pit; in other styles of smokers, mop as soon as you remove the livers. Serve the tidbits piping hot.

"BEST LITTLE PORKHOUSE IN MEMPHIS"

A few years after it opened, Jim Neely's Interstate won the title of "Best Little Porkhouse in Memphis" in a two-month survey conducted by reporters at the *Memphis Commercial Appeal*. That perked up business, which was mighty slow when Neely put out his shingle in 1980. Back then, he says, "my wife and I could watch a whole movie between customers." In more recent years, *USA Today* pronounced the restaurant's pork sandwich the best in the country and *People* magazine ranked the barbecue overall as the second best in the land. Better hurry by.

In the old Kreuz Market in Lockhart, Texas, "diners" ate standing, cutting their hunks of meat with a knife chained to a counter. The restaurant added some tables later, and now has moved to a big new location, but you still place your order at the pit and by the pound. The barbecue comes on butcher paper, with a choice of white bread or saltine crackers. A separate station sells sides such as onions and pickles, and Big Red, the soft drink of choice. If you want barbecue sauce, you'd better sneak it in, because they don't abide it here.

Chicken from Hell

These potent stuffed chiles will spice up anyone's life. MAKES 1 DOZEN

1 large boneless, skinless chicken breast half, pounded thin and sliced into 12 sections

1 tablespoon vegetable oil

2 tablespoons Wild Willy's Number One-derful Rub (page 26), Smoky Salt (page 29), Southwest Heat (page 32), or other savory seasoning blend

12 large fresh jalapeños or yellow güero chiles

1/2 medium onion, in slivers

6 slices bacon, halved

Boydesque Brew (page 368) or other barbecue sauce (optional)

1. About 1½ hours before you plan to barbecue, toss the chicken with the oil in a small bowl. Sprinkle the dry rub over it and stir to coat. Refrigerate, covered, for 1 hour.

2. Prepare the smoker for barbecuing, bringing the temperature to 200°F to 220°F.

3. Split the jalapeños along one side and seed them. Stuff a section of chicken breast and a sliver or two of onion in each, wrap with a half piece of bacon, and secure the tidbit with a toothpick.

4. Place the chicken in the smoker and cook until the bacon is crisp, 30 to 40 minutes.

5. These are extremely hot when served with the jalapeño still in place, so proceed cautiously. Tender mouths may find the chicken plenty potent eaten alone or perhaps with a barbecue sauce, such as Boydesque Brew.

VARIATION: QUAIL FROM HELL The preparation works with game birds, too. Substitute quail or dove breast for chicken if you wish.

More than 80 percent of the households in the country own an outdoor grill, according to the Barbecue Industry Association. The figure jumps as the size of a family increases, soaring over 90 percent in families of four in one recent year. A solid majority of those households cook outside year-round, most often on gas grills.

BBQ Bacon and Eggs

This notion came from our barbecue buddy Wayne Whitworth, who has fired up many a pit around dawn. These dandy breakfast sandwiches will get anyone through to lunch. SERVES 6

6 thin slices fully cooked Canadian bacon

6 large eggs

Tabasco or Cholula hot sauce, or a pinch of Wild Willy's Number One-derful Rub (page 26) or Cajun Ragin' Rub (page 29)

Table salt and freshly ground black pepper

6 English muffins or biscuits, split, buttered, and toasted

1. Prepare the smoker for barbecuing, bringing the temperature to 200°F to 220°F.

2. Let the Canadian bacon sit, covered, at room temperature for 15 to 20 minutes.

3. Place the Canadian bacon slices in the smoker and cook until warmed through and fragrant from the smoke, about 15 minutes. Transfer the Canadian bacon to a greased 6-cup muffin pan, tucking each slice into the bottom of a cup. Crack an egg over each slice of Canadian bacon, keeping the yolks intact and sunny looking. Splash with enough hot sauce to wake you up, and add a sprinkle of salt and pepper. Place the muffin tin in the smoker and cook until the eggs are lightly set, or otherwise cooked to your taste. We like them still a bit runny at the yolk's center, 30 to 35 minutes.

4. Remove the bacon-egg combo from each cup, arrange between muffin halves, and serve.

VARIATION: BBQ BREAKFAST BOWLS Smoke the Canadian bacon as in the recipe but skip putting it in the muffin tin. Scramble the eggs instead and pan-fry some chunky red potatoes. Layer in shallow bowls the English muffin halves, a layer of Canadian bacon slices, the potatoes, scrambled eggs, and some shredded cheese and salsa on top.

BBQ tip To make cleaning easier, spray the muffin tin with oil before using. If you suspect you might want to make this recipe frequently, dedicate one muffin tin that you don't mind turning dark from the smoke.

Smoked Trout on Apple Slices

We like to make this with local wild trout caught by our fisherman friend Raymond Holmes. You can get good results, though, with farm-raised trout from the supermarket. **MAKES ABOUT 3 DOZEN**

DRESSING

1/4 cup olive oil

1/4 cup vegetable oil

2 1/2 tablespoons white wine vinegar

2 tablespoons minced shallots

1 teaspoon prepared horseradish

1/2 teaspoon Dijon mustard

3/4 teaspoon kosher salt or coarse sea salt

Four 8-ounce butterflied boned trout, with or without heads, or 8 ounces trout fillets

1 green-skinned apple

1 red-skinned apple

Tiny dill sprigs (optional)

1. About 2 hours before you plan to smoke the trout, combine the dressing ingredients in a blender and puree until smooth.

2. Place the trout, lying open, in a shallow, nonreactive dish. Drizzle each fish with about 1 tablespoon of the dressing. Cover the trout and refrigerate for about 1 1/2 hours.

3. Prepare your smoker for barbecuing, bringing the temperature to 200°F to 220°F.

4. Remove the trout from the refrigerator and let them sit, covered, at room temperature for 15 to 20 minutes.

5. Transfer the fish to the smoker, skin sides down. Cook the trout until opaque and easily flaked, 35 to 45 minutes. When the fish is cool enough to handle, slice or flake it into neat bite-size chunks. (The trout can be chilled for at least 1 hour if you wish to serve it cold.)

6. Halve and core the apples. Cut each vertically into slices about 1/3 inch thick. Place a chunk of trout on each apple slice. Moisten each with a little drizzle of the remaining dressing. Top with a bit of dill, if you wish, and serve.

A SOLEMN RESPONSIBILITY

At cooking competitions sanctioned by the Kansas City Barbeque Society, the judges take an oath about their job. It goes something like, "I solemnly swear to objectively and subjectively evaluate each barbecue meat that is presented to my eyes, my nose, and my palate. I accept my duty so that truth, justice, excellence in Barbeque, and the American Way of Life may be strengthened and preserved forever."

007 Shrimp

A true "seafood cocktail," these shrimp are enhanced by James Bond's favorite drink, the vodka martini. **SERVES 4 TO 6**

1 pound large shrimp (24 to 30)

JAMES BOND'S BASIC BARBECUE MARINADE
1½ cups vodka
½ cup dry vermouth
3 tablespoons vegetable oil
3 tablespoons minced onion
Juice of 1 large lemon

Lemon wedges, for garnish

1. Prepare the smoker for barbecuing, bringing the temperature to 180°F to 200°F.

2. Peel the shrimp, leaving the tails on. Clean and, if desired, devein them. Place the shrimp in a shallow, nonreactive dish or a plastic bag.

3. In a large glass measuring cup, combine the marinade ingredients. Pour the marinade over the shrimp and let the shrimp marinate at room temperature for 30 minutes.

4. Drain the shrimp and arrange them on a small grill rack. Place in the smoker as far from the fire as possible. The shrimp should be done in 20 to 25 minutes, but watch them carefully. They are ready when opaque, slightly firm, and lightly pink on the exterior. Serve them hot or chilled, garnished with lemon.

Succulent Bacon-Wrapped Shrimp

Sara Perry wrote a book called *Everything Tastes Better with Bacon* (2002, Chronicle Books). Who are we to disagree? **MAKES 2 DOZEN**

2 dozen peeled large shrimp, with tails left on

Minced zest and juice of 1 lemon

Pinch or 2 of salt

12 slices bacon, halved crosswise, par-cooked until limp and just beginning to brown

Mango-Habanero Hellfire (page 387) or other habanero hot sauce (optional)

1. Prepare your smoker for barbecuing, bringing the temperature to 180°F to 200°F.

2. Toss the shrimp with the lemon zest and juice. Wrap each shrimp with bacon, covering the sides of the shrimp pretty thoroughly, and then skewer the wrapped shrimp on a small bamboo skewer. Place on a small grill rack or on the cooking grate and smoke until the bacon is cooked through and crispy and the shrimp still juicy, 25 to 30 minutes. Serve immediately with Mango-Habanero Hellfire sauce on the side if you wish.

VARIATION: PROSCIUTTO-WRAPPED SHRIMP
If you don't want to bother with par-cooking bacon, get yourself 4 to 6 ounces thinly sliced prosciutto. Cut the slices in half crosswise, then wrap around the marinated shrimp and proceed as above.

BBQ tip Bamboo skewers will hold up better for any smoked dish if they've been soaked in water for at least a few minutes before lacing them with food.

Scallops on a Stick

SERVES 4 TO 6

1 pound sea scallops, cut into bite-size pieces if needed

SCALLOP MARINADE
1/4 cup sake or dry sherry
2 tablespoons peanut oil
2 teaspoons packed brown sugar

10-ounce can water chestnuts, drained and blanched
4 to 6 scallions, sliced into 3/4-inch lengths
Plum Good Slopping Sauce (page 387) or West Coast Wonder barbecue sauce (page 379) (optional)

1. Prepare your smoker for barbecuing, bringing the temperature to 180°F to 200°F.

2. Place the scallops in a plastic bag or shallow dish. Combine the marinade ingredients and pour the mixture over the scallops. Let the scallops sit at room temperature for 20 to 30 minutes.

3. Thread the scallops on bamboo skewers interspersed with water chestnuts and scallion pieces. Arrange the skewers on a small grill rack or baking sheet. Place in the smoker as far from the fire as possible. Cook until the scallops are cooked through and opaque, about 15 minutes.

4. Serve immediately, with Plum Good Slopping Sauce or West Coast Wonder barbecue sauce if you wish.

SERVING SUGGESTION Make lunch out of the scallops by serving them with rice and Asian Vegetable Slaw (page 428). For dessert, serve orange slices zipped up with a sprinkling of triple sec.

Texas Terrine

A great way to use leftovers, this glorified meatloaf relies on already smoked meat. Unlike many of our appetizers, it keeps well for several days. SERVES 8 OR MORE

1¼ pounds smoked meat, preferably 2 or 3 meats, such as brisket, pork shoulder, ham, chicken, or turkey, chilled

3 ounces pork fat, chilled

2 tablespoons unsalted butter

1 medium onion, minced

2 garlic cloves, minced

¾ cup fresh cornbread crumbs or other bread crumbs

¼ cup minced fresh cilantro

2 to 3 tablespoons milk

1½ tablespoons jalapeño mustard or other hot spicy mustard

1 tablespoon Worcestershire sauce

1 tablespoon chili powder

1 large egg, lightly beaten

Kosher salt or coarse sea salt and freshly ground black pepper to taste

⅓ cup chopped, roasted green New Mexican, Anaheim, or poblano chiles, preferably fresh or frozen (see BBQ tip on page 151)

Toasted cornbread slices, crackers, or crusty country-style white bread

Bar-B-Q Ranch Sauce (page 375) or Jalapeach Barbecue Sauce (page 384) (optional)

1. Preheat the oven to 325°F.

2. In a food processor or meat grinder, mince or grind the meats and pork fat together. Transfer the meat to a bowl.

3. Warm the butter in a small skillet over medium heat. Add the onion and garlic and sauté briefly until softened. Spoon the mixture over the meat. Add the bread crumbs, cilantro, milk, mustard, Worcestershire sauce, chili powder, and egg, mixing well. Fry up 1 to 2 teaspoons of the meat mixture in a small skillet to check the seasoning. Mix in salt or pepper as needed.

4. Pat half of the meat into a 7 x 3-inch loaf pan. Scatter the chiles over the loaf and top with the rest of the meat. Pat the meat down firmly.

5. Place the loaf pan in a larger baking pan and half-fill the baking pan with hot water. Bake the terrine in the water bath for 70 to 75 minutes. Let the terrine cool at room temperature for 20 minutes.

6. Cover the terrine with foil and weight it down with a couple of bottles of barbecue sauce or cans from your pantry. Refrigerate the meat for at least 2 hours, but preferably longer. Like a meatloaf, the terrine improves with age for a few days.

7. Serve chilled with toasted cornbread, crackers, or other bread. If you want to offer sauce on the side, the most compatible choices are Bar-B-Q Ranch Sauce and Jalapeach Barbecue Sauce.

PART THREE

GREAT ACCOMPA- NIMENTS FROM INDOORS

BARBECUE SAUCES

SAUCES ARE CONTENTIOUS. SOME SMART PEOPLE, SUCH AS THE PROS AT THE CALIFORNIA CULINARY ACADEMY, SAY THAT SAUCES DEFINE THE NATURE OF BARBECUE. IF YOU DON'T SERVE ONE ON YOUR FOOD, THEY CLAIM, YOU ARE "SMOKE COOKING" INSTEAD OF BARBECUING. OTHER SMART PEOPLE MAINTAIN THAT IF SOMETHING ISN'T WORTH EATING WITHOUT A SAUCE, IT DOESN'T DESERVE THE NAME BARBECUE. TO THEM, USING A SAUCE IS AKIN TO SKINNY-DIPPING IN YOUR SKIVVIES.

Even if you come down firmly on the side of saucing, you'll soon discover that everyone who agrees with you is talking about a different potion. The styles of barbecue sauce across the country are more numerous and varied than the vices of Washington, D.C. Most regions have a favored style, and within that tradition, each pitmaster has a special twist or two. The only common denominator is a resolute conviction among the inventors and fans that nobody else knows a damned thing about making sauce.

Perhaps everyone is a little right and a little wrong. Most good barbecue doesn't require any sauce to enhance its flavor, but it can often benefit from several different styles of sauce, depending on personal preferences. Our recipes cover the major regional variations and a few offbeat options. Experiment with them to craft your own concoction. Even if you prefer your barbecue bare, you're certain to find that your own sauce is the best one ever brewed.

Boydesque Brew

Kansas City is the sauce capital of the country, where they practically pave the streets with the stuff. In a town full of famous brand names, the late Otis Boyd made the best unheralded barbecue sauce in Kansas City. He didn't pass around his recipe, of course, but our rendition is a tasty imitation. MAKES ABOUT 2 CUPS

6-ounce can tomato paste

3/4 cup water

1/4 cup white vinegar

1/2 medium onion, minced

1 tablespoon packed brown sugar

1 to 2 teaspoons prepared horseradish (optional)

1 teaspoon ground allspice

1 teaspoon celery salt

1 garlic clove, minced

1/2 teaspoon ground anise

1/2 teaspoon freshly ground black pepper

1/4 teaspoon ground cinnamon

1/8 teaspoon cayenne

Mix all the ingredients in a saucepan and bring to a simmer. Reduce the heat to low and cook until the onions are tender and the mixture thickens, 25 to 30 minutes. Refrigerate the sauce overnight to allow the flavors to mingle and mellow. Use the sauce warm or chilled. It keeps, refrigerated, for a couple of weeks.

Struttin' Sauce

Over the last half century, Kansas City pitmasters perfected a spicy, sweet sauce, thick with tomatoes, that ultimately became the most common and popular style nationally. When you look for a commercial sauce in a supermarket today, Kansas City–style will probably dominate the aisle. Few of the packaged products, however, rival the originals, still served in Bar-B-Q joints all over town, or good homemade variations on the same theme. This version is modeled on the sauce that Ollie Gates created years ago for his thriving small chain of Gates Bar-B-Q restaurants.

MAKES ABOUT 2 1/4 CUPS

1 tablespoon vegetable oil

1 medium onion, chopped

2 garlic cloves, minced

1 cup canned tomato puree

3/4 cup cider vinegar

3/4 cup water

6 tablespoons packed brown sugar

4 to 6 tablespoons chili powder

1/4 cup tomato paste

3 tablespoons Worcestershire sauce

3 to 4 teaspoons celery salt

1 tablespoon yellow mustard

1 tablespoon freshly ground black pepper

1 tablespoon corn syrup

1 tablespoon pure liquid hickory smoke (optional)

In a saucepan, warm the oil over medium heat. Add the onion and garlic and sauté until they are softened, about 5 minutes. Mix in the remaining ingredients, reduce the heat to low, and cook the mixture until it thickens, approximately 30 minutes. Stir frequently. If the consistency is thicker than you prefer, add a little more water. Use the sauce warm or chilled. It keeps, refrigerated, for a couple of weeks.

SERVING SUGGESTION Kansas City sauces really shine on barbecued ribs, but they can also enhance grilled hamburgers, baked brisket, fried sausage, boiled crawfish, or even fresh scallions.

STEPPING OUT WITH GEORGE AND OLLIE GATES

You have to love the logo at Gates & Sons Bar-B-Q restaurants in Kansas City. A gent with a big smile, in top hat and tails, struts down the street carrying a cane in one hand and a take-out bag of barbecue in the other. George Gates got his start in the barbecue business about the end of World War II, and his son Ollie followed behind him in 1958. They remain legends of the craft in Kansas City.

Vaunted Vinegar Sauce

If you're one of the millions of Americans who have never tried anything except tomato-based barbecue sauces, a taste of this could be a real revelation. Thin, vinegary sauces of this style are as indigenous to the Southeast as summer humidity—and a lot more enjoyable, particularly on pork. A pig couldn't ask for a finer demise.

MAKES ABOUT 2 CUPS

2 cups cider vinegar or white vinegar

2 tablespoons granulated sugar or packed brown sugar

2 teaspoons kosher salt or coarse sea salt

1 teaspoon freshly ground black pepper

1 teaspoon cayenne or crushed red chile flakes

Combine all of the ingredients in a bowl and stir to dissolve the sugar. Serve at room temperature or chilled. The sauce keeps indefinitely.

YE OLDE KETCHUP

This type of vinegar sauce is probably a direct descendant of early English ketchups, which were made with vinegar in combination with mushrooms, walnuts, oysters, and other ingredients, but never with tomatoes. It can double as a mop, unlike tomato-based sauces, which are rarely applied before the last hour of cooking because they burn.

Carolina Red

The geographic gradation of sauces in North Carolina is fascinating. Toward the eastern shore, pitmasters favor a vinegar style, such as our Vaunted Vinegar Sauce (page 370), while their colleagues on the opposite, western border are inclined toward a thick, sweet-sour, ketchup-based sauce. This "Red" from the central Piedmont region is right in between, blending the best of the rest of the state. **MAKES ABOUT 2 CUPS**

1½ cups cider vinegar
½ cup ketchup
½ teaspoon cayenne or crushed red chile flakes
1 tablespoon sugar
1 teaspoon table salt

Combine all of the ingredients in a bowl and stir to dissolve the sugar. Serve at room temperature or chilled. The sauce keeps indefinitely.

Golden Mustard Barbecue Sauce

In South Carolina and Georgia, mustard-based sauces provide the strongest competition to vinegar mixtures. Start with the smaller amount of mustard and keep adding until it suits you. **MAKES ABOUT 2 CUPS**

1 cup white vinegar
⅓ cup water
½ to ¾ cup yellow mustard
½ medium onion, minced
¼ cup canned tomato puree
1 tablespoon paprika
6 garlic cloves, minced
1½ teaspoons table salt
½ teaspoon cayenne
½ teaspoon freshly ground black pepper

Mix the ingredients in a saucepan and bring to a simmer. Reduce the heat to low and cook until the onions are tender and the mixture thickens, 20 to 25 minutes. Use the sauce warm or chilled. It keeps, refrigerated, for a couple of weeks.

VARIATION: HONEY-MUSTARD BARBECUE SAUCE
Substitute an equal amount of honey for the tomato puree. Skip the paprika and the garlic if you like.

You can't beat the name and you can't beat the sauce, at least if you're partial to pigs and mustard. Maurice's Piggie Park, with 14 locations now in South Carolina, sells its golden sauces online at piggiepark.com. In the past, when the never-timid founder Maurice Bessinger was in charge, your delivery might come wrapped in a Confederate flag or packaged with a sermon about the Great Pitmaster in Heaven. His family heirs say they now keep the focus strictly on the barbecue.

Old-Fashioned High-Cholesterol Great-Tasting Southern Sauce

Not so common today, barbecue sauces based on butter and other fats frequently flavored pork in the past. MAKES ABOUT 2 CUPS

6 tablespoons bacon drippings

6 tablespoons unsalted butter

1 medium onion, chopped

1/2 cup white vinegar

Juice of 2 lemons

2 tablespoons Worcestershire sauce

2 teaspoons freshly ground black pepper

1 teaspoon dry mustard

1 teaspoon kosher salt or coarse sea salt

In a saucepan, melt the bacon drippings and butter over medium heat. Add the onion and sauté until quite soft, about 5 minutes. Mix in the remaining ingredients, reduce the heat to low, and simmer for 5 minutes. Use the sauce warm. It keeps, refrigerated, for at least a week.

SERVING SUGGESTION We think the old butter-based sauces are too rich for pork, but this one works well with smoked or grilled chicken or steak and with some vegetables, particularly smoked onions and steamed broccoli.

Smoked Butter

Yep, you smoke the butter. The result is great for layering extra flavor on barbecued fish, seafood, and vegetables. You can also use it to top grilled foods, from chicken breasts to corn on the cob, or for sautéing. If you like, add a handful of minced fresh herbs or minced garlic to the butter. MAKES 1/2 CUP

1/2 cup unsalted butter, cut in 2-tablespoon chunks
A light sprinkling of kosher salt or coarse sea salt

1. Prepare your smoker for barbecuing, bringing the temperature to 180°F to 200°F.

2. Arrange the butter in a shallow, smoke-proof dish. Place in the smoker as far from the heat as possible, and cook for about 15 minutes. Use the melted smoked butter as is or chill until it begins to firm. Form it into a log or other shape, cover, and refrigerate for up to several days.

BBQ tip We suggest unsalted butter in most recipes, even ones where we add salt, too. Salt acts as a preservative, so salted butter keeps longer but it doesn't necessarily keep its sweet fresh flavor throughout its shelf life. Also, salted butters can vary a good bit in their sodium level. Adding the precise amount of salt you like gives you control over the result. For longer life, unsalted butter can be frozen for several months.

AN ARKANSAS TREASURE

One of Bill Clinton's favorite barbecue sauces comes from McClard's Bar-B-Q in Hot Springs, Arkansas. The McClard family got the recipe in 1928 when they were running a tourist court along the highway. A boarder traded the secrets of the sauce for his $10 monthly rent, inspiring the McClards to fire up their pit for the public. The children and grandchildren of the founders still adhere strictly to the original recipe, now locked in a safe deposit box.

Memphis Magic

The center of mid-South barbecue, Memphis offers a range of sauces that take the high middle ground between Eastern and Western styles. Like this version, they are often medium-bodied mixtures, moderate in sweet, heat, and everything else except taste. MAKES ABOUT 2 CUPS

3 tablespoons unsalted butter

1/4 cup minced onion

1 cup white vinegar

1 cup tomato sauce

1/4 cup Worcestershire sauce

2 teaspoons sugar

1 teaspoon table salt

1/2 teaspoon freshly ground black pepper

1/8 teaspoon cayenne or crushed red chile flakes

Dash of Tabasco or other hot pepper sauce

In a saucepan, melt the butter over medium heat. Add the onion and sauté until the onion begins to turn golden, 6 to 8 minutes. Stir in the remaining ingredients, reduce the heat to low, and cook until the mixture thickens, approximately 20 minutes. Stir frequently. Use the sauce warm. It keeps, refrigerated, for a couple of weeks.

HAVE SOME OF MY BRAND

When you're ready to create a signature sauce of your own, seek a savory balance of sweet, sour, and spicy flavors. The sweetening can come from regular or brown sugar, honey, maple syrup, molasses, cane syrup, hoisin sauce, or even Coca-Cola. Common sour ingredients include lemon or lime juice, tamarind concentrate, and vinegar—cider, raspberry, wine, white, rice, or sherry, among others. Add onions, garlic, chili powder or chiles, mustard, cumin, ginger, pepper, curry powder, or just about anything else from the spice rack. Salt or salty ingredients such as soy sauce are optional, according to taste. Remember always that a great sauce complements rather than masks the flavor of food.

Bar-B-Q Ranch Sauce

A lot of Texans eat their barbecue without a sauce, or with just meat juices laced with cayenne, but others prefer a robust sauce full of Southwestern seasonings.

MAKES ABOUT 4 CUPS

1 tablespoon vegetable oil

2 cups chopped onions

2 to 3 minced fresh jalapeños

2 to 3 minced fresh serrano chiles

8 garlic cloves, minced

1 cup ketchup

3/4 cup Worcestershire sauce

3/4 cup strong black coffee

1/3 cup molasses

1/4 cup cider vinegar

1/4 cup freshly squeezed lemon juice

1/4 cup chili powder

2 tablespoons yellow mustard

1 1/2 teaspoons cumin

1 1/2 teaspoons table salt

1. In a saucepan, warm the oil over medium heat. Add the onions, jalapeños, serranos, and garlic and sauté over medium heat until everything is softened. Mix in the remaining ingredients and bring the sauce to a simmer. Cover and cook for 35 to 40 minutes. Allow the sauce to cool briefly.

2. Strain the sauce and puree the solids in a food processor. Return the pureed mixture to the sauce, stirring thoroughly. Refrigerate the sauce overnight to allow the flavors to mingle and mellow. Use the sauce warm or chilled. It keeps for weeks.

SERVING SUGGESTION If you don't want to slop up your 'Q', use the sauce on potatoes. It makes a good topping on baked spuds, along with other favorite condiments, or stir the sauce into cottage fries or hash browns while they cook to give the potatoes an outdoorsy ranch flavor.

Memphis offers a range of sauces that take the high middle ground between Eastern and Western styles

Espresso Barbecue Sauce

This sauce will certainly wake up brisket but is even better with pork of all varieties.

MAKES ABOUT 4 CUPS

1 tablespoon vegetable oil

1 tablespoon unsalted butter

1½ cups chopped onions

1 or 2 minced fresh serrano chiles

4 garlic cloves, minced

1 cup ketchup

1 cup espresso or 1 heaping tablespoon espresso powder stirred into 1 cup hot water

3 tablespoons molasses

¼ cup white vinegar

2 teaspoons chili powder

1 teaspoon kosher salt or coarse sea salt

1 teaspoon sugar

¼ teaspoon Worcestershire sauce

1. In a saucepan, warm the oil and butter over medium heat. Add the onions, serrano, and garlic and sauté until everything is softened, about 10 minutes. Mix in the remaining ingredients and bring the sauce to a simmer. Cover and cook for 35 to 40 minutes. Allow the sauce to cool briefly.

2. Strain the sauce and puree the solids in a food processor. Return the pureed mixture to the sauce, stirring thoroughly. Refrigerate the sauce overnight to allow the flavors to mingle and mellow. Use the sauce warm or chilled. It keeps for weeks.

SAUCES TO SEEK OUT

Two of the mid-South's finest commercial sauces—Wicker's and Corky's—get wide regional distribution and enjoy a limited national market. Wicker's, which hails from Hornersville, Missouri, calls itself "the great American barbecue sauce from the little Missouri town." Check out the company's story and place an order at wickersbbq.com. The equally illustrious Corky's comes from a Memphis restaurant of the same name. Buy it at one of the small chain's three locations or online at corkysmemphis.com.

Peppery Sweet Onion Sauce

One of our very regular go-to accompaniments. Darned fine on brisket and beef ribs, but also try it with smoked shrimp. MAKES ABOUT 3 CUPS

1/4 cup unsalted butter

2 cups minced sweet onions

2 garlic cloves, minced

1/4 cup packed light brown sugar

1 cup ketchup

1 cup water

1/4 cup cider vinegar

2 tablespoons Worcestershire sauce

2 tablespoons freshly ground black pepper

1 tablespoon Dijon mustard

1 1/2 teaspoons kosher salt or coarse sea salt

1. In a saucepan, warm the butter over medium-low heat. Add the onions and garlic and sauté slowly, stirring frequently, until the onion bits are quite soft and beginning to turn golden, 12 to 15 minutes. Mix in the sugar and cook for about 2 minutes more to caramelize some of the onion bits. Stir in the remaining ingredients and bring the sauce to a simmer. Cover and cook for 30 minutes. We like this a bit on the thin side. Allow the sauce to cool briefly. Use the sauce immediately or refrigerate it overnight for the flavors to mingle and mellow a bit more.

2. Use the sauce warm or chilled. It keeps for weeks.

Black Sauce

Around Owensboro, Kentucky, a dark, thin, and tangy sauce like this is usually served on or with the barbecued mutton. It also works well with other dishes, such as our Mustard 'n' Lemon Chicken (page 191). MAKES ABOUT 2 1/4 CUPS

1 cup Worcestershire sauce

1 cup white vinegar

2 tablespoons freshly squeezed lemon juice

2 garlic cloves, minced

2 tablespoons packed brown sugar

4 teaspoons freshly ground black pepper

1/2 teaspoon ground allspice

Combine the ingredients in a saucepan and heat over medium heat. Simmer the mixture for about 10 minutes. Serve the sauce hot or at room temperature. It keeps, refrigerated, for several days.

Sauce Olé

A chunky, salsa-style sauce that enhances barbecued pork, smoked turkey, or our Nachos Blancos (page 342). MAKES ABOUT 2 1/4 CUPS

3/4 cup canned crushed tomatoes

2 small Roma or other plum tomatoes, chopped

1/2 medium red onion, chopped

1/2 cup chopped roasted green chiles, preferably New Mexican, Anaheim, or poblano, fresh or frozen (see BBQ tip on page 151)

1/2 cup water

2 to 3 tablespoons freshly squeezed lime juice

2 tablespoons chopped fresh cilantro

1 tablespoon olive oil

1/2 teaspoon ground cumin

1/2 teaspoon table salt

1. Combine the ingredients (starting with just 2 tablespoons of the lime juice) in a saucepan and bring the mixture to a simmer over medium heat. Cook for approximately 10 minutes, enough to slightly thicken the sauce. The vegetables should soften a little yet still stay crisp-tender. Taste and add additional lime juice if desired. Refrigerate the sauce for at least 1 hour to allow the flavor to develop.

2. Serve the sauce chilled. It keeps, refrigerated, for several days.

VARIATION: GREEN SAUCE OLÉ Substitute an equal amount of pureed fresh or canned tomatillos for the canned crushed tomatoes and reduce the amount of lime juice to 1 1/2 to 3 teaspoons

West Coast Wonder

This Asian-American hybrid works wonders with duck, lamb, fish, and seafood.

MAKES ABOUT 1 3/4 CUPS

1 cup hoisin sauce

1/2 cup rice vinegar

1/4 cup reduced-sodium soy sauce

2 tablespoons Dijon mustard

2 teaspoons peeled and minced fresh ginger

1 teaspoon ground anise

2 garlic cloves, minced

Combine the ingredients in a saucepan and warm them over low heat for about 10 minutes. Serve the sauce hot or at room temperature. It keeps, refrigerated, for several weeks.

SERVING SUGGESTION Thin the sauce with a little water and use it in a stir-fry with broccoli, scallions, red bell peppers, and sliced water chestnuts.

Moonlite and Moonshine

Catherine and Hugh Bosley opened the Moonlite Bar-B-Q in Owensboro, Kentucky, in 1963. Lacking restaurant experience, they just pretended they were having company for dinner. These days the company numbers in the thousands on weekends, many making the hour-plus trek from Louisville to load up their plates at the copious buffet. Among the treats, one of our favorites is the vodka-based hot sauce, great on mutton and other red meat. It inspired this fiery concoction of our own.

MAKES ABOUT 2 1/2 CUPS

3/4 cup white vinegar

3/4 cup vodka

1/2 cup Tabasco or other hot pepper sauce

1/4 cup canned tomato puree

1/4 cup water

1/4 cup crushed chile caribe or other crushed dried red chile of moderate heat

3 tablespoons cayenne

2 tablespoons ground red chile, preferably ancho

Combine the ingredients in a saucepan and heat over medium heat. Simmer the mixture for about 20 minutes, until it's thickened a bit. Serve the sauce warm or chilled, remembering that a little goes a long way. Full of natural preservatives, the sauce keeps indefinitely in the refrigerator.

MOONLITE BY MAIL

Moonlite Bar-B-Q hosts a website (moonlite.com) as bountiful as the restaurant's buffet. You can purchase all of Moonlite's sauces there, including the Very Hot Sauce we used as our model in the recipe. If you want to go hog-wild with your order, get a pound or two of Moonlite's meat, some frozen burgoo, and maybe a restaurant cookbook, too.

Bour-B-Q Sauce

Another boozy Kentucky inspiration, this sauce uses the state's native whiskey instead of vodka. MAKES ABOUT 3 CUPS

1/4 cup unsalted butter

1/4 cup vegetable oil

2 medium onions, minced

3/4 cup bourbon

2/3 cup ketchup

1/2 cup cider vinegar

1/2 cup freshly squeezed orange juice

1/2 cup pure maple syrup

1/3 cup molasses

2 tablespoons Worcestershire sauce

1/2 teaspoon freshly ground black pepper

1/2 teaspoon kosher salt or coarse sea salt

In a saucepan, melt the butter with the oil over medium heat. Add the onions and sauté until they begin to turn golden, about 5 minutes. Mix in the remaining ingredients, reduce the heat to low, and cook the mixture until it thickens, approximately 40 minutes. Stir frequently. Serve the sauce warm. It keeps, refrigerated, for a couple of weeks.

Cinderella Sauce

We originally developed this for our barbecued beef short ribs but decided it was too good to limit to one dish. It also transforms other mundane cuts of meat, from pork spareribs to chicken drumsticks. MAKES ABOUT 2 1/2 CUPS

1 1/2 cups ketchup

1 cup beer

3/4 cup cider vinegar

1/4 cup minced fresh cilantro

3 tablespoons packed brown sugar

2 tablespoons Worcestershire sauce

2 garlic cloves, minced

2 teaspoons ground cumin

1 1/2 teaspoons ground anise

1 1/2 teaspoons kosher salt or coarse sea salt

1 teaspoon Tabasco or other hot pepper sauce

Mix all the ingredients in a saucepan and bring the liquid to a simmer. Reduce the heat to low and cook the mixture until it thickens, approximately 40 minutes. Stir frequently. Use the sauce warm. It keeps, refrigerated, for a couple of weeks.

Creole Classic Barbecue Sauce

Snappy as a zydeco band, this sauce features the flavors of Louisiana.

MAKES ABOUT 3 CUPS

1 tablespoon vegetable oil

1 medium onion, chopped

1/2 medium green bell pepper, chopped

2 celery ribs, chopped

3 garlic cloves, minced

1 cup canned crushed tomatoes

1 cup chicken or beef stock

2/3 cup cider vinegar

1/2 cup pecan pieces

6 tablespoons Creole mustard, such as Zatarain's

3 tablespoons packed brown sugar

2 tablespoons chili sauce

1/2 teaspoon Tabasco or other hot pepper sauce

1/2 teaspoon freshly ground black pepper

1/2 teaspoon ground white pepper

1/2 teaspoon cayenne

Table salt to taste

In a saucepan, warm the oil over medium heat. Add the onion, bell pepper, celery, and garlic and sauté until everything is softened, about 5 minutes. Mix in the remaining ingredients, reduce the heat to low, and cook until the mixture thickens, approximately 30 minutes. Stir frequently. Let the sauce cool briefly. Spoon the sauce into a blender and puree it until smooth. If the consistency is thicker than you prefer, add a little water. Use the sauce warm or chilled. It keeps, refrigerated, for at least a week.

A SAUCY READ

Rich Davis and Shifra Stein of Kansas City wrote a fine book on barbecue, *The All-American Barbecue Book* (1988, Vintage). They present a collection of recipes from pitmasters across the country and give a good overview of differences in regional styles. As you might expect from Davis, the creator of the original K. C. Masterpiece sauce, the information on sauce is particularly strong.

Jamaican Barbecue Sauce

This light but intensely flavored sauce goes well with salmon and most varieties of white fish. You can find the sweet-sour tamarind concentrate in Caribbean, Latin American, or Asian markets if it's not available in your grocery store.

MAKES ABOUT 1 3/4 CUPS

2 cups seafood stock

5 tablespoons honey

2 tablespoons tamarind concentrate

2 tablespoons peeled and minced fresh ginger

2 tablespoons Jamaican Jerk Rub (page 32) or other jerk seasoning

Combine the ingredients in a saucepan and bring the mixture to a boil over high heat. Reduce the heat and simmer the sauce until it's reduced by one-third, approximately 10 minutes. Serve the sauce warm. It keeps, refrigerated, for several days.

VARIATION: FIERY JAMAICAN BARBECUE SAUCE
To make the sauce hotter, in true Jamaican fashion, add part of a minced habanero or Scotch bonnet chile. Proceed cautiously because these are among the most blistering chiles known.

Smoked Onion Sauce

Shot through with bits of real smoked onion, this sauce is great with many foods, especially burgers and good cuts of pork. MAKES ABOUT 2 CUPS

1 tablespoon vegetable oil

1 large onion, smoked as for Better-Than-French Onion Soup (page 277), chopped

2 garlic cloves, minced

1 cup canned tomato puree

3/4 cup cider vinegar

3/4 cup water

6 tablespoons molasses

3 tablespoons packed brown sugar

3 tablespoons tomato paste

3 tablespoons Worcestershire sauce

1 tablespoon yellow mustard

2 tablespoons chili powder

2 teaspoons freshly ground black pepper

1 teaspoon table salt

In a saucepan, warm the oil over medium heat. Add the onion and garlic and sauté until the garlic is soft, about 3 minutes. Mix in the remaining ingredients, reduce the heat to low, and cook the mixture until it thickens, approximately 30 minutes. Stir frequently. If the consistency is thicker than you prefer, add a little more water. Use the sauce warm or chilled. It keeps, refrigerated, for a couple of weeks.

Jalapeach Barbecue Sauce

Fruit flavors are a relatively recent trend in barbecue sauces. This one sizzles with jalapeños and soothes with peaches. MAKES ABOUT 2 CUPS

16-ounce can peaches in heavy syrup, undrained

1/4 cup minced onion

3 tablespoons minced pickled jalapeños

2 teaspoons pickling liquid from jar or can of pickled jalapeños

2 tablespoons peach chutney, or mango chutney in a pinch

2 teaspoons packed brown sugar

1/2 teaspoon Worcestershire sauce

1/2 teaspoon table salt

1/4 teaspoon ground cumin

Mix the ingredients in a saucepan and bring the liquid to a simmer. Reduce the heat to low and cook the mixture until the onions are tender and the sauce thickens, 25 to 30 minutes. Use the sauce warm or chilled. It keeps, refrigerated, for a couple of weeks.

SERVING SUGGESTION For a different start to the day, serve bacon glazed with Jalapeach Barbecue Sauce. Bake thick-sliced strips of bacon for about 10 minutes at 350°F. Then brush both sides with the sauce and continue cooking for another 5 to 7 minutes per side.

Apple City Apple Sauce

This is our variation on a splendid sauce created by the Apple City BBQuers from Murphysboro, Illinois. MAKES ABOUT 2 1/2 CUPS

1/2 cup unsalted butter

1 medium onion, minced

2 1/2 cups apple juice or cider

2 tablespoons molasses

2 tablespoons Worcestershire sauce

2 tablespoons cider vinegar

2 tablespoons tomato paste

1/2 teaspoon chili powder

1/2 teaspoon ground cinnamon

1/2 teaspoon kosher salt or coarse sea salt

In a heavy saucepan, melt the butter over medium heat. Add the onion and sauté for a couple of minutes, until the onion is softened. Mix in the remaining ingredients, reduce the heat to low, and cook the mixture until it reduces by about one-quarter, approximately 30 minutes. Stir frequently. Serve the sauce warm. It keeps, refrigerated, for a couple of weeks.

SERVING SUGGESTION The sauce makes a fine glaze for apples. Sauté slices of apples in butter, adding a little apple cider as they soften. Then cover the slices with a few tablespoons of sauce and continue to cook until a glaze forms. We like the apple slices for breakfast or as a side dish with pork later in the day.

Alabama Great White

Big Bob Gibson Bar-B-Q in Decatur, Alabama, serves the original version of this sauce on barbecued chicken. In a similar manner, we put it on our Alabama Smoked Chicken Sandwich (page 204), but we also offer the sauce with many other foods. **MAKES ABOUT 1½ CUPS**

1 cup mayonnaise (the real stuff—no Miracle Whip here)

2 tablespoons vinegar, preferably cider

1 tablespoon water

1 tablespoon coarsely ground black pepper

3/4 teaspoon table salt

Pinch or two of onion powder

Pinch or two of cayenne

Whisk together the mayonnaise with about 1 tablespoon of the vinegar until smooth. Add the remaining ingredients, including the rest of the vinegar, and whisk until well combined. Serve immediately, or chill for up to a couple of weeks.

VARIATION: SOUTHWESTERN GREAT WHITE People in Decatur may not like this, but we sometimes add ½ cup sour cream and about ¼ cup minced fresh cilantro to Alabama Great White and serve it with California Dreamin' Fish Tacos (page 256) or any other smoked or grilled fish.

Lime-Mint Barbecue Sauce

As refreshing as a cool summer shower, this sauce mates well with lamb, salmon, or trout. **MAKES ABOUT 2 CUPS**

1/4 cup unsalted butter

1/4 cup minced scallions

1/4 cup minced celery

1 garlic clove, minced

1½ cups brewed mint tea made from 3 mint tea bags

1 cup freshly squeezed lime juice

Zest of 4 limes

1/4 cup honey

1 tablespoon brown mustard

In a heavy saucepan, melt the butter over medium heat. Add the scallions and sauté for a couple of minutes, until softened. Mix in the remaining ingredients, reduce the heat to low, and cook the mixture until it reduces by about half, approximately 40 minutes. Stir frequently. Serve the sauce warm or chilled. It keeps, refrigerated, for a couple of weeks.

South Florida Citrus Sauce

A zingy combo, flavored with citrus and horseradish, this is a winner on chicken, pork, shrimp, and meaty white fish such as red snapper. MAKES ABOUT 2 CUPS

1/2 cup unsalted butter

1 cup cider vinegar

1 cup canned tomato puree

5 tablespoons prepared horseradish

Juice of 4 limes

Juice of 1 medium orange

3 tablespoons packed brown sugar

1 tablespoon Worcestershire sauce

1 teaspoon kosher salt or coarse sea salt

Mix the ingredients in a saucepan and bring the liquid to a simmer. Reduce the heat to low and cook the mixture until it thickens, approximately 40 minutes. Stir frequently. Serve the sauce warm or chilled. It keeps, refrigerated, for a couple of weeks.

SERVING SUGGESTION Try the sauce on chilled boiled shrimp, as a substitute for the standard cocktail sauce. If you're in a flamboyant mood, toss it tableside with the shrimp and bits of onion and avocado.

Hoisin BBQ Sauce

You could probably brush this Chinese-inspired sauce on a piece of lumber and we would like it. It goes even better with pork and chicken. MAKES ABOUT 2 CUPS

1 cup hoisin sauce

1/2 cup reduced-sodium soy sauce

1/2 cup packed brown sugar

1/4 cup rice vinegar

2 tablespoons toasted sesame oil

1 teaspoon ground ginger

1/2 teaspoon freshly ground black pepper

Mix the ingredients in a saucepan and bring the liquid to a simmer. Reduce the heat to low and cook the mixture until it thickens and reduces by about one-quarter, approximately 10 minutes. Stir frequently. Serve the sauce warm or chilled. It keeps, refrigerated, for a couple of weeks.

Plum Good Slopping Sauce

The name lays the claim. MAKES ABOUT 2 CUPS

16-ounce to 17-ounce can plums in heavy syrup, undrained

1/4 cup minced scallions

1 tablespoon yellow mustard

1 teaspoon molasses

1/2 teaspoon ground red chile, preferably New Mexican or ancho

1/4 teaspoon table salt

Dash of Worcestershire sauce

Mix the ingredients in a saucepan and bring the liquid to a simmer. Reduce the heat to low and cock the mixture until it thickens, approximately 20 minutes. Stir frequently. Serve the sauce warm or chilled. It keeps, refrigerated, for a couple of weeks.

Mango-Habanero Hellfire

For a really hot time, ring this number. Don't forget to practice safe cooking, wearing rubber gloves when handling the searing habanero, which is a natural mate to mango and other fruit flavors. MAKES ABOUT 1 1/2 CUPS

1 large ripe, juicy mango, peeled, pitted, and chunked

3 scallions, chunked

3 tablespoons freshly squeezed lime juice

1 1/2 teaspoons molasses

1/2 teaspoon minced habanero or Scotch bonnet chile, or more to taste

1/2 teaspoon table salt

1/4 teaspoon dried thyme

1/8 teaspoon ground allspice

Place all the ingredients in a blender. Puree, adding 1 to 2 tablespoons of water if needed to make the process go smoothly. Avoid standing directly over the blender or taking a deep breath of the pungent chile aroma. Use the sauce immediately or chill for up to a couple of days.

TRADITIONAL SIDE DISHES AND BREADS

WHAT PITMASTERS SERVE ON THE SIDE HAS A LOT TO DO WITH WHAT THEY SERVE IN THE CENTER, AND THAT HAS A LOT TO DO WITH WHERE THEY HAPPEN TO BE HOLDING FORTH. SOMEWHERE IN THE COUNTRY, SOMEONE OFFERS ALMOST ANYTHING YOU CAN IMAGINE, FROM PIG SNOUTS TO TAMALES.

OUR RECIPES COVER THE MOST TRADITIONAL DISHES, PLUS A FEW OF THE MOST UNUSUAL, BUT WE DON'T ALWAYS fix them in a purely old-fashioned way. In some cases we've spiced up the preparation a bit to help finish off the flavor of a dish so that it can stand alone as well as sit on the side. Despite the occasional embellishments, the recipes remain true to their tradition. You'll find them worthy of serving on any barbecue plate, anywhere in the country.

Creamy Coleslaw

The barbecue belt never needed iceberg lettuce. When most of the country started down the road to radicchio in the 1950s, 'Q' lovers remained faithful to America's original crunchy green salad, coleslaw. This is a classic version of the dish, updated for contemporary tastes but still similar to the old *cool sla* that many early settlers ate with meat. SERVES 6 TO 8

1 cup half-and-half

1/2 cup sugar

6 tablespoons cider vinegar

2 tablespoons mayonnaise

2 garlic cloves, minced

1 teaspoon kosher salt or coarse sea salt, or more to taste

1 medium head cabbage, grated

2 to 3 carrots, grated

In a lidded jar, shake together the half-and-half, sugar, vinegar, mayonnaise, garlic, and salt until well blended. Place the cabbage and carrots in a large bowl, pour the dressing over the vegetables, and toss together. Chill the slaw for at least 1 hour. It keeps well for several days.

STANDARD-SETTING BURGOO

Western Kentucky is the heart of burgoo country, and the town of Owensboro claims to be the capital. George's Bar-B-Q in Owensboro did indeed make the best restaurant version we've ever had when we visited several years ago.

Lexington, North Carolina, is the only town in the country that has given its name to a single type of barbecue. Since the turn of the century—when the burg's first joint opened in a tent across from the courthouse—a succession of pitmasters have maintained a consistent tradition by training their heirs as they cooked. Today as then, the Lexington style is pulled and chopped pork shoulder served with a mild tomato and vinegar sauce, topped off with a mound of red coleslaw made with the same sauce. It's so good that a town of 20,000 supports about two dozen barbecue restaurants.

Lexington Red Slaw

Coleslaw is so linked to the 'Q,' some pitmasters like to flavor it with a dollop of barbecue sauce. That's particularly popular in the Piedmont region of North Carolina, home of this colorful version. SERVES 6 TO 8

1 cup mayonnaise

3 tablespoons Carolina Red (page 371) or other Lexington/Piedmont-style tomato-based barbecue sauce

2 to 3 tablespoons sugar

1 tablespoon ketchup

1 tablespoon cider vinegar

1 teaspoon table salt, or more to taste

1 medium head cabbage, grated

In a lidded jar, shake together the mayonnaise, barbecue sauce, sugar, ketchup, vinegar, and salt until well blended. Place the cabbage in a large bowl. Pour the dressing over the cabbage and toss together. Chill the slaw for at least 1 hour. It keeps well for several days.

Brunswick Stew

Brunswick stew is as old as barbecue. Early British settlers in the Southeast cooked both kinds of food, and in that region the two are still served together. "A good Brunswick stew," according to one venerable source, "is made of practically everything on the farm and in the woods, including chicken, beef, veal, squirrels, okra, beans, corn, potatoes, tomatoes, butter beans, vinegar, celery, catsup, sugar, mustard, and enough red pepper to bring tears to your eyes." This version leaves out the squirrel meat—though some swear it's essential for authenticity—and it starts with smoked chicken rather than an uncooked bird. SERVES 10 TO 12

2¹/2-pound to 3-pound smoked chicken, such as Chicken on a Throne (page 188), or substitute the same size uncooked chicken

1 pound boneless pork loin, cubed

¹/4 pound sliced bacon, chopped fine

10 cups water

4 large baking potatoes, peeled

3 tablespoons unsalted butter

3 medium onions, chopped

Two 10-ounce packages frozen lima beans or 2¹/4 cups fresh limas

1¹/4 cups fresh green beans, cut in ³/4-inch lengths

5 tablespoons Worcestershire sauce

2 tablespoons yellow mustard

4 teaspoons coarsely ground black pepper

1 tablespoon kosher salt or coarse sea salt

1 teaspoon cayenne, or more to taste

1. Place the chicken, pork loin, and bacon in a large stockpot. Pour the water over the meats and bring to a simmer. Cook, uncovered, for 1 hour.

2. While the meats simmer, slice 3 of the potatoes in thirds and place them in a saucepan with enough water to cover. Bring the potatoes to a boil and cook until soft, about 20 minutes.

Drain and mash the potatoes with the butter. Set aside.

3. Remove the chicken from the pot. When cool enough to handle, discard the skin and bones and shred the chicken into bite-size pieces.

4. Return the chicken to the pot along with the mashed potatoes. Cut the remaining potato into bite-size chunks and add it to the pot. Add the remaining ingredients to the pot and continue to simmer over medium-low heat for 1¹/2 hours, stirring frequently. Add more water if the stew appears dry. The chicken and pork should be tender enough to fall apart, blending with the soft vegetables into a thick ragoût. The stew can be served immediately, but it reheats or freezes well.

SERVING SUGGESTION While Brunswick stew accompanies 'Q' in some areas, it also makes a satisfying main dish, especially on a rainy fall evening. We like to offer it with a selection of breads, including Blue Corn Muffins (page 412) and Sweet Potato Biscuits (page 411).

Kentucky Burgoo

The Kentucky equivalent of Brunswick stew, burgoo is a living legacy, a hearty and peppery concoction from the past that's still a passion in the state. Some say the odd name has French or Turkish origins, but one authority suggests that it was just a slurred pronunciation of "bird stew." **SERVES 10 TO 12**

2¹/2-pound to 3-pound smoked chicken, such as Chicken on a Throne (page 188), or substitute the same size uncooked chicken

1¹/2 pounds beef or veal shanks

1 pound smoked mutton or lamb (or substitute 1¹/2 pounds uncooked lamb shanks)

12 cups (3 quarts) water

1 tablespoon kosher salt or coarse sea salt

3 cups canned tomato puree

2¹/2 cups shredded cabbage

3 large baking potatoes, peeled, if you wish, and chopped

2 medium green bell peppers, seeded and chopped

2 large onions, chopped

3 to 4 medium carrots, sliced thin

3 large celery ribs, chopped

3 garlic cloves, minced

1/4 cup sherry vinegar

1 tablespoon A.1. steak sauce (original flavor)

2 teaspoons freshly ground black pepper

3/4 teaspoon cayenne, or more to taste

2¹/2 cups sliced okra, fresh or frozen

2 cups corn kernels, fresh or frozen

1. Place the chicken, beef or veal shanks, and mutton or lamb in a large stockpot. Pour the water over the meats, sprinkle in the salt, and bring the mixture to a simmer. Cook, uncovered, for 1¹/2 hours.

2. Remove the chicken and meats from the pot. When cool enough to handle, discard the skin, fat, and bones, and shred the chicken and meats into bite-size pieces.

3. Return the chicken and meats to the pot. Add the remaining ingredients, except for the okra and corn. Continue to simmer over medium-low heat for 2 more hours, stirring frequently. Add the okra and corn and cook for at least 1 more hour, preferably 2. Add more water if the stew appears dry.

4. As with Brunswick stew, the ingredients should be cooked down and no longer easily identifiable. The stew can be served immediately, but it is even better reheated the following day.

AN AMERICAN CLASSIC

In *Fading Feast* (1979, Farrar, Straus & Giroux), a commemoration of disappearing regional American foods, Raymond Sokolov calls Brunswick stew "the most famous dish to emerge from the campfires and cabins of pioneer America." Like some of the other foods Sokolov describes, it seems to be on the road to revival.

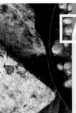

A THOROUGHBRED STEW

The winner of the Kentucky Derby in 1932, a home-state horse, was Burgoo King. The owner named the thoroughbred after a famous Lexington burgoo cook, James T. Looney.

Kansas City Baked Beans

Boston has no monopoly on baked beans. This is how they cook them out west in Kansas City, where barbecue sauce is a key ingredient and a few local "burnt" brisket ends sometimes add a powerful smoky flavor. SERVES 6 TO 8

1 pound dried navy beans, soaked for 4 hours in water and drained

6 cups water

1 teaspoon kosher salt or coarse sea salt, plus more to taste

4 slices bacon, chopped

1 medium onion, chopped

2 medium bell peppers (preferably 1 red and 1 green), seeded and chopped

1 cup Struttin' Sauce (page 369), Smoked Onion Sauce (page 383), or other tomato-based barbecue sauce, or more to taste

1 cup apple cider

1/3 cup molasses

1/4 cup yellow mustard

1 to 2 tablespoons cider vinegar

1 cup shredded Burnt Ends (page 115) (optional)

1. In a large, heavy saucepan, combine the beans and water. Bring the water to a boil over high heat, and then reduce to a simmer. Cook slowly, stirring up from the bottom occasion-ally for at least 2 to 3 hours, depending on the beans. Stir in the salt after the beans have softened. Add more water if the beans begin to seem dry. The beans are ready when they mash easily but still hold their shape. Drain the beans.

2. Preheat the oven to 325°F.

3. In a skillet, fry the bacon until crisp. Remove the bacon with a slotted spoon and drain it. Add the onion and bell pepper to the rendered bacon drippings and sauté until soft.

4. Transfer the bacon and the onion mixture to a greased Dutch oven or other baking dish. Mix in the remaining ingredients and the beans. Bake, covered, for about 1 hour. Uncover and bake until the liquid is thickened and bubbly, an additional 15 to 30 minutes. Serve hot. The beans reheat especially well.

Flash-Fried Okra

Fried in this old Southern fashion, okra becomes the Cinderella of vegetables, transformed from its humble and homely ways into a majestic mate for the 'Q.' SERVES 4

1 to 1¼ pounds fresh okra pods, preferably under 2½ inches each

2 teaspoons table salt

½ teaspoon freshly ground black pepper

2 cups cornmeal, preferably stone-ground

Oil for deep-frying, preferably peanut

Hot pepper sauce, such as Texas Pete or Tabasco

1. Place the okra in a bowl and cover with ice water. Add 1 teaspoon of the salt. Refrigerate for 30 minutes to plump the okra.

2. Spoon the cornmeal onto a plate and stir the pepper and remaining 1 teaspoon salt into it.

Drain the okra and cut into thin rounds.

3. Pour the oil into a heavy saucepan, to a depth of at least 3 inches Heat the oil to 360°F.

4. Dredge the okra in the seasoned cornmeal. Place batches of it in a strainer and shake lightly to knock off excess cornmeal. Fry until the cornmeal deepens slightly in color, 30 seconds to 1 minute, stirring occasionally to fry evenly. Drain the okra and serve it immediately, accompanied by hot sauce.

okra is transformed from its humble and homely ways

DON'T WHISTLE THAT TUNE

In the chuck-wagon days, cowboys called beans "whistle berries" because of their antisocial gas-producing effect. The Coca-Cola in the pintos supposedly helps to muffle the whistling, which you can also accomplish with epazote, an herb that's sometimes called Mexican tea. Of course, it's always best to avoid beans altogether before a dance.

Cowpoke Pintos

Meanwhile, down on the ranch, they wouldn't eat a navy bean even if Dolly Parton baked it. If you prefer your beans *borracho* (drunken), replace the soft drink with beer. SERVES 6 TO 8

1 pound dried pinto beans, soaked overnight in water to cover

8 cups (2 quarts) water

12 ounces Coca-Cola, Dr Pepper, or beer

14.5-ounce can whole tomatoes, undrained

2 medium onions, chopped

3 slices bacon, preferably a smoky slab variety, chopped

3 tablespoons chili powder

2 tablespoons Worcestershire sauce

1 tablespoon ground cumin

4 garlic cloves, minced

3 to 4 fresh serranos or jalapeños, chopped

1 teaspoon kosher salt or coarse sea salt, or more to taste

1 cup sliced barbecued sausage (optional)

1. Once the beans have soaked overnight, drain them well.

2. In a Dutch oven or stockpot, combine all of the ingredients except the salt and sausage. Bring the liquid to a boil over high heat and then reduce to a simmer. Cook slowly, stirring up from the bottom occasionally, for at least 2 to 3 hours, depending on your batch of beans. Add more water if the beans begin to seem dry. Stir in the salt and the sausage, if you are using it, in the last 30 minutes of cooking. The beans should still hold their shape but be soft and just a little soupy.

3. Serve the beans in bowls with a bit of the cooking liquid. The beans reheat especially well.

SERVING SUGGESTION With slices of Cracklin' Cornbread (page 408) and romaine lettuce tossed with the vinaigrette used in Hand Salad (page 420), these beans are hearty enough for a weeknight supper.

VARIATION: WAYNE'S WONDERFUL $50 BEANS Barbecue expert Wayne Whitworth often kids us about the $100 fish (a beauty of a 10-pound wild-caught Alaskan salmon) we ordered for one of his visits, telling us we "oughta learn to fish." Here's his delicious extravagance, equally worth the investment: Eliminate the Coke, tomatoes, bacon, and sausage from the recipe. Before you start, rub down a fully cooked 10-pound bone-in ham with 1/3 cup coarsely ground black pepper. Let the ham sit at room temperature for at least 1 hour, or refrigerate it overnight. Place the ham in a large stockpot. Fill the pot with water to cover the ham by several inches. Let the pot simmer over low heat for about half of the day, covered, until the meat literally falls apart. Remove the meat and bones. Increase the pintos to 3 pounds and add them and the rest of the ingredients to the ham broth. Cook as directed above, adding to the beans at the end as much shredded ham as you like.

Not Deli Dills

Especially in Arkansas and Mississippi, some pitmasters substitute pickles for okra as their fried green vegetable. The idea may sound strange, but the first bite will delight. SERVES 6

4 large dill pickles, sliced into rounds about 3/4 inch thick

1 cup all-purpose flour

1 teaspoon baking powder

Table salt and freshly ground black pepper to taste

1 large egg, lightly beaten

1 cup buttermilk

Oil for deep-frying, preferably peanut

1. Blot any moisture from the surface of the pickles.

2. In a medium-size bowl, stir together the flour, baking powder, salt, and pepper.

3. Combine the egg and buttermilk in a small bowl, and then pour the mixture into the dry ingredients. Stir just to combine.

4. Pour the oil into a heavy saucepan, to a depth of at least 3 inches. Heat the oil to 375°F.

5. Dip the pickles in the batter and fry a few at a time until golden brown, about 2 minutes. Drain the pickles and serve immediately.

FRIED PICKLES AND BOILED PEANUTS IN CHICAGO?

Yes ma'am, at Charlie McKenna's rather new Lillie's Q. A graduate of the Culinary Institute of America as well as a big-time winner on the competitive barbecue circuit, Chef Charlie went back to his roots at the restaurant. His grandmother Lillie taught him Southern cooking as a kid at her home in South Carolina, and he learned about barbecue from his father, Quito, a seasoned pitmaster. Phil Vettel, the restaurant critic for the *Chicago Tribune*, says Charlie's barbecue sauce is the best he has ever tasted.

Southern food authority John T. Edge tracked down dueling stories about the origins of the fried dill pickle. As he relates in *Southern Belly* (2000, Hill Street Press), one crowd gives the credit to the Hollywood Café in Robinsonville, Mississippi, where an overwhelmed cook supposedly started frying dill pickle slices in desperation one day when he had a rush on the dining room and ran out of catfish. Bob Austin declares that's a "damn lie." He claims he invented the dish in Atkins, Arkansas, at his Duchess Drive In, which was located across the street from a pickle plant. After staring out the window at that plant for years, Austin says his mind started "wandering" and he began toying around with a batter that would make pickles as good as everything else he fried.

Candied Sweet Potatoes

About as down-home as a dish can be, this gooey Southern classic is like a vegetable dessert. SERVES 6

1 cup mini marshmallows

3/4 cup bourbon or other sour-mash whiskey

2 to 2 1/2 pounds sweet potatoes (about 3 medium), baked or boiled, still warm

1/4 cup unsalted butter, preferably

1/4 cup milk

1/4 cup freshly squeezed orange juice

1/4 cup packed brown sugar

1/2 teaspoon table salt

1/2 teaspoon ground cinnamon

1. In a small bowl, combine the marshmallows with the bourbon. Soak the marshmallows for 20 to 30 minutes, stirring occasionally.

2. Preheat the oven to 350°F. Grease a medium-size baking dish.

3. Peel the sweet potatoes, if desired. In a large bowl, mash or whip the potatoes with the butter. Pour any bourbon not yet absorbed by the marshmallows into the potatoes. Add the remaining ingredients, except the marshmallows, mixing until well incorporated.

4. Spoon the potatoes into the baking dish. Scatter the marshmallows over the potatoes. Bake, uncovered, until heated through to the ooey-gooey stage, 25 to 30 minutes. Serve warm.

Country Collard Greens

Another sweetened Southern vegetable dish, these greens may be the perfect accompaniment to barbecue. The combination of the two offers a blend of honey, smoke, and spice that would be the envy of any honky-tonk angel. SERVES 8

8 cups (2 quarts) water

3 to 3¹/₂ pounds collard greens or kale, tough stems removed and leaves roughly chopped

1 smoked ham hock (about 1 pound)

4 medium onions, chopped

2 medium green or red bell peppers, seeded and chopped

²/₃ cup cider vinegar, preferably unrefined

1 tablespoon honey

3 garlic cloves, minced

1 tablespoon coarsely ground black pepper

2 teaspoons Tabasco or other hot pepper sauce, or more to taste

2 teaspoons celery seeds

Combine all of the ingredients in a large pot and bring to a boil. Cover and simmer for about 2 hours. With a slotted spoon, remove the ham hock. When the hock is cool enough to handle, pick the meat from it in small chunks or shreds and return it to the pot. Reheat the greens briefly, if necessary. Serve warm with some of the liquid (the "pot likker"). Leftovers keep for several days.

Smashed Potato Bake

As some barbecue joints have tried to upscale their image to family dining establishments, the side dishes have become a little more broad-ranging. Kids (or at least our grandkids) like to help make this take on the twice-baked potato. SERVES 6

2¹/₂ pounds small potatoes, about 1¹/₂ inches in diameter, preferably a combination of red- and brown-skinned varieties

¹/₄ cup unsalted butter or Smoked Butter (page 373), melted

Kosher salt or coarse sea salt and freshly ground black pepper or Wild Willy's Number One-derful Rub (page 26)

6 ounces mild cheddar cheese, grated, or more to taste

2 tablespoons minced fresh chives, or more to taste

Sliced pickled jalapeños (optional)

Sour cream (optional)

1. Cover the potatoes with water in a large pan, salt generously, and bring to a boil over high heat. Reduce to a simmer and cook until tender when pierced with a fork, about 20 minutes. Drain the potatoes. Place them in a single layer in a 9 x 13-inch pan. Smash each potato lightly

with a meat mallet or heavy fork. Expose the flesh but avoid totally squashing them.

2. Preheat the oven to 375°F.

3. Drizzle the melted butter over the potatoes, season with salt and pepper, and bake for 5 min-utes. Sprinkle the cheese, chives, and optional jalapeños over the potatoes. Return to the oven until heated through with melted cheese, about 10 minutes more. Serve immediately, with sour cream on the side if you wish.

Buttermilk Onion Rings

Barbecue legends, such as Leonard Heuberger of Memphis and Sonny Bryant of Dallas, among others, liked crispy buttermilk-soaked onion rings with their ribs and brisket. Sweet onions are particularly good in this recipe. SERVES 4

3 large onions, preferably sweet

3 to 4 cups buttermilk

1 cup all-purpose flour

1 cup cornmeal, preferably stone-ground

2 teaspoons kosher salt or coarse sea salt

2 teaspoons onion powder

2 teaspoons chili powder

1 teaspoon sugar (if not using sweet onions)

Oil for deep-frying, preferably peanut

1. Cut the onions into ¼-inch-thick slices. In a nonreactive dish, soak the onions in the buttermilk for 30 to 60 minutes.

2. In a brown paper sack, combine the flour, cornmeal, salt, onion powder, chili powder, and, if needed, sugar. Drain the onions lightly and dredge them in the seasoned flour.

3. Pour at least 4 inches of oil into a heavy saucepan. Heat the oil to 375°F. Fry the onions, in batches, until golden, 2 to 3 minutes. For the crispiest results, drain on paper towels and spread on a serving platter rather than piling them into a basket, where they could become soggy. Serve immediately.

Famous French Fries

Anyone can fry potatoes, but few people know how to make great French fries. The secret is a few extra steps, all worth the time in extra flavor. Increase the number of potatoes and other ingredients as needed for additional eaters. SERVES 1

1 to 1¹/₂ medium baking potatoes

Ice cubes

Peanut oil or lard for deep-frying

Kosher salt or coarse sea salt and/or Cajun or Creole seasoning, or Smoky Salt (page 29)

1. Wash the potatoes and, if you wish, peel them. (We prefer the peels on, and besides, it's less work.) Slice them into fat matchsticks, about ³/₈ inch wide, and toss them into a bowl of cold water. Soak the potatoes in the water for at least 1 hour and preferably 2, to eliminate much of the starch. Pour off the water, add more cold water to cover, and toss in a half dozen ice cubes. Soak the potatoes in the ice water to firm them back up, about 30 minutes. Drain them well on a dishtowel or sturdy paper towels, drying off each matchstick. Then roll the potatoes up in another dry towel. You want no remaining moisture.

2. Pour the oil into a large, heavy saucepan, to a depth of at least 4 inches. Heat the oil to 340°F. Add the potatoes in batches and partially fry them for 4 minutes. They should just begin to color. Drain the potatoes. This step can be done up to 30 minutes before eating.

3. Just before serving, reheat the oil to 360°F. Fry the potatoes again until golden brown, 3 to 4 minutes. Drain the potatoes again. Sprinkle the salt or seasoning into a brown paper sack, add the potatoes, and shake. Serve the fries hot.

VARIATION: FAMOUS WET FRIES For the height of excess, top the fried potatoes with melted cheese and a dollop of your favorite tomato-based barbecue sauce. (We use Struttin' Sauce, page 369.) For extra pizzazz, add a few slices of fresh or pickled jalapeño.

SPONGY WHITE VEGGIES

Many Bar-B-Q joints take pride in not cooking anything except their meat. In these cases, the side dishes are limited to items that don't require much except cutting—such as onions, tomatoes, jalapeños, and dill pickles. Our friend Toni Sikes, who grew up in Alabama, says that if you ordered vegetables at her favorite barbecue restaurant, you would get a few slices of white bread.

Prize Pilau

Spelled and pronounced a dozen different ways, this chicken-and-rice dish probably landed in Charleston, South Carolina, about 1680 and spread across the South as rice cultivation moved westward. Pilau is unusual for the region because of its French and Spanish overtones, but it's been a favorite in the barbecue belt for more than three centuries. The recipe really benefits from the use of homemade stock.

SERVES 6 TO 8

2$^1/_2$-pound to 3-pound whole chicken

4 cups chicken stock, preferably homemade

4 cups water

1$^1/_2$ teaspoons kosher salt or coarse sea salt (if the stock is unsalted; otherwise, reduce the salt to taste)

1$^1/_2$ teaspoons freshly ground black pepper

3 tablespoons bacon drippings or unsalted butter

1$^1/_2$ cups chopped green bell peppers

1 cup sliced scallions

1 cup chopped celery

1 teaspoon Worcestershire sauce

1 teaspoon Tabasco or other hot pepper sauce

2 cups uncooked white rice

1. Place the chicken in a stockpot. Pour the stock and water over, sprinkle in the salt and pepper, and bring the mixture to a simmer. Cook, uncovered, for 45 to 50 minutes. The chicken should be done, but not falling apart.

2. Preheat the oven to 350°F.

3. Remove the chicken from the pot. Increase the heat to high and reduce the cooking liquid to 2$^1/_2$ cups. Skim the fat from the cooking liquid. When the chicken is cool enough to handle, discard the skin, fat, and bones, and shred the chicken into bite-size pieces. Reserve both the cooking liquid and the chicken.

4. In a Dutch oven or other flameproof baking dish, warm the bacon drippings or butter over medium heat. Add the remaining ingredients, except the rice, and sauté until the vegetables are tender.

5. Stir the rice into the vegetables and pour the cooking liquid over the mixture. Scatter the chicken over the top. Cover the pilau and bake until the liquid is absorbed and the rice is soft, about 2 hours. Stir the pilau and serve it warm.

SERVING SUGGESTION Although pilau pairs with barbecue in the Carolinas, we find its subtle and distinctive flavors are shown off best when the dish takes center stage. We prefer it as a main dish with Sweet and Sour Cukes (page 420), Succotash Salad (page 425), or other vegetable salads.

Hot Tamales

By all geographical rights, tamales should be a Southwestern side dish with barbecue, but it's actually the Mississippi Delta that specializes in them. Mexican laborers who came to pick cotton in the early twentieth century probably brought the germ of the idea. Only a skinny cousin to a Tex-Mex or New Mexican tamale, they are usually made with yellow cornmeal rather than masa harina. MAKES 24 TAMALES

MEAT FILLING

1 tablespoon bacon drippings

3/4 pound ground pork or beef

2 garlic cloves, minced

1/4 cup chili powder

3/4 teaspoon table salt

1/4 teaspoon dried oregano, preferably Mexican

1/4 teaspoon cumin seeds, toasted and ground

3/4 cup beef stock

TAMALES

6-ounce package dried corn husks

4 cups cornmeal, preferably yellow stone-ground

1 1/2 cups beef stock

1 cup water, or more if needed

1 1/4 cups vegetable oil or solid vegetable shortening

1 1/2 teaspoons table salt

1. In a heavy skillet, warm the bacon drippings over medium heat and add the meat and garlic. Brown the meat, then add the chili powder, salt, oregano, cumin, and stock. Simmer over medium heat until the mixture has thickened but is still moist, about 20 minutes. Watch carefully toward the end of the cooking time, stirring frequently so it does not burn. Reserve the mixture. It can be made a day ahead.

2. To prepare the corn husks, soak them in hot water to cover in a deep bowl or pan. After 30 minutes the husks should be softened and pliable. Separate the husks and rinse them under warm running water to wash away any grit or brown silks. Soak the husks in more warm water until you are ready to use them.

3. Pour the cornmeal into another large bowl. Add the stock, water, oil, and salt. Mix with a sturdy spoon, powerful electric mixer, or with your hands until smooth. When well blended, the mixture should have the consistency of a moist cookie dough.

4. To assemble the tamales, hold a corn husk flat on one hand. With a rubber spatula, spread a thin layer of the cornmeal mixture across the husk and top it with about 1 tablespoon meat filling. Roll the husk into a tube shape and tie the two ends with strips of corn husk. (It should resemble a party favor.) Repeat the procedure until all the meat and cornmeal mixture are used.

5. Steam the tamales, standing them on end or crisscrossed over water in a large saucepan or small stockpot. Don't pack the tamales too tightly. Cook the tamales until the cornmeal

mixture is firm and no longer sticks to the corn husk, 50 to 60 minutes. Unwrap one tamale to check its consistency.

6. The tamales should be eaten warm after first removing the corn husk.

SERVING SUGGESTION Try the tamales as a main dish served with San Antonio Cactus and Corn Salad (page 421) and Key Lime Pie (page 447).

VARIATION: ARKANSAS TAMALE SPREAD McClard's in Hot Springs, Arkansas, serves this belly-buster. Layer a platter with corn chips and top with a few tamales, then a healthy portion of your favorite kind of chopped barbecued beef. Spoon chili beans over all, and finish with chopped onion and grated cheese. Alka-Seltzer makes a good dessert.

Mayme's Macaroni and Cheese

While fettuccine, penne, and orzo may be the rage in some American restaurants, modest elbow macaroni still outsells them all. Combined with cheese as a time-honored comfort food, it offers a good foil to the smoky richness of barbecued meats. Cheryl's grandmother, Mayme Luthy Alters, perfected this version, though without our addition of the Tabasco, which would have sent Grandfather Clifford through the ceiling. SERVES 6

12 ounces elbow macaroni, cooked al dente
2 tablespoons unsalted butter
3 large eggs
1 cup buttermilk
1 cup evaporated milk
1 1/2 teaspoons dry mustard
1/2 teaspoon Tabasco or other hot pepper sauce
1/2 teaspoon freshly ground black pepper
1/4 teaspoon table salt
2 cups grated sharp cheddar cheese (8 ounces)

1. Preheat the oven to 350°F. Grease a medium-size baking dish. Toss the warm macaroni with the butter.

2. In a medium-size bowl, beat the eggs lightly and add the buttermilk, evaporated milk, dry mustard, Tabasco, pepper, and salt. Mix well. Stir in the macaroni and the cheese and pour the mixture into the prepared dish.

3. Bake, uncovered, until the macaroni and cheese is lightly firm and browned, about 30 minutes. Serve warm. Any leftovers should be reheated gently to avoid developing the consistency of galvanized rubber.

DON'T SPILL THE SAUCE ON MY BLUE SUEDE SHOES

The Bop-N-Quers contest team from Memphis devised a barbecue smoker shaped like a jukebox. When we stopped by at a cook-off, the group had set up a dance floor in its barbecue area and was bopping away the day while the 'Q' browned. They didn't win at that event, but they looked like they had more fun than anyone who took home a prize.

Peppery 'Pups

These red pepper hushpuppies are a Carolina barbecue specialty. Because of their crunch, they may go better with the 'Q' than with fried fish, the more common mate.

SERVES 4 TO 6

¾ cup cornmeal, preferably white stone-ground
⅓ cup all-purpose flour
¾ teaspoon sugar
½ to 1 teaspoon cayenne
½ teaspoon baking powder
¼ teaspoon baking soda
¼ teaspoon table salt
½ cup buttermilk
¼ cup minced onion
1 large egg, lightly beaten
Peanut oil for deep-frying

1. In a medium-size bowl, stir together the cornmeal, flour, sugar, cayenne, baking powder and soda, and salt. Mix in the buttermilk, onion, and egg.

2. Pour enough oil in a skillet to measure at least 2 inches in depth. Heat the oil to 350°F. Gently spoon in the hushpuppy batter by the tablespoon. Try a test pup first. It should quickly puff up and, when done, be deep golden brown on the outside. Cut into the first one to make sure it is cooked through. Adjust the heat if necessary.

3. Drain the hushpuppies and serve hot.

Jalapeño Poppers

Like the hushpuppies, these little firecrackers also offer a good crunch, but with a creamy interior that offsets the jalapeño heat. MAKES ABOUT 1 DOZEN

12-ounce jar pickled whole jalapeños (about 12 large chiles)

2 ounces cream cheese, softened

2 tablespoons shredded mild cheddar cheese

3/4 cup cornmeal, preferably stone-ground

1/4 cup extra-fine stone-ground cornmeal (sometimes called corn flour), preferably, or all-purpose flour

1/2 teaspoon Smoky Salt (page 29), seasoned salt, or table salt

1 large egg

2 tablespoons milk

Vegetable oil

Sauce Olé (page 379) or other salsa (optional)

1. Slit each of the jalapeños along one side from top to bottom. Mash the cheeses together in a small bowl. Nudge a heaping teaspoon of cheese into each pepper, being sure to push the cheeses into the tops and bottoms of the pods. (The exact amount of cheese will vary with the size of your chiles.) This is easiest using your fingers, but afterward wash your hands well with soap and water before touching your eyes, lips, or other sensitive skin. Combine the two cornmeals and the salt on a plate.

2. Whisk the egg and milk in a bowl until light and very foamy. Dunk the jalapeños into the egg mixture and then into the cornmeal mixture, rolling to coat evenly, and then repeat so that each has a double coating of egg and cornmeal. Transfer to a greased baking sheet and chill for 10 to 30 minutes.

3. Pour several inches of oil into a high-sided skillet or saucepan and heat the oil to 360°F. Fry the jalapeños, a few at a time (so that the oil temperature doesn't drop drastically) until deep golden and crisp, 1 to 1½ minutes. Drain and serve immediately, with salsa on the side if you wish.

VARIATION: BAKED JALAPEÑO POPPERS If you're trying to manage too many cooking chores at once, you may find that baking the poppers works better for you than frying them. The crust isn't as crisp, but they still pop in your mouth. When you remove the stuffed jalapeños from the fridge, spritz them lightly with vegetable oil spray. Bake in a preheated 375°F oven directly on the chilled baking sheet until deep golden, 10 to 12 minutes.

Cracklin' Cornbread

An old Southern favorite, cracklings are crunchy slivers of pork skin or other bits of meat left after fat has been rendered. Using bacon will be easier for most home cooks and will result in a similar flavor. If you're feeling virtuous about fat, or having a vegetarian boss to dinner, eliminate the bacon and substitute a tablespoon of vegetable oil for the rendered fat. SERVES 6 TO 8

3 slices bacon, chopped

1½ cups cornmeal, preferably stone-ground

½ cup all-purpose flour

3 tablespoons sugar

1 tablespoon baking powder

1 teaspoon baking soda

¾ teaspoon table salt

1½ cups buttermilk

3 large eggs, lightly beaten

1 cup fresh or frozen corn kernels

2 tablespoons unsalted butter, melted

1. Preheat the oven to 400°F.

2. In a cast-iron skillet, fry the bacon over medium-low heat until very crisp. With a slotted spoon, remove the bacon and drain it. Pour out all but 1 tablespoon of the rendered bacon fat. Keep the skillet warm.

3. In a medium-size bowl, stir together the cornmeal, flour, sugar, baking powder and soda, and salt. Pour in the buttermilk and eggs and mix by hand until lightly but thoroughly blended. Stir in the corn, bacon, and melted butter.

4. Pour the batter into the warm skillet. Bake until the cornbread's edges are brown and the top has lightly browned, about 20 minutes. A toothpick inserted in the center should come out clean. Serve warm.

VARIATION: CRACKLIN' CORNCAKES The batter, thinned with an additional ¼ to ½ cup buttermilk, can be fried into corncakes, a barbecue accompaniment in some areas of the upper South. Use a griddle or a large skillet and a film of bacon drippings or vegetable oil for frying over medium heat, like pancakes.

PASS THE BLAND BREAD, PLEASE

Old-fashioned white bread and similar hamburger-style buns are easily the favorite breads to eat with barbecue. The very characteristics that many people disdain—the blandness and sponginess—are a perfect foil for barbecue sauce. Even so, we'll take cornbread with our 'Q' any day.

Buttermilk Biscuits

In contrast to so many commercial versions, a superior biscuit should be a sky-high puff of dough as light as a cumulus cloud. These beauties achieve that ethereal texture and taste, while soaking up barbecue juices with the best of the white breads. If you just can't abide the idea of lard, replace it with butter, but know that you are messing with tradition, texture, and taste.

MAKES ABOUT EIGHT 3-INCH OR TWELVE TO FOURTEEN 2-INCH BISCUITS

2 cups soft-wheat flour, such as White Lily, or 1 3/4 cups all-purpose flour plus 2 tablespoons cake flour

1 1/2 tablespoons sugar

2 teaspoons baking powder

1/2 teaspoon baking soda

1/2 teaspoon table salt

3 tablespoons lard, well chilled

2 tablespoons solid vegetable shortening, such as Crisco, well chilled

1 cup buttermilk, well chilled

1. Position the baking rack in the middle of the oven and preheat the oven to 450°F. Grease a baking sheet.

2. Sift together the dry ingredients into a large bowl. Repeat the sifting three times. With a pastry blender or large fork, blend in the lard and shortening, working lightly until a coarse meal forms. Pour in the buttermilk and stir together just until a sticky dough forms.

3. Flour your hands and a pastry board or counter. Turn the dough out and knead it lightly, four to six times. Pat out the dough to a thickness of about 1/2 inch. Cut with a 2-inch or 3-inch biscuit cutter or round cookie cutter.

4. Transfer the biscuits to the baking sheet, arranging so that they just touch one another. Bake until the biscuits are raised and golden brown, about 10 minutes, turning the baking sheet at the halfway point from front to back for even browning. Serve immediately.

INDEPENDENT SPIRIT

Rosedale Bar-B-Que, near downtown Kansas City, proudly promotes its birth on July 4, 1934. Anthony Rieke founded the lunchroom-cum-bar and designed his own pits, including a rotisserie smoker for ribs that he tested first by riding in it himself.

A WELL-KNOWN SECRET

A miraculous product from barbecue country, soft-wheat flours like White Lily have been the secret to great Southern biscuits for more than a century. Soft-wheat flours absorb less liquid than all-purpose or hard-wheat flours, creating lighter, flakier biscuits. For help in finding a source for soft-wheat flour, go online to whitelily.com.

Sweet Potato Biscuits

A lovely shade of orange and very moist, these biscuits stay a little more compact than their buttermilk cousins. If you must, substitute shortening for the lard.

MAKES TWELVE TO FOURTEEN 2-INCH BISCUITS

8 ounces cooked sweet potato, well chilled

$1/3$ cup buttermilk, well chilled

1 cup soft-wheat flour, such as White Lily, *or* 1 cup all-purpose flour with 1 tablespoon replaced by cake flour

$1^1/2$ teaspoons baking powder

1 teaspoon sugar

1 teaspoon chili powder

$1/2$ teaspoon table salt

$1/4$ teaspoon baking soda

3 tablespoons lard, well chilled

1. Position the baking rack in the middle of the oven and preheat the oven to 450°F. Grease a baking sheet.

2. Puree the sweet potato and buttermilk together in a food processor or blender.

3. Sift the dry ingredients together into a bowl.

With a pastry blender or large fork, cut in the lard until the mixture resembles coarse meal. With a spoon or spatula, fold in the sweet potato. Blend well with the dry ingredients but don't overmix.

4. On a floured board or counter, knead the dough lightly, about 20 turns of the dough over itself. Pat out the dough to a thickness of about $1/2$ inch and cut with a 2-inch biscuit cutter or round cookie cutter.

5. Transfer the biscuits to the baking sheet. Bake until the biscuits are raised and lightly browned on the top edges, about 14 minutes, turning the baking sheet at the halfway point from front to back for browning. Serve hot.

The biggest challenger to white bread at barbecue joints may be saltine crackers. They are particularly popular in places that serve meat by the pound and don't feature a sauce. Instead of the dainty four-pack you might get with soup in a regular restaurant, the pitmaster is likely to toss you and a mate a full, long bag of crackers directly out of the box.

Blue Corn Muffins

These slightly sweet and delicately flavored muffins are not truly traditional, but they go well with lighter smoked fare, such as fish and fowl. Substitute yellow cornmeal if you can't find the blue variety from the Southwest. MAKES 1 DOZEN

3/4 cup unsalted butter, softened

1/3 cup sugar

4 large eggs

1/2 cup milk

1 to 2 fresh jalapeños, minced

3/4 cup shredded mild cheddar cheese (3 ounces)

3 ounces cream cheese or fresh, mild goat cheese

1 cup all-purpose flour

1 cup blue cornmeal, preferably stone-ground

2 1/2 teaspoons baking powder

1 teaspoon table salt

2 tablespoons poppy seeds

1. Preheat the oven to 375°F. Grease a muffin tin.

2. Cream together the butter and sugar with an electric mixer or food processor. Add the eggs, milk, jalapeños, and cheeses, mixing well after each addition. Sift together the flour, cornmeal, baking powder, and salt. Spoon the dry mixture into the batter about one-third at a time, again mixing well after each addition. Stir in the poppy seeds at the end.

3. Spoon the batter into the prepared muffin tins. Bake until a toothpick inserted in the center comes out clean, 22 to 25 minutes. Serve warm or at room temperature.

Yeast Buns

Buns are probably not technically an accompaniment, but they are, of course, a key piece of any classic barbecue sandwich. When you go to the effort of cooking meat for hours, you may want to surround it by something more than plain old supermarket white bread. Don't be intimidated by the yeast. Anyone who can make barbecue can sure mix up buns. We make them in the oven while the meat's in the smoker. The recipe began with one from the good folks at King Arthur Flour, the flour we use for nearly all our baked goods. MAKES 8 LARGE BUNS

1 cup lukewarm water

2 tablespoons unsalted butter, softened

1 large egg, at room temperature

1 tablespoon instant-rise yeast

3½ to 3¾ cups unbleached all-purpose flour

3 tablespoons sugar

1¼ teaspoons table salt

2 tablespoons melted unsalted butter

1. In a stand mixer fitted with a dough hook, combine the water, softened butter, egg, and yeast. (If you don't have a stand mixer, you can mix and knead the dough by hand in a large sturdy bowl.) When mixed, add 3½ cups flour and the sugar and salt. Mix on medium speed for several minutes, until a soft, smooth dough forms. If the dough is too wet to form properly, add up to the remaining ¼ cup of flour.

2. Cover the dough with a clean dishtowel and set in a warm place. Let it rise until doubled in size, 1 to 2 hours.

3. Punch the dough down and divide it into 8 equal balls. Flatten each ball with your palm until it is about 3 inches across. Line a baking sheet with a silicone mat or parchment paper. Arrange the buns on the baking sheet, spacing them evenly apart. Cover with the dishtowel and let rise until puffy and soft, about 1 hour.

4. Preheat the oven to 375°F. Brush the buns with the melted butter, avoiding smooshing them down as you brush.

5. Bake until golden brown, 15 to 18 minutes. Cool on the baking sheet for a couple of minutes, then remove them from the baking sheet to a baking rack and let them cool. Split them in half horizontally when ready to use. The buns are best eaten the day they are made.

SIDE-DISH SALADS AND RELISHES

ANY PITMASTERS WHO LIMIT THEIR ACCOM-PANIMENTS TO TRADITIONAL BARBECUE SIDE DISHES ARE BEING BLINDED BY THEIR OWN SMOKE. MANY KINDS OF FOOD GO GREAT WITH BAR-BECUE, FROM DOWN-HOME PICNIC SPECIALTIES TO CRE-ATIVE, CONTEMPORARY CONCOCTIONS.

UNLIKE THE DISHES IN THE CHAPTER ON SMOKE-SCENTED SALADS, PASTAS, AND PIZZAS, WHICH MAKE AN AMPLE MEAL IN THEMSELVES, THE SALADS AND RELISHES here go on the side of the plate as a vibrant supplement to the main course. They help round out a barbecue feast with complementary tastes that add new dimensions to the dinner. You can even enjoy them without barbecue, but they contrast particularly well with smoky flavors, which bring out the best of their refreshing garden goodness.

Southern Caesar Salad

The classic Caesar salad contains some things, such as a coddled egg, that don't seem right at a barbecue. This variation gets extra zing from onions. SERVES 4 TO 6

SOUTHERN CAESAR DRESSING
1 1/2 cups extra-virgin olive oil
5 to 6 garlic cloves
2 tablespoons freshly squeezed lemon juice
2 tablespoons sherry vinegar
1 tablespoon Dijon mustard
1 teaspoon anchovy paste
1/4 teaspoon coarsely ground black pepper

2 to 3 medium onions, cut in thick slices
2 to 3 heads romaine, dark green outer leaves reserved for another purpose
1/2 cup grated Romano cheese

1. Blend the oil and garlic in a blender or food processor. Strain the oil through a fine-mesh strainer and discard the garlic bits. Pour the oil and remaining dressing ingredients back into the blender or food processor and blend until thick. Set aside.

2. Place the onions in a shallow dish in a single layer. Pour about 1/2 cup of the dressing over the onions and allow them to marinate for at least 30 minutes.

3. Prepare a grill or broiler. Drain the onions and grill or broil them until lightly browned and well softened, 8 to 10 minutes. Watch them carefully, as they should caramelize lightly but not burn. Toss the onions with an additional tablespoon or two of dressing and set aside to cool.

4. In a large bowl, toss the romaine leaves gently with enough dressing to coat, reserving the rest of the dressing for other salads. (Leftover dressing keeps for several weeks.) Transfer the lettuce to a decorative platter and top it with the onion slices. Sprinkle the cheese over the salad and serve.

SERVING SUGGESTION On weekends when we're barbecuing for much of the day, we like this for lunch, accompanied by Sweet Potato Biscuits (page 411) or any good loaf of bread.

California Crunch

The combination of ingredients comes from the West Coast, but the taste and texture of this salad travel easily to other terrains. SERVES 4 TO 6

CALIFORNIA DRESSING

1 ripe avocado, peeled, pitted, and cut into chunks

2 tablespoons freshly squeezed lemon juice

1/2 cup sour cream or plain yogurt

6 tablespoons vegetable oil

1 garlic clove, minced

1 teaspoon chili powder

1/2 teaspoon sugar

1/4 teaspoon table salt, or more to taste

1/4 teaspoon freshly ground black pepper

1 medium head romaine lettuce, sliced into thick ribbons

2 ripe medium tomatoes, chopped

1 ripe avocado, peeled, pitted, and sliced

1/2 cup pitted black olives, sliced

1 cup corn chips

1/2 medium onion, cut in very thin rings

1/2 cup grated Monterey Jack or pepper Jack cheese

1. Combine all the dressing ingredients in a blender and puree until smooth.

2. In a bowl, toss the romaine, tomatoes, avocado, and olives with about half of the dressing. Top the salad with the corn chips, onion, and cheese, arranged attractively. Serve immediately, with additional dressing on the side. If the dressing thickens too much, mix a bit of water into it.

THE MEX-ITALIAN SALAD

Something in the origin of the Caesar salad may explain why the classic version is not quite right for barbecue. Caesar Cardini, an Italian chef, created the salad in the Roaring Twenties in a restaurant he owned in Tijuana, Mexico. Southern Californians partying in the city depleted most of the food in the kitchen, so Cardini threw together what remained and convinced the tipsy patrons that it was a special new dish. The Hollywood crowd adopted the idea and made the salad a star.

Killed Salad

Generations of Southern cooks doused leaf lettuce with a heap of hot bacon drippings, more than a smidgen of sugar, and a splash of vinegar. This is a homey but slightly more sophisticated take on the original idea. Most people know it as a "wilted salad," but some Southerners have always called it "killed salad."

SERVES 4 TO 6

GLAZED BACON

4 slices bacon, preferably a smoky slab variety

1 tablespoon honey

1 tablespoon yellow mustard

Dash of cider vinegar

BACON VINAIGRETTE

Extra-virgin olive oil

1 garlic clove, minced

3 tablespoons cider vinegar

1 tablespoon honey

Table salt and freshly ground black pepper to taste

10 to 12 cups torn leaf lettuce

1. Preheat the oven to 350°F.

2. Arrange the bacon in a single layer on a baking sheet with sides. Bake the bacon for 10 minutes, and pour off all rendered fat into a glass measuring cup.

3. In a small bowl, mix the honey, mustard, and vinegar. Spread half of the mixture on top of the bacon, and return the meat to the oven for another 7 to 8 minutes. Turn the bacon over and spread it with the remaining glaze mixture. Bake until the bacon is medium-brown and crispy, another 6 to 7 minutes. Watch carefully for the last few minutes to avoid burning. Cool briefly. Chop or crumble the bacon.

4. Add enough olive oil to the rendered bacon fat to make ½ cup. Warm the bacon fat and oil mixture over medium heat in a small skillet. Add the garlic and sauté it briefly. Add the remaining dressing ingredients and heat through, stirring until the honey dissolves.

5. Place the greens in a salad bowl and pour the warm dressing over them. Toss lightly. Like cooked spinach, the lettuce will reduce substantially in volume. Sprinkle the bacon over the salad and serve the salad hot or at room temperature.

SERVING SUGGESTION Granny served her version of this salad with a Sunday ham and, maybe in the spring, batter-fried mushrooms hunted by the whole family. We like it on summer evenings with crusty rolls and Peach Melba Ice Cream (page 466) or Mojito Sorbet (page 466).

Burstin' with Black-Eyed Peas Salad

From the hoppin' John of the Deep South to the Texas caviar served in Dallas, the black-eyed pea is featured in some of the favorite dishes of the barbecue belt. While we've never met a black-eyed pea we didn't like, they really shine in this salad.

SERVES 4 TO 6

1 pound black-eyed peas, dried or frozen

4 to 6 cups chicken stock

1 to 2 teaspoons crab boil seasoning or barbecue dry rub, such as Wild Willy's Number One-derful Rub (page 26) or Seafaring Seafood Rub (page 28)

1 small bell pepper, preferably red, seeded and diced fine

6 scallions, sliced

BLACK-EYED PEA VINAIGRETTE

$1/3$ cup vegetable oil

3 tablespoons freshly squeezed lime juice

1 tablespoon cider vinegar, preferably unrefined

1 tablespoon tomato-based barbecue sauce

1 to 3 teaspoons packed brown sugar

1 to 2 pickled jalapeños, minced

2 garlic cloves, minced

1 teaspoon chili powder

1 teaspoon freshly ground black pepper

1 teaspoon kosher salt or coarse sea salt, or more to taste

$1/2$ teaspoon ground cumin

1. In a large saucepan, cover the peas by at least 1 inch with stock, sprinkle in the crab boil seasoning, and bring to a boil over high heat. Reduce the heat to a simmer and cook until the peas are tender, anywhere from 45 minutes to $1\frac{1}{2}$ hours, depending on your peas. Frozen peas generally cook faster. Stir occasionally, and add more stock or water if the peas begin to seem dry before they are done.

2. Drain the peas. In a large bowl, toss them with the bell pepper and scallions.

3. In a blender or food processor, mix the vinaigrette ingredients. Pour over the peas.

4. Refrigerate, covered, for at least 2 hours and preferably overnight. The peas taste best the following day. Serve them chilled.

SERVING SUGGESTION Always offer black-eyed peas on New Year's Eve or Day, as solid a guarantee as you can get for good luck in the months ahead. To ring in the year in style, serve the peas with a Creole Crown Roast (page 91) and Cranberry-Ginger Crumble (page 456).

Hand Salad

At a fancy affair, the hostess would probably call this crudités. Our version might be a little too crude for her tastes, though. SERVES 8 TO 10

BARBECUE VINAIGRETTE

$1/2$ cup freshly squeezed orange juice

$2 1/2$ to 3 tablespoons tomato-based barbecue sauce, preferably a variety that isn't overly sweet or flavored with pure liquid smoke, such as Memphis Magic (page 374)

2 teaspoons Worcestershire sauce

1 garlic clove, minced

$1/2$ cup corn oil, preferably unrefined

Table salt and freshly ground black pepper to taste

A batch of easily handled raw vegetables—asparagus stalks, carrot sticks, scallions, cucumber chunks, broccoli florets, summer squash slices, center leaves of romaine, cherry tomatoes

A healthy sprinkling of barbecue dry rub, such as Southwest Heat (page 32) or Cajun Ragin' Rub (page 29), or Smoky Salt (page 29) or other seasoned salt

1. In a food processor, combine the orange juice, barbecue and Worcestershire sauces, and garlic. Drizzle in the oil, continuing to process, until combined. Add salt and pepper to taste.

2. Arrange the vegetables on a platter. Sprinkle dry rub over them to taste. Pour the salad dressing into a bowl. Serve the veggies as finger food, for people to dunk in the dressing. Leftover dressing keeps for at least a week.

Sweet and Sour Cukes

A cooling combo no matter how hot it gets outdoors. SERVES 6

2 medium cucumbers, peeled and chopped

1 medium red-ripe tomato, chopped

1 medium green bell pepper, seeded and chopped

1 large onion, chopped

1 cup white vinegar

$2/3$ cup sugar

$1/2$ teaspoon table salt

$1/2$ teaspoon freshly ground black pepper

In a large bowl, toss the vegetables together. Add the remaining ingredients and stir well. Refrigerate the salad for at least 30 minutes, stirring again before serving. The salad keeps well for a couple of days.

San Antonio Cactus and Corn Salad

A Southwestern delicacy for centuries, prickly pear cactus deserves to be better known in other regions. Look for it in the Mexican food section of the supermarket in jars labeled *nopales* or *nopalitos*. Here succulent strips of the cactus enhance summer sweet corn. SERVES 6

4 medium ears of corn, smoked, grilled, roasted, or boiled

1 1/2 cups nopalitos, drained and diced

3/4 cup peeled and diced cucumber

1 to 2 Roma or other plum tomatoes, chopped

1/4 cup chopped celery

2 tablespoons sliced scallions

2 tablespoons minced fresh cilantro

NOPALITOS DRESSING

3 tablespoons extra-virgin olive oil

1 tablespoon freshly squeezed lime juice

1 fresh serrano or jalapeño, minced

1/4 teaspoon table salt

Lettuce leaves

1. Slice the kernels from the ears of corn. Place the corn in a medium-size bowl and mix in the nopalitos, cucumber, tomatoes, celery, scallions, and cilantro.

2. In a small lidded jar, shake together the dressing ingredients and pour over the vegetables. Serve the salad at room temperature or chilled, on the lettuce leaves.

SERVING SUGGESTION The salad can double as a salsa or relish. Try it—without the lettuce—on crisp tortilla chips or warm corn tortillas as an appetizer.

OKLAHOMA'S FIRST FAMILY OF BARBECUE

The original Van's Pig Stand in Shawnee brags of being "the oldest family-owned restaurant in Oklahoma." The Vandegrift clan has a modern building nowadays, but they still use barbecue recipes developed for the grand opening in 1930. Jerry Vandegrift once summed up the restaurant's history succinctly, saying, "We've gone through who knows how many wars, fires, and that sort of thing."

Boarding House Macaroni Salad

This is the only kind of pasta salad you should have the nerve to serve with real barbecue. SERVES 6 TO 8

1 pound macaroni, preferably small elbows or shells, cooked al dente and drained

6 to 8 ounces mild or medium cheddar cheese, cut in small cubes

1½ cups baby peas, fresh or frozen

1 medium green bell pepper, seeded and chopped

1 medium onion, chopped

⅔ cup sweet pickle relish

¼ cup mayonnaise

¼ cup plain yogurt

¼ cup chopped pimientos

Ground white pepper to taste

In a large bowl, mix all the ingredients. Refrigerate, covered, for at least 1 hour to develop the flavors. The salad keeps well for several days.

THE WORLD'S BEST POTATO SALAD SANDWICH

Nobody forgets a takeout rib sandwich from C & K Barbecue in St. Louis. A flattened scoop of potato salad sprawls under the top slice of white bread, making an inherently messy meal into total mayhem. For a meat plate, you may want the smoky ribs or the great chicken, but many of the locals prefer deep-fried slices of pig snouts as crunchy as cracklings.

When a group of U.S. pitmasters challenged Soviet cooks in a barbecue contest in 1990, the winners were the Wild Boars of Walls, Mississippi, a team headed by Gene and Patti McGee. Estonians hosted the cook-off, but they never stood a chance against Mississippi masters.

Tangy Buttermilk Potato Salad

Potato salad is a sure-fire way to a woman's heart. Men and kids like it, too.

SERVES 6 TO 8

5 medium baking potatoes, peeled

1/2 green bell pepper, chopped

6 radishes, grated

4 hard-boiled eggs, grated

1/3 cup chopped sweet pickles

3 tablespoons juice from a jar of sweet pickles

4 scallions, sliced

BUTTERMILK DRESSING

3/4 cup mayonnaise

1/2 cup buttermilk

2 garlic cloves, minced

2 tablespoons chopped fresh parsley

4 teaspoons yellow mustard

1 teaspoon freshly ground black pepper

1/4 teaspoon table salt, or more to taste

1. In a large pan of boiling salted water, cook the potatoes over high heat until tender, 15 to 20 minutes. Drain the potatoes, rinse them in cold water, and drain them again. Set the potatoes aside to cool.

2. Place the bell pepper, radishes, eggs, pickles, pickle juice, and scallions in a large bowl. Chop the cooled potatoes into bite-size chunks and add them to the bowl, mixing lightly.

3. In a blender, combine the dressing ingredients. Pour about three-quarters of the dressing over the potatoes and stir together until well blended. Add more dressing to taste, or a little more salt to adjust the salad to your liking. Cover and chill for at least 2 hours or, even better, overnight. Serve cold. The salad keeps well for several days.

VARIATION: HOT AND SPICY BUTTERMILK POTATO SALAD If you can find a "hot and spicy" variety of sweet pickles, try them in the salad for extra punch. Otherwise, add a minced serrano or jalapeño or two to the salad when you add the green bell pepper.

Hot German Potato Salad

German settlers in central Texas contributed heavily to the strong barbecue tradition of the area. They also brought Old Country traditions with them in dishes like this, which is a stalwart favorite in both of our families. SERVES 6 TO 8

8 medium red-skinned potatoes, peeled if desired

1 1/2 celery ribs, chopped fine

1/2 green bell pepper, chopped fine

1 hard-boiled egg, grated

1/3 cup chopped fresh parsley

4 slices slab bacon, chopped

1/2 medium onion, chopped

2 teaspoons all-purpose flour

1/2 teaspoon table salt, or more to taste

1/4 teaspoon freshly ground black pepper

3/4 cup beer

6 tablespoons cider vinegar

4 teaspoons sugar

1 tablespoon brown mustard

1. In a large pan of boiling salted water, cook the potatoes over high heat until tender, 15 to 20 minutes. Drain the potatoes, rinse them in cold water, and drain them again. Set them aside to cool.

2. Place the celery, bell pepper, egg, and parsley in a large bowl. Slice the potatoes thick and add them.

3. Fry the bacon in a skillet over medium heat until browned and crisp. With a slotted spoon, remove the bacon, drain, and reserve it. Add the onion to the warm bacon drippings and cook briefly until softened. Sprinkle in the flour, salt, and pepper and stir to combine. Pour in 1/2 cup of the beer, the vinegar, sugar, and mustard, and bring to a boil. Reduce the heat and simmer for 2 to 3 minutes.

4. Pour the sauce over the potato mixture and toss to combine. The salad should look moist but not runny. If it seems dry, add some or all of the remaining beer. Taste and adjust the seasoning. The vinegar tang should come across as assertive but not aggressive. Add the bacon shortly before serving. Serve hot.

SERVING SUGGESTION For a hearty lunch while barbecuing, try the German potato salad with the sandwich we call a German burrito—a flour tortilla wrapped around a smoked link sausage and loaded with mustard and onions. Beer would be optional only if you're French.

Among the small number of great drive-ins left in the country, the Beacon in Spartanburg, South Carolina, is in a class by itself. It's a better tribute to controlled chaos than central Manhattan, and the staff may hustle you along with more verve and determination than a New York cabbie. The kitchen cooks everything that's considered edible in the state, but many of the thousands of people who show up on weekend nights come for the barbecue, heaped on skyscraper sandwiches.

a distinctive take on an outdoor-party bean salad

Succotash Salad

You and your guests will love this distinctive take on an outdoor-party bean salad.

SERVES 6 OR MORE

8 ounces fresh thin young green beans, trimmed, halved or cut in thirds on the diagonal

2 cups cooked baby limas, butter beans, or shelled edamame (baby soybeans), fresh or frozen

2 cups cooked corn kernels

2 celery ribs, chopped fine

2 large shallots, minced

2 tablespoons minced fresh parsley

SUCCOTASH SALAD DRESSING

6 tablespoons extra-virgin olive oil

1 1/2 teaspoons Dijon mustard

1/4 teaspoon table salt, or more to taste

Pinch or 2 of sugar

2 tablespoons cider vinegar

1. Steam the green beans over simmering water for a brief few minutes, just until tender. Run cold water over the beans to retain their bright green color, and drain. Transfer the green beans, limas, corn, celery, shallots, and parsley to a large bowl.

2. Prepare the dressing, whisking together the ingredients in a medium-size bowl. Pour the dressing over the salad, toss until combined, and chill, covered, for at least 1 hour. Serve chilled or at room temperature.

Sweet Sally's Sweet Potato Salad

The sweet potato makes an attractive alternative to Irish spuds in salads. Our version bathes sweet potato chunks in a zesty dressing featuring smoky chipotle chiles. This is dedicated to the memory of Sally Martin, an English friend who moved to the Southwest and started putting chipotles in everything short of afternoon tea.

SERVES 6

CHIPOTLE DRESSING

1/3 cup freshly squeezed lime juice

1/4 cup canned chipotle chiles in adobo sauce

1 tablespoon ketchup

1 1/2 teaspoons Dijon mustard

1 garlic clove, minced

1/3 cup extra-virgin olive oil

2 large or 4 small sweet potatoes (about 2 pounds total), peeled and cut into bite-size chunks

1 medium bell pepper, preferably red, seeded and chopped

1 celery rib, chopped

6 to 8 scallions, sliced thin

2 tablespoons chopped fresh cilantro

Table salt and coarsely ground black pepper to taste

1. Combine all the dressing ingredients, except for the oil, in a food processor and puree. Drizzle in the oil and continue to process until you have a thick dressing. Reserve.

2. In a large pan of boiling salted water, cook the sweet potatoes over medium-high heat until tender, 10 to 12 minutes. Drain the potatoes, rinse them in cold water, and drain them again. Set them aside to cool briefly.

3. Combine the bell pepper, celery, scallions, cilantro, and sweet potatoes in a large bowl, mixing lightly. Pour about three-quarters of the dressing over the potato mixture and toss to combine. The result should look moist but not runny. If it seems dry, add the remaining dressing. Taste and season with salt and pepper.

4. Cover and chill for at least 2 hours or, even better, overnight. Serve cold. The salad keeps well for several days.

MUST BE YANKEES

For a different perspective on barbecue secrets, take a look at Matt Kramer and Roger Sheppard's *Smoke Cooking* (1967, Hawthorn Books). It's a terrific resource book, devoted to barbecue cooking methods, but the authors seem completely unaware of real barbecue. They call their technique "smoke roasting" and label it "a revolution in outdoor cooking."

Kraut Salad

Paul Bosland, the reigning academic authority on chiles, once specialized in sauerkraut. He changed fields when he decided that kraut wasn't a growth industry. Apparently not enough folks had tried this kind of salad. SERVES 6

16 ounces sauerkraut, preferably not a canned variety

2/3 cup sugar

1/3 cup cider vinegar

1/2 cup sliced water chestnuts

1/2 medium onion, chopped

1/2 small green bell pepper, chopped

1/2 small red bell pepper, chopped

2 carrots, shredded fine

2 celery ribs, chopped

2 tablespoons vegetable oil

1 tablespoon mustard seeds

Dash of ground cloves

1. Drain the sauerkraut, rinse it, and drain it again. Place the kraut in a large bowl.

2. In a small saucepan, heat the sugar and vinegar together until the sugar has dissolved. Pour the mixture over the kraut and toss well. Add the remaining ingredients and toss the salad again. Refrigerate, covered, for at least 1 hour. Serve chilled. The salad keeps well for several days.

Asian Vegetable Slaw

When the seasonings of your main dish wander toward the Far East, this sprightly combo makes a welcome accompaniment. SERVES 6 TO 8

ASIAN VEGETABLE DRESSING

3/4 cup rice vinegar

3/4 cup water

6 tablespoons sugar

1/3 cup dry sherry

1 tablespoon peeled and minced fresh ginger

1/2 teaspoon kosher salt or coarse sea salt

1 small dried hot red chile (optional)

5 lightly packed cups shredded napa cabbage or bok choy, or a combination

6 ounces snow peas, stemmed and sliced into thirds lengthwise

4 medium carrots, grated

1 large red bell pepper, seeded and sliced into matchsticks

3 scallions, halved lengthwise, then sliced on the diagonal into inch-long sections

1. Combine the dressing ingredients in a small saucepan. Bring to a boil over high heat, then reduce the heat to a simmer and cook for 5 minutes. Cool to room temperature, then discard the chile if it was used.

2. Toss together the remaining ingredients in a large bowl. Pour the dressing over the vegetables and mix well. Chill for 30 minutes and serve.

The Bosley family calls their Owensboro barbecue restaurant "Kentucky's Very Famous Moonlite." The acclaim is real, and you'll see why if you try the Moonlite's mountainous buffet, three long tables crowded with coleslaw, gelatin salads, burgoo, green beans, macaroni, cornbread with sorghum, mutton, beef, pork, chicken, and enough desserts to put a dieter into shock. The food is superb and it all costs about the same as a hot dog at Yankee Stadium.

Arty Rice Salad

When Cheryl first moved south to barbecue country, right after college, this was one of the first salads she ate. It remains a sentimental favorite. SERVES 6

2 cups cooked white rice

6-ounce jar marinated artichoke hearts, sliced thin, with marinade

1/3 cup mayonnaise

2 celery ribs, chopped fine

1/4 cup sliced pimiento-stuffed green olives

2 tablespoons chopped red bell pepper or pimiento

2 tablespoons minced fresh parsley

3 scallions, sliced thin

1 pickled jalapeño, minced

1 teaspoon curry powder

Pinch of sugar

Lettuce leaves (optional)

In a large bowl, mix the rice with the other ingredients, except the lettuce. Refrigerate, covered, for at least 30 minutes. Serve chilled, on top of the lettuce leaves if desired.

SERVING SUGGESTION For a cheery lunch while your meat smokes for dinner, serve the salad mounded in red bell pepper halves and pass Blue Corn Muffins (page 412) as an accompaniment.

Mango and Avocado Salad

This duo mates particularly well with tropically inspired main dishes. SERVES 6

CELERY SEED DRESSING

1/4 cup sugar

1/4 cup honey

1/4 cup white vinegar

2 tablespoons freshly squeezed lemon juice

2 teaspoons grated onion

1 teaspoon dry mustard

1 teaspoon paprika

1/2 teaspoon table salt

1 cup vegetable oil

2 tablespoons celery seeds

Shredded red cabbage

3 ripe mangoes, sliced

3 ripe Hass avocados, peeled, pitted, and sliced

1. In a food processor or blender, combine all the dressing ingredients except the oil and celery seeds. Pour in the oil and continue processing until the dressing is thick and well blended. Spoon in the celery seeds and process just until incorporated.

2. Make a bed of shredded cabbage on a serving platter. Arrange the mangoes and avocados decoratively on the cabbage. Drizzle some dressing over the salad and serve the salad with the remaining dressing on the side.

3. The dressing keeps, refrigerated, for a couple of weeks and complements any fruit salad. Process again before using if it separates.

'Nana Nut Salad

We had almost forgotten this childhood favorite until we stumbled onto it in the buffet line at the Moonlite Bar-B-Q in Owensboro, Kentucky. SERVES 6

1/2 cup sugar

1 egg yolk, lightly beaten

3 tablespoons white vinegar

1/2 cup Miracle Whip salad dressing (not mayonnaise)

6 medium bananas, sliced

1/2 cup chopped salted peanuts

Additional chopped peanuts (optional), for garnish

1. In a small, heavy saucepan, combine the sugar, egg yolk, and vinegar. Warm over low heat, stirring constantly, until the sugar dissolves and the mixture thickens. Remove from the heat and mix in the Miracle Whip.

2. Combine the bananas and peanuts in a large bowl. Spoon the dressing over the salad and mix well. Top with additional peanuts if you wish. The salad is best eaten within a couple of hours.

Devil-May-Care Eggs

Despite their own heat, these little numbers will cool you down on a blistering summer day. If you can't find spicy sweet pickles in your area, use regular sweet pickles and up the jalapeño ante. MAKES 24 EGGS

12 hard-boiled eggs

3 tablespoons mayonnaise

2 tablespoons hot and spicy sweet pickles, chopped

2 tablespoons minced pickled jalapeño

2 tablespoons minced fresh cilantro

4 teaspoons Dijon mustard

1 tablespoon minced scallions

1 to 2 teaspoons curry powder (optional)

Table salt to taste

Cilantro sprigs, for garnish

1. Halve the eggs lengthwise. Remove the yolks and place them in a bowl. Reserve the egg whites. Using a fork, crumble the yolks. Stir in the remaining ingredients. Adjust the seasonings to taste.

2. Spoon the yolk mixture into the egg whites or, for a more festive look, pipe the mixture with a pastry tube. Refrigerate the eggs, covered, until serving time. Arrange on a platter surrounded by cilantro.

VARIATION: SIMPLY SCRUMPTIOUS DEVILED EGGS When other dishes are heavily seasoned, you might want a less-adorned egg. Eliminate the pickles, jalapeño, cilantro, and scallions. Add 2 more tablespoons of mayonnaise and reduce the curry powder to $1/4$ to $1/2$ teaspoon. Sprinkle with paprika for 1950s nostalgia, and arrange on watercress or other greens.

A KANSAS CITY MASTER

Few people have won more barbecue cooking awards than Paul Kirk, the Kansas City "Baron of Barbecue." A big winner at the American Royal competition, the Jack Daniel's World Championship Invitational Barbecue, and even the Irish Cup International, Kirk generously shares his secrets with others through cooking classes and books. Check out his thorough tome titled *Paul Kirk's Championship Barbecue Sauces* (1997, Harvard Common Press).

Okra Pickles

We've always liked the crunchy little spurt that comes when munching on these pickles. They make us chuckle a little, too, reminding us about the "Fighting Okras" of Delta State University in Mississippi, nicknamed for their green jerseys.

MAKES ABOUT 5 PINTS

2 pounds small whole okra

3 cups cider vinegar

1 cup water

2 tablespoons pickling salt or 2 heaping tablespoons kosher salt

2 teaspoons white wine Worcestershire sauce or 1 teaspoon regular Worcestershire sauce

1 teaspoon Tabasco or other hot pepper sauce

5 small whole dried chiles, preferably cayenne or pequín

5 garlic cloves

5 fresh dill heads

1¼ teaspoons mustard seeds

1. In a large bowl, soak the okra in cold water for about 1 hour to plump them.

2. While the okra soak, sterilize five pint canning jars according to the manufacturer's directions.

3. Shortly before the okra finishes its bath, combine the vinegar, water, salt, Worcestershire sauce, and Tabasco in a medium-size saucepan and bring the mixture to a boil.

4. While the pickling liquid simmers, drain the okra. With clean hands, snugly pile the okra vertically into the sterilized jars, leaving about ½ inch space at the top of each jar. Add a chile, garlic clove, dill head, and portion of the mustard seeds to each jar. Arrange the okra and the spices attractively.

5. Ladle the hot pickling liquid over the okra in each jar, covering the okra but leaving about ½ inch headspace. Seal.

6. Process the jars in a boiling water bath for 10 minutes. Let the pickles sit for at least a week, and preferably several weeks, before serving.

SERVING SUGGESTION Make the pickled okra part of a dazzling relish tray for a Monday night football game. Load a platter with a mix of pickles and chowchows, supplementing your homemade goodies with a few store-bought selections if needed.

Humphrey Bogart's famous line, "Here's looking at you, kid," is a feeling you can't escape at Roy's Hickory Pit BBQ in Hutchinson, Kansas, where many of the diners sit at a big circular communal table facing one another. A dozen or so enthusiastic folks chow down on 'Q' at once, producing a chorus of lip smacking you can hear all the way to Wichita.

Bodacious Bread-and-Butter Pickles

A friend making these the same weekend that she acquired a new kitten liked both so well that she named the cat "Pickles." MAKES 3 PINTS

3 pounds unpeeled plump pickling cucumbers, 4 to 5 inches long, sliced into 1/4-inch rounds

1 large sweet onion, or mild onion, sliced into 1/4-inch rings and separated

1 medium red bell pepper, sliced into 1/4-inch rings

2 fresh medium jalapeños (optional), sliced into 1/4-inch rings

About a dozen ice cubes

3 tablespoons pickling salt or 3 heaping tablespoons kosher salt

2 1/4 cups packed brown sugar

1 1/2 cups cider vinegar

2 garlic cloves, slivered

2 teaspoons yellow mustard seeds

2 teaspoons black peppercorns

2 teaspoons celery seeds

1 1/2 teaspoons ground turmeric

1. Sterilize three pint canning jars according to the manufacturer's directions.

2. Stir together the cucumbers, onion, bell pepper, and jalapeños in a large nonreactive bowl. Toss with the ice cubes. Sprinkle the mixture with the salt and toss again lightly. Set aside at room temperature for 3 hours. The cucumbers will release a good bit of water during this time.

3. Pour off the cucumber mixture's liquid. Rinse well with cold water and drain again.

4. Combine the brown sugar, vinegar, garlic, and remaining spices in a large, heavy pan. Bring to a boil over high heat. Spoon the cucumber mixture into the liquid and bring back to a full boil. Ladle the pickles into each jar, covering them in syrup, and dividing the spices among the jars. Leave 1/2 inch headspace. Seal.

5. Process the jars in a boiling water bath for 10 minutes. Refrigerate the pickles for at least a week before eating. The pickles keep at least several months.

Carolina Jerusalem Artichoke Pickles

Jerusalem artichokes have nothing to do with the Holy Land or artichokes. These tubers, sometimes known as sunchokes, are kissing cousins to the sunflower. The knobby little fists taste slightly sweet and offer a pleasant crunch. You can find them fresh in well-stocked produce sections from winter through spring, and at farmers' markets in the late fall. **MAKES ABOUT 5 PINTS**

3 cups cider vinegar

2/3 cup water

2/3 cup packed brown sugar

1 tablespoon pickling salt or 1 heaping tablespoon kosher salt

1 teaspoon whole allspice, bruised

1/2 teaspoon ground turmeric

3 pounds Jerusalem artichokes, well scrubbed but unpeeled, sliced about 1/4 inch thick

1 medium onion, sliced and pulled into individual rings

5 small whole dried chiles, preferably cayenne or pequín

5 whole cloves

2 teaspoons mustard seeds

2 teaspoons celery seeds

1. Sterilize five pint canning jars according to the manufacturer's directions.

2. In a large saucepan, combine the vinegar, water, sugar, salt, allspice, and turmeric. Bring the syrup to a boil and boil for 3 to 5 minutes.

3. With clean hands, snugly pile the artichoke slices and onion rings into the sterilized jars, leaving about 1/2 inch space at the top. Add a chile, a clove, and equal portions of the mustard and celery seeds to each jar.

4. Ladle the hot pickling liquid over the artichokes, covering the artichokes but leaving about 1/2 inch headspace. Seal.

5. Process the jars in a boiling water bath for 10 minutes. Let the pickles sit for at least a week, and preferably several weeks, before you indulge.

A GREAT PIT STOP

Right along old Route 66, now Interstate 40, in Clinton, Oklahoma, Jigg's Smokehouse looks like a frontier cabin painted with smoke. The pitmasters will smoke anything that moves and sell it to you by the pound, along with jars of chowchow and other superb relishes.

Wonderful Watermelon Pickles

Hard to find at a local grocery outside the South, these morsels will make you a believer if you try them once. Just save the rind from the next watermelon you eat and take a little time over the following three days to complete a series of simple steps. MAKES ABOUT 8 PINTS

THE FIRST DAY

Rind of one large watermelon

3/4 cup pickling salt or heaping 3/4 cup kosher salt

1 gallon water

THE SECOND DAY

6 cups granulated sugar

4 cups white vinegar

2 cups packed brown sugar

2 lemons, sliced thin

1 tablespoon whole cloves

1 tablespoon whole allspice

4 sticks cinnamon, broken more or less in half

1/4 teaspoon mustard seeds

THE FIRST DAY

1. This is the toughest part of the process. Cut the watermelon rind into manageable chunks. Scrape all the remaining red watermelon meat from the inside of the rind. Then pare off the hard green skin of the outer rind with a small knife. It's not difficult, but it takes a while. Cube the rind into bite-size pieces. You should have about 16 cups.

2. In a large bowl, dissolve the salt in the water. Transfer the rind cubes to the salted water. Find an out-of-the-way corner of your kitchen for the bowl and then weight the rind down with a plate to keep it submerged. Soak the cubes for about 24 hours.

THE SECOND DAY

3. Combine all the remaining ingredients in a large saucepan and bring them to a boil, simmering the syrup for about 5 minutes.

4. While the syrup simmers, drain the rind cubes, rinse them, and drain them again. Rinse the bowl the cubes were soaking in and return the cubes to the bowl. Pour the hot syrup over the cubes, return the bowl to its original resting place, cover it lightly, and let it sit for another 24 hours, more or less.

THE THIRD DAY

5. Sterilize eight pint canning jars according to the manufacturer's directions.

6. Pour the cubes and syrup into a large pan and bring the mixture to a boil. With a slotted spoon, pack the cubes lightly into the prepared jars, dividing the lemon slices and spices equally among the jars. Pour the syrup over the cubes, covering them but leaving about 1/2 inch headspace. Seal.

7. Process the jars in a boiling water bath for 10 minutes. Allow the pickles to sit for at least a week, and preferably several weeks, before serving.

Quick Carrot Pickles

No canning or even long waiting time is needed for these tasty and tangy little carrot sticks. MAKES ABOUT 2 CUPS

2¹/2 cups water

1 teaspoon kosher salt or coarse sea salt

¹/2 pound carrots cut into sticks, or whole baby carrots

¹/2 cup rice vinegar

3 tablespoons sugar

1 teaspoon dried dill (optional)

¹/2 teaspoon yellow mustard seeds

4 to 6 black peppercorns

2 whole cloves

1. Pour 2 cups of the water into a medium-size saucepan and add the salt. Bring to a boil over high heat. Add the carrots and cook for about 2 minutes, just shy of crisp-tender. Drain the carrots, rinse them in cold water, and drain again. Place the carrots in a heatproof nonreactive bowl.

2. Using the same saucepan, rinsed out, combine the remaining ingredients with the remaining ¹/2 cup water and bring to a boil. Pour the mixture over the carrots and let them cool to room temperature. Chill for at least several hours. The carrots will keep for several weeks at least. Drain before nibbling.

Green Tomato Chowchow

A mustard-based relish, chowchow comes in more varieties than the pickup trucks in the parking lot at a stock-car race. This is one of our favorites. MAKES ABOUT 5 PINTS

2 pounds green tomatoes (4 to 5 medium)

1¹/2 pounds cauliflower (1 to 1¹/2 heads)

1 pound sweet onions, or other mild onions

2 large bell peppers, preferably 1 red and 1 green, halved and seeded

2 fresh jalapeños

3 tablespoons pickling salt or 3 heaping tablespoons kosher salt

2¹/2 cups cider vinegar

1¹/2 cups sugar

2 tablespoons pickling spice

1 tablespoon celery seeds

1 tablespoon mustard seeds

2 teaspoons dry mustard

¹/2 teaspoon ground ginger

1. Chop all the vegetables in batches in a food processor. Chowchow is generally chopped fine, but stop short of pureeing it. You want some remaining chunkiness and fresh vegetable texture.

2. Place all the vegetables in a large bowl and sprinkle with the salt. Let the vegetables sit for at least 2 hours and up to 4 hours, stirring occasionally. They will release a good bit of liquid while they rest. Drain them but don't rinse.

3. Sterilize five pint canning jars according to the manufacturer's directions.

4. Bring the vinegar, sugar, and spices to a boil in a large pan or stockpot. Reduce the heat and simmer for 10 minutes. Add the vegetables and continue simmering for another 10 minutes. Bring the mixture to a rolling boil and boil for 2 to 3 minutes. Spoon the hot chowchow into the prepared jars, leaving 1/2 inch headspace. Seal.

5. Process the jars in a boiling water bath for 10 minutes. Let the chowchow sit for at least a week, and preferably several weeks, to develop its flavor before serving.

SERVING SUGGESTION For our tastes, nothing is better with barbecued meat inside a sandwich than chowchow, which cuts and complements the richness of almost any smoked food.

Squash Relish

Another fine idea from Cajun country, this sweet-sour relish is as zippy as a Justin Wilson quip. MAKES ABOUT 4 PINTS

12 cups (3 quarts) water
2/3 cup pickling salt or heaping 2/3 cup kosher salt
8 cups chopped yellow squash
3 cups sugar
2 cups white vinegar
2 1/2 tablespoons celery seeds
2 1/2 tablespoons mustard seeds
2 cups chopped onions
2 cups chopped bell peppers, preferably 1 red and 1 green
6 scallions, sliced

1. Sterilize four pint canning jars according to the manufacturer's directions.

2. Stir together the water and salt in a large bowl until the salt has dissolved. Add the squash to the brine and soak it for 1 hour. Rinse the squash, drain it, and rinse and drain it again.

3. In a stockpot, bring the sugar, vinegar, celery seeds, and mustard seeds to a boil. Stir in the squash and other vegetables and bring the mixture back to a boil.

4. Pack the mixture into the prepared jars, leaving 1/2 inch headspace, and seal.

5. Process the jars in a boiling water bath for 10 minutes. The relish is best after it sits for at least 2 weeks.

Corn and Watermelon Pickle-lilli

Cambridge, Massachusetts, chef Chris Schlesinger, and food writer John Willoughby, both big fans of real barbecue, came up with the model for this unusual relish for their terrific book, *The Thrill of the Grill* (1990, William Morrow). We've tinkered a bit with the original version to tailor it to smoked food. The texture is best when you chop the pickles and vegetables not much larger than the corn kernels.

MAKES ABOUT 2 CUPS

2 medium ears of corn, smoked, roasted, or boiled

1 cup Wonderful Watermelon Pickles (page 435) or store-bought watermelon pickles, chopped fine

1/2 medium red onion, chopped

1/2 medium red bell pepper, chopped

1/2 cup cider vinegar

1/4 cup packed brown sugar

3/4 teaspoon chili powder

1/2 teaspoon ground cumin

1 tablespoon minced fresh cilantro

1. Slice the kernels from the ears of corn. In a medium-size bowl, combine the corn and watermelon pickles.

2. Place the remaining ingredients, except the cilantro, in a small saucepan and bring the mixture to a boil. Boil for 1 minute and then pour the mixture over the corn and watermelon pickles. Refrigerate the relish for at least 1 hour. Stir in the cilantro just before serving.

SERVING SUGGESTION When you've got smoked turkey leftovers, make a sandwich on toasted sourdough with sharp cheddar cheese and this relish.

FUSION FOOD

Piccalilli refers to any one of many highly seasoned relishes. Chowchows are similar, but usually have mustard among their ingredients. The concoctions ultimately go back to India in origin. British colonists there brought the basic ideas back home to England, and they then sailed across the Atlantic to American shores before the War of Independence.

Canning requires only a few pieces of equipment, none terribly expensive. The essentials are a big lidded canning pan or a large stockpot, and canning tongs for gripping jars going in and coming out of steaming water. A wide-mouthed canning funnel is also useful but not a necessity. Use the size jars suggested in recipes, since changes can affect a product's processing time. Let the processed jars cool undisturbed for 12 hours. Check the seals and refrigerate any jars that have not sealed. Store in a cool, dry place.

Bourbon Peaches

Bourbon adds a smoky sweetness to many good foods, especially tender peaches fresh from the tree. Serve them whole alongside any plate of 'Q.' SERVES 4 TO 6

2 pounds peeled small to medium peaches, ripe yet still firm

2 cups sugar

2 cups water

1/2 cup bourbon, plus an optional additional 2 tablespoons

1 cinnamon stick

8 to 10 peppercorns

1. Combine the peaches, sugar, water, ½ cup bourbon, cinnamon stick, and peppercorns in a heavy saucepan. Bring the mixture to a rolling boil over high heat. Boil until the peaches can be pierced easily with a fork, but before they soften, about 5 minutes.

2. Remove the pan from the heat and let it cool to room temperature. Refrigerate the peaches in the syrup for at least 24 hours. Weight the peaches with a saucer, if necessary, to keep them submerged. Taste the peach syrup and, if desired, add the optional 2 tablespoons bourbon. Serve chilled or at room temperature. The peaches keep well, refrigerated, for up to a week, and they soften in texture.

DOWN-HOME DESSERTS

BARBECUE DEMANDS DESSERT, EVEN IF IT'S NO MORE THAN A COUPLE OF PACKAGED PEANUT PATTIES OR A FRIED PIE PICKED UP ON THE WAY OUT OF A BAR-B-Q JOINT. SWEET FOLLOWS SMOKE AS NATURALLY AS AMOROUS EYES TRACK AFTER TIGHT JEANS.

THE BEST DESSERTS FOR A BARBECUE PIG-OUT ARE THE OLD AMERICAN FAVORITES. THESE ARE UPDATED RECIPES, DEVELOPED SPECIFICALLY TO PROVIDE A PERFECT FINISH FOR A SMOKY MEAL.

Prodigal Pecan Pie

Nothing finishes a barbecue meal better than a sinfully rich pecan pie. This recipe is heavily influenced by John Thorne, author of many notable cookbooks and food articles, who came up with the method for making the filling so lusciously dense.

SERVES 6 TO 8

1 cup packed dark brown sugar

2/3 cup cane syrup, preferably, or 1/3 cup light corn syrup and 1/3 cup molasses

4 tablespoons unsalted butter

3 tablespoons dark rum

1/2 teaspoon pure vanilla extract

1/2 teaspoon table salt

4 large eggs

2 tablespoons half-and-half

2 generous cups pecan pieces

Unbaked 9-inch pie crust

Pecan halves

1. Preheat the oven to 350°F.

2. In a large, heavy saucepan, combine the brown sugar, syrup, butter, rum, vanilla, and salt. Heat to the boiling point, stirring frequently. Boil for 1 minute, stirring constantly. Remove the pan from the heat and let the mixture cool.

3. In a bowl, beat the eggs with the half-and-half until light and frothy. Beat the egg mixture into the cooled syrup until well incorporated. Stir in the pecans. Pour the filling into the pie crust. Top with a layer of pecan halves.

4. Bake until a toothpick inserted into the center comes out clean, 45 to 50 minutes. Serve warm or at room temperature.

PORK AND PIE

De Valls Bluff, Arkansas, used to be the finest food stop on Interstate 40 between Little Rock and Memphis, and it's still pretty good. Until recently, you could start with a pork sandwich at Craig's Bar-B-Q and then wander across the street to a simple building with a hand-painted "Pie Shop" sign. In an annex to her home, Mary Thomas made some of the best pies in the South, including a pecan delight that she called a Karo Nut Pie. Mary retired in 1999, but Craig's continues to smoke marvelous meat.

In 1992, when we were traveling across the country researching the original edition of this book, the pie-eating contest was one of the most memorable events at the Owensboro, Kentucky, International Bar-B-Q Festival. That year, 13-year-old Roger Morris took home the $100 prize by holding his breath and scarfing a banana-cream pie in enormous mouthfuls. Still hungry, Roger entered the mutton-eating contest a few minutes later, trying to down an entire barbecue sandwich in one bite.

Run for the Roses Pie

Traditionally served to celebrate the Kentucky Derby, this pie provides a triple-crown finish to any barbecue. SERVES 6 TO 8

1 cup packed brown sugar

2/3 cup cane syrup, preferably, *or* 1/3 cup light corn syrup and 1/3 cup molasses

3 tablespoons unsalted butter

3 tablespoons Kentucky bourbon

1/2 teaspoon pure vanilla extract

1/2 teaspoon table salt

4 large eggs

2 tablespoons half-and-half

2 cups walnut pieces

1/3 cup chocolate chips

Unbaked 9-inch pie crust

1. Preheat the oven to 350°F.

2. In a large, heavy saucepan, combine the brown sugar, syrup, butter, bourbon, vanilla, and salt. Heat to the boiling point, stirring frequently. Boil for 1 minute, stirring constantly.

Remove the pan from the heat and let the mixture cool.

3. In a bowl, beat the eggs with the half-and-half until they are light and frothy. Beat the egg mixture into the cooled syrup until well incorporated. Stir in the walnuts and the chocolate chips. Pour the filling into the pie crust.

4. Bake until a toothpick inserted into the center comes out clean, 45 to 50 minutes. Serve warm or at room temperature.

SERVING SUGGESTION On Derby Day serve Almost Owensboro Mutton (page 158) on sandwiches and a big pot of Kentucky Burgoo (page 393). Wash them down with Derby Day Mint Juleps (page 473) and present this pie for the grand finale.

Peanutty Pie

Some peanut pies are similar in consistency to a pecan pie. We prefer this creamy, cool style with barbecue. SERVES 6 TO 8

CRUST

1¹/4 cups graham cracker crumbs (about 16 crackers)

2 tablespoons granulated sugar

5 tablespoons unsalted butter, melted

1 cup whipping cream

8-ounce package cream cheese, softened

1¹/4 cups creamy peanut butter (don't use a natural or freshly ground type)

1 tablespoon pure vanilla extract

1 cup confectioners' sugar

¹/3 cup chopped peanuts, preferably honey-roasted

Chocolate sauce (optional)

1. Preheat the oven to 350°F.

2. In a bowl, stir together the graham cracker crumbs and granulated sugar. Pour in the butter and stir to combine.

3. Pat the mixture into the bottom and sides of a 9-inch pie pan. Bake for 10 minutes, until lightly set. Put the crust aside to cool.

4. Whip the cream in a bowl until stiff. In another bowl, beat together the cream cheese, peanut butter, vanilla, and confectioners' sugar. Fold in the whipped cream and blend well. Spoon the filling into the graham cracker crust and sprinkle the peanuts over the pie. Refrigerate, covered, for at least 2 hours, or overnight.

5. To gild the lily, serve with a spoonful of your favorite chocolate sauce. The pie keeps well for several days.

DO WE HAVE TO EAT AGAIN?

Still largely reliable, the 1988 *Real Barbecue* by Greg Johnson and Vince Staten (Harper & Row) is a first-rate guide to 100 of the top barbecue joints in the country. The authors logged 40,000 miles researching the book and estimated that they ate 200 pounds of barbecue and consumed some 629,200 calories.

BARBECUE NETWORKING

An active and growing organization, the National Barbecue Association (nbbqa.com) brings together restaurateurs, caterers, equipment manufacturers, sauce makers, and backyard cooks. For a $50 individual enthusiast membership or a $175 business membership, you receive the monthly newsletter, *National Barbecue News*, and an invitation to an annual conference and trade show.

Wild Huckleberry Pie with Coconut Crumble

You aren't likely to find huckleberries in a grocery store, but they grow wild in many parts of the country and occasionally show up in farmers' markets during summer months. For a reasonable alternative in appearance and taste, substitute blueberries and reduce the amount of sugar. SERVES 6 TO 8

4 cups huckleberries

2/3 to 3/4 cup sugar for the filling, plus an additional 1/3 cup for the topping

3 tablespoons instant tapioca

Juice of 1 lemon

Pinch of nutmeg

Unbaked 9-inch pie crust

1/3 cup all-purpose flour

3 tablespoons unsalted butter, softened

1/3 cup shredded unsweetened coconut

1. Preheat the oven to 425°F.

2. In a large bowl, stir together the huckleberries and enough sugar to make the berries taste sweet with a tart edge. Add the tapioca, lemon juice, and nutmeg. Spoon the fruit into the pie shell.

3. Bake the pie for 15 minutes, then reduce the heat to 375°F and continue baking for an additional 18 to 20 minutes.

4. While the pie bakes, mix the flour, butter, coconut, and remaining 1/3 cup sugar in a small bowl. Remove the pie from the oven and sprinkle the coconut mixture evenly over the top.

5. Return the pie to the oven for 25 to 30 more minutes, covering the crust with aluminum foil if it begins to get overly dark. When done, the topping should be crisp and golden brown. Serve warm.

Key Lime Pie

When someone serves you a "Key lime pie" these days, what you're actually getting is likely a dishonest version. It can be a great pie, but it's rarely made with the wonderfully distinctive Key limes anymore because Florida's commercial crop was wiped out in a 1926 hurricane. Until recently, most stores in the States carried only Persian limes, which are more similar to lemons. Look for the true Key limes, which are tiny sour gems, in well-stocked produce sections or in Caribbean, Latino, or Mexican markets. They're often labeled *limones*. SERVES 6 TO 8

CRUST

1¼ cups graham cracker crumbs (about 16 crackers)

2 tablespoons sugar

4 teaspoons minced lime zest

5 tablespoons unsalted butter, melted

1 pint heavy cream

14-ounce can sweetened condensed milk

6-ounce can frozen limeade concentrate, thawed

6 tablespoons freshly squeezed lime juice, preferably from Key limes

1/8 teaspoon pure vanilla extract

Lime slices, for garnish

1. Preheat the oven to 350°F.

2. In a bowl, stir together the graham cracker crumbs, sugar, and 2 teaspoons of the lime zest. Pour in the butter and stir to combine.

3. Pat the mixture into the bottom and sides of a 9-inch pie pan. Bake for 10 minutes, until lightly set. Put the crust aside to cool.

4. With an electric mixer, whip the cream until very stiff. Add the condensed milk, limeade concentrate, lime juice, vanilla, and remaining 2 teaspoons lime zest and continue beating until well combined. Pour the filling into the pie shell. Garnish with the lime slices. Refrigerate the pie for at least 4 hours, and preferably overnight. Serve chilled.

SERVING SUGGESTION The creamy pie is perfect after spicy smoked dishes such as Pit Pot Roast (page 144), Jerk Burgers (page 151), or Peppered Catfish (page 246).

VARIATION: MANGO-TOPPED KEY LIME PIE Skip the lime slice garnish. Neatly dice 1 ripe, plump mango, and toss it with about 2 teaspoons more lime juice and 1 teaspoon minced lime zest. After the finished pie has chilled for at least 3 hours, top with the mango mixture. Mound it just in the center of the pie so that the pale green filling can still show in a large circle around it.

Lemon Pudding Ice Cream Pie

Tangy, fruity, icy, creamy, crunchy—every bite yields a new and scrumptious taste sensation. SERVES 6 TO 8

LEMON PUDDING

3/4 cup sugar

2 tablespoons cornstarch

1/8 teaspoon table salt

3/4 cup water

5 large egg yolks, lightly beaten

6 tablespoons freshly squeezed lemon juice

Zest of 1 lemon

2 tablespoons unsalted butter

CRUST

1 cup graham cracker crumbs (about 14 crackers)

1/3 cup pecan pieces

2 tablespoons sugar

Zest of 2 lemons

5 tablespoons unsalted butter, melted

4 cups vanilla ice cream, softened

2 tablespoons pecan pieces (optional), for garnish

1. To prepare the pudding, mix the sugar, cornstarch, and salt in a heavy saucepan. Pour in the water, stirring to combine. Warm the mixture over medium-low heat, stirring constantly until hot but short of boiling. Place the egg yolks, lemon juice, and zest in a small bowl and gradually add about 1/2 cup of the hot mixture to the yolks. Stir the egg mixture back into the saucepan. Cook slowly and stir constantly, gradually bringing the pudding just to a boil over 7 to 10 minutes. Remove the pudding from the heat and whisk in the butter. The pudding should be somewhat thick but will thicken further while it cools. Refrigerate the pudding for at least 1 hour.

2. Preheat the oven to 350°F.

3. To prepare the crust, combine the graham cracker crumbs, pecans, sugar, and lemon zest in a food processor and process until crumbly. Pour in the butter and process just to combine.

4. Pat the mixture into the bottom and sides of a 9-inch pie pan. Bake for 10 minutes, until lightly set. Put the crust aside to cool.

5. When both the pudding and pie shell are cool, assemble the pie. Pack about half of the ice cream into the pie shell. Top it with about half of the pudding. Place the pie in the freezer for 15 minutes. Remove from the freezer and spoon the remaining ice cream over the pudding, smoothing it. Decoratively swirl spoonfuls of the remaining pudding over the ice cream, leaving some ice cream exposed. Sprinkle pecans over the top if you wish.

6. Freeze the pie for 2 hours or longer. Let it sit at room temperature for 5 to 10 minutes before serving.

Pan-Fried Pies

Fried pies are always popular with barbecue. Most versions are deep-fried, but we like them cooked this way, which is the leading style around Owensboro, Kentucky.

SERVES 8

CRUST

2 cups all-purpose flour

1 teaspoon table salt

6 tablespoons lard or solid vegetable shortening, well chilled

6 tablespoons unsalted butter, well chilled

5 to 7 tablespoons ice water

1 1/2 cups dried peaches

1 1/2 cups water

1/2 cup peach jam

1/4 cup finely minced pecans

Butter for pan-frying

1. With a food processor, combine the flour and salt. Add the lard and butter and process until a crumbly meal forms. Pour in the water, a couple of tablespoons at a time, processing until the dough just barely holds together. Form the dough into a ball and wrap it in plastic. Refrigerate the dough for at least 30 minutes, and up to 2 days.

2. Combine the peaches and water in a heavy saucepan. Simmer the fruit over low heat until it is plump and soft and most of the water is absorbed, about 25 minutes. Add more water if needed.

3. Drain the peaches and chop them fine. Transfer the peaches to a small bowl. Stir in the jam and the pecans and reserve the mixture.

4. On a floured pastry board or counter, roll out the dough 1/8 inch to 1/4 inch thick. Cut the dough into rounds with a 3-inch biscuit cutter.

5. Divide the peach filling among the dough rounds. Moisten the dough's edges with water and fold the pies into half-moons. Crimp the edges with a fork.

6. Just before serving, melt enough butter in a heavy skillet over medium heat to come up about one-third of the way on the pies. Pan-fry the pies until lightly browned and cooked through on both sides, 8 to 10 minutes. Serve hot.

VARIATION: DEEP-FRIED PIES These are crustier, and that's a joy to many people. Deep-fry the little pockets of fruit in 350°F vegetable shortening or oil until golden.

S'more Quesadillas

Any chocolate fan will love this easy, homey take on s'mores, the classic campfire treat. If we're barbecuing with our pit, we warm these on the top of the firebox, but you can also cook them on a grill or indoors on a griddle or in a skillet. SERVES 8

4 thin flour tortillas

Four 1.55-ounce milk chocolate candy bars, such as Hershey bars

1 cup mini marshmallows

1 cup mini graham crackers (such as those shaped like little teddy bears) or regular graham crackers broken into bite-size bits

1. If the tortillas are too stiff to fold in half easily, warm them for a few seconds on a griddle or in a skillet until they are pliable. Cover half of each tortilla with an equal portion of chocolate, marshmallows, and graham crackers. Fold the empty portion of the tortillas over the filled portion, and secure with a toothpick.

2. Warm on a medium-hot griddle or skillet, and cook 2 to 3 minutes per side, until the chocolate and marshmallows are melted and gooey, and the tortillas are crisp and golden in spots. Serve immediately, cutting each into four wedges. Offer plenty of napkins.

Fruit Pizza

This one is bound to keep your guests smiling to the end. SERVES 8

CRUST

3/4 cup unsalted butter, softened

1/2 cup confectioners' sugar

1 1/4 cups all-purpose flour

8-ounce package cream cheese, softened

4 ounces almond paste

1/4 cup granulated sugar

1 large egg

1 teaspoon pure vanilla extract

1/2 teaspoon pure almond extract

3 to 3 1/2 cups colorful mixed fruit (strawberry halves, blueberries, raspberries, kiwi slices, pineapple chunks, apricot halves, orange or tangerine sections with their membranes removed)

1 cup currant or apricot jelly

1 tablespoon freshly squeezed lemon juice

1 tablespoon brandy or triple sec

1. Preheat the oven to 350°F. Grease a 12-inch pizza pan.

2. In a food processor or an electric mixer, combine the butter and confectioners' sugar. Add the flour and mix well. Flatten out the soft dough with your hands and press it into the prepared pan, forming a thin layer.

3. Bake the crust until lightly browned and firm, 16 to 18 minutes.

4. While the crust bakes, beat together the cream cheese, almond paste, granulated sugar, egg, vanilla, and almond extract with an electric mixer. Pour the mixture over the crust, smoothing it with a spatula.

5. Bake the pizza until the topping is lightly set, about 10 minutes. Cool the pizza.

6. An hour or two before serving, arrange the fruit decoratively over the pizza. In a small, heavy saucepan, heat together the jelly, lemon juice, and brandy until the jelly melts. Brush the jelly mixture over the fruit.

7. Refrigerate the pizza for 1 to 2 hours. Serve the chilled pizza cut into wedges.

rhubarb offers a tangy contrast to a smoked meal

Rhubarb Crunch

Rhubarb offers a tangy contrast to a smoked meal. Food writer Marilynn Marter inspired this homey preparation. SERVES 6

¾ cup all-purpose flour
¾ cup rolled oats
½ cup packed brown sugar
6 tablespoons unsalted butter, melted
2 teaspoons ground anise
1 teaspoon ground cinnamon
3 cups chopped rhubarb, fresh or frozen
½ cup granulated sugar
1 tablespoon cornstarch
½ cup water
½ teaspoon pure vanilla extract

1. Preheat the oven to 350°F. Grease an 8-inch square pan.

2. In a small bowl, mix the flour, oats, brown sugar, butter, anise, and cinnamon. Press half of the mixture into the pan, reserving the rest. Place the rhubarb over the crumb mixture.

3. In a small saucepan, stir together the granulated sugar and cornstarch. Add the water slowly, stirring to avoid lumps. Warm the sauce over medium heat, cooking until it is clear and lightly thickened, 3 to 5 minutes. Remove the sauce from the heat and stir in the vanilla. Pour the sauce over the rhubarb. Top the sauce with the remaining crumb mixture.

4. Bake until the rhubarb appears bubbly and the topping crunchy, about 55 minutes. Serve warm or at room temperature.

Texas Peach Cobbler

Texans like their peach cobblers with an abundance of juicy fruit and a biscuit-like batter topping that's crunchy on the surface and doughy inside. SERVES 8 TO 10

FILLING

12 to 14 ripe medium peaches (about 3 1/2 pounds), peeled, pitted, and sliced

1/4 cup sugar

1 tablespoon freshly squeezed lemon juice

2 teaspoons ground cinnamon

3/4 teaspoon ground ginger

3/4 teaspoon pure vanilla extract

BATTER

1/4 cup unsalted butter

1 1/4 cups all-purpose flour

3/4 cup sugar

2 teaspoons baking powder

1 cup milk

Peach Melba Ice Cream (page 466) or softly whipped cream (optional)

1. Preheat the oven to 350°F.

2. In a bowl, mix all the filling ingredients. Set the fruit aside to draw out the juices while preparing the batter. Cobbler filling should be a bit juicier than most pies.

3. For the batter, melt the butter in a 9 x 13-inch baking dish, either in the oven or on the stove.

4. In another bowl, stir together the flour, sugar, and baking powder and add the milk. Mix until lightly blended. Spoon the mixture evenly over the melted butter. Don't stir it, which eliminates the development of crunchy edges. Pour the peach filling evenly over the batter.

5. Bake for 45 minutes. As the cobbler cooks, the batter oozes up and around the fruit, crowning the cobbler with a moist golden brown crust. Serve warm. If you're a certified hedonist, top it with ice cream or whipped cream.

SERVING SUGGESTION Stage a Texas ranch-style barbecue. Put out plentiful quantities of Little Devils (page 344) in bowls and pass Chicken from Hell (page 359). The centerpiece has to be Braggin' Rights Brisket (page 111), supplemented, if you like, by Hill Country Links (page 93). Round out the meal with Cowpoke Pintos (page 397), Creamy Coleslaw (page 390), a tray of pickled jalapeños and onion slices, and this juicy cobbler. Offer beer by the keg and Turquoise Margaritas (page 477) by the pitcher.

VARIATION: BLACKBERRY COBBLER Make a blackberry cobbler by substituting berries for the peaches and eliminating the ginger. For ourselves, we would also add 1/4 teaspoon nutmeg.

Chipotle Cherry Cobbler

For a special Fourth of July dinner, add some fireworks to this early summer delight. We developed it as part of a summer article for *New Mexico Magazine*. SERVES 8

FILLING

1³/4 pounds pitted fresh sweet cherries or three 10-ounce packages frozen sweet cherries, with juice

1¹/2 to 2 teaspoons ground dried chipotle chile

1¹/2 teaspoons freshly squeezed lemon juice

Scant ¹/4 teaspoon pure almond extract

³/4 cup sugar

2 teaspoons cornstarch

TOPPING

³/4 cup all-purpose flour

³/4 cup sugar

¹/4 cup plus 2 tablespoons almond flour or meal

³/4 teaspoon baking powder (reduce to ¹/2 teaspoon at altitudes over 6,000 feet)

Pinch of salt

10 tablespoons unsalted butter, chilled and cut into little bits

2 large eggs

³/4 teaspoon pure vanilla extract

¹/4 teaspoon pure almond extract

2 tablespoons slivered almonds

1. Preheat the oven to 375°F. Grease a shallow medium-size baking dish.

2. Mix the filling ingredients in a large bowl and set aside.

3. Prepare the topping in a food processor, first pulsing together the flour, sugar, almond flour, baking powder, and salt. Scatter the butter over the dry ingredients and pulse quickly several times to combine. Add the eggs and both extracts and pulse again, just to combine.

4. Give the filling another stir and pour it into the prepared dish. Scatter the topping over the filling, leaving it a bit uneven and with a few spots uncovered. Top with the almonds.

5. Bake until the topping is golden brown and the fruit filling bubbly, 35 to 45 minutes. Serve warm.

CUTTING DOWN ON THE CALORIES

When you're in the mood for a lighter fare to finish a barbecue feed, toss together a platter of juicy seasonal fruit, or turn directly to the last recipe in this chapter, The Best Cure for a Southern Summer (page 469). Consider also a smoked fruit from the Garden of Eatin' chapter, or a sweet beverage from our Cool and Cheery Drinks.

Long-on-Strawberries Shortcake

While summer strawberries are always good over shortcake, the treat is twice as good with fruit in the cake, too. SERVES 8 TO 10

CAKE

2 cups cake flour, sifted

1 tablespoon baking powder

1/2 teaspoon table salt

1 tablespoon poppy seeds

1 1/2 cups granulated sugar

3/4 cup unsalted butter, softened

3 large eggs, separated

3/4 cup water

1/4 cup crushed fresh ripe strawberries

1 teaspoon pure almond extract

TOPPING

1 cup whipping cream

About 1/3 cup confectioners' sugar

2 pints fresh ripe strawberries, sliced

1. Preheat the oven to 350°F. Grease and flour two 9-inch round cake pans. Cut waxed paper or parchment circles to fit the pans, place in the pans, and grease and flour them again.

2. To make the cake, stir together the flour, baking powder, and salt in a bowl. Stir in the poppy seeds.

3. With an electric mixer, cream together the sugar and butter. Add the egg yolks, beating well after each addition. Combine the water with the crushed strawberries and almond extract. Add the fruit and liquid to the butter mixture in thirds, alternating with the dry ingredients. Continue beating the batter until all ingredients are well incorporated.

4. With the mixer and clean beaters and bowl, beat the egg whites until stiff. Fold them into the batter.

5. Pour the batter into the prepared pans and bake until a toothpick inserted in the center comes out clean, about 20 minutes. Cool the layers for about 5 minutes before removing them from the pans. Cool the layers on cake racks.

6. Prepare the fruit topping while the cake cools. Whip the cream and 1 tablespoon of the confectioners' sugar. Refrigerate until ready to use. Combine the sliced strawberries with the remaining confectioners' sugar, a tablespoon or two at a time, to the desired sweetness.

7. To assemble the cake, transfer one layer to a serving plate. Top with half of the berries and spread half of the whipped cream over them. Repeat with the remaining ingredients. Serve immediately.

PIN A CONGRESSIONAL MEDAL OF HONOR ON THAT PIG

Short Sugar's Pit Bar-B-Q in Reidsville, North Carolina, won a congressional barbecue contest in 1982. Representatives from North and South Carolina got into a spat about which state had the best 'Q' and settled it with a barbecue duel. A dozen of the top joints from each state sent samples to Washington, and a jury of congressional peers awarded top honors to Short Sugar's—for the pork as well as the name.

Cranberry-Ginger Crumble

Here's a great dish to go with a fall barbecue, during the season when you can easily find garnet cranberries to pair with snappy ginger. For a nice enhancement, top the crumble with softly whipped cream flavored with a big pinch of ground ginger.

SERVES 8

Two 12-ounce bags cranberries, fresh or frozen

1 cup granulated sugar

1/4 cup ground ginger

16 thin gingersnap cookies

3/4 cup old-fashioned oats

1/3 cup packed brown sugar

1/2 cup unsalted butter, chilled

1/4 teaspoon table salt

1. Preheat the oven to 350°F. Butter an 8-inch square baking dish. Place the cranberries in the dish. Mix the sugar and ginger, and pour evenly over the cranberries.

2. Break each of the gingersnaps into several pieces and transfer them to a food processor. Pulse several times, until you have coarse crumbs, then add the oats, brown sugar, butter, and salt, and process just until coarse and crumbly.

3. Spoon the gingersnap topping evenly over the cranberries, packing it down lightly. Bake until the topping is crunchy and the cranberry mixture thick, 45 to 50 minutes. Serve warm.

Peanut Butter Cake

A recipe from Southern food authority Nathalie Dupree inspired our version of this cake-eater's cake. SERVES 12

CAKE

2 cups cake flour

1¼ teaspoons baking soda

1 teaspoon baking powder

½ teaspoon table salt

¾ cup granulated sugar

½ cup packed brown sugar

⅓ cup creamy peanut butter (don't use a natural or freshly ground type)

⅓ cup unsalted butter, softened

1¼ cups buttermilk

2 large eggs, separated

1 teaspoon pure vanilla extract

FROSTING

¼ cup unsalted butter

1 cup granulated sugar

½ cup packed brown sugar

½ cup evaporated milk

1 cup creamy peanut butter (don't use a natural or freshly ground type)

1. Preheat the oven to 350°F. Grease and flour two 9-inch round cake pans. Cut waxed paper or parchment circles to fit the pans, place them in the pans, and grease again.

2. To make the cake, in a medium-size bowl, sift together the flour, baking soda, baking powder, and salt, and set the mixture aside.

3. With an electric mixer, cream together the sugars, peanut butter, and butter. Add the sifted dry ingredients in batches, alternating with the buttermilk, egg yolks, and vanilla.

4. With the mixer and clean beaters and bowl, beat the egg whites until very foamy. Fold the whites into the batter by hand.

5. Pour the batter into the prepared pans. Bake until a toothpick inserted in the center comes out clean, 30 to 35 minutes. Cool the layers for about 5 minutes before removing them from the pans. Cool the layers on cake racks.

6. Prepare the frosting after the cake is cool, since the frosting thickens quickly. In a heavy saucepan, melt the butter over medium heat. Add both sugars and the evaporated milk and bring to a boil over high heat. Boil for 5 minutes. Remove from the heat and immediately stir in the peanut butter, mixing well.

7. To assemble the cake, place one layer of the cake on a decorative serving platter. Spread just the top of the layer with half of the frosting. Add the second cake layer and again frost just the top. The cake is best the day it's made.

South Georgia Pound Cake

Like barbecue, pound cake made an early American appearance in Colonial Virginia. It spread from that area to other states, which often developed treasured local variations. This sour cream rendition was influenced by an heirloom Georgia recipe.

SERVES 8 TO 10

3 cups all-purpose flour

1/4 teaspoon table salt

1 pound unsalted butter, softened

2 cups sugar

2/3 cup sour cream

1 tablespoon pure vanilla extract

1/2 teaspoon pure lemon extract

5 large eggs

1. Preheat the oven to 350°F. Grease and flour a 10-inch Bundt pan or tube pan.

2. Sift together the flour and salt.

3. With an electric mixer, cream together the butter and sugar. When well blended, mix in the sour cream and the vanilla and lemon extracts. Beat in the eggs one at a time, alternating them with the flour mixture.

4. Spoon the batter into the prepared pan. Bake until the cake is golden and a toothpick inserted in the center comes out clean, 60 to 65 minutes. Let the cake sit for 10 minutes, then invert onto a cake rack to finish cooling. Serve warm or at room temperature.

SERVING SUGGESTION In honor of the cake's origin, top it with fresh peaches or our Bourbon Peaches (page 439).

HEAVENLY PIE

Lindsey's in North Little Rock, Arkansas, is known for both its barbecue and its light, flavorful fried fruit pies. Bishop D. L. Lindsey of Church of God in Christ opened the first of the two restaurants in 1956, and both have been in his family ever since. You'd better like soda pop with your 'Q,' because there's no beer here.

The post-barbecue candy of choice in many Southern states is actually a kind of cake that is called a pie—a Moon Pie. Made solely by the Chattanooga Bakery in Chattanooga, Tennessee, it's a gooey fistful of marshmallow sandwiched between graham cracker–style cookies coated in chocolate or other flavorings. They likely took their name from an early salesman's comment about them being "as big as the moon." If you aren't lucky enough to live in Tennessee, Arkansas, Mississippi, or another Moon Pie stronghold, you can order them online by the case at moonpie.com.

Becky's Pineapple Cake

The Glenmar Plantation Bed & Breakfast near Springfield, Kentucky, once served us a cake similar to this for afternoon snacking. It's as simple as it is scrumptious.

SERVES 8

CAKE

2 cups all-purpose flour

2 cups granulated sugar

2 large eggs

2 teaspoons baking soda

20-ounce can crushed pineapple with juice or syrup

1 cup chopped pecans

1½ teaspoons pure vanilla extract

¼ teaspoon table salt

FROSTING

8-ounce package cream cheese, softened

½ cup unsalted butter, softened

2 cups confectioners' sugar

1½ teaspoons pure vanilla extract

1. Preheat the oven to 350°F. Grease a 9 x 13-inch baking pan.

2. In a large bowl, stir together all the cake ingredients. Pour the batter into the prepared pan. Bake until a toothpick inserted in the center comes out clean, about 35 minutes.

3. With an electric mixer, beat together the cream cheese and butter. Mix in the confectioners' sugar and vanilla and beat until smooth. Spread the cake with the frosting. The cake can be frosted warm or cool. It keeps well for 2 days, refrigerated. Bring to room temperature before serving.

Black Walnut Cake

From the Carolinas to Kansas City, black walnuts are prized for their rich pungency. They're worth seeking out, but if you can't find them, substitute the more common English variety. The inspiration for this cake comes from an old recipe included in Beth Tartan's classic *North Carolina and Old Salem Cookery* (1955, University of North Carolina Press). SERVES 12

CAKE

3 cups all-purpose flour

1½ teaspoons ground ginger

1 teaspoon baking soda

½ teaspoon ground cinnamon

½ teaspoon table salt

1 cup cane syrup, preferably, *or* ½ cup molasses and ½ cup light corn syrup

1 cup unsalted butter, softened

3 large eggs

1 cup buttermilk

1 teaspoon pure vanilla extract

FROSTING

1 cup granulated sugar

1 cup packed brown sugar

½ cup buttermilk

¼ cup unsalted butter

1 cup black walnut pieces

¾ cup dried currants or chopped raisins

1½ teaspoons pure vanilla extract

1. Preheat the oven to 350°F. Grease and flour two 9-inch round cake pans. Cut waxed paper or parchment into circles to fit the pans, place in the pans, and grease again.

2. In a medium-size bowl, sift together the flour, ginger, baking soda, cinnamon, and salt.

3. With an electric mixer, cream together the syrup and butter. Beat in the eggs. Add the sifted dry ingredients in batches, alternating with the buttermilk and vanilla, and continue beating until well mixed.

4. Pour the batter into the prepared pans. Bake the cakes until a toothpick inserted in the center comes out clean, 25 to 30 minutes. Cool the layers for about 5 minutes before removing them from the pans. Cool the layers on cake racks.

5. To prepare the frosting, combine the sugars, buttermilk, and butter in a heavy saucepan. Bring the mixture to a boil and boil for several minutes, until thickened. Remove from the heat and mix in the walnuts, currants, and vanilla.

6. To assemble the cake, place one layer of the cake on a decorative serving platter. Spread just the top of the layer with half of the frosting. Add the second cake layer and again frost just the top. The cake is best served the day it's made, but if tightly covered, leftovers will remain moist for another day.

SERVING SUGGESTION Because of the cake's density and richness, it's best after a lighter barbecue meal, perhaps Kingly Salmon (page 232) or Mint Trout (page 244).

Candy Bar Cheesecake

The only dessert offered in many Bar-B-Q joints is candy from a rack near the door. Here's a way to go that Mounds bar one better—in a classier dessert form.

SERVES 10 TO 12

CRUST

5 to 6 ounces chocolate wafer cookies

1 cup shredded sweetened coconut

2 tablespoons sugar

1/4 cup unsalted butter, melted

FILLING

1 pound cream cheese, softened

3/4 cup canned cream of coconut

1/2 cup shredded sweetened coconut

3 large eggs, lightly beaten

1/2 teaspoon pure vanilla extract

TOPPING

8 ounces bittersweet or dark sweet chocolate

2 tablespoons unsalted butter

2 tablespoons canned cream of coconut

1. Preheat the oven to 350°F.

2. In a food processor, combine the cookies, coconut, and sugar, and process until crumbly. Pour in the butter and process just to combine.

3. Pat the mixture into the bottom of a 9-inch springform pan. Bake the crust for 10 minutes, until lightly set. Put the crust aside to cool.

4. Reduce the oven temperature to 300°F.

5. In a food processor or electric mixer, combine the cream cheese, cream of coconut, and coconut. By hand, stir in the eggs, one at a time until fully incorporated, and then add the vanilla. Pour the filling into the crust. Fill a baking pan or dish with water and place it on the lowest rack in the oven. Bake the cheesecake on the center rack until lightly set, about 1 hour. Let the cake sit at room temperature for about 15 minutes, then cover it and chill for at least 1 hour.

6. Remove the cheesecake from the refrigerator. In a small, heavy saucepan, melt together the topping ingredients. Remove the mixture from the heat and spread it gently over the top of the cheesecake. Return the cheesecake to the refrigerator for at least 3 more hours or overnight.

7. Before serving, allow the cheesecake to sit for 10 to 15 minutes at room temperature. Remove the springform sides from the pan. Slice the cheesecake with a warm knife, to cut through the chocolate topping most easily, and serve.

Bozo's is a legendary name in Tennessee barbecue, founded in 1923 by Thomas Jefferson "Bozo" Williams. Located in the small town of Mason, the restaurant features pork plates and sandwiches that are good enough to draw fans from Memphis, which has a hundred or so joints of its own and calls itself the "Pork Barbecue Capital of the World."

Sweet Potato Pudding

If you've ever had sweet potato pie, you won't be surprised that the spuds also make a superb pudding, topped here with a praline crunch. SERVES 6 TO 8

PRALINE

1/2 cup chopped pecans

1/4 cup chopped crystallized ginger

1/4 cup packed brown sugar

2 tablespoons unsalted butter, softened

PUDDING

2 1/2 cups baked sweet potatoes (about 3 medium potatoes), flesh scooped from the skin

1/2 cup packed brown sugar

4 large eggs

1/3 cup milk

2 tablespoons unsalted butter, melted

2 tablespoons pure vanilla extract

1 tablespoon cane syrup or dark corn syrup

1 tablespoon light or dark rum

1/2 teaspoon table salt

1/2 teaspoon ground cinnamon

1/2 teaspoon ground ginger

1. Preheat the oven to 350°F. Grease a 1 1/2-quart baking dish.

2. In a small bowl, combine the pecans, ginger, brown sugar, and butter. Reserve the mixture.

3. With an electric mixer, beat together all the pudding ingredients until smooth and light. Pour the pudding into the baking dish.

4. Bake for 25 minutes. Sprinkle the reserved praline mixture over the pudding and bake until the pudding is set and slightly puffed, another 20 to 25 minutes. The top will sink as the pudding cools. Serve warm or at room temperature.

SERVING SUGGESTION Serve the pudding as the finale for a Thanksgiving feast featuring Worth-the-Wait Turkey (page 210) and all the trimmings.

'Nana Pudding

Certainly a kid-friendly dessert, this old favorite also appeals to any adult who hasn't had too much sophistication training. SERVES 6 TO 8

PUDDING

1 cup sugar

2 tablespoons cornstarch

Pinch of table salt

6 large egg yolks

2¹/₂ cups whole milk, heated

2 teaspoons pure vanilla extract

12-ounce box vanilla wafers

5 to 6 bananas

MERINGUE

6 large egg whites

¹/₈ teaspoon cream of tartar

Pinch of table salt

3 tablespoons sugar

1. To make the pudding, stir together the sugar, cornstarch, and salt in the top pan of a double boiler. Mix in the egg yolks and place the pan over its simmering water base. Pour in the warm milk gradually, stirring constantly. Continue to stir frequently as the pudding cooks. It will gradually thicken, usually in about 15 to 20 minutes, but don't rush it. The pudding is done when it coats a spoon and slides off slowly. Remove the pan from the heat and stir in the vanilla.

2. Preheat the oven to 350°F.

3. While the pudding cools, arrange a layer of vanilla wafers at the bottom of a shallow 1¹/₂-quart baking dish. Slice the bananas thin and layer half over the cookies. Spoon half of the pudding over the banana slices. Repeat with the remaining cookies, bananas, and pudding. Tuck more cookies around the sides of the dish as well. We normally use only about two-thirds of the box of cookies, but some people manage more.

4. To make the meringue topping, beat the egg whites with an electric mixer. When the egg whites begin to froth, add the cream of tartar and salt. Gradually beat in the sugar and continue beating until the whites form a stiff-peaked meringue.

5. Crown the assembled pudding with the meringue, heaping it high in the center. Bake until the meringue is firm and golden brown, 15 to 18 minutes.

6. Cool for 30 minutes before serving. Refrigerate the pudding if you plan to hold it longer than that. Leftovers can be kept for another day, although the bananas will darken somewhat.

Santa Fe Capirotada

Most versions of bread pudding come from the French New Orleans tradition, which involves a liberal use of eggs and cream. This version hails from farther west, in New Mexico, and it gets its richness from butter and cheese. A similar version is offered by the Santa Fe School of Cooking in some of its classes. SERVES 8

1/2 cup raisins

1/2 cup brandy

10 to 12 slices white bread, torn in small pieces and toasted

1/2 cup chopped pecans, toasted

1 cup shredded cheddar or Monterey Jack cheese (4 ounces)

4 tablespoons unsalted butter

1 tart apple, peeled, cored, and chopped

2 cups sugar

2 1/2 cups hot water

1 cup apple cider

2 teaspoons pure vanilla extract

1 teaspoon canela (Mexican cinnamon) or ground cinnamon

1/2 teaspoon ground nutmeg

Pinch of cloves

Whipped cream (optional), for garnish

1. Place the raisins in a small bowl and pour the brandy over them. Set aside to soften for at least 20 minutes.

2. Preheat the oven to 350°F. Butter a 9 x 13-inch baking dish. Arrange the bread in the baking dish. Top the bread with the pecans and the cheese, mixing both in lightly. Scatter the raisins over the cheese and add any brandy not absorbed by the fruit.

3. In a small skillet, warm 2 tablespoons of the butter. Add the apple and sauté until softened.

Spoon the apple over the raisins.

4. Pour the sugar into a large, heavy saucepan. Warm it over medium-high heat until the sugar melts and turns a deep golden brown, 8 to 10 minutes. Stir occasionally to assure even melting. Carefully pour the hot water into the melted sugar. Steam will rise as the water hits the sugar and the mixture will partially solidify. Continue cooking it until the sugar becomes liquid again, stirring occasionally. Add the cider, vanilla, spices, and remaining 2 tablespoons butter to the syrup.

5. Ladle the hot syrup over the bread. The syrup should be about equal in level to the bread itself. Push the bread into the syrup if any isn't already coated.

6. Bake the pudding until the syrup has been absorbed and the cheese has melted into the pudding, 20 to 25 minutes. Serve hot, topped with whipped cream if you wish.

SERVING SUGGESTION Serve the bread pudding following a barbecue of Southwestern Cabrito (page 175), or a simpler meal of Green Chile Chicken Soup (page 208) and salad.

VARIATION: COCONUT BREAD PUDDING WITH RUM Eliminate the cheddar, apples, cider, nutmeg, and cloves. Substitute rum for the brandy. Along with the pecans, sprinkle the bread with 1 cup unsweetened coconut shreds. Add a 14-ounce can coconut milk to the caramelized sugar after it becomes liquid again, as you would have added the cider. The syrup may look a little mottled, but don't worry. Add all 4 tablespoons of the butter at this point. Complete as above.

Booker's Bourbon Mint Ice Cream

This is a little like a creamy, frozen mint julep. We named it after the late Booker Noe, grandson of Jim Beam and Master Distiller for more than 40 years at the big family business in Clermont, Kentucky. SERVES 4 TO 6 (MAKES 1 QUART)

6 tablespoons bourbon

¼ cup minced fresh mint

1 pint half-and-half

1 cup heavy cream

¾ cup sugar

5 large egg yolks

1 tablespoon pure vanilla extract

1. In a small saucepan, warm the bourbon with the mint over medium heat. Remove the bourbon from the heat and allow it to steep for 15 minutes. Strain the bourbon into the top pan of a double boiler. Add the remaining ingredients and place the pan over simmering water. Warm the custard mixture, whisking until well blended. Continue heating, frequently stirring up from the bottom, until the mixture thickens. Expect the process to take about 15 minutes. Do not boil the custard. Remove the pan from the heat and strain the custard.

2. Transfer the custard to an ice cream maker and process according to the manufacturer's directions. Freeze it until serving time. The ice cream is best eaten within several days.

SERVING SUGGESTION Serve the ice cream over South Georgia Pound Cake (page 458) and garnish with fresh mint. Sip a small-batch premium bourbon, such as Booker's, after dessert.

WE CAN TOAST TO THAT

Booker Noe's company, Jim Beam, is the oldest continuing business in Kentucky, founded by farmer Jacob Beam shortly after he moved to the frontier territory in 1788. We don't know for sure, but it's likely that Jacob liked barbecue as much as his bourbon and that he preferred both to ice cream.

Peach Melba Ice Cream

At the height of the barbecue season, peaches and raspberries reach a peak of fragrance and succulence. At our home, many of the ripest go immediately to this delightful ice cream. MAKES 1 QUART

2 pounds ripe, juicy peaches, peeled and pitted

1 cup fresh raspberries, pressed through a sieve or food mill

1/2 cup sugar

2 teaspoons freshly squeezed lemon juice

3 large eggs

1 cup half-and-half

4 drops pure almond extract

2 drops pure vanilla extract

1. Cut half of the peaches into bite-size chunks and put them and all their juices in a large bowl. Place the remaining peaches in a food processor and puree them. Pour the puree over the peach chunks and stir together with the raspberries, 1 tablespoon of the sugar, and the lemon juice.

2. Whisk together the remaining sugar and the eggs in a heavy saucepan. Gradually whisk in the half-and-half and the extracts. Place over medium-low heat and warm until small bubbles form at the edge of the pan, stirring frequently. Don't let the mixture actually come to a boil. Pour the custard over the peach-raspberry mixture, stir, and chill for at least 1 hour and up to a day.

3. Transfer the custard mixture to an ice cream maker and process according to the manufacturer's directions. Freeze it until serving time. The ice cream is best eaten within several days.

Mojito Sorbet

The Cuban cocktail is soaring in popularity today as quickly as a new Bruce Springsteen song. The beverage is just as good, or maybe better, turned into a refreshing ice to serve after a spicy meal. MAKES 1 QUART

3 cups water

2 cups sugar

1 1/2 cups lightly packed fresh mint leaves

1 cup light rum

6 tablespoons freshly squeezed lime juice

3 to 4 dashes bitters (optional)

1. Warm the water, sugar, mint, and 3/4 cup of the rum in a saucepan over medium heat until bubbles form at the rim. Remove the rum mixture from the heat and allow it to steep for 15 minutes. Strain the rum mixture and stir in the

lime juice, remaining ¼ cup rum, and optional bitters.

2. Transfer the mixture to an ice cream maker and process according to the manufacturer's directions. Freeze it until serving time. (It freezes rather softly because of the rum.) The flavor is best within a day or two.

Ice-Sicles

These two-toned frozen pops cool down the young and the young at heart. Investing in an inexpensive set of frozen pop molds makes them a breeze to prepare.

MAKES 8 OR MORE FROZEN POPS

About 1¼ cups mango or mango-orange juice or nectar

½ pint strawberries

1 to 2 teaspoons sugar

1. Using half of the mango juice, pour an equal amount into each of 8 pop molds. Tap the molds on the counter to eliminate any air pockets. Cover with the little lids that come with most molds. Insert sticks into the openings in lids, unless the lids actually form their own handles. Freeze until lightly set, at least 30 minutes.

2. Puree the strawberries and sugar in a blender. Spoon the strawberry puree over the mango juice, dividing all of it among the molds. Tap the bottom of the molds, and return to the freezer again until lightly set, at least 30 minutes.

3. Top with the remaining mango juice, distributed equally among the pops. Tap the bottom of the mold, and freeze again until firmly set, at least 1 more hour. (The pops keep for up to 2 weeks before their flavor fades.)

4. To unmold, gently squeeze the bottom or sides of each mold with one hand while pulling on the stick with the other. If they don't come out easily, soak the molds for just a second or two in hot water, and try again. Serve immediately, with plenty of paper napkins.

VARIATION: WATERMELON ICE-SICLES Puree 1 cup chopped watermelon instead of strawberries, using the sugar if the sweetness needs a little lift.

BBQ tip You can make frozen pops out of any fruit juice that appeals to you, or use yogurt or softened ice cream. While pops can be made out of a single liquid, we think they're more fun with a mix of colors. Just remember to let the first color set up in the freezer before adding the next.

Brazen Rum-Raisin Sauce

If you don't want to make your own ice cream or other frozen dessert, whip up a batch of this to go over several meals' worth of store-bought vanilla or other compatible ice cream. It can also top pineapple spears, South Georgia Pound Cake (page 458), or even your breakfast pancakes. MAKES 2 CUPS

1/2 cup raisins
1/2 cup dark rum
3/4 cup water
1/4 cup light corn syrup
1/4 cup packed brown sugar
Pinch of ground allspice or nutmeg (optional)

Combine the raisins and rum in a medium-size saucepan and let them sit for 10 to 15 minutes. Stir in the remaining ingredients and bring to a boil over high heat. Reduce the heat to a simmer and cook until a thin sauce is formed, about 5 minutes. It will thicken as it cools. Use immediately, or chill for later use. The sauce keeps for up to a couple of weeks.

The Best Cure for a Southern Summer

As much as we love the previous desserts, we're not sure that any of them beat cold watermelons, so naturally sweet that they were once processed into sugar. Ice down a big melon and forget heat, humidity, and your air-conditioning bill.

SERVES 3 OR MORE

1 watermelon

1. Chill the melon in the refrigerator or iced down in a tub. Slice and serve.

2. Save the leftover watermelon rind to turn into Wonderful Watermelon Pickles (page 435).

COOL AND CHEERY DRINKS

IT CAN GET PRETTY DAMN HOT COOKING OUTSIDE. YOU'RE CONTENDING WITH THE SUN, THE WOOD OR CHARCOAL FIRE, THE SMOKE, AND MAYBE EVEN A LOT OF HOT AIR FROM SOME EXPERT HELPER LIKE YOUR SPOUSE. IF IT DOESN'T DRIVE YOU TO DRINK, YOU PROBABLY HAVEN'T MET ENOUGH GOOD TEMPTATIONS IN YOUR LIFE. TRY THESE.

Bloody Bud

Beer is the beverage of choice for most pitmasters, particularly light-bodied American brews, such as Budweiser. To keep up with the crowd at a barbecue cook-off, you start bending your elbow about the time you light your fire in the morning. If that sounds too early, or if your cranium is still complaining about the night before, drink your first beer like a Bloody Mary. It may not exactly cure a hangover, but it'll at least shock that sucker into submission. SERVES 2

12 ounces ice-cold beer

12 ounces tomato or V8 juice, chilled

1 tablespoon Worcestershire sauce

Several splashes of Tabasco or other hot pepper sauce

1/2 teaspoon celery salt

1/2 teaspoon barbecue dry rub, preferably a spicy one such as Southwest Heat (page 32)

Pour half of the beer, tomato juice, Worcestershire sauce, and Tabasco into each of two tall iced tea glasses. Top each glass with half of the celery salt and the dry rub. Drink, don't sip.

SERVING SUGGESTION A full hangover cure includes some Up and At 'Em Lamb Sausage (page 168) and Buttermilk Biscuits (page 410).

beer is the beverage of choice for most pitmasters

HIGH TIMES IN MISSISSIPPI

When we attended the Delta Jubilee Barbecue Cooking Contest in Clarksdale, Mississippi, a few years back, the judges gave awards for two tangentially related achievements. The group that won the "Party 'til Ya Oink" trophy seemed to be pretty tight the next morning with the folks who took the prize for the best Bloody Mary.

The origin of the mint julep is obscure, but Kentucky has claimed credit for the invention since the early nineteenth century. Old lore about the drink suggests many secrets for success, such as picking the mint in the dewy cool of the early morning, using cold spring water "pure as angels are," and, most important, serving the julep in a silver goblet.

Derby Day Mint Julep

Mint juleps have been the traditional drink of the Kentucky Derby since the founder of Churchill Downs, Colonel Meriwether Lewis Clark Jr., started the race in 1875. On Derby Day, special bars at the track sell thousands of juleps to the spectators. Some people think the concoction is too sweet, some say it's too strong, but you'll always find a julep in the winner's circle in the bluegrass and bourbon state. SERVES 10 TO 20

MINT SYRUP
1 cup water
1 cup sugar
1 cup loosely packed fresh mint leaves

Kentucky bourbon
Mint sprigs, for garnish

1. In a saucepan, bring the water, sugar, and mint to a boil, and boil the mixture until the sugar is dissolved and the liquid is clear. Set the syrup aside to steep as it cools. Strain before using. The syrup keeps in a covered jar in the refrigerator for several weeks.

2. Make juleps individually. For each serving, fill an 8-ounce glass with crushed ice. Add a half-tablespoon of the mint syrup—or as much as a full tablespoon if you like your juleps on the sweet side—and 2 ounces bourbon. Stir gently to frost the glass, garnish with a sprig of mint, and serve at once.

SERVING SUGGESTION No Derby Day party is complete without a bowl of Kentucky Burgoo (page 393).

Jack Daniel's hosts one of the most prestigious barbecue cook-offs each fall in Lynchburg, Tennessee, a little over an hour south of Nashville. You must be invited to enter the competition, and you won't get that honor without winning other important contests first. Spectators numbering in the tens of thousands descend on the village (population 361) each October. It's a good thing they come for a taste of something other than whiskey because Lynchburg is in a dry county.

Lynchburg Cooler

Kentucky may be the home of bourbon, but Tennessee also produces its share of good whiskey, including the Jack Daniel's made in the small burg of Lynchburg.

SERVES 2

2 ounces Jack Daniel's or similar sour-mash whiskey

1 ounce brandy

1 ounce light rum

1 ounce water

1½ teaspoons sugar

4 twists of lemon peel

1. In a cocktail shaker or lidded jar, combine all of the ingredients except the lemon peel and shake until the sugar dissolves.

2. Pour over ice cubes in old-fashioned glasses. Top with the lemon peel. Serve immediately.

V.W.

Nothing tastes better than watermelon in the summertime, even in a beverage.

SERVES 2

3 ounces vodka

2 cups pureed watermelon or watermelon juice

Confectioners' sugar (optional)

Half-fill two tall 10-ounce to 12-ounce glasses with ice. Pour in the vodka and the juice. Stir and taste. If the watermelon wasn't particularly

sweet, you may want to add a touch of confectioners' sugar. Mix in the sugar, if needed, and serve immediately.

SERVING SUGGESTION The perfect appetizer to eat with a V.W. is Mouthwatering Watermelon Morsels (page 347).

Mexican Martini

The city of Austin has become a serious barbecue bastion in recent years and is widely known for its "Keep Austin Weird" mentality. Get into the same spirit with this purely Austin cross between a margarita and a martini. Weird and delicious both. Adjust the sweetness as you see fit. SERVES 2

Pimiento- or jalapeño-stuffed olives

Lime wedges

Kosher salt or coarse sea salt

6 ounces reposada or añejo tequila

3 ounces freshly squeezed lime juice

2 to 3 ounces Cointreau

1 ounce freshly squeezed orange juice

1 ounce olive jar brine

Handful of ice cubes

1. Skewer together an olive or 2 or 3 on a toothpick or mini bamboo skewer with a lime wedge for each of two martini glasses. Place kosher salt, about 1 tablespoon, on a saucer. Rub another lime wedge around the rim of each glass and dunk the rim of each glass in the salt.

2. Place the remaining ingredients in a cocktail shaker and give a good 20 seconds' worth of shaking. Pour into prepared martini glasses, add garnishes, and serve. *Salud.*

Firewater

Some major American chefs offer variations on this theme under different names at pretty steep prices. You can make your own, and earn your own fame, for a much lower cost. SERVES A PARTY

1 liter decent vodka

3 to 4 fresh serranos or jalapeños, split

Twists of lime peel or green olives, preferably jalapeño-stuffed, for garnish

1. In a bottle or jar, combine the vodka and chiles and cover. Let the mixture steep at room temperature for a minimum of 3 days.

2. Transfer the vodka to the freezer and allow it to chill thoroughly. (It won't freeze.) Serve straight up or over ice, garnished with a twist of lime or olive, martini style.

SERVING SUGGESTION To soothe your throat, munch on smoked cheese, such as Can't Wait Queso (page 340) or Unholy Swiss Cheese (page 341).

LOVE THEM TEXAS TALES

In addition to being a champion pitmaster, Obie Obermark has written for several barbecue publications and was instrumental in founding the International Barbecue Cookers Association, one of the largest membership organizations of its kind. If you run into him at a cook-off, don't worry about a lag in the conversation. Always outgoing, Obie definitely has the gift of gab.

Yankee Shooter

The barbecue contest circuit is full of colorful characters, but none is more entertaining than Obie Obermark, the lean, tall Texan who invented the Yankee Shooter. To fix the Shooter right, you have to use Yankee Blaster, one of a score or so barbecue spice mixes that Obie makes and sells (obiecue.com). Our suggestion for a substitute works in a pinch, but it's not the genuine article. SERVES 1

Yankee Blaster spice mix or an equal combination of cayenne and crushed chile de árbol

Shot of high-quality tequila

1. Add 1 to 7 shakes of Yankee Blaster to the tequila or the same number of tiny pinches of the substitute spice mix. Yankee Blaster is named for its heat level, so beware. Obie himself takes a full 7 shakes but doesn't recommend it to anyone who isn't a veteran of jalapeño-eating contests.

2. Cover the glass with your hand and shake it vigorously, one shake per dose of the dry spices. Gulp the contents immediately and completely, trying to remain upright.

Apricorita

A specialty margarita, this is a frozen version with a fruity tang. SERVES 2

2 ounces high-quality tequila

1 ounce apricot brandy

3/4 ounce freshly squeezed lime juice

1 tablespoon honey, or more to taste

1 1/2 cups cracked ice

1 fresh apricot, halved (optional), for garnish

In a blender, combine the tequila, brandy, lime juice, and honey and blend until well combined. Add the ice and blend until smooth. Pour into tulip-shaped champagne glasses and garnish with apricot halves if you wish. Serve immediately.

Turquoise Margarita

This is a festive take on the margarita, perfect for a barbecue party. SERVES 1

Kosher salt or coarse sea salt

Lime wedge

1½ ounces high-quality tequila

1 ounce blue Curaçao

¾ ounce freshly squeezed lime juice

1. Place a thin layer of salt on a saucer. Rub the rim of an 8-ounce glass with the lime wedge and immediately dip the rim into the salt.

2. Pour the tequila, Curaçao, and lime juice into a cocktail shaker or lidded jar, add several pieces of cracked ice, and shake to blend. Pour into the prepared glass and serve.

SERVING SUGGESTION Little Devils (page 344) are made to match any tequila drink.

Sangrita Maria

In Mexico, bartenders often serve shots of tequila with a side glass of sangrita, a zippy tomato and citrus mixture. We're too lazy to wash two glasses when one will do, so we just combine the ingredients into a south-of-the-border Bloody Mary. SERVES 4

2 cups tomato juice

½ cup high-quality tequila

½ cup freshly squeezed orange juice

2 tablespoons freshly squeezed lime juice

1 tablespoon chopped onion

2 teaspoons Worcestershire sauce

1 fresh serrano or jalapeño, chopped

Celery salt

Barbecue dry rub, such as Wild Willy's Number One-derful Rub (page 26) or Southwest Heat (page 32) (optional)

Whole serranos and lime wedges, for garnish

Combine the tomato juice, tequila, citrus juices, onion, Worcestershire sauce, and chile in a blender. Blend the mixture briefly until well combined. Pour it into tall glasses filled with ice cubes. Shake a little celery salt over each drink and, if you wish, a bit of dry rub, too. Garnish with a serrano chile attached by a toothpick to a lime wedge.

Smoked Tomato Bloody Mary

When you want to wow your friends at brunch, smoke the season's best tomatoes for the juice to make the drinks. They may start calling you mixologist as well as pitmaster. SERVES 4

1½ to 1¾ pounds red-ripe tomatoes

5 ounces vodka

2 tablespoons freshly squeezed lime juice

2 teaspoons Worcestershire sauce, or to taste

1 teaspoon Tabasco sauce, or to taste

1 teaspoon grated horseradish, or to taste

¼ teaspoon freshly ground black pepper

1 lime wedge

1 tablespoon Smoky Salt (page 29) or kosher salt

1 teaspoon celery salt, plus more for serving

Whole pickled okra such as Okra Pickles (page 432), cherry tomatoes (yellow and red are nice together), pimiento-stuffed olives, leafy celery sticks, and/or additional lime wedges

1. Prepare the smoker for barbecuing, bringing the temperature to 200°F to 220°F.

2. Place the tomatoes in a shallow smoke-proof dish or heavy-duty foil tray with edges turned up tightly. Transfer the tomatoes to the smoker and cook until the tomatoes are warmed through and skins have split, 20 to 30 minutes.

Carefully remove the tomatoes from the smoker to avoid losing any of their copious juices. Set the tomatoes aside to cool in the pan. (The smoked tomatoes can be refrigerated for several hours.)

3. Combine the tomatoes and their juice, vodka, lime juice, Worcestershire sauce, Tabasco sauce, horseradish, and pepper in a blender. Blend the mixture briefly until well combined. Taste and adjust seasonings if you wish.

4. Stir together the smoked salt and celery salt on a saucer. Run the lime wedge around the rim of four tall glasses. Dunk each glass's rim into the combined salts. Fill each glass with ice cubes, then pour the drink mixture over. Shake a little celery salt over each drink. Spear together on toothpicks or bamboo skewers some combo of garnishes, a mini salad of sorts, as guests wish.

THE SCANTIEST OF INSPIRATIONS

A decade or more ago, the Jack Daniel Distillery decided to sponsor a barbecue cook-off team headed by Mike "Fish" Fisher, a technician at the whiskey plant. Cooking on a huge smoker in the shape of a Jack Daniel's bottle, the group took up their hobby with genuine enthusiasm after they were invited to barbecue for a bikini contest in Nashville.

Bar-B-Q joints sell plenty of sweetened tea, but they are often big on soft drinks as well. If you want to evoke the right feeling at home, serve RC Cola instead of Coke or track down a carton of Big Red, a popular barbecue drink in central Texas.

Iced Sunshine

A bright, perky tequila drink, perfect for sunrise and sunset alike. SERVES 2

2 tablespoons simple syrup, or more to taste (see BBQ tip)

2 cups freshly squeezed pink grapefruit juice (from about 4 large grapefruit)

1/4 cup high-quality tequila, preferably silver

Splash of grenadine

In a cocktail shaker or lidded jar, combine the simple syrup, fruit juice, and tequila. Pour the mixture over ice in tall glasses. Add a splash of grenadine to the top of each drink and serve.

BBQ tip To make simple syrup, combine equal amounts of sugar and water and bring the mixture to a boil until the sugar dissolves. Cool. The syrup keeps indefinitely in the fridge.

Maui Mai Tai

A couple of these and you'll feel as balmy as a Hawaiian breeze. SERVES 1

1 1/2 teaspoons simple syrup

1 ounce dark rum

1 ounce light rum

1 ounce freshly squeezed lemon juice

1/2 ounce Curaçao or other orange-flavored liqueur

1 1/2 teaspoons orgeat syrup (an almond-flavored syrup available at well-stocked liquor stores) or amaretto liqueur

Fresh pineapple spear, lime wedge, and fresh mint sprig, for garnish

Little paper parasol, to make your friends giggle (optional)

Combine the simple syrup, rums, lemon juice, Curaçao, and orgeat syrup in a cocktail shaker or lidded jar and shake well. Pour the drink over ice in a double old-fashioned glass. Garnish as desired and serve.

SERVING SUGGESTION Mai Tais go great before a Hawaiian seafood dinner, such as Kohala Tuna Steaks (page 253) or Jungle Prince Scallops (page 266).

Peachy Daiquiri

Here's the best use for canned peaches we've ever found. SERVES 4

16-ounce can peaches in heavy syrup, undrained

1 cup light rum

Juice of 1 to 2 limes

2 cups cracked ice

Lime slices, for garnish

Combine the peaches with their syrup, rum, lime juice, and ice in a blender and blend until smooth. Pour the drink into tulip-shaped champagne glasses, garnish with lime slices, and serve.

VARIATION: MANGO DAIQUIRI Substitute an equal-size can or jar of mangoes and juice for the peaches.

Plumb Loco Coco Punch

You'll probably jibber like you're plumb loco if you drink more than two of these.
SERVES 4

1 cup dark rum

1/2 cup canned cream of coconut

1/4 cup Mint Syrup (see Derby Day Mint Julep, page 473)

1/4 cup milk or half-and-half

1 tablespoon pure vanilla extract

4 cups cracked ice

Mint sprigs, for garnish

Place the rum, cream of coconut, syrup, milk, vanilla, and ice in a blender and blend until the mixture is smooth. Pour the drink into tall glasses, garnish with mint, and serve.

LOST OUR VOTE

On a hot day at the barbecue pit, our thirst sometimes reminds us of an old Prohibition politician, the one who promised voters that he would make their state so dry the residents would have to prime their mouths to spit.

The New Braunfels Smokehouse (online at nbsmokehouse.com) is one of the best mail-order sources in the country for smoked food. Though the company established its reputation by brine-curing most of its products—using a dry rub only on beef brisket and pork ribs—the food is cooked in a barbecue style rather than smoke-cured. Originally a local brewery in the German-American community of New Braunfels, Texas, the business switched to smoking during Prohibition.

Cold Buttered Rum

Here's an ice cream alternative to the winter favorite, filling enough to replace dessert. SERVES 1

1¹/₂ ounces dark rum

1 large scoop butter pecan ice cream

¹/₂ cup cracked ice

Dash of bitters

Sprinkle of nutmeg

Orange slice, for garnish

In a blender, combine the rum, ice cream, ice, and bitters and blend until smooth. Pour the drink into a balloon-shaped wine glass. Sprinkle it with nutmeg, garnish with the orange slice, and serve immediately.

SERVING SUGGESTION With any spicy barbecue meal, Cold Buttered Rum makes a refreshing after-dinner drink.